Studies in Energy, Resource and Environmental Economics

This book series offers an outlet for cutting-edge research on all areas of energy, environmental and resource economics. The series welcomes theoretically sound and empirically robust monographs and edited volumes, as well as textbooks and handbooks from various disciplines and approaches on topics such as energy and resource markets, the economics of climate change, environmental evaluation, policy issues, and related fields. All titles in the series are peer-reviewed.

Machiel Mulder

Economics of Energy Transition

Principles, Policies and Stakeholders

Springer

Machiel Mulder
Professor of Energy Economics
Department of Economics and Business
University of Groningen
Groningen, The Netherlands

ISSN 2731-3409 ISSN 2731-3417 (electronic)
Studies in Energy, Resource and Environmental Economics
ISBN 978-3-032-29009-0 ISBN 978-3-032-29010-6 (eBook)
https://doi.org/10.1007/978-3-032-29010-6

This Springer imprint is published by the registered company Springer Nature Switzerland AG
The registered company address is: Gewerbestrasse 11, 6330 Cham, Switzerland

'As for the future, your task is not to foresee it, but to enable it.'

Antoine de Saint-Exupery

Statement on the use of AI

This book has been written without the help of any AI tools, which means that the conceptualisation of the book, structuring of the text, collection and analysis of both literature and data, design and construction of graphs, as well as the writing, editing and proofreading have been done by the author himself (with the support of various people mentioned in the foreword). The author only indirectly made use of AI, for example when using search engines. Additionally, the publisher used an AI tool to construct the Alt Texts to describe graphs and other visual images, which have been checked, and if needed, corrected by the author.

Preface

Energy transition refers to one of the fundamental changes taking shape within current societies, and which is why it receives a lot media attention. The news items cover, for instance, projects in offshore wind parks, which are planned, just realised or cancelled because of financial reasons. Companies active in the fossil-energy business also frequently attract media attention with questions regarding their future development strategy. Operators of electricity grids which are struggling to connect new users, such as charging points for electric vehicles, have to explain why the capacity of their grids has not been expanded in time. All such changes in energy systems require investments and result in costs, which have to be paid in one way or another. As a result, the distributional consequences of energy transition are frequently subject to debate. To address the various types of problems related to the transition of energy systems, governments are asked to step in and help, for instance, businesses to realise profitable business cases for investments in renewable energy, to enable energy-intensive industries to remain competitive in international markets while decarbonizing their production processes, or to support residential households in taking energy-efficiency measures.

The above examples show a number of things. First of all, energy transition affects almost everyone in society, from large, internationally operating companies to residential households. Secondly, the examples show that energy transition is about the decisions various types of organisations and individuals have to make. Firms have to invest in new production technologies or transportation grids, or they have to move away from their conventional way of producing, transporting or consuming energy. Energy users, both firms and individuals, may want to reduce their expenditures on energy when prices become too high or governments stimulate them to do so through energy taxes or support schemes. Governments face decisions regarding the way and the intensity with which they want to intervene in energy systems. Should they stimulate particular technologies, support energy-intensive industries, help with the development of energy networks, or should they simply leave it to market parties?

In order to answer these kinds of questions, an economic perspective can be useful. After all, economics is the science of choices. Through an economic lens, one sees that everyone is always forced to make decisions because we have to deal with scarce commodities. Applied to the field of energy, we see that all kinds of organisations and individuals are constantly making choices about how to produce, transport, store or consume energy. All these decisions together shape the development of energy systems, which are in constant flux as a result.

When we use this economic perspective to understand energy transition, it seems to be a useful addition to the widely adopted interpretation of energy transition. In that interpretation, energy transition is defined as the change of energy systems towards a particular direction, such as more renewables and less fossil-fuel based. While that definition is formulated in terms of a particular outcome, in an economic perspective, the focus is on the process. After all, organisations and individuals are making their own choices regarding energy systems, and these decisions need not necessarily be geared in a particular direction. This can simply be deduced from the fact that countries have quite different energy systems without explicit energy-transition policies. If that is the situation, why should all countries pursue the same energy system and use the same objectives regarding energy transition? And, how can the economic lens help to better understand what energy transition is or how it could be organised?

The objective of this book is to contribute to answering questions like these. In this book, I want to discuss what we actually mean by energy transition, what are economically valuable arguments to pursue energy transition, and how it can be realised in an effective and efficient way. Because I intend to discuss energy transition in a more general way, throughout this book I do not speak about 'the' energy transition, as that would refer to a particular, well-defined movement within energy systems. Instead, by not using the article 'the', I refer to the energy transition as a concept.

This book is the result of many years of experience in the field of energy economics. I have done quite a lot of research and given many lectures to a wide variety of audiences. This was done from various positions, for example, at the Agricultural Economics Research Institute, the Netherlands Bureau for Economic Policy Analysis, the Netherlands Authority for Consumers & Markets, and the University of Groningen. In particular in my current positions as professor of Energy Economics in Groningen, and director of the Energy Transition program of the University of Groningen Business School, I have been really lucky to meet so many (BSc, MSc, executive MBA, as well as PhD) students with whom I could discuss the economic perspective on energy transition. In addition, I really benefitted from all the discussions and collaborations with colleagues at the above institutes as well as from collaborations with external stakeholders, such as in advisory committees on energy policy. Actually, the idea for the outline of this book originated from a session at a large energy company in November 2024. In that session, I presented my views on the economics of energy transition to a group of more than 100 staff members with mainly an engineering background. The lively discussions during this session inspired me to start writing this book.

This book strongly benefitted from the feedback I received on the manuscript. I am very grateful to the following persons in particular who made some time to read (parts) of the manuscript and share their feedback with me. Thanks a lot, Jilles van den Beukel, Thijs Broekhuizen, Matteo Di Castelnuovo, Peter Dijkstra, Paul Giesbertz, Roeland van Gilst, Roweno Heijmans, Gerben Hieminga, Marijne

Timmers, Ton Schoot Uiterkamp, Arjen Veenstra and Edwin Woerdman. Their comments and suggestions have really helped me to make the book more clear, more up to date and more to the point. The finishing touch as proofreader of the manuscript was carried out by Sylvie van Wijk and Team Scriptium, for which I am very grateful. Of course, I remain fully responsible for any remaining errors or shortcomings in this book.

I also want to thank Georg Erdmann, Anne Neumann and Andreas Loeschel as the editors of the book series Studies in Energy, Resource and Environmental Economics for their positive response and support for this book. Similarly, I am very grateful to Johannes Glaeser and Niko Chtouris of Springer for their support throughout the process, from the initial idea until its realisation. I also thank Divyalakshmi Ganesan and Nandhitha P, Production Editor and Production Supervisor, respectively, at Springer, for carefully managing the process of producing this book.

Finally, I am grateful to my family, friends and colleagues showing interest in the progress of my book over the past year. Most of all, I am very grateful to my wife, Mieke, for supporting me in many respects, listening to my stories about the progress and making suggestions. Without her love and care, it would not have been possible to write this book.

Groningen/The Hague, The Netherlands Machiel Mulder
July 2026

Contents

List of Figures

List of Tables

List of Boxes

Economics of Energy Transition: An Introduction

1

1.1 Introduction

The objective of this book is to explore the concept of energy transition from an economic perspective. Energy transition is generally seen as a fundamental change in the way societies use energy. This change refers to many aspects and includes many different stakeholders, and, therefore, it has to be analysed from various perspectives. One of these is the economic perspective. This perspective is helpful in thinking about why societies should realise a transition in energy systems, and how this could be done. After introducing the central topic of this book, this chapter ends by introducing the organisation of the book, including the target group, the learning objectives and the outline.

1.2 Background

1.2.1 Energy Systems

Box 1.1 Energy Sources and Carriers
There are many types of commodities that can carry energy (so-called energy carriers), but there is a smaller number of commodities that are also a source of energy. The latter are called 'energy sources' or 'primary energy carriers'. This group consists of commodities that can be seen as natural gifts. These energy carriers include fossil-energy resources, such as coal, oil and gas, but also renewable resources, such as wind, sunshine, biomass, hydro- and wave energy. When a primary energy carrier is converted into another type of commodity, a secondary energy carrier may result. Examples of these are

M. Mulder, *Economics of Energy Transition*, Studies in Energy, Resource and Environmental Economics, https://doi.org/10.1007/978-3-032-29010-6_1

electricity that is made out of fossil-energy or renewable resources, hydrogen that is made, through Steam-Methane Reforming (SMR), out of natural gas, and fuels like gasoline and diesel that are produced from fossil energy. When a secondary energy carrier is converted into another energy carrier, the result is a tertiary energy carrier. An example of this is hydrogen that is made out of electricity (and water) through electrolysis.

A fundamental economic difference between primary energy carriers on the one hand and secondary and tertiary energy carriers on the other, is that the latter two have to be produced, which implies that the costs of supplying these carriers are related to the costs of using a primary energy carrier. For instance, the costs of making electricity with a gas-fired power plant are related to the costs of burning gas. Consequently, when the price of gas increases, the price of electricity may also increase, although the precise relationship depends on the characteristics of the electricity market (see Sect. 3.5).

Energy systems can be defined as the complete set of relationships between the primary supply and the final use of energy carriers. As there exist several types of energy carriers, such as oil, gas, electricity and hydrogen (see Box 1.1), there are also several sets of relationships. Each set can be seen as a supply chain, starting with the upstream activities of exploration until the downstream activity of using energy (see Fig. 1.1). Exploration not only refers to the search for the non-renewable resources coal, oil and natural gas, but also to finding the best locations to install wind turbines or to produce geothermal heat. Once a resource or location has been discovered and developed, the next step in the supply chain is the production of energy. Depending on the type of energy carrier, transport can be carried out by pipelines and/or by ships and trucks. As production and consumption of energy are often not simultaneous, storage is an important component of supply chains, either in the same type of energy carrier or, through conversion, into another type.

There also exist relationships among/between supply chains, referred to as sector coupling. For instance, natural gas is supplied to the end-users of that energy carrier, but also to producers in the supply chain of electricity, where it is used in gas-fired power plants. The heat, which is produced as a by-product by power plants, can be used to heat industrial or residential buildings, which is another example of sector coupling. This complete set of relationships, both within and between supply chains, can be defined as an energy system.

1.2.2 Energy Transition as System Change Seen from Various Perspectives

Technically speaking, an energy transition can be defined as a change in the characteristics of energy systems. This change can refer to the shares of the various types of energy carriers in the energy mix, but also to different ways of organising the

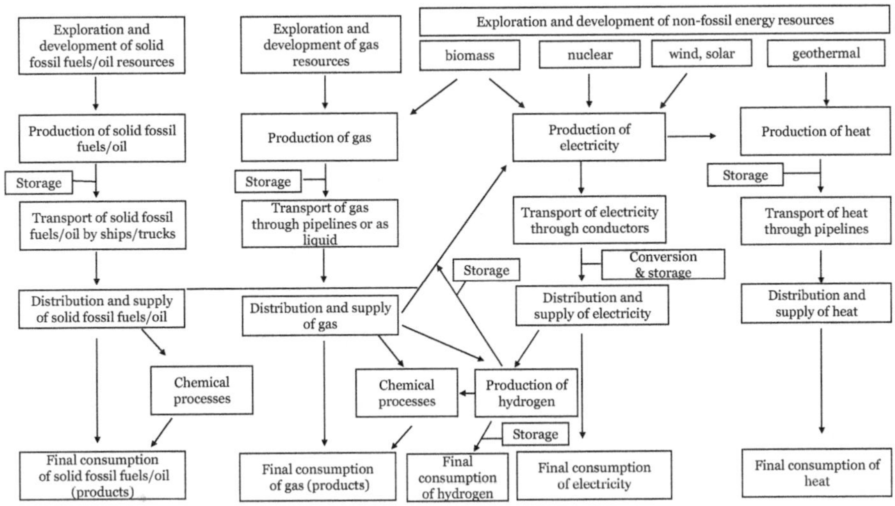

Fig. 1.1 Supply chains and sector coupling within an energy system

system. Although energy transition is increasingly seen as a fundamental change in the way societies deal with their need for energy, the question remains to what extent this also requires a completely different way of organising energy systems. Generally, this question is answered positively. In order to replace fossil-energy-based systems by systems which hardly emit greenhouse gases, for instance, it is often said that huge changes within society are required. Not only the technologies for the production, transport and storage of energy need to change, but also the way energy systems and energy markets are organised have to be redesigned, while both businesses and residential consumers need to change the way they use energy. Because of the wide scope of these required changes, they can only be fully realised when all parts of societies are involved, ranging from international energy businesses to residential consumers and local governments. Hence, energy transition is generally seen as a fairly radical change of energy systems.

As energy transition relates to many different aspects of energy systems, many different perspectives are relevant. Not only the technological aspects of how energy can be produced, transported and stored, but also various other aspects play a crucial role. For instance, legal frameworks in which firms and consumers operate determine what they are legally allowed to do. Moreover, behavioural aspects, referring to how people tend to behave and respond to each other as well as to actions of firms and governments, also shape the development of energy systems. Hence, in order to analyse energy transition in its entirety, various academic perspectives have to be used, as each perspective sees reality through a particular lens (see Fig. 1.2).

It is, for instance, expected that electricity will become way more important as an energy carrier in future energy systems. As a consequence, the technical functioning of electricity grids is becoming a more crucial component of energy systems. One has, therefore, to understand electrical aspects of electricity systems, which can be

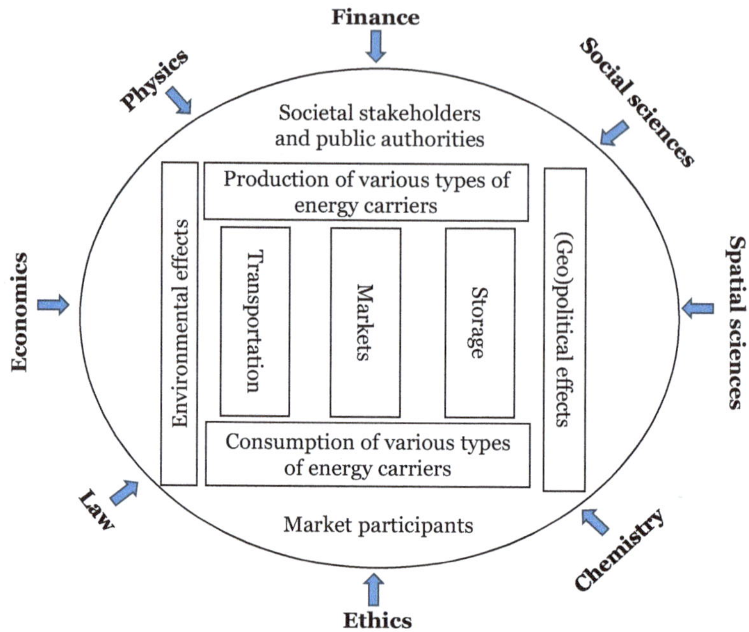

Fig. 1.2 Various academic perspectives on transitions in energy systems, consisting of supply chains for various types of energy carriers and various types of actors

done by using the lenses of physics and, in particular, electrical engineering. Electricity systems consist of a set of components that generate and use electrical energy. This energy consists of electromagnetic fields. Most of the continental European grid (ranging from Denmark to Portugal, Poland and Turkey)[1] is based on Alternating Current (AC), with a synchronous frequency of approximately 50 Hertz (Hz). Within this system, the frequency needs to be maintained at a constant level, which occurs when total load is permanently equal to total generation. The physical design of the electricity grids affects the options for economic users connected to that grid. The same holds, although to different extents, for the design of the infrastructures for the transport of other energy carriers, such as gas, heat and hydrogen.

Another aspect of energy systems that is relevant for the analysis of energy transition is the spatial dimension, which refers to the best location for production facilities, such as wind turbines, and the distance between production units and consuming appliances. The location of industries and consumers affects options of both parties to participate in energy systems, such as for the use of hydropower or wind turbines. After all, production units are located in a particular place, such as in a rural, urban or offshore area, with particular physical characteristics such as altitude and climate. The location is also relevant insofar as it relates to the ability to

[1] Next to this continental grid in Europe, there are synchronous zones in the UK, Ireland, the Nordic countries and the Baltic States.

make use of transportation grids. All generating and consuming units of electricity within a region are connected to the same grid and, as a result, are physically connected and influence each other. The units themselves also require some space, but to what extent depends on their physical characteristics.[2] Depending on their required space and location, their functioning is related to how the space is used in the neighbourhood. Until recently, electricity systems were characterised by centralised generation in which a limited number of power plants were responsible for the majority of electricity generation, while the load was spread over many locations within countries. In future electricity systems, also the generation will be increasingly spatially spread out and closer to the consumption. The more different types of producers and users are located in close proximity to each other, the more options for mutual collaboration, so-called industrial symbiosis.

At the end of the day, the operation of all the various types of units in energy systems is carried out by humans. These humans can be employees at an energy company, but everyone is also a private person using energy. The fact that the use of energy is related to human behaviour makes that the social-sciences perspective is also relevant. In this perspective, an analysis is made of psychological and social factors that affect the behaviour of people. This behaviour does not only refer to the choices they make, but also to their attitude towards their social and natural environment. Here, the attention is not only directed at the people that work in energy supply, transport or delivery companies, but also at individuals that consume energy or live in the neighbourhood of the companies and, as a result, may face some consequences thereof. These people may have views or feelings, so-called values, regarding what is important to them, for example about the sustainability of electricity generation, the security of supply or the costs of consumption. These different values may result in different behaviour, such as the extent to which people support or oppose particular developments, like the construction of nuclear-power plants. Through that behaviour, they may influence each other, as people can be seen as social animals.

As mentioned above, all considerations in society have to be translated into legal rules, otherwise society cannot function properly. These legal rules are based on a number of legal principles. In the case of energy law, they include, amongst others, the principle of national resource sovereignty and the principle of access to modern energy services (Heffron et al., 2018). The translation of these principles into legal rules determines to a large extent in what way economic agents can take particular measures. Operators of an electricity grid, for instance, are subject to regulatory oversight in many countries, which means that their economic behaviour is affected by the rules implemented by governments.

The behaviour of people, including the choices they make regarding the use of scarce resources, as well as the legal framework they are subject to, can be analysed

[2]There exist large differences in land use between electricity-generation technologies. Nuclear uses the least space per unit of electricity production, while hydropower uses the most (Ritchie, 2022). Fossil-fuel power plants may not need so much space themselves, but for the mining of the fuels, in particular coal, the land use is much more extensive.

from what is called a positive approach. In this approach, the objective is to describe what people are doing, feeling and thinking, how they influence each other and what the underlying factors are. One can also look at these aspects from a more normative perspective, such as ethics. In this perspective, one wonders to what extent certain behaviour is just, fair or morally right. Is it just, for instance, that producers of renewable electricity may make high profits at the expense of consumers? Is it morally right to use nuclear power, knowing that there will be nuclear waste for thousands of years? These types of questions can be answered by argumentation, based on academic literature[3] and/or discussions with those involved.

1.2.3 Economic Perspective

Although all the above, and other, academic perspectives are very relevant and useful to understand how to realise an energy transition, this book focuses on the economic perspective. This book focuses on the economic perspective not only because it can provide useful insight in how to realise the transition, but also because it is rather misinterpreted. It is often said that economics is only directed at profit and economic growth, while for a sustainable (energy) future we need a change in the way societies are organised: 'system change, no climate change' as is sometimes said by environmentalists.[4] The economic perspective is also often equated to the analysis of financial costs and revenues, but that is also not correct, as we will show later on in more detail. Moreover, economics is sometimes seen as a theoretical, ivory-tower science as it assumes all individuals are rational, while we all know real behaviour is often based on emotions and intuition, not on rational calculations of costs and benefits. If all these perceptions of the economic lens would be correct, it would indeed be better to analyse and realise energy transition without this perspective. In this book, however, we will show the contrary by explaining and illustrating how the economic lens can provide a very useful perspective on how to understand as well as realise energy transition.

The economic discipline does not prescribe that societies pursue economic growth or that individual firms strive for profit maximisation. Fundamentally, the economic perspective is about how people (and firms and other types of organisations) deal with scarcity. A firm that wants to produce renewable electricity, for instance, generally has several options, such as using wind turbines or solar panels. That firm may also have various options to sell the produced electricity to others.

[3] See for instance Redgwel and Rajamani (2018) who analyse the international justice aspects related to energy systems, paying attention to, amongst others, the inter-generational equity and the allocation of responsibilities. These authors define a just global energy system as system 'that is safe, reliable, fair, affordable, and also sustainable for current and future generations and the natural world'.

[4] See for instance the organisation of North American so-called eco-socialists who collaborate in the network 'System Change Not Climate Change', based on the idea that 'capitalism is driving climate change and that a radical international grassroots movement can stop it' (Source: https://systemchangenotclimatechange.org/points-of-unity/).

The choices that agents make and how they interact with each other is the focus of economic analysis. In this analysis, use is made of various theoretical concepts like rationality, profit maximisation, welfare and perfect competition. These concepts are not meant to describe actual behaviour, but function as (theoretical) benchmarks to analyse what happens in reality systematically.

One of the key economic concepts in the analysis of energy transition is the idea that welfare is based on the degree to which individual humans (in their various roles) are successful in meeting their demands, and that this degree can only be determined by individuals themselves. Individuals form their own preferences regarding what they like and what they do not like. These preferences are the basis for the choices individuals make. If we depart from the assumption that everyone wants to pursue the realisation of her/his own needs and that no one else can really assess what is important to her/him, then intervening in the decisions of others, such as regarding their energy-related choices, is not so straightforward. The fundamental question here is: why should a government (i.e. a society) intervene in the decisions taken by individuals? What are the arguments to do so, and if the arguments are convincing, what are the best ways to intervene?

The economic framework we use to answer questions like these is based on microeconomic theory. This theory focuses on the choices economic agents make regarding the use of scarce commodities and how they interact with each other regarding the allocation of these commodities. Microeconomics can, therefore, also be seen as the intermediate layer between business economics, which focuses on the optimising behaviour of firms, and macroeconomics, which analyses the interaction between the aggregates of individual behaviour.

Because of its clear and systematic theoretical framework, this economic perspective can be very helpful in understanding what happens in society and to advise what societies (in particular governments) could do to, for instance, realise a transition in energy systems. The value of the economic analysis for actual decision-making in societies also results from the fact that the economic discipline has developed methods to integrate insights from other disciplines in its analysis. A crucial element in this method is that costs and benefits are not restricted to those effects which have a market price. After all, many effects of societal projects have so-called unpriced effects, such as noise, or effects on air quality and landscape. Such effects have to be included in an analysis, so the optimal decision for society can be made. The economic approach offers techniques to integrate such aspects into an integrated analysis. The objective of this book is to provide insight in the concepts and methods used in economics and how these can be used to understand whether and how societies should pursue a transition of energy systems.

1.2.4 Economic Perspective on Change of Energy Systems

Above, we have said that an energy transition can be understood as a change of energy systems, but how can such system change be analysed from an economic perspective? When it is said that energy systems need to change in order to realise an energy transition that contributes to societal objectives, it is often unclear what is meant by system change. It may refer to changing the behaviour of people such that they make other choices and have different objectives. It may also refer to changing the organisation of systems, in particular the role of markets and governments. System change may also be seen as changing the circumstances stakeholders are operating in. How feasible is it to realise these various types of changes, and how could they be realised? Let us briefly discuss each of these types of system changes.

1.2.4.1 System Change as Changing the Objective Functions

Sometimes it is stated that other stakeholders should change their objective functions in order to realise the common goal of energy transition. For instance, shareholders of large fossil-fuel companies should not focus on dividends, but should allow companies to use the profits to invest in renewable-energy projects. Or, residential consumers should consume fewer products or make more use of public transport instead of private cars. Such claims about what others should do are often made by environmental lobby groups or non-governmental organisations (see Box 1.2). Such wishes regarding what others should do are, however, at odds with the fundamental economic theorem, as just discussed above, that no one can judge what others should prefer, as we cannot deem what others' preferences are. Any intervention in what others should do may reduce the overall welfare (in the broader meaning of the word). Therefore, one needs to have arguments that show that the choices made by (some) consumers result in a lower overall welfare and that, therefore, intervention by society, i.e. by the government is warranted.

Individual preferences, though, are not constant, as they may change under the influence of new information and experiences. This also explains the role education can play. When people are better informed on, for instance, the relationship between energy consumption and climate change, they may be more willing to adapt their choices. Nevertheless, changing the objectives and preferences of stakeholders is an uncertain and complex approach to realise a fundamental change of energy systems without lowering the overall societal welfare.

1.2.4.2 System Change as Changing the Organisation

An alternative approach to realise systemic change is to change the way energy systems are organised. The organisation of these systems refers to the type of ownership (e.g. public versus private), how the commodities are allocated (e.g. through markets or centralised allocation) and to what extent the various types of stakeholders are involved in the decision-making process. The choices which are made regarding the organisation of energy systems strongly affect the options stakeholders have to participate in various parts of energy systems. In order to change the organisation of energy systems, public interventions may be needed.

Public agencies could, for instance, change the way the energy carriers are allocated by replacing a centralised governance system by a liberalised system in which market forces take care of the coordination of the allocation, or the other way around. The former movement occurred in many countries at the end of the twentieth and start of the twenty-first century, based on the idea that in liberalised systems

Box 1.2 Environmental Groups Calling for Behavioural Change

The fact that a reduction in the use of fossil energy is needed to realise a reduction in global carbon emissions is used as argument by environmental lobby groups to call for behavioural change on the side of agents active in energy supply chains. These groups want that energy companies, but also other companies in the supply chains, such as financial institutions, reduce their activities in the field of fossil energy. As an example of what these groups can do, one can look at the actions of the Dutch NGO *Milieudefensie*. Supported by many other groups and individuals, this NGO started a lawsuit against Shell in order to force the company to comply with the Paris Agreement by reducing all its emissions by 45% in 2030 (see website Milieudefensie). The total emissions include not only the emissions resulting from its own operations (the so-called Scope 1 emissions), but also the emissions related to the use of electricity (the so-called Scope 2 emissions) and the emissions related to the use of their products (the so-called Scope 3 emissions) (see Appendix B for a discussion of the three Scopes of emissions). This NGO also wants, amongst others, that the ING bank stops financing fossil-energy projects.

The claims on individual (fossil-energy) companies to move away from fossils may originate from moral considerations, namely that everyone should take responsibility to reduce harm to others, such as later generations. When discussing the value of such claims, however, one also has to discuss the effectiveness. How effective is it for the realisation of the societal climate goals to address individual companies to reduce their fossil-energy activities? In the case of fossil-energy production, it is relevant to know that as long as states issue licences for the exploration, development and production of fossil-energy resources, the individual actions by one company may not have any influence on global fossil-energy production and, hence, global carbon-dioxide emissions. The role of stakeholders to contribute to the transition of energy systems will be further discussed in Chap. 5, while Chap. 4 analyses the efficiency of various types of policy measures to incentive stakeholders to make other choices regarding their activities in energy supply chains.

there is more competitive pressure to innovate, improve efficiency and pass the resulting benefits onto consumers. Currently, there is a policy shift reversing earlier moves towards market liberalisation, with renewed emphasis on increasing public influence in decision-making around energy systems. This shift is partly due to concerns that privately owned, commercial firms operating in liberalised markets may be too oriented towards short-term profits at the expense of long-term public objectives. In addition, privately owned firms may become so large and powerful that they are able to influence government decision-making in such a way that they are less oriented towards realising societal objectives. This so-called governmental capture by powerful firms is a risk that must be continuously addressed, also when markets are liberalised.

A government may also decide that particular activities within energy systems should be subject to closer governmental oversight, because of concerns about affordability of energy or security of supply. An example of such government intervention is the regulation of electricity grid operators' tariffs because of the natural-monopoly character of their business (see Sect. 4.2.2). Another example is municipalities that increase their influence on the local energy system by, for instance, developing their own district-heat networks.

While in the above examples the focus is on the distribution of responsibilities among public agencies on the one hand and market parties on the other, it is also possible that groups of market parties want to change the way they have to deal with market processes. Agents may, therefore, decide they want to change the system themselves by implementing alternative organisational structures. An example is a local community that wants to be independent from the grid or commercial suppliers. Another example refers to households that do not want to make use of the (commercial) energy markets and, therefore, develop their own organisational structure for the exchange of energy. In order to facilitate such developments, energy communities and concepts like energy sharing have been introduced into legal frameworks in the European Union. A question, however, is to what extent such local energy communities contribute to the efficiency of the electricity market as they strongly restrict the options for exchange among market parties (see Section 5.4.9 for a further discussion of this issue).

Although agents may want to operate within an alternative organisation of the energy system, this does not imply that the basic principles of these systems can also (easily) be changed. For instance, the use of electricity grids is based on electrotechnical laws which state, among others, that the electromagnetic frequency of an alternating-current (AC) system is determined by the balance between the total injection and total withdrawal of electricity and that, hence, every appliance connected to the grid affects this frequency. This means that a local electricity grid also needs to take care, in one way or another, of the balancing requirement. If in a local grid, the generation of electricity is mainly based on solar panels and wind turbines for instance, the balancing task will be challenging, to say the least, when there is no physical connection to the main grid. After all, in order to supply electricity to consumers when there is no wind or sunshine, the local grid needs to take care of alternative generation or storage technologies.

When in such a grid, the participants want to exchange electricity among themselves, they also need to deal with basic economic principles. One such principle is the budget constraint everyone is facing, which means that somehow there needs to be a relationship between the financial revenues and financial costs, otherwise activities are (economically) not sustainable. Both revenues and costs remain related to what happens outside a local energy system, unless such a system is a complete autarky. The agents in a local system also have to deal with national legal frameworks, which constrain the options of individual agents. For instance, in such frameworks it may be prescribed that a grid operator needs to be unbundled from production activities, that consumers should be protected against abuse of market power from the producers and that the conditions for exchange should be transparent and non-discriminatory.

1.2.4.3 System Change as Changing the Circumstances

Aside from trying to change the preferences of individual agents and the organisation of energy systems, one could also try to realise system change by changing the circumstances in which other agents operate. This approach is completely in line with the common economic principle that agents want to pursue their own objectives, as it only tries to influence the conditions for these agents. If the conditions can be changed, this approach for system change can be effective. For instance, if an individual agent successfully develops a more efficient renewable-energy technology, such as electrolysers or solar panels, or storage technologies, such as batteries, other agents can use these technologies which may trigger an energy transition. After all, the adaptation of these new technologies by other agents may foster, for instance, the electrification and replacement of natural gas by low-carbon hydrogen. Another example is that shareholders, who want to stimulate renewable energy, provide their capital to a company in that business against more favourable conditions, such as a lower required rate of return. This way to realise a change in energy systems is the most closely linked to the economic perspective, as this lens focuses on how to induce economic agents to make different decisions than they otherwise would. Explaining and clarifying this perspective is the main objective of this book.

1.3 Organisation of the Book

1.3.1 General Approach

In order to pursue this objective, this book approaches the topic of energy transition by paying attention to four different aspects. These aspects consist of (a) the general economic principles which are needed to use an economic lens, (b) whether governments should intervene in energy systems, (c) the way governments can efficiently intervene in energy systems and (d) the role of various types of stakeholders in these systems and how they (can) contribute to the transition of energy systems. The core of this book consists of assessing commonly used arguments for transition of energy systems.

As the objective of this book is to discuss energy transition in a more conceptual and fundamental way, most of the time the article 'the' will not be used when talking about energy transition. That is only done when reference is made to a specific kind of energy transition. In addition, in order to illustrate economic mechanisms or particular phenomena, various types of examples will be used. These examples can be related to global developments, such as in the average global oil price, or to specific developments in a particular region, such as the gas price in the Netherlands. These examples are, however, not meant to describe or analyse a particular development, but to support the reader in understanding a particular economic reasoning.

1.3.2 Target Group and Learning Objectives

The target group of this book consists of both final year undergraduate and graduate students, as well as professionals working in the field of energy transition. Those with a background in economics can use this book to learn more about applying their economic knowledge to the topic of energy transition. Those with another academic background can use this book to learn more about energy transition from an economic perspective, and if there is an economic rationale to pursue such a transition, how it can be realised in an effective and efficient way.

After studying the content of this book, readers should be able to distinguish the economic perspective from other academic perspectives. They should also be able to apply this perspective in analysing the need for societies and governments to intervene in energy systems and how such interventions can be realised efficiently. Readers will also understand the various types of stakeholders in energy systems and the different roles they play, and to what extent each of them can successfully contribute to an energy transition.

1.3.3 Outline of this Book

The body of this book consists of four chapters, next to this introductory chapter and the concluding chapter. In Chap. 2, the economic perspective on energy systems is introduced. After discussing the basic economic concepts, the focus moves to the question of what is meant by 'energy transition'. How is the concept generally defined, and what is the economic definition? In this chapter, we will first show that energy systems are constantly changing. Hence, energy transition is not the same as a change in energy systems. It will become clear that energy transition can be defined as the intervention of governments in how firms, households and other types of organisations deal with energy. The basic economic principle for this analysis is that, in theory, individual economic agents should be completely free to form their own preferences and make their own choices. This principle departs from the assumption that everyone is well-informed, that no one is subject to psychological biases and that there are no externalities. When these conditions are met, everyone will make the optimal decisions, notably those decisions which are fully in line with their own objectives. When in such a situation, a government would intervene by forcing agents to make a different choice, which would result in a lower societal welfare.

However, if all these stakeholders pursue their own objectives, why should governments intervene? This question is central to Chap. 3, where we analyse economic arguments to pursue an energy transition, answering the key question: why should societies/governments intervene in energy systems to realise a fundamental change? This topic is analysed from the public-interest perspective, which assumes that governments want to maximise social welfare instead of pursuing their own interests, and that they are not captured by interest groups. In this chapter, we discuss four arguments often used to plea for energy transition. These arguments refer to the depletion of energy resources, the dependence on energy imports, the volatility of energy prices and the climate effects of using fossil energy. The first two arguments are related to security of supply, the third one to the affordability of energy and the last one to sustainability. These three aspects, often mentioned by governments, are their main objectives for energy policy (International Energy Agency, 2025).

When the rationale(s) for intervening in how stakeholders deal with energy have become clear, the next question is how this could be done in an economically efficient way. This is the topic of Chap. 4. Here, we will discuss the concept of efficiency, what it actually means, and how it is related to other societal criteria, such as effectiveness and fairness. Here, we explore, for all the above arguments for energy transition, how the intended changes in energy systems can be realised in an economically efficient and effective way.

After the preceding discussion on the system level, in Chap. 5, we zoom in to the various types of stakeholders in energy systems. Here, we discuss what they can do to contribute to the energy transition. To what extent can an individual energy-intensive industry, grid operator, electricity producer, financial institution or household effectively contribute to realising the transition of energy systems?

Finally, Chap. 6 summarises the main conclusions and provides some recommendations for both research and policy.

Exercises

1. What is the economic relevance of differentiating between primary, secondary and tertiary energy carriers?
2. What is meant by sector coupling?
3. Explain why energy systems should be analysed from various (academic) perspectives to successfully realise energy transition projects?
4. What is the essence of the economic perspective on energy transition?
5. Why is the concept of system change not really useful for understanding changes in energy systems?

References

Heffron, R. J., Rønne, A., Tomain, J. P., Bradbrook, A., & Talus, K. (2018). A treatise of energy law. *Journal of World Energy Law and Business, 11*, 34–48. https://doi.org/10.1093/jwelb/jwx039

International Energy Agency (2025). *World Energy Outlook 2025.*

Redgwel, C., & Rajamani, L. (2018). And justice for all? Energy justice in international law. In I. del Guayo (Ed.), *Energy justice and energy law*. Oxford University Press. https://doi.org/10.1093/oso/9780198860754.003.0004

Ritchie, H. (2022). *How does the land use of different electricity sources compare?* OurWorldinData.org

Economic Perspective on Energy Transition

2

2.1 Introduction

Energy transition can be looked at from various perspectives. The widely adopted interpretation of energy transition refers to the physical changes in the way we satisfy our need for energy. This refers in particular to the replacement of fossil energy by renewable energy, but this can also refer to making energy systems less dependent on international markets or making energy prices less volatile for consumers (Sect. 2.2). This chapter introduces the economic perspective on energy transition, by departing from the basic economic principles related to scarcity and optimising behaviour of economic agents (Sect. 2.3). It will become clear that the economic definition is quite different from the widely adopted interpretation, but that this perspective is useful to understand the rationales for pursuing energy transition, the drivers behind energy systems and how energy transition can be realised in an economically efficient way. In order to illustrate this, Sect. 2.4 shows that energy systems are constantly in flux. In Sect. 2.5, we explain the economic perspective on energy transition, while in Sect. 2.6 the economic concepts to formulate energy-transition policies are discussed. Sect. 2.7 concludes.

2.2 Widely Adopted Interpretation of Energy Transition

Energy transition is generally understood as the realisation of fundamental changes within energy systems. Energy systems used to be based on the exploitation of fossil-energy resources, in particular coal, oil and gas. Because of their limited availability within the Earth's crust, these resources are also called non-renewable resources. Energy systems are now increasingly using energy carriers which do not have a limited resource availability, like solar and wind energy, and that is why these

M. Mulder, *Economics of Energy Transition*, Studies in Energy, Resource and Environmental Economics, https://doi.org/10.1007/978-3-032-29010-6_2

are also called renewable-energy resources.[1] These energy resources also differ from the conventional non-renewable-energy carriers in another respect: they hardly result in greenhouse gas emissions. These emissions only occur during the construction and demolition of the installations, but not during their actual use. Consequently, the increased use of renewable-energy resources results in energy systems which are based on energy resources which will not be exhausted in the foreseeable future and which also hardly contribute to climate change. That is why such energy systems are often called sustainable,[2] both in terms of the durability of the supply, but also in its minimal consequences for the living conditions on Earth.

The increased use of renewable energy does, however, not automatically imply a decline in the use of fossil-energy resources, since the global demand for energy is still increasing. In many global regions, investments in renewable energy coincide with investments in conventional fossil-energy production capacity in order to meet the growing demand for energy.[3] This implies that in practice, increased capacities of renewable energy may not always refer to the replacement of fossil energy by renewable energy, but rather meeting the growing demand for energy with higher shares of renewables (see also Yergin et al., 2025). As a result, energy addition may be a better term to define the recent changes in energy systems than energy transition.

Next to changing the composition of various types of energy resources in energy systems, energy transition may also refer to changing the spatial dimension of energy systems. Since in particular oil and gas are only available in a limited number of places, the use of these energy carriers results in international dependencies. Many developed countries used to import large amounts of energy from a few exporting countries, giving the latter a strong position not only in global energy markets, but also in international political relations. When oil and gas are being replaced by renewables, these international dependencies may also change. Hence, energy transition may also refer to changing international relations within energy systems.

In addition to these changes in the origins of the energy carriers, the widely adopted interpretation of energy transition also refers to changes in the use of energy. This change in particular refers to the intensity of energy use, which means how much energy is used to produce a particular amount of work. By reducing this energy intensity, the overall use of energy may be reduced and, as a result, have an effect on the remaining availability of energy, the emission of greenhouse gases and the international energy dependencies.

---

[1] It is important to realise the difference in meaning of energy resources versus energy carriers. See further on this issue Box 1.1.

[2] The concept of sustainability seems to be a clear and straightforward concept, but it isn't. To determine what is good for later generations, one should also know what their preferences and technical and economic abilities are. For instance, later generations may have way more technological options to use energy efficiently, making it less relevant to save energy carriers for the future. This notion is relevant for the discussion on the social costs of carbon (see Box 3.1).

[3] This is also the conclusion of Fressoz (2025), who states in his historical analysis that the growing use of new energy carriers (like renewable electricity) did not replace the conventional energy carriers (like coal, oil and natural gas), but that this growth coincided with a higher demand for energy.

The common denominator in these widely adopted approaches of energy transition can be expressed in physical terms. Seen from this perspective, energy transition refers to installing renewable assets like wind farms or solar parks, the abolition of fossil-fuel assets, investing in electricity grids, replacing gasoline cars by fully electric cars or making appliances more energy efficient (see Box 2.1). By all these kinds of physical measures within energy systems, the use of fossil energy can be reduced and the amount of renewable-energy production increased.

Box 2.1 The German *Energiewende*

Germany was one of the first countries that formulated ambitious targets regarding the transition of its energy system, the so-called *energiewende* (This box is based on Unnerstall (2017)). This political project to radically change the energy system was formally launched by the German government in 2010/2011. This project consisted of three main pillars: (a) the shutdown of nuclear power plants by 2022, while they had a market share of 23% in 2010, (b) the expansion of renewable energy in electricity generation from 17% in 2010 to 35% by 2030 and at least 80% by 2050, and (c) an increase in energy efficiency at a growth rate of 1.6% per year.

The German government had four different motives to pursue this change of the German energy system. These motives were (a) to reduce carbon emissions because of the threat of climate change, (b) to reduce the risks related to nuclear energy, (c) to reduce the dependence on import of fossil fuels in order to foster security of supply and (d) to promote innovation and export opportunities for the German industry. On top of these four motives, some groups in the German society also wanted to break up the market power of the big four energy companies by promoting decentralisation of energy production. The motives related to climate change and security of supply are shared with many other countries, but in particular the motive related to phasing out nuclear energy is unique to Germany.

For the realisation of the policy targets, the German government formulated three basic principles to guide the design of policy measures. These principles were (a) safeguarding security of supply, (b) ensuring cost-efficiency and affordability and (c) preserving a market economy.

In 2025, the objectives of the Energiewende are to a large extent realised. The nuclear power plants have been shut down, the share of renewables in total German electricity generation has increased to about 55%, while the total amount of electricity generation has decreased, which is partly due to a more efficient consumption (see Fig. 2.1).

(continued)

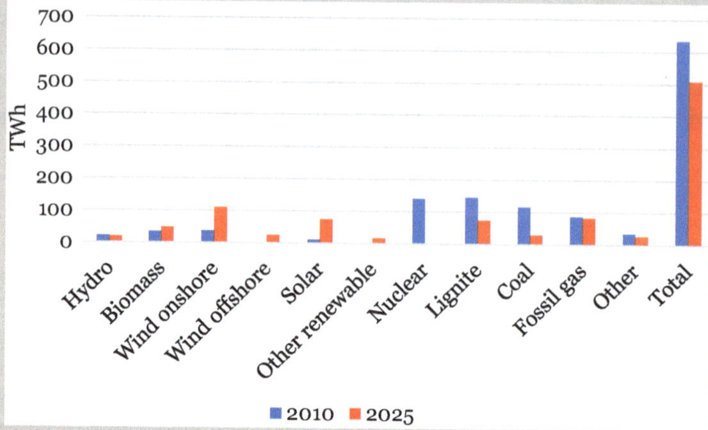

Fig. 2.1 Electricity generation by technology in Germany in 2010 and 2025 (in TWh) (Source: Agora (2026))

Box 2.2 Energy-Transition Objectives of Governments

Energy-transition objectives of governments are generally formulated in physical terms related to the use of energy. Countries and international institutions all over the world have formulated such targets. We mention the policy targets of the European Union, China and Brazil, here, by way of example.

The objectives of the European Union regarding the energy transition consists of the following targets regarding the emission of greenhouse gases, the share of renewables and the energy efficiency (European Commission, 2023). The emissions of greenhouse gases should be reduced by at least 55% by 2030 compared to 1990 levels, with the objective to realize a net-zero emissions economy by 2050. Moreover, the share of renewables in the total EU energy consumption should be at least 42.5% by 2030. In addition, the efficiency of energy use should be improved by 11.7% by 2030. Member States have to implement measures to assure that on average the energy savings are at least 1.49% per year in the period 2024–2030. These general targets are translated into more specific targets for separate industries within the EU, such as for transport, residential buildings and the public sector.

China has also formulated a number of energy-transition targets. Its ambition is that the emission of greenhouse gases reaches its maximum level by 2030 in order to decline until net-zero by 2060. Regarding the use of non-fossil fuels, the ambition is that this share is increased to 25% by 2030 and 80% by 2060. In addition to these targets, there are also targets regarding the carbon intensity of electricity generation and industry (CREA, Centre for Research on Energy and Clean Air, 2025).

(continued)

Box 2.2 (continued)

Brazil has the ambition to reduce its overall level of greenhouse gas emissions between 59% and 67% by 2035 compared to 2005 levels, in order to have a net-zero economy by 2050 (IRENA, 2025). In order to realise these targets, Brazil focuses on the expansion of the electricity system, the gradual replacement of fossil fuels with electrification and advanced biofuels, and the expansion of biofuel production with carbon capture and storage (CCS). The latter measure is needed to remove carbon from the air to compensate for positive emissions.

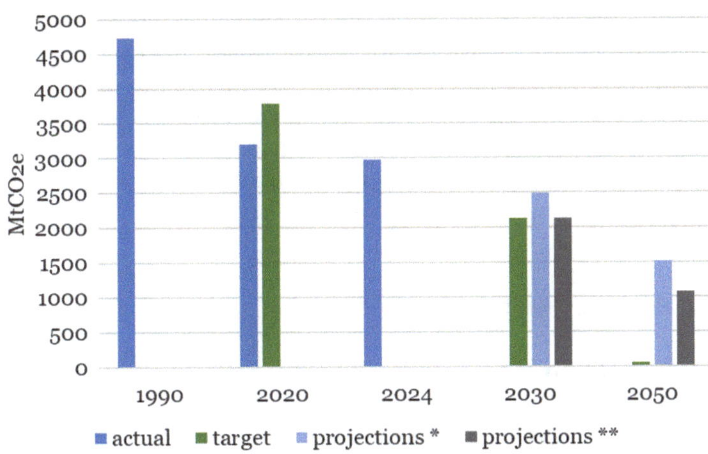

Fig. 2.2 Realised, projected and targeted emissions of greenhouse gases in the EU-27. Note: projections* stands for projections based on existing policy measures, and projections** refers to projections based on additional policy measures (Source: European Environmental Agency (2025))

This widely adopted approach to energy transition is also reflected in the way governments formulate their policy objectives regarding energy transition. These objectives are generally expressed in terms of the share of renewable energy of the total domestic energy consumption, the energy intensity, the installed renewable capacity, the total number of coal-fired power plants that will be closed or the scale of the electricity grids expansion (see Box 2.2).

Defining energy transition in physical terms is useful as it provides a focus on what has to be done at the end of the day. In order to be less dependent on fossil energy or to reduce the emissions of carbon, reducing the use of fossil energy can be effective, and the same holds for increasing the efficiency of energy consumption. This definition of energy transition in physical terms helps to monitor the progress in realising the policy targets. Figure 2.2 shows, as an example, the monitoring of the EU-27 goal regarding the reduction of greenhouse gas emissions. As the total emissions in the EU-27 was 4727 million tons of CO_2-equivalents ($MtCO_2$-e), the target of 55% reduction by 2030 means that the emissions should not be higher than 2131 $MtCO_2$-e. The projected emissions for that year are, however, a bit higher, based on existing policy measures. In case of additional policy measures, however, the target can be reached. For 2050, the gap between projected emissions and the target of net-zero emissions is large, which means that more policy measures are needed in order to realise that target.

Although the definition in physical terms is useful to monitor the realisation of policy targets, this approach is less useful to see how this can be realised. After all, in most countries energy systems are not operated by a central operator who determines what kind of resources to use and how to use the various types of energy carriers. Even in countries without liberalised energy markets, there are still many decisions individual stakeholders have to make, such as how much energy they want to consume in their factory and for what purpose. In countries with liberalised energy markets, there are many decision-making units who can decide what they want to do, not only in terms of consumption, but also in terms of production, storage and trade. Because of the role of all the individual stakeholders who influence the pathway of energy systems, energy transition should not only be looked at from a physical or engineering perspective, but also from a social-sciences perspective and in particular the perspective of economists.

2.3 Economic Perspective

2.3.1 Introduction

The economic perspective does not define energy transition in physical terms, but in terms related to the behaviour of so-called economic agents. In order to understand the economic definition of energy transition, we first have to look more closely at the basic concepts in the economic analysis.

2.3.2 Economic Agents Pursuing their Objectives

The starting point in any economic analysis is the assumption that individuals and organisations, i.e. economic agents, are constantly making choices about how to deal with scarce resources in order to pursue their own objectives (see e.g. Varian, 2003). These objectives can be various, such as maximisation of profits or shareholder value, to stay in business for a long period of time or to contribute to society. It is important to realise that economists do not assume or prescribe that economic agents need to maximise their financial benefits. This is often misunderstood by the general public and even by scholars from other academic perspectives (see e.g. Bolderdijk & Steg, 2014). Frequently, it is said that economists only tend to look at financial variables, and, hence, the economist's perspective is too narrow, resulting in a biased view. This interpretation of what economists focus on is, however, incorrect. In the economic perspective, everyone is completely free to determine her/his own objectives, as economists do not judge the decisions made by economic agents. In other words, for the economic analysis, it does not matter what the objectives of individual economic agents are or which choices they make.[4]

The key assumption in economic analysis is that all economic agents want to maximise their own objectives, which are called utility. In order to do so, all agents, no matter what their objectives are, have to make choices, because the resources they can use are scarce. By scarcity, it is meant that these resources can be used in alternative ways and that these alternative uses compete with each other. For instance, time is a resource which is available to all of us. As human beings, we have to decide how to utilise that resource. Such decisions may be well thought of or just result from intuitions. How time is actually used doesn't matter for the fact that the time, such as a particular hour or day, can only be used for one (or a few more) purposes but not for all potential destinations. Whether we like it or not, as humans we have to deal with the scarce availability of our resources, and this is precisely the object of the economic perspective. If a resource were unlimitedly available to us, the economic analysis would not be relevant.[5] The economic perspective is only relevant when the availability of resources is constrained. Basically, the economic analysis is focused on how the allocation of such scarce resources is carried out.

The fact that almost all resources are scarce implies that using a resource in a particular direction results in so-called opportunity costs. This is the economic term for the missed benefits of making a particular choice regarding the use of a particular resource. If you decide, for instance, to use a particular hour to read a book, you cannot use that hour any more to do something else, like reading a newspaper or attending a concert. As there could be many alternative utilisations of that same hour, there are also many different types of costs of not choosing each of these uses, so there are many different estimates of the missed benefits. Some alternative uses may be very valuable to you, others much less. The highest benefit you could achieve by doing something else (than, in this example, reading the book) is seen as the opportunity costs of that activity. After all, if you would not read that book, you could have enjoyed the benefits of the so-called best of the other potential uses. So, the opportunity costs of doing something (i.e. the first-best choice) are defined as the missed benefits of the second-best alternative.[6]

---

[4] Hence, economics as an academic discipline tends to follow a positive approach instead of a normative approach, in which it is said how people and firms should behave.

[5] Note that the concept of unlimited availability does not refer to physical abundance, but to the fact that a choice related to the use of resources, does not have any consequences for the remaining choice options for oneself or others in the same moment in time or in the future. Such resources are called non-economic goods. An example of such goods are gifts of nature which are freely available to everyone, such as air and sunshine, although both may be scarce in particular circumstances, at particular places or at particular times.

[6] This definition of opportunity costs implies that it is something different than financial costs. The latter concept refers to financial sacrifices to realise something, which is related to the opportunity costs of money. After all, the budget need to pay these financial costs could also be used for a different destination. There may, however, be more (non-financial) missed opportunities due a particular choice, as is discussed in the above example.

It is essential to realise that opportunity costs can exist even when there are no market prices. Actually, for being a cost or not, it doesn't matter whether economic agents have to make financial sacrifices. The latter occurs when the cost refers to things that are exchanged on a market, which means that there exist market prices which can be used to determine the monetary value of the sacrifice. When the sacrifices to obtain something refer to things which are not exchanged on a market or that are not priced by, for instance, government agencies, that does not imply that the costs do not exist. In such a situation, the cost still occurs, but it is only experienced differently, such as less time available for something else or a deterioration in the experienced air quality. It is relevant, though, to realise that such non-financial costs (or benefits) can often be expressed in financial units, through different estimation methods, such as conjoint choice experiments (see Box 2.9).

Box 2.3 Estimating the Value of Preferences Based on the Concept of Opportunity Costs

The actual behaviour regarding choices may indicate so-called revealed preferences, which refer to the benefits agents expect to receive from particular choices. If an economic agent makes a particular choice, e.g. to install solar panels on the roof of her house, then we conclude that the benefit this person attaches to this decision is apparently higher than the opportunity costs, otherwise it would be an irrational decision. The opportunity costs consist, in this case, not only of the costs related to the investment in solar panels (e.g. interest rates of a loan needed to finance the investments), but also the effort the person has to make. This effort may refer to choosing the supplier of the equipment and analysing the characteristics of the contract it offers. If, in this example, all the financial costs of the investment are 1000 euro and the time needed to choose a supplier and contract type is 10 h, we only need to know what the costs of 1 h is in order to determine the minimum value of the expected benefits of the solar panels. Suppose that this person earns 15 euro per hour, then the opportunity costs of the time needed for making the choice regarding the retailer and contract type can be estimated at 150 euro. Altogether, the opportunity costs of the solar panels in this simplistic case are 1150 euro. Hence, we can assume that the person attaches at least a benefit of 1150 to having the solar panels, otherwise we cannot understand why the person would have made the choice to install the solar panels, unless there are some clear factors which hinder the agent to make the best decisions, such as a lack of information or even misinformation, besides the presence of psychological factors, like loss of aversion or status-quo bias. This way of estimating the minimum value agents attach to certain things is based on the opportunity costs they have to make.

Opportunity costs form a crucial economic concept which can be used to analyse the behaviour of economic agents and estimate the value of their preferences (see Box 2.3). Estimates of the value economic agents attach to something on the basis of the opportunity costs are related to another fundamental economic concept: rationality. Economists assume that in principle all agents act rationally, which may seem to be an odd assumption as we all know that people of flesh and blood are driven by many factors, including their own emotions and social circumstances. It is clear that we as human beings generally do not make extensive analyses of all potential pros and cons, and all costs and benefits of the various choice options we face.

Even companies cannot be seen as fully rational entities as their decisions are often inspired by many irrational factors[7]. If this is the case, what do economists mean by the term rational behaviour?

Rationality in economics refers to the fundamental assumption that in principle everyone wants to pursue his/her own objectives and that all decisions they make are directed towards that objective. These decisions can be based on emotions or another non-rational factor, but the background and motivation for decisions are actually not so relevant. The basic approach in economics is to assume that the behaviour of others as it is observed is consistent with their objectives. The reason why this assumption is a powerful analytical tool easily becomes clear: if this assumption is not made, it is more difficult, if possible at all, to determine to what extent decisions of agents contribute to their welfare. Suppose, someone makes financial costs plus some personal effort to replace a gas boiler with a heat pump in her house. In return that person may face a reduction in the future expenditures on heating while also some environmental benefits may be expected. If we do not assume that the person behaves rationally, we can't assume anything about the net value she attaches to the heat pump. Without the rationality assumption, we would actually have no clue to what extent decisions of economic agents contribute to their utility. Instead, if we depart from the assumption of rationality, we can conclude that apparently the (sum of the) expected financial and environmental benefits outweigh the (sum of the) financial and personal sacrifices to realise the replacement of her in-house heating system. Maybe that conclusion is not correct, but that should become clear from information on other factors.

Decisions by economic agents may not be rational as a result of a number of factors. One of these factors is an inability to digest all relevant information. Because of a lack of information or even misinformation, agents may make decisions which do not appear to be beneficial to themselves. In terms of the above example, the person may believe that the environmental benefits of replacing a gas boiler with a heat pump are significantly higher than what they in reality are. Such errors in decision-making can, however, not be attributed to a lack of (economic) rationality, but to a lack of information. Improving the quality of information and transparency, therefore, can result in better decisions, i.e. decisions which are more in line with the objectives of economic agents.

[7] Also macroeconomic developments can result from an accumulation of irrational human behaviour, such as the animal spirits playing a central role in the macroeconomic analysis of the economies of the 1930s by John Maynard Keynes (1936).

Box 2.4 Behavioural Economics Research in the Field of Energy
From behavioural economics, we learn that the actual behaviour of individual economic agents can be subject to various kinds of psychological factors, which means that their decisions do not always conform with the assumption of economic rationality. Such insights are useful for improving the design of, for instance, policy instruments which are meant to influence the decisions economic agents make regarding the use of energy. To obtain these insights, increasingly research is being conducted to test how individual agents actually respond to changes in the design of policy instruments or financial contracts.

Carrol et al. (2022), for instance, show that the way in which consumers are informed about the costs of their energy use affects their willingness-to-pay for energy efficiency measures. A discrete choice experiment shows that when individuals receive information about the long-term costs, they have a higher willingness-to-pay for these measures than when the information is provided on a short-term (bimonthly) basis.

From the research of Jacobsen and Stewart (2022), it appears that the complexity of pricing schemes negatively affects the responsiveness of consumers. Their experiment shows that consumers respond strongly to price signals when these are presented in isolation, but when consumers receive several price signals, which give the similar messages, their responsiveness is much lower. This result suggests that consumers are less able to oversee more complex pricing systems, and therefore respond less.

Another reason why decisions of economic agents may not be consistent with their own objectives is linked to psychological factors (see Box 2.4). Even when people want to pursue their own objectives, they can make inconsistent decisions as a result of various types of psychological biases, such as status-quo biases, loss aversion and choice overload (Dijkstra, 2020). The status-quo bias refers to the notion that individuals generally have a preference for choices that favour the current situation and, therefore, choose not to change anything. The loss-aversion bias means that individuals prefer choices that do not incur a loss over choices that may result in losing something. The choice-overload bias refers to the stress individuals may experience when they have to make a choice from many options: a higher number of options may reduce the satisfaction of the choice they make.

From behavioural economics research, it also appears that individuals tend to make irrational decisions when they are forced or stimulated to take them in a short period of time (see Kahneman, 2013). All these insights on the irrationality in actual individual decision-making are very relevant for both businesses (who make use of this limited rationality in order to make more profit) and governments (to protect consumers against the risk of making suboptimal decisions).

2.3.3 Coordination of the Behaviour of Individual Agents

Economic agents make choices regarding the use of scarce resources, and these decisions follow from the objective to optimise their own outcomes, although agents may be subject to several psychological biases, as we have seen in the previous section. As the circumstances in which the economic agents operate constantly change, their optimal choice may also change. For instance, if the price of gasoline changes, an individual may make other choices regarding his transport. The changing decisions of individual economic agents, in turn, may affect the circumstances they have to operate in. For instance, if many individual agents respond to higher gasoline prices by switching to electric cars or more frequently making use of public transport, the prices of electric cars may increase, just as the price of electricity, while public transport may become more crowded.

These examples show that the optimising behaviours of individual economic agents influence each other through their impact on the costs of the scarce resources, at least when these resources have a limited availability. For those resources which are unlimitedly available, the use by one agent would have no impact on the availability for others. Such resources are, therefore, called non-rivalrous. When such resources are also non-excludable, meaning that no one can be excluded from using it, economists call them public goods. An example of such a good is a dike to protect a region against flooding from a river or sea. Once the dike is there, everyone in that region is protected, no one is exempted. The flip side of such public goods, however, is that no one has an incentive to make costs to realise them. This is why for the category of public goods specific regulatory arrangements are needed, which will be further discussed in Chap. 4.

For most goods, however, it holds that the availability is constrained, which means that using them in one way affects the options for using them in other ways. Hence, for these goods, the choices individual agents make influence each other. The crucial question is how to organise the allocation of these so-called scarce commodities in such a way that it results in the optimal use in a society. As a solution to this allocation problem, the economic discipline has formulated a crucial theorem: the optimising behaviour of all economic agents collectively results in the highest possible welfare,[8] when the coordination mechanisms function perfectly (see e.g. Varian, 2003). One condition for this is that all relevant factors are taken into account when the allocation decisions are made. This is realised when all markets are complete,[9] resulting in market prices for all relevant factors. Another condition is that the allocation process is not influenced by other factors, such as some agents have more (negotiating or market) power than others, which enable them to steer the allocation in the direction of their preferences. The conditions for well-functioning markets will be further discussed in Sect. 3.2.

---

[8] In economics, welfare is something different from well-being. The latter refers to the subjective experience of the quality of life, while welfare refers to the way economic agents satisfy their needs by using scarce goods. The economic concept of welfare also differs from financial income (see Box 2.5).

[9] In economics, complete markets refer to the theoretical concept of markets without any transaction costs and the presence of perfect information.

The coordination mechanisms are generally called markets, where agents who can supply a commodity can meet those who want to buy them. When all conditions for well-functioning markets are met, this process results in the optimal allocation. This means that this allocation results in the highest possible welfare. Here, it is important to realise that the economic concept of welfare is not defined in terms of national income or gross domestic product, but in terms of the net benefits economic agents derive from using and exchanging commodities (see Box 2.5).

Given an initial distribution of resources with different characteristics, such as for instance fossil-energy resources or wind farm locations, the application of these

Box 2.5 Economic Growth, Income and the Measurement of Welfare

In the popular interpretation of welfare, it is measured through the income we earn. This holds both on the level of individual economic agents and on the level of economies. For individuals, a higher income is generally seen as a measure for higher welfare as it allows for a higher standard of living to be achieved. In the case of the aggregated economies (i.e. countries), the common metric for income is the Gross Domestic Product (GDP). GDP can be measured in three different ways, notably as (a) the sum of added value of all industries in an economy; (b) the sum of income earned by all consumers and firms in an economy, independent of whether that income is earned domestically or abroad; and (c) the total sum of consumers and governments spending, plus the investments by business and exports, minus imports (see Fig. 2.3 for an example of the values for the Dutch economy in 2025). The fact that GDP can be calculated using different approaches, indicates it is based on a set of accounting rules. Hence, GDP is a metric from the national account systems.

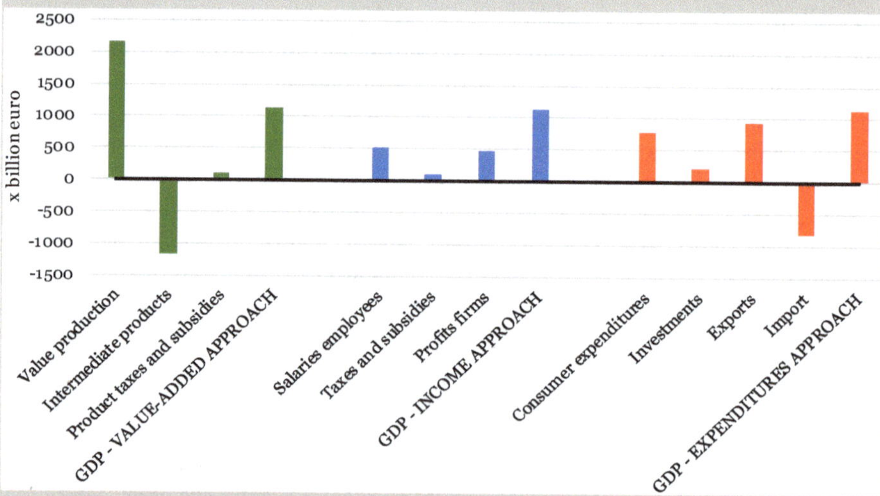

Fig. 2.3 GDP of the Dutch economy in 2025, according to three different measurement methods (Source: CBS/Statline)

(continued)

Box 2.5 (continued)

From a more conceptual, economic perspective, however, welfare is something different. It is not equal to the value of the goods that we produce, the income that we earn or the money that we spend. Welfare has to do with the satisfaction of our needs and the sacrifices we make to obtain that satisfaction. One of the sacrifices we make to earn an income is that we spend time and/or make some efforts. These sacrifices are not necessarily fully accounted for in the GDP or individual income calculations, as only the financial reward is included. In addition to that, both satisfaction and sacrifices are not restricted to financial variables. The benefits of conducting a particular activity may also consist of the pleasure of doing that activity, while the costs may also consist of time spent, which is not paid for.

Hence, income measures on an individual, firm and economy level are important for daily decisions regarding the utilisation of our resources because of the budget constraints we are all facing, but these measures do not reflect the actual welfare which theoretical economics refer to. In order to estimate the impact of, for instance, policy measures on welfare, we need to conduct social cost-benefit analyses, which are based on the fundamental economic concept of welfare (see Box 4.6 for more about this method).

resources results in the highest possible welfare when priority is given to the cheapest resources. It would be a loss of potential welfare (i.e. higher costs for society) if a more expensive resource would be used while a less expensive resource would remain unused. Figure 2.4 shows how the application of this rule maximises the

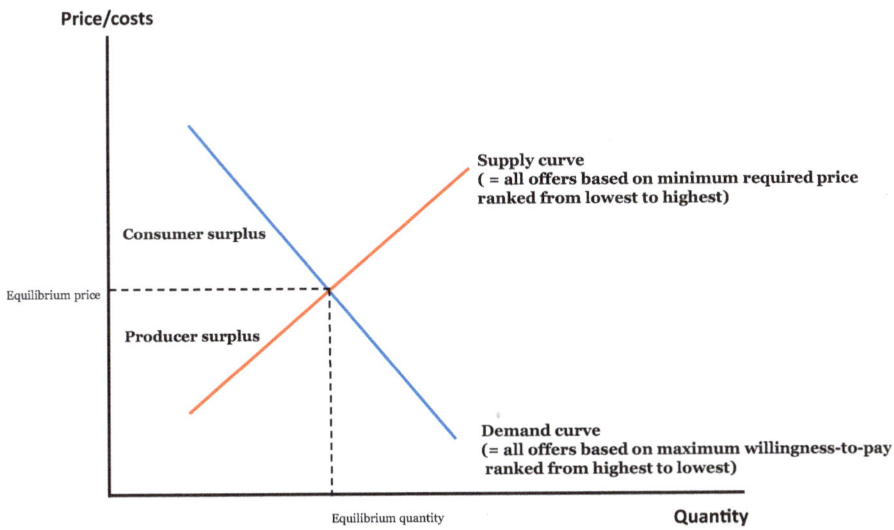

Fig. 2.4 Markets as coordination devices that result in maximum welfare when a number of conditions are met

so-called producer surplus. This surplus measures the difference between the market price that suppliers receive and the costs they have to make. The greater the use of the cheapest options, the higher the producer surplus. If more expensive options would be used, the produce surplus would be less.

The total welfare resulting from the allocation of resources also includes the consumer surplus, which is measured as the difference between the value economic agents attach to a commodity and the price they have to pay for it. In order to maximise consumer welfare, and hence total welfare, it is crucial that the commodities are used by those agents which attach the highest value to it. After all, suppose that a commodity is allocated to someone who hardly values it, while someone else with a much higher value is not able to obtain the commodity, then the total welfare would be below its potential. In economic terms, the allocation is not efficient.

If commodities are allocated based on these principles, the so-called Pareto optimum is realised. This optimum entails that it is impossible to improve the situation for someone without making it worse for someone else. It is important, however, to realise that the Pareto optimum can only be determined for a given initial distribution of the resources. For any other initial distribution, other optimal allocations can be found. The optimal allocation through markets only occurs when a number of conditions hold, as will be discussed in Sect. 3.2. It is important to realise that the concept of optimal allocation through markets must be seen as a theoretical benchmark, which can be used to analyse real markets.

Markets are not the only type of mechanisms that can be used for allocating scarce commodities. Another kind of mechanism to coordinate how a group of economic agents allocate a scarce resource is through centralised management. The problem with such an allocation method, however, is that the central agency which is responsible for achieving the optimal allocation generally does not have all the information about the potential benefits as well as all the potential costs for all the (potentially) involved economic agents. As a result, such centralised coordination mechanisms easily result in a suboptimal allocation.[10]

For energy carriers, top-down allocation methods were fairly common in many countries until the liberalisation of energy markets. Centralised agencies were responsible for the allocation of electricity, for instance, using technical-economics models minimising the overall system costs. In many emerging countries, energy is still allocated through centralised systems, but in most developed countries the allocation of energy carriers is based on market principles, as will be discussed in Sect. 2.4.4.

---

[10] A centralized system of planning and coordination can be successful in realising in a high economic growth, but that may go at the expense of efficiency, as was shown by the historical economic development of the Soviet Union (Gregory & Stuart, 1981).

2.4 Energy Systems Are Constantly Changing

2.4.1 Introduction

The fact that economic agents are pursuing their own objectives, whatever these objectives may be, and that they respond to the (market) circumstances they operate in, has as a consequence that the structure and characteristics of economies change all the time. This holds also for energy systems. Over the past centuries, energy systems have changed very strongly. The composition of the use of primary energy carriers, i.e. the so-called energy mix, today is completely different from those of the past (see Sect. 2.4.2). These changes were triggered by technological developments and changes in relative energy prices (see Sect. 2.4.3). These changes in prices are related to the development of liquid marketplaces (see Sect. 2.4.4). In addition, energy systems have increasingly become international, with producers and consumers connected to each other through extensive physical infrastructures and liquid international marketplaces (see Sect. 2.4.5). The characteristics of the firms active in the energy supply chains have also changed quite strongly over the past period. For instance, supply chains with vertically integrated firms dominating the market in one country have been transformed into supply chains with various types of firms, including internationally operating firms specialised in only one part of the energy supply chain (see Sect. 2.4.6).

2.4.2 Changes in Total Energy Use and Energy Mix

Over the past one and a half centuries, huge changes occurred in the use of energy. The total global energy consumption increased dramatically since the start of industrialisation around 1850. The total global primary energy consumption grew from about 10,000 TWh in 1850 to about 185,000 TWh in 2024 (see Fig. 2.5). Together

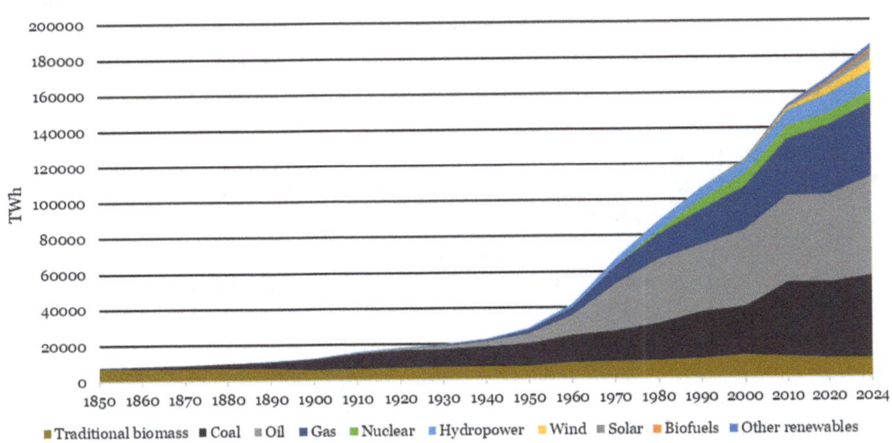

Fig. 2.5 Global primary energy consumption by source, 1850–2024 (Source: Our World in Data, using data from Energy Institute (2026))

with this growth, the composition of the energy mix also changed significantly.[11] Two centuries ago, the global energy consumption mainly consisted of biomass, but one century later the share of biomass decreased due to the strong growth in the use of coal in industrial processes.

After World War II, the use of oil increased significantly, in particular due to the rise in the use of oil products as transport fuel. About 50 years ago, natural gas became an important primary energy carrier, while simultaneously nuclear energy became a new primary energy source. While the contribution of to the total energy mix continued to increase, the amount of nuclear energy remained stable, implying that its relative share has declined. Since the start of this century, the renewable energy sources wind and solar show a growth in their share of the total energy supply. Despite the recent strong growth in renewables, their share in the total primary energy consumption is still fairly limited. From Fig. 2.5, we can clearly conclude that the new energy carriers did not really replace the old ones, but that they were added to the energy system, as was already mentioned in Sect. 2.2.

Box 2.6 Measurement of Final-Energy Use

The energy consumed by end-users is called final-energy use. This use typically consists of various types of energy carriers. When households burn natural gas to heat their premises, this refers to the final use of a primary energy carrier. When they use electricity or gasoline, this final use refers to the use of secondary energy carriers, as both energy carriers are produced from primary energy carriers. Note that even when a household uses electricity that is produced by its own solar panels, it uses a secondary energy carrier as this electricity is generated from the energy included in sunshine. Households use a tertiary energy carrier when they use an energy carrier such as hydrogen that is produced through electrolysis.

Final-energy use can be measured as the energy that is consumed, but it can also be measured as the underlying primary energy. For the final consumption of primary carriers, this can be measured directly through the energy content of these carriers, but for renewable electricity this is not the case. If the final-energy use of renewable electricity would be measured on the basis of its energy content (e.g. the kWh of electricity produced by solar panels), the comparison with the final-energy use of primary energy (e.g. the kWh of electricity produced by a gas-fired power plant) would not be correct. After all, the latter coincides with energy losses, in particular through the production of heat. In order to obtain a fair comparison of the final-energy use of different types of energy carriers, the so-called distribution method can be

(continued)

[11] The share of the various types of energy carriers in the total primary energy consumption is measured through the so-called distribution method (see Box 2.6).

Box 2.6 (continued)
used. In this method, it is assumed that the production of renewable-energy carriers are subject to similar energy losses as fossil fuels (see Energy Institute, 2026). In this way, an estimate of the primary consumption of renewable energy is obtained which can be compared with the primary consumption of fossil energy.

Note that the final energy use refers to the energy delivered to end-consumers, but this energy is generally still converted into a form that is actually used, the so-called useful energy. Electricity, for instance, is converted into light from a lightbulb or into power of an appliance, while natural gas can be converted into heat through a gas boiler. Also in this final stage of energy-supply chains, energy is lost because of conversion losses, such as through the heat of lightbulbs and appliances.

2.4.3 Technological Developments and Changing Energy Prices

Past changes in the energy mix were driven by a combination of rising energy demand, resulting from industrialisation and the development of modern transport, and shifts in the availability of energy resources (see also Petit, 2017). These shifts affected the relative prices of different energy carriers. The discovery of coal resources, together with the development of technologies to mine these resources in the midst of the nineteenth century, gave a boost to the supply of coal. This increase in the availability of coal facilitated the industrial revolution in the nineteenth century, which started in England. Because of the high energy content of coal compared to traditional biomass,[12] this supply fostered human activities which needed more energy, in particular industrial processes which needed high temperatures or feedstock (e.g. the use of cokes for the production of steel).

A similar development happened when oil resources[13] were discovered which could be exploited at relatively low costs (i.e. making crude oil available at lower costs), which resulted in a relatively strong decline in the oil price (see Fig. 2.6). At the same time, technological innovations fostered the production of oil products like gasoline (through refining processes). The widespread availability and the low production costs of oil were a strong incentive for the use of that energy carrier, in particular in the then upcoming activity of motorised transport. This strong growth in the consumption of oil came to an end in the oil market crises during the 1970s, in which oil prices surged.

[12] See Appendix A for the technical characteristics of various types of energy carriers.

[13] Oil and natural gas are found in geological reservoirs that contain hydrocarbons, which are organic compounds based on hydrogen (H) and carbon (C). When oil is produced from a reservoir, also natural gas may come up, and when the operators do not want the gas, they used to flare it. Because of environmental regulation, the flaring of gas has to be reduced (see IEA, https://www.iea.org/energy-system/fossil-fuels/gas-flaring)

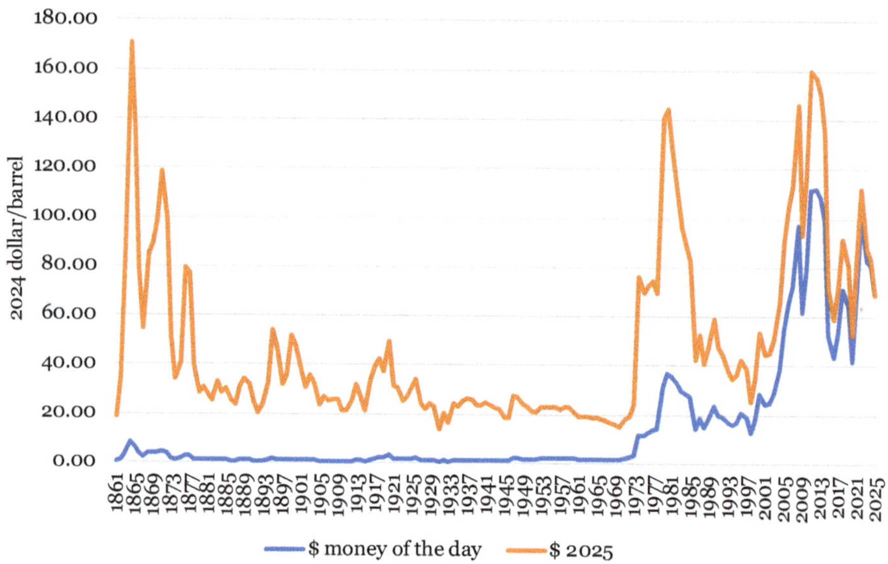

Fig. 2.6 Average annual crude oil prices, 1861–2025, in dollars per barrel (in money of the day as well as corrected for inflation using 2025 dollar value) (Source: Energy Institute based on S&P Global Energy - Statistical Review of World Energy (2026))

The crises in the oil market in the 1970s were caused by a number of factors. Prior to these crises, global oil demand experienced a long period of strong growth starting already in the 1960s, which made countries more dependent on oil, while the global supply capacity hardly increased. Because the oil was mainly supplied by a few oil-producing countries, this increase in oil demand created a dependence of the oil-consuming countries on these countries. The majority of the oil-producing countries formed a cartel called the Organisation of Petroleum Exporting Countries (OPEC), with the objective to jointly manage the supply of oil in order to raise market prices and, hence, the profits for the oil-producing countries. This cartel agreement was quite successful for many years of their existence in keeping the global oil price above competitive levels.[14]

The resulting high oil prices led, however, also to various types of responses by other market parties. First of all, the high oil prices were an incentive for other countries and firms to search for oil resources outside the OPEC, such as in the North Sea and in the US. The production costs in these regions were significantly higher than the ones in several OPEC countries. Without the cartel interventions resulting in the higher oil prices, these fields would not have been developed as that would not have been profitable. After all, as the OPEC cartel successfully raised the oil price above the levels of the production costs in regions like the North Sea and the Gulf of Mexico, it became profitable to explore those resources.

[14] In some periods, however, the OPEC cartel was not able to raise the oil price (see Sect. 2.4.4).

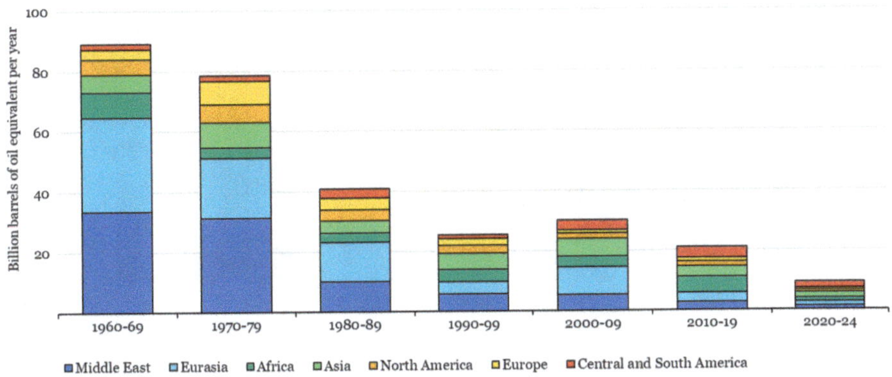

Fig. 2.7 Discoveries of conventional oil and gas, per region, average per year for each period, 1960-2024 (Source: IEA (2025))

These increased exploration activities are reflected in data on the number of discoveries across various global regions. In the 1960s, the majority of oil and gas discoveries were in the Middle East and Eurasia (i.e. Caspian region and Russian Federation), but during the oil crises of the 1970s, the share of Asia and Europe in the global discoveries increased strongly (see Fig. 2.7). From this figure, it is also clear that the annual number of discoveries has fallen below the levels of the 1960s and 1970s, reflecting that the majority of the oil and gas resources have now been discovered.

Another effect of high prices of particular energy carriers, like oil, is that they trigger the substitution with other energy carriers. This substitution occurred both on the supply and demand side. An example of supply-side substitution triggered by the high oil prices during the oil crisis of the 1970s was the incentive to explore for natural gas, which led to the discovery of new gas resources. On the demand side, end-users substituted oil with gas and nuclear, like in the electricity-generation sector. These developments clearly show how one (big) event in one energy market, i.e. the actions by OPEC countries, is able to trigger massive changes within energy systems.

That the global portfolio of natural resources is constantly changing is also reflected in Fig. 2.8, which shows the ageing of the natural gas fields since 2000. In 2000, about 10% of all the gas fields were already in production for more than 50 years, but gradually this share reduced. In 2024, about 70% of the producing gas fields were in production for less than 20 years, with a significant number of fields in production since only a few years, which is likely related to the extremely high gas prices in the period 2021–2023. These changes in the average age of the producing gas fields are an indication of the exploration activities in the upstream gas industry.

The previous examples show that technological innovations and economic developments interact closely. This is also reflected in recent developments in renewable-energy technologies. The costs per unit of production for wind and solar electricity have decreased sharply over the past decades, measured through the so-called Levelised Costs of Energy (LCOE) (see Box 2.7).

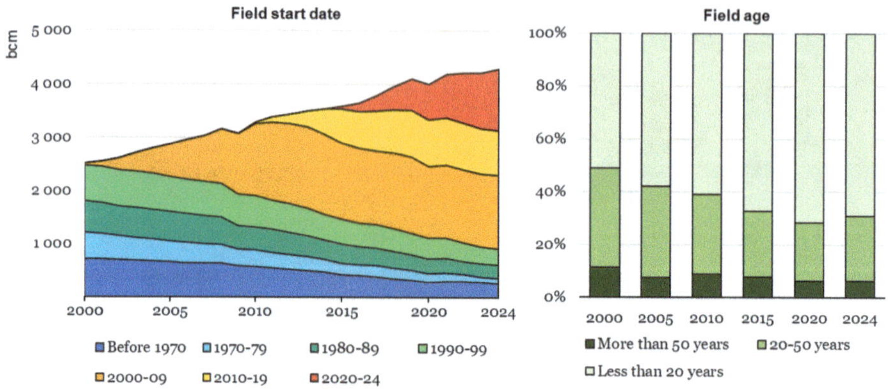

Fig. 2.8 Global natural-gas production by start date and age, 2000–2024 (Source: IEA (2025))

Box 2.7 Levelized Costs of Energy (LCOE)

In order to compare the costs of different technologies, it is common to use the metric Levelized Costs of Energy (LCOE). This measure shows the present value of the total costs over the lifetime of a production facility in relation to the present value of the production volume during that period. The formula is:

$$\text{LCOE} = \frac{\sum_t^T \frac{\text{Costs}_t}{(1+r)^t}}{\sum_t^T \frac{\text{Production}_t}{(1+r)^t}}, \tag{2.1}$$

where t is the index for year, T stands for total (expected) lifetime of the plant (e.g. in years) and r is the discount rate. *Costs* stands for all costs, including investments, operational and maintenance costs and decommissioning costs (in, e.g. a million euro). *Production* stands for the total production per year (in, e.g. Megawatt-hour (=MWh)). Both Costs and Production are divided by $(1 + r)^t$ in order to express the future values of costs and production in the current value of money, i.e. to discount the future numbers. Note that the discounting of the future production volumes in physical units is related to the discounting of future (financial) revenues. The calculation of the LCOE is based on the break-even condition that the discounted value of the revenues should at least be equal to the discounted value of the future costs. The LCOE can therefore be seen as the break-even value of the average future price (P) of production (IEA/NEA, 2020). Hence, the LCOE is the value of P which makes that the present value of the future revenues is equal to the present value of the future costs:

(continued)

Box 2.7 (continued)

$$\sum_{t}^{T} P * \frac{\text{Production}_t}{(1+r)^t} = \sum_{t}^{T} \frac{\text{Costs}_t}{(1+r)^t} \tag{2.2}$$

It is, however, important to realise that for a full comparison of the economics of various technologies, one should not only look at the costs, but also at the revenues. A solar PV park, for instance, may have a much lower LCOE than a nuclear power plant, but it generally also realises much lower revenues (see Veenstra et al., 2026). The latter is due to the so-called market-value factor. This factor describes how the capture price (i.e. the price that actually can be realised) of a technology develops in relation to the market share of that technology. The higher the share of solar PV in an electricity system, the lower the price it realises as many solar PV systems in a region (market zone) are producing when the sun shines, which reduces the electricity price. This effect does not occur with nuclear power plants, as their operation does not depend on weather circumstances, although there is some dependence on the availability of cooling water. For a further discussion of the market-value factor, see Sect. 2.5.4.

This decrease is partly due to economic incentives provided by government through support schemes. That governmental support triggered learning effects and economies of scale. These effects were stronger in the solar PV industry than in the wind turbine industry, which is due to a number of factors (see Fig. 2.9). One of them is that PV installations can be produced modularly. This means that they can be made in small units on industrial scale, after which the units can be easily combined to realise large solar PV parks. This is different for wind parks, as they consist of a smaller number of large units. A related aspect is that the production of wind turbines is raised by making them taller which results in a higher production, i.e. a higher capacity factor (as wind turbines with higher height capture more wind).[15] Hence, this increase in the capacity factor is realised with a higher capital expenditure. On the contrary, a higher capacity factor for solar PV units is realised through a higher efficiency of converting the solar energy into electric energy, without necessarily raising the capital expenditures.

As for other generation technologies, the development was less stimulated, and their average costs per unit of production show less pronounced changes. The LCOE of nuclear seems even to have increased, which may be related to the increased uncertainty around the realisation of projects, resulting in higher construction durations as well as higher discount rates. For conventional fossil-fuel power plants, the LCOE does not show a clear decline, but this is also related to the fact that the

[15] The capacity factor is the ratio between the actual aggregated production versus the technically maximum production. For instance, a wind turbine of 10 MW capacity has a technically maximum annual production of (10 × 8760 =) 87,600 MWh. If the actual production realised in a year is 40,000 MWh, then the capacity factor is 40,000/87,600 = 0.45.

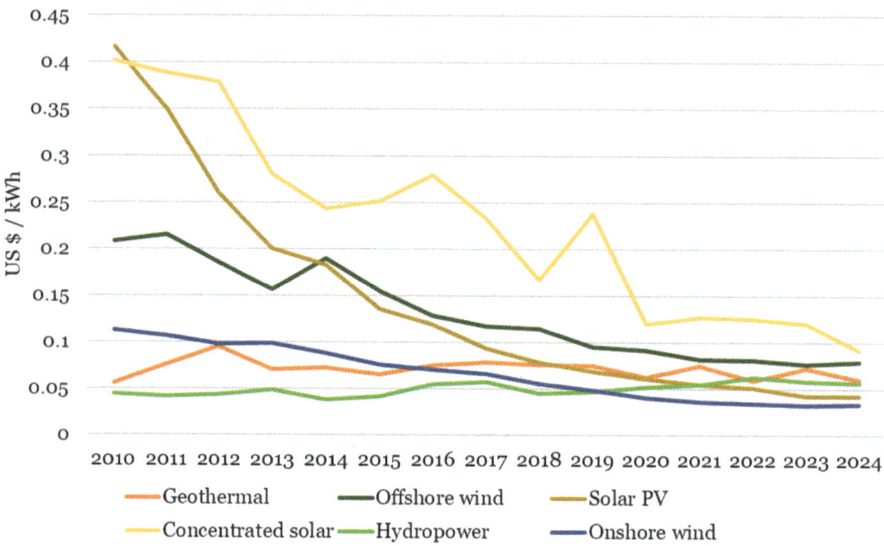

Fig. 2.9 Levelised costs of energy (LCOE) of renewable electricity generation technologies, 2010–2024, average per year (Source: Our World in Data)

LCOE of these technologies not only relates to the capital intensity, but also to the variable costs. The latter depends strongly on the prices of fossil fuels. Because these prices are volatile, this also causes the LCOE to fluctuate.

2.4.4 Development of Marketplaces

A crucial component of the evolution of energy systems is the development of marketplaces. In order to exchange a commodity among economic agents, there needs to be a possibility to meet each other, to collect information on what others want to offer or buy and conclude contracts. The facilities that enable these exchanges of information and commodities are called marketplaces. For oil and coal, such marketplaces already exist for many decades, although they were initially of a more bilateral and regional nature. After the development of the first commercial oil wells in the USA, the informal organisation of the trade was quickly replaced by the introduction of local exchanges where brokers acted as intermediaries between sellers and buyers.[16] Gradually, the marketplaces for oil and also coal became more international where producers, consumers, traders and other types of economic agents from all of the world can participate. As a result, the international trade in these energy carriers results in prices all over the world which are closely interconnected.

[16] The first commercial field started to produce in 1859 in Pennsylvania and the first exchange became operational in 1878. For a description of the history of the trade in oil see: https://oilregionlibraries.org/the-oil-exchange-national-transit/

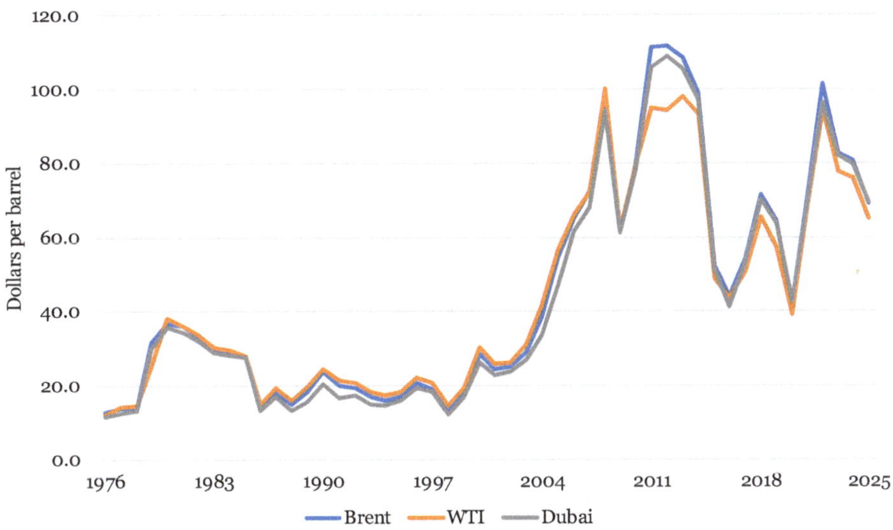

Fig. 2.10 Average annual crude oil spot prices, per type of oil, 1976–2025 (Source: Energy Institute based on S&P Global Energy - Statistical Review of World Energy (2026). Note: Brent stands for a basket of crude oil from various fields in the North Sea, Dubai for a basket from the Middle East and WTI (West Texas Intermediate) from the Texas region in the USA)

Although the physical characteristics of oil coming from the Middle East (Dubai), the North Sea (Brent) or the Gulf of Mexico (WTI) differ to some extent,[17] their prices are strongly related to one another through international trade (see Fig. 2.10). For well-functioning, large-scale and internationally organised market-places, the trade needs to be standardised. This is achieved through so-called exchanges, where a limited number of products, such as contracts for delivery in the upcoming month or calendar year, are defined for which market parties can submit bids to offer or buy.

Despite the development of liquid international marketplaces, the oil markets were and still are prone to the (ab)use of market power. Initially, the oil market was dominated by a few so-called majors or large companies. Standard Oil, for instance, dominated about 90% of the refined oil in the USA at the end of the nineteenth century.[18] The powerful role of the major oil companies has been taken over by the group of oil-producing countries in the OPEC. The market power of this cartel is, however, not unrestricted, as we have seen in the past. During periods of relatively low oil demand, it is difficult for the cartel to operate coherently, as in such situations, individual members have an incentive to cheat, i.e. not to stick to cartel

[17] The differences in oil coming from various fields refer to the density, i.e. the mass per unit of volume, and the sulphur content. Oil from the Middle East generally has more sulphur (and is therefore called 'sour') as well as a higher density, and is therefore called 'heavy' (see Mulder, 2023).

[18] Sources: Oilprice.com; https://oilprice.com/Energy/Energy-General/The-Complete-History-Of-Oil-Markets.html.

agreements to produce less (Zweifel et al., 2017). In addition to that, the more liquid and transparent marketplaces are, the more difficult it is for firms or countries to dominate the market, as other market parties have more options to choose from.

In contrast to oil and coal industries, where marketplaces were initiated already more than a century ago, in natural gas and electricity industries, marketplaces are more recent. The relatively late introduction of marketplaces here is due to the fact that the transport of these energy carriers is more bounded by physical infrastructures. These infrastructures have to be carefully managed, particularly because of the requirement to permanently maintain system balance. Therefore, centralised management is crucial. Until a few decades ago, in many countries, utility companies were responsible for both the operational decisions regarding power plants and the operation of the electricity grid. A similar situation holds for the gas sector, where the operator of the gas transportation infrastructure was also involved in the production and sales of gas.

Later on, however, it became clear that economic agents could be given the freedom to make their own decisions regarding investments in power plants and exploration in new gas fields, and to make the operational decisions on how to use them. In many countries, this resulted in a process of liberalisation, which includes the establishment of wholesale and retail markets for electricity and natural gas. Although these markets differ in their precise design, as seen with nodal electricity markets in several states in the US and zonal markets in Europe, the basic idea of all electricity and gas markets is that economic agents can decide for themselves in which technologies they want to invest, how much electricity or gas they want to sell and under what conditions. The functioning of these markets depends, however, on the well-functioning of the underlying network, which makes these markets quite different from the coal and oil markets.

The markets for gas and electricity, but also for hydrogen and heat, can only function properly when there is sufficient network as well as production capacity, while the networks always need to be in balance (see Fig. 2.11). The development of markets for the network-based energy markets, therefore, requires the implementation of regulations in order to guarantee these so-called reliability conditions (see Mulder, 2023).

A typical example of such a development is the creation of virtual hubs in the European gas market, such as the Net Balancing Point in the UK, the Title Transfer Facility (TTF) in the Netherlands and the Trading Hub Europe (THE) in Germany (see Fig. 2.12). In such hubs, market participants can trade in ownership rights of gas molecules somewhere within a network, without the need to bother with the presence of sufficient transportation capacity (Keller et al., 2022). It is the task of the grid operator to take care of that, next to taking care of system balance and the quality of the gas that is injected into the grid.

Such developments in the governance of networks and marketplaces have strongly facilitated the international trade in both natural gas and electricity. For hydrogen, the international trade is still in an infant stage, but may become more important as a result of energy-transition policies promoting that energy carrier. In the case of heat markets, there exist only a number of small-scale markets, on the

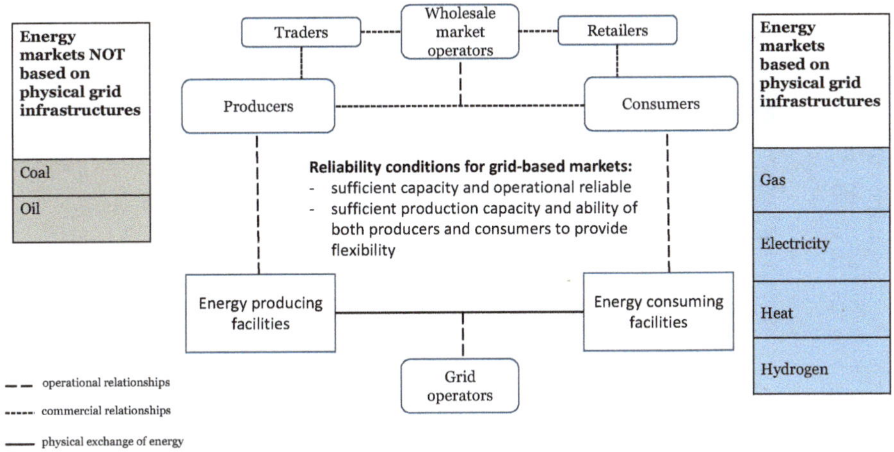

Fig. 2.11 Functioning of network-based energy markets depends on a number of reliability conditions

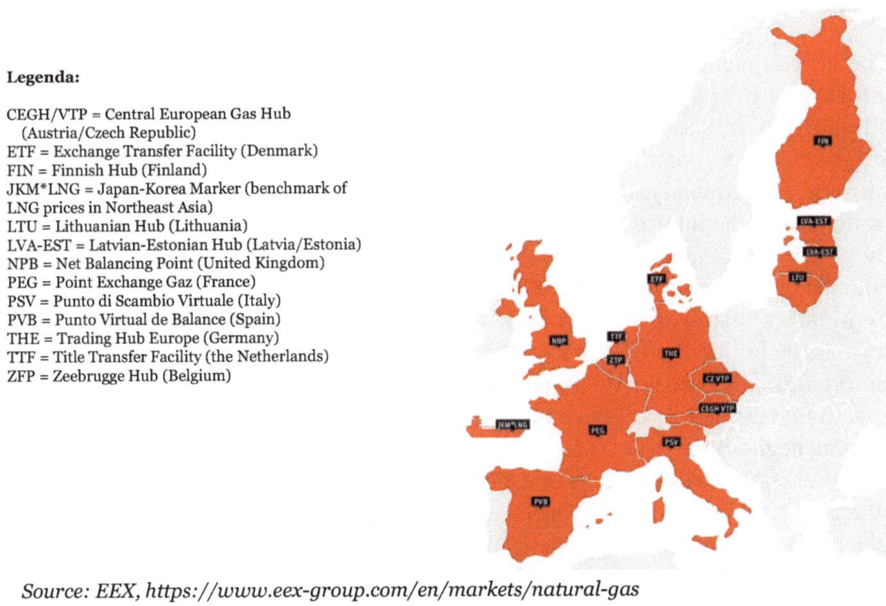

Fig. 2.12 Virtual hubs for European gas spot trading, operated by the European Energy Exchange (EEX) (Source: EEX, https://www.eex-group.com/en/markets/natural-gas)

level of municipalities or regions within countries. The local operation of heat markets is related to the high transport costs and energy losses during transport, which make it not economical to have markets on a larger spatial scale.

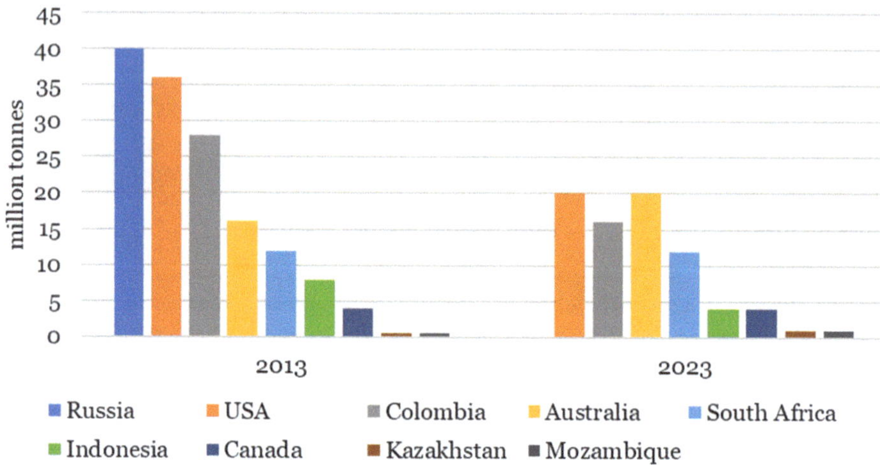

Fig. 2.13 Annual net import of hard coal in the EU, 2013 and 2023 (Source: Eurostat)

2.4.5 International Integration of Markets

The development of marketplaces is strongly related to the development of the infrastructure for international transport. The development of large and cost-efficient oil and coal vessels enabled producers to supply their commodities to users all around the globe, contributing to the development of global markets for these energy carriers. Consequently, the buyers in this market obtained more options to choose from. Hence, the improvement in the international transport options raised the ability of economic agents to respond to changing circumstances. As a result of this, both the oil and coal market have become global markets. The hard coal[19] imported by Member States of the European Union, for instance, originates from various regions, including the USA, Colombia, South Africa and Australia (see Fig. 2.13). Before Russia's invasion of Ukraine, Russia used to be the primary supplier of hard coal to Europe. However, since the invasion, its role in the supply of coal to Europe became negligible.

For energy carriers which were mainly transported through physical grid infrastructures, the possibilities for international exchange developed more slowly. Electricity and natural gas systems used to be more regional due to the physical constraints on transport. Gradually, however, these systems have also become more international. The national gas markets within Europe, for instance, have increasingly become integrated, as can be observed from the rather synchronous movements of the gas prices across various countries. Figure 2.14 shows that the average gas prices in the NBP market in the UK and the TTF market in the Netherlands are

[19] Hard coal is also called anthracite. This is coal with a high carbon content, but also a high energy content. This type of coal is mainly used for making coke which is used in smelting iron ore in order to make steel. In this process, the carbon of the coal is used to remove the oxygen from the iron ore. See Sect. 5.4.5 how the steel industry can decarbonise its processes.

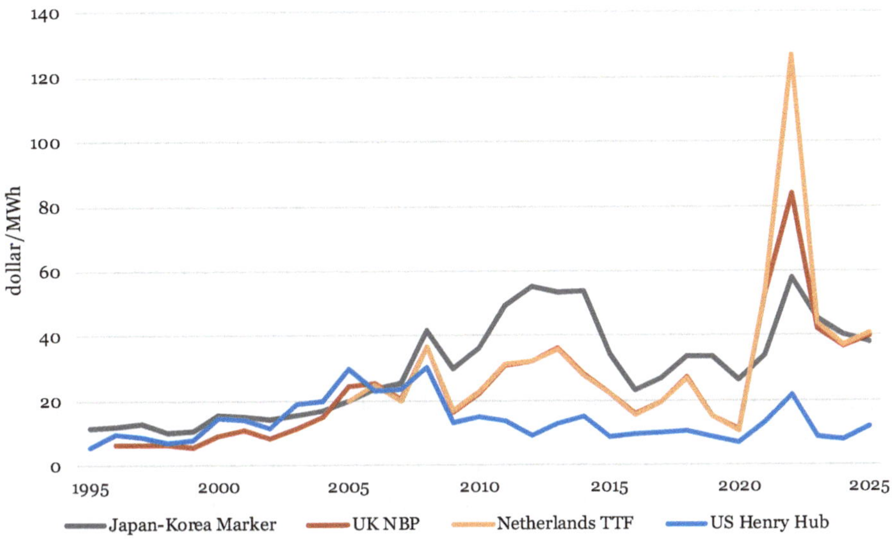

Fig. 2.14 Average annual natural-gas prices in a number of marketplaces, 1995–2025 (Source: Energy Institute based on S&P Global Energy - Statistical Review of World Energy (2026))

fairly similar most of the time. Only during the energy crisis of 2022, the difference between the gas prices between these countries was significant, with the highest gas prices on the Dutch TTF. The high prices in the Netherlands resulted from the strong reduction in gas coming from Russia, which affected the gas markets on the continent more strongly than the UK gas market. Although gas exports from the UK to Northwest Europe increased to benefit from these high prices, the limited capacity of the cross-border transport lines prevented the UK from fully exploiting the price differences. As the gas trade between Europe and other parts of the world, such as the Henri Hub in the USA, is done through LNG (Liquefied Natural Gas) which is more expensive, and also subject to physical constraints regarding terminals and vessels, there still exists fairly large international price differences between the US and Europe, but the price differences between the European and Asian gas market have become smaller in recent years.

In many parts of the world, electricity systems have also become increasingly internationally integrated. In Europe, the national systems are physically connected to each other since the 1950s, not only because of reliability concerns, but also to increase the fuel efficiency of power plants (UCTE, 2010). Since the 1990s, these cross-border connections have been strongly extended and made available for commercial purposes.[20] Currently, the electricity markets in most European countries

[20] Cross-border transmission capacity can be extended by physical measures, i.e. investing in physical grid capacity, as well as by increasing the efficiency of the utilisation of the existing capacity. In Europe, the latter has been done through so-called flow-based market coupling, which means that the electricity markets in various market zones are cleared by taking into account the physics of the flow of electricity through the grid. Despite the strong increase in cross-border transmission

are linked to each other, although cross-border transmission constraints still exist and may result in large international price differences within Europe from time to time.[21] This strong degree of international integration gives economic agents the option and the incentive to respond to changes somewhere within Europe. For instance, a dry winter season in Norway resulting in low hydro reservoir levels and, hence, high electricity prices, may also raise the prices in other European countries. Such an increase in prices may trigger consumers in these countries to reduce their consumption, while producers are incentivised to raise their production. See Box 2.8 for the relationship between international trade and international price differences in electricity markets.

Box 2.8 International Integration of Electricity Markets

A major development in energy systems during the past decades is the increasing international integration of electricity markets. In the past, systems for electricity were mainly organised at a local or sub-national level, although with some physical interconnections because of both economic and reliability considerations. The limited regional scope of these systems was related to the fact that the exchange of these energy carriers was based on the use of physical grids. When electricity markets in Europe were introduced, they became more international by making use of the existing connection capacities. Gradually, international trade was fostered by extending the available cross-border capacity. The extension in this capacity was realised by investments in the physical transport capacity as well as by increasing the efficiency of the utilisation of the existing technical capacity. Since cross-border capacities are also meant to address reliability issues, a part of the technical transmission capacity is reserved for emergency situations in which the frequency of a grid can only be maintained or restored through international cooperation. In addition to that, grid operators reserve a part of the cross-border capacity to handle so-called transit and loop flows. These are unplanned flows of electricity resulting from physical laws determining the flow of electricity in a meshed grid.

The remaining part of the transport capacity can be allocated for commercial uses, i.e. international exchange to benefit from international price

(continued)

capacity, international price differences may still occur when the market circumstances in the various market zones are strongly different, such as in terms of marginal production costs and tightness of the market. See Mulder (2023) for a further discussion on this topic.

[21] The European integration of electricity market is hampered by the complex legal architecture of cross-border trade as well as delays in the implementation, according to the European Court of Auditors (2023). Rumpf (2020) also argued that the legal framework gave insufficient incentives for the transmission system operators to reduce cross-border bottlenecks, as they are more directed at relieving congestion within their market zone instead of congestion between market zones.

Box 2.8 (continued)

differences. This allocation process can be carried out through explicit auctioning, in which market parties buy cross-border transport capacity in advance, but this easily results in inefficient use. The latter happens when parties which have bought cross-border transport capacity are not actually continuously using that capacity, since there may not always be arbitrage opportunities. By allocating the cross-border capacity in an implicit way, the efficiency may improve significantly. In this method, the capacity allocation is done jointly with the clearing of electricity markets.

The more cross-border capacity is available to market parties, the more options for international price arbitrage exist and the less international price differences occur. This relationship between possibilities for international trade and price differences is reflected in the Law-Of-One-Price (LOOP). This law says that, in absence of bottlenecks in international trade, the price differences among countries will not exceed the actual transport costs. Even when countries use completely different production technologies, such as hydropower versus fossil fuel power plants, the electricity prices in these countries are similar to each other when there is sufficient cross-border capacity and no (marginal) transmission costs. This also implies that the presence of international price differences must be attributed to the presence of bottlenecks on the borders and not to differences in production technologies or load patterns.

Another implication of the above relationship is that the profitability of investments in international transport capacity depends on the potential for international trade, i.e. the differences in production costs and load patterns. When countries have fairly similar generation portfolios and load patterns, the electricity prices will be fairly similar as well, even without international trade. This means that there will not be many options for price arbitrage. Investing in international transport capacity can, therefore, in particular be efficient when the countries involved utilise different generation technologies or have different load patterns. Such an investment generates welfare benefits when expensive technologies (in the high-cost country) are replaced by less-expensive technologies (in the low-cost country). These productive efficiency effects may coincide with distributional effects which may make it politically challenging to extend cross-border capacity. In addition to the benefits in productive efficiency, the investments in cross-border capacity may also result in reduced price volatility (i.e. lower risk) and more competition among producers. This results in lower prices for end-users.

2.4.6 Organisation of Energy Supply Chains

Together with the liberalisation and internationalisation of energy systems, the organisation of energy supply chains changed significantly. This holds in particular for the energy markets which are based on networks, i.e. natural gas and electricity markets. In order to realise a fair competitive playing fields for all suppliers of these commodities, the grids need to be operated by independent operators. It was quite common in many countries prior to the liberalisation, that the operator of the natural gas or electricity grid was also active in the production and supply to end-users. If this had remained unchanged, these vertically integrated companies would have a strong competitive advantage compared to other firms that were only active in production or supply.

Therefore, in many countries where the markets are liberalised, the grid operators have been unbundled from commercial activities. This enables these operators to fully focus on the management of the grid and treat all grid users equally, in a non-discriminatory way. This so-called unbundling of the grid operators can be done in different ways. Some countries, like Belgium, France and Germany, choose for a relatively weak form of legal unbundling, which means that the grid operator is a separate entity but owned by a holding company which is also active in commercial activities (Meletiou et al., 2018). Other countries, including the Netherlands, choose for a stronger form of unbundling, notably full ownership unbundling, both for the transmission and the distribution grids.[22] This kind of unbundling means that the owner of a grid operator may not be active in commercial activities at all.

Another dimension of the organisation of energy supply chains refers to the type of ownership of companies. In many countries, energy firms used to be entirely owned by public authorities, such as the state or regional governments. Energy was seen as a utility which could only be served by public entities. Countries appear, however, to have different views on the importance of having public shareholders of energy companies, and in particular the grid operators. In some countries, such as the Netherlands, all grid operators are fully publicly owned, while in others, such as Germany and the UK, there is a mixture of publicly and privately-owned grids. In the economic literature, however, there is no clear evidence which type of ownership is most favourable for the development of energy markets or the functioning of energy grids (Rekker et al., 2024).

Furthermore, the energy supply chains have also changed in terms of the number and size of firms. The liberalisation of markets facilitated the entrance of new (smaller) firms, which competed with the incumbent (generally larger) firms. The internationalisation made it possible for firms from other countries or even global regions to enter markets, making the composition of the supply much more diverse. The production of fossil-energy resources is now carried out by a large number of firms from all over the world, while in the past these resources were mainly exploited by national energy companies. Figure 2.15 shows how the oil and gas fields on the Norwegian continental shelf are distributed across various operators. It appears that

[22] In the case of electricity, the transmission grids refer to the (very) high voltage grids, while the distribution girds refer to the medium and low-voltage grids. The former form the backbone, used for long-distance transport, while the latter are used to connect decentralized grid users. In the case of gas, transmission grids are called transport grids, which refer to the high-pressure grid, while the distribution grids refer to the medium and low-pressure grids.

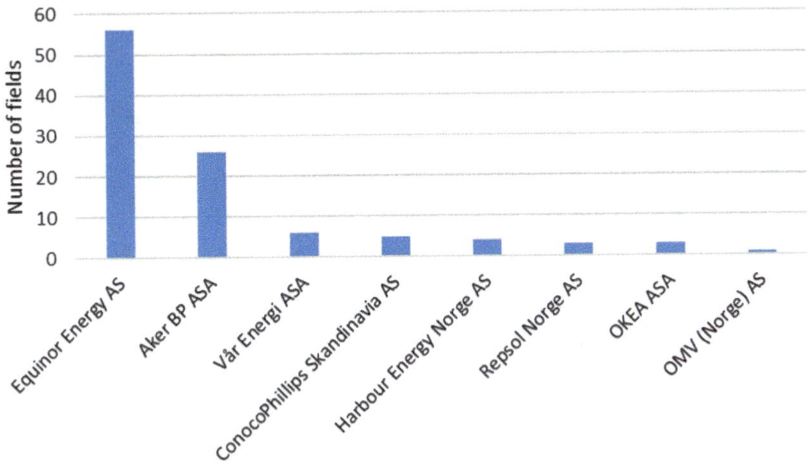

Fig. 2.15 Number of Norwegian oil and gas fields in production by various types of operators, by the end of 2024 (Source: https://www.norskpetroleum.no/en/facts/field/)

there are several firms active in this region with backgrounds in various European countries and the USA.[23]

Also in the electricity industry, many changes have occurred. Incumbent firms, for instance, have acquired power plants in other countries, which makes them more international. This implies that the above-mentioned international integration of electricity markets is complemented with an internationalisation of companies (see also the discussion of the transitions of E.ON and Vattenfall in Chap. 5). Electricity firms are also making choices regarding the portfolio of their generation plants, which affects their sensitivity to external developments. For instance, firms may respond to declining prices of gas relative to the price of coal by investing more in gas-fired power plants. As a result, the share of gas-fired power plants in their generation portfolio increases, which make their costs more sensitive to movements in the international gas price. Their overall profitability, however, is much less sensitive to these prices when the electricity prices are mainly determined by the marginal costs of gas-fired power plants as marginal production units[24].

Firms also respond to changing price volatility by investing in flexible assets, such as flexible open-cycle gas turbines (OCGT) or batteries. These assets can be used to profitably respond to the occurrence of low and high prices, resulting from the fluctuating production circumstances for renewable assets such as wind turbines and solar panels. Hence, in an electricity system with high shares of renewables, firms have stronger incentives to invest in flexible assets.

[23] Such as ConocoPhillips from the USA, Harbour Energy from the UK, and Repsol from Spain.

[24] After all, in such circumstances a rising price of gas implies a rising price of electricity as well.

2.4.7 Conclusion

Looking at the past developments in energy systems, it is clear that change is a permanent characteristic. Under the influence of economic, political and technological developments, current energy systems are in many aspects different from those centuries or even decades ago. Hence, energy systems are constantly changing. These changes are, however, not the same as energy transitions.

2.5 Energy Transition is not equal to changing Energy Systems

2.5.1 Economic Definition of Energy Transition

All the above changes within energy systems—in terms of energy mix, technological developments, international dimension, organisation of supply chains and business, and development of markets—have a huge impact on what these systems look like. These changes, however, are not the same as energy transition from an economic perspective, although they do partly result from economic factors like changes in relative prices. The changes in energy mixes, the organisation of international markets and other aspects, mainly show that energy systems, just as many other systems, are constantly changing in response to changing circumstances and decisions made by economic agents. In this chapter, we will show that energy transition from an economic perspective is something different from the ongoing changes in energy systems.

In the economic definition of energy transition, we have to refer to the basic components of the economic analysis. These basic components consist first of all of the economic agents who are constantly making choices about how to deal with scarce resources. These agents are assumed to maximise their own objectives, whatever they may be. In making these decisions they can decide to collaborate with each other, in one way or another, as that can enable them to make more efficient choices by exchanging commodities or providing services to each other. Agents are also competing with each other to obtain the same resources or to provide goods or services to other agents. These activities of agents, constantly making choices and interacting with each other, result in the allocation of scarce commodities across uses and users.

Using this economic perspective, energy transition must be seen as a set of interventions in the process of allocating energy commodities among various potential users and uses. These interventions can be done to reach particular objectives, such as the reduction of carbon emissions or to be less dependent on fossil energy. Hence, from an economic perspective energy transition can be defined as the process of intervening (by society or governments) in the optimising behaviour of economic agents regarding the use of energy carriers, to reach particular public objectives in an efficient way. Hence, the economic perspective on energy transition includes two components: intervening in the choices economic agents make and doing this efficiently. With this focus on intervening in choices of economic agents in an efficient way, the economic perspective offers a valuable additional contribution to other perspectives, such as technical or ethical (see Box 2.9).

Energy-transition policies differ from regulating energy markets, as the latter is meant to improve the functioning of these markets without specific objectives regarding the outcomes of these markets (see Mulder, 2023). Energy-transition policies, however, consist of policy interventions directed at realising particular objectives. Hence, energy-transition policies are a specific category of interventions in energy markets. In Chap. 4, where we will evaluate the efficiency of various types of energy transition policy measures, we will also make the relationship to general energy policies clearer.

In the remainder of this chapter, we will explain how changes in energy systems, as discussed in the previous section, can be analysed using a number of economic concepts. First, we will dive into the economics behind changes in the energy intensity of economies, and the economic incentives for economic agents to invest in renewable energy. Then, we will introduce some economic concepts to analyse the impact of policy measures on changing economic agents' decisions.

Box 2.9 The Economic Concept of Efficiency in Relation to the Concept of Fairness

Efficiency is a central concept in economics, referring to productive efficiency (i.e. using the most efficient technologies), allocative efficiency (i.e. market prices are related to marginal costs and goods are allocated to those who most value the goods) and dynamic efficiency (i.e. innovation resulting in movements of the technological frontier). A specific concept is cost-efficiency, which refers to the amount of (government) expenditure needed to realise a particular objective.

According to the basic microeconomic theory, well-functioning markets results in the optimal allocation of goods, while they also provide incentives to economic agents to become more productively efficient and to innovate. In such markets, firms can only become more profitable by either reducing the costs of their production or by improving the quality of their products, which enables them to charge higher prices. Note that the process of markets fostering the productive and dynamic efficiency also consists of changes in the industry structure. This means that the competitive process may make less competitive firms, i.e. firms having relatively high costs, unprofitable. This may result in the exit of these firms from the market. As a result, over time, the industrial composition changes in response to competitive pressure fostering efficiency.

An efficient production of goods and efficient allocation does not only contribute to the overall welfare of a society, but it may help make societies fairer, although fairness and efficiency are two different dimensions of societal well-being. When overall welfare increases, due to lower production costs and/or more innovative products, more wealth is, in principle, available

(continued)

Box 2.9 (continued)

for more agents to share in. One can, of course, not state that welfare and fairness are necessarily positively related, as the latter is strongly related to the distribution of welfare and how the various economic agents participate in societal activities. In other words, a country with a relatively low income can be perceived as fair and a country with a high level of income as unfair, when the distribution of the wealth is very unequal and many people may not be able to participate in the decisions-making process. As an example of the latter type of country, we can refer to the USA, where the average income per capita is much higher than in most other countries, but the distribution of income is, in comparison to many other developed countries, more unequal, as many citizens do not have access to basic services, such as healthcare (see: https://nashbio.com/).

2.5.2 Understanding Changes in Energy Intensity

As we have seen in the previous section, activities of economic agents to, for instance, install renewable energy or to insulate buildings, do not necessarily belong to energy transition when we look at this phenomenon from an economic perspective. Such activities may be triggered by a government's policy measures, and, hence, may be seen as a tool for realising their objectives regarding renewable energy or energy efficiency. However, such activities may also result from other factors. This becomes clear when we look more closely at past developments in the energy intensity of economies.

Even without any government policies stimulating energy efficiency, economic agents may experience market incentives to reduce their energy use per unit of product. This is in particular the case when energy prices are relatively high, as is clearly reflected in historical evidence. During past periods of relatively high energy prices, firms and households took more measures to reduce their energy consumption.[25] Higher prices improve the business case for energy efficiency measures, which stimulates economic agents to take measures to reduce their energy consumption. This can be deduced, for instance, from the response of natural gas users in Europe to the extremely high gas prices during the gas crises in the years 2021–2023. The surge in international wholesale gas prices raised the end-user prices for both industries and residential households, and in response, both groups adapted their gas consumption. This occurred in various ways. Residential households lowered the temperature in their premises, other economic agents who used gas for heating did the same. Next to that, industries that used gas as input for their processes, like heating or feedstock, reduced their economic activity, as the input prices of their production process became too high for a profitable exploitation. Other industries, such as

[25] The response in the demand by economic agents to changes in the prices can be measured through the so-called price elasticities (see Sect. 2.6.3).

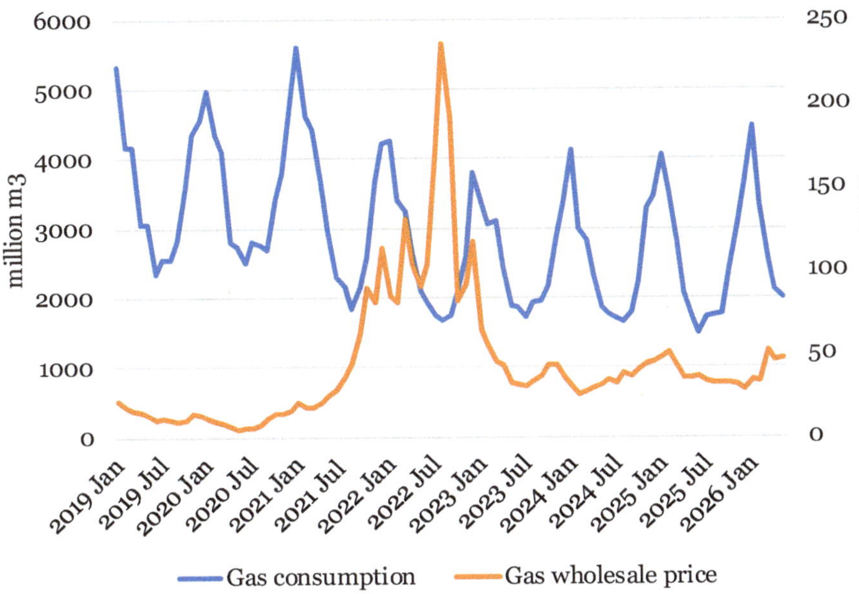

Fig. 2.16 Average monthly natural-gas wholesale price in the Dutch TTF and total monthly consumption of natural gas (not-temperature corrected) in The Netherlands, per month, Jan 2019–Jun 2026 (Sources: gas consumption: Statline CBS: gas price: Elexys)

electricity generation, switched to other energy carriers, in particular coal. All these responses together strongly reduced the aggregate consumption of natural gas.

As an example, Fig. 2.16 shows the monthly average of the day-ahead gas prices as well as the aggregated gas consumption in the Netherlands. We can see that, together with the increase in gas prices starting in 2021, the total gas consumption (including the consumption by the energy industry) decreased strongly[26]. This resulted not only in much lower winter peaks, but also in lower summer lows. One may have expected the gas consumption to increase again when the gas prices dropped after the summer of 2023, but this happened only partially. This may have partly been due to behavioural changes, such as residential households that became used to a lower temperature, but there are also more structural changes induced by the high gas prices. Households which have insulated their houses have structurally reduced their heat consumption. The same holds for industrial users who took investment decisions which reduced their use of gas, by making their processes more energy efficient or reverting to other energy carriers, such as electricity. The latter also holds, for instance, for households who replaced their gas boiler with a heat pump to heat their houses. In addition to these more or less permanent changes on the level of agents, there were also some structural changes within the economy, such as highly energy-intensive industries that lost market shares due to their high

[26] For a full analysis of the relationship between gas price and gas consumption, one needs to control for other factors, such as outside temperature and the influence of taxes on end-user prices.

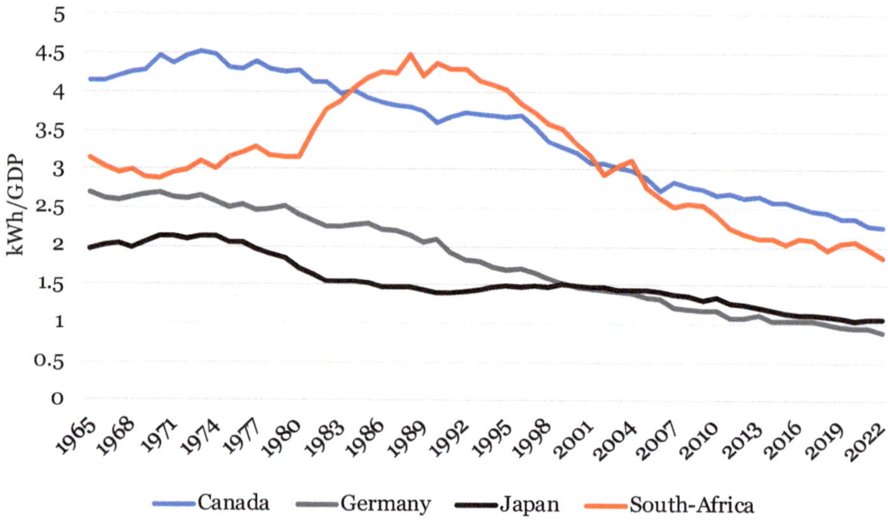

Fig. 2.17 Average annual energy intensity in a number of countries, 1965–2022 (in kWh/dollar GDP) (Source: Our World in Data. Note: GDP is adjusted for inflation and differences in living costs between countries)

costs. Less energy-intensive firms on the other hand became more competitive. All these permanent and structural changes were also facilitated by the fact that the wholesale gas prices remained significantly above the pre-energy crisis levels, although at much lower levels compared to those during the energy crisis.

Also on a macroeconomic level, we can see a clear relationship between energy prices and the energy intensity of economies. Since the oil crises of the 1970s, the energy intensity in many countries has reduced significantly. On a global level, the energy intensity is reduced by more or less 50%, which means that in order to earn the same income now, about half as much energy is needed as 50 years ago. Of course, there are large differences among countries depending on their level of economic development, industrial structure and organisation of their energy systems. Figure 2.17 shows that in Japan, the energy intensity of the economy has always been on a relatively low level, while in Canada this intensity was significantly above that of other developed countries. This difference can be attributed to variations in the availability of domestic resources (which is low in Japan and high in Canada), affecting the relative price of energy usage. This figure also shows that a country like South Africa first saw an increase in energy intensity, which was related to its stage of the economic development, in which the contribution of energy-intensive activities as industry and transport increased. Later on, this country also showed a decrease in energy intensity, due to among others energy-efficiency measures. A similar belt shape development in the macroeconomic energy intensity occurred earlier in developed countries. The UK already realised the peak in its energy intensity around 1870, while the energy intensity in the USA peaked around 1910

(Pepermans et al., 2023). Since then in both countries, the energy intensity gradually declined to about a quarter of these peak levels.

From the above examples, we learn that a reduction in energy intensity results from two different types of underlying developments: improvements in energy efficiency at the level of the agent or the technology and changes in the composition of economic activities.

As an example of the former group of developments, we can refer to households which are taking energy-efficiency measures to reduce the costs for heating their houses, or to car manufacturers improving the efficiency of the engines of their cars to make them more attractive for their customers.

The second group of developments, contributing to changes in the energy intensity of countries, refer to changes in the industrial structure. High energy prices make energy-intensive products more expensive compared to products which are produced with a lower energy usage. As a result, the relative product prices change, which trigger economic agents to change the mix of their consumption package. Energy-intensive industries face, as a result of higher energy prices, more economic challenges, while less energy-intensive industries may see an improvement in their competitive position. All these changes in decisions by economic agents result in a lower energy intensity, which automatically also results in much lower energy use and emission levels.

These relationships between energy intensity, technical energy-efficiency improvements and structural changes can also formally be described. The total energy consumption (*E*) in a country can be seen as a function of energy intensity (*ei*) and the total realised income (*Y*):

$$E_t = ei_t * Y_t \tag{2.3}$$

Energy intensity (*ei*), which is defined as the amount of energy (*E*) that is used per unit of income (*Y*), can be expressed as a function of the energy use per unit of income per type of activity (*i*) and the economic structure, i.e. the share of the incomes from various activities in the total economy (Gorus & Karagol, 2022; UNIDO, 2015):

$$ei_t = \frac{E_t}{Y_t} = \sum_i \left(\frac{E_{it}}{Y_{it}}\right) * \left(\frac{Y_{it}}{Y_t}\right) = \sum ee_{it} * sa_{it} \tag{2.4}$$

Using this formula, one can state that the energy intensity of an economy in a particular period (*t*) results from, on the one hand, changes in the energy efficiency (*ee*) of all the various types of activities and, on the other, the share of each activity (*sa*) in the economy.

Using this decomposition method, one can estimate the impact of the various factors behind the changes in the energy intensity. In a long-term panel analysis on 27 OECD countries, Gorus and Karagol (2022) find that the energy intensity in this region in 2018 was 62.5% compared to 1980, which results are in line with what we discussed above in relation to Fig. 2.17. These authors find that the reduction in energy intensity in the 27 OECD countries is due to efficiency measures within

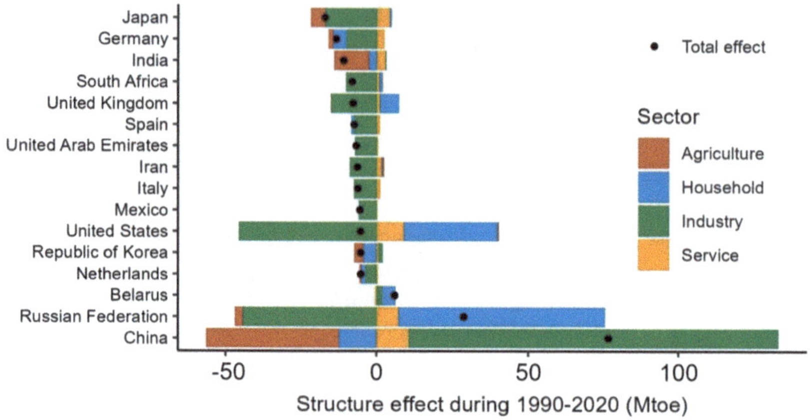

Fig. 2.18 Change in energy consumption due to structural changes, per country, 1990–2020 (Source: Jain (2025))

industries, while the industrial structure contributed negatively to the overall energy intensity reduction. This means that the share of energy-intensive industries in the OECD increased, but that this effect is more than neutralised by technical efficiency measures in various types of industries. On a country level, however, there appears to be large variation in these results.

A similar conclusion was found by Croner and Frankovic (2018), who conclude that the decline in energy intensity in a group of 40 major economies can mainly be attributed to technological improvements and only for a small extent to structural changes within economies. The explanation for the almost negligible contribution of structural changes on the energy intensity of groups of countries is related to international trade. Changes in (energy) prices affect competitive conditions in various countries, and in response, the market shares of countries in particular industries change. In countries, for instance, having relatively low energy costs, energy-intensive industries may grow, while they may decline in countries where these costs are relatively high. Because of the changing international production conditions, firms may also move to other international locations. As a result of these developments, the industrial structure of a country may change strongly, but on a global level, however, the industrial structure may change much less.

This effect can be clearly seen in Fig. 2.18, which is derived from Jain (2025). In many countries the industrial change had a negative impact on the total energy consumption, but in China the industrial growth had a strong positive effect, while the agriculture industry in this country reduced its total energy consumption. These developments refer to the industrialisation of the Chinese economy. At the same time, the US and Russian economy became less industrialised, while its households were responsible for a strong growth in energy consumption. From the above economic analysis of developments in energy intensity, it appears that they result from both technical efficiency improvements and changes in the industrial structure. Both changes are related to changes in relative prices. Hence, even without specific policy measures, the energy intensities of economies change.

2.5.3 Understanding Price Formation and Incentives for Investments

In order to understand changes in energy systems, one also needs to understand how energy markets function and how firms are incentivised to invest in new capacity and, as a result, contribute to changing energy systems. Therefore, we now briefly discuss the relationship between price formation and incentives for investments.

Trade in energy markets is typically conducted in terms of the amount of energy carriers, measured through energy units (e.g. MWh) or the physical quantity of the energy carrier, such as weight (e.g. tonne) or volume (e.g. m^3). The market transactions, therefore, result in prices in terms of these units, such as euro per MWh, dollar per ton or euro per m^3. The energy prices affect the revenues of energy suppliers and, hence, their profits. These profits form, in turn, the basis for the profitability of investments in new production facilities, which can be seen as capacities to supply energy. These capacities can be measured in terms of, for instance, MW. This implies that the profitability of these investments in production capacity depends, in the case of absence of government support, on energy prices which result from market transactions. An investment is expected to be profitable when the present value of the expected net revenues, resulting from the product prices (p) and marginal costs (c) from operation during the lifetime (T) of the investment (I), exceeds the present value of the costs of the investment. This is shown by the following equation, where r stands for the discount rate and t for years:

$$\sum_{t}^{T} \frac{I_t}{\left(1+r\right)^t} \le \sum_{t}^{T} \frac{p_t - c_t}{\left(1+r\right)^t} \tag{2.5}$$

Hence, when the expected net revenues are such that its present value is sufficient to compensate for the costs of the investments, an economically rational firm will make the investment, while it will not make the investment when the net revenues are not sufficient. As the net revenues are based on the volume of the produced energy, but are needed to compensate for the costs of the capacity, one may wonder to what extent energy markets provide appropriate return on investments. This boils down to the question to what extent energy prices and incentives for investments are related to each other.

In a competitive market with sufficient supply capacity, energy prices are only based on the marginal costs of the marginal supplier (in case the market-clearing prices are set on the basis of pay-as-clear). After all, when one supplier would ask a price which exceeds the marginal costs[27], a competitor with the same marginal

[27] Marginal costs are the costs of supplying one extra unit. In case of a gas-fired power plant, for instance, these costs refer to the costs of burning gas. These costs depend on the conversion efficiency of the turbine, the price of gas and, depending on the implemented climate policy, the costs of emitting carbon. Note that the fixed costs of a power plant do not play a role in price setting, as these costs are sunk, which means that they do not depend on the amount or timing of production.

production costs could easily outcompete that firm by asking a lower price. Due to competition, the market price will not exceed the marginal costs, which implies that the price will not generate any return on fixed costs.

For an individual firm operating in a large competitive market, the market prices do not change whether that firm invests or not. That is also the reason to call individual firms in such a market price-takers. At a market level, this is, however, different. When many firms decide not to invest because of the expected net revenues being insufficient, this may in the future, result in more scarcity in the market and so-called scarcity prices. Scarcity prices are prices which exceed the marginal costs of supply, and they occur when the demand exceeds the available capacity. Hence, scarcity prices generate operational profits which can be used to compensate for the fixed costs.

Scarce capacity to supply energy has to be allocated in one way or another. Without the presence of a market, this can be done through, for instance, allocation rules such as first-come-first-served or priority rules. When a market exists, this allocation is done through its price mechanisms. When demand exceeds available supply, energy prices rise to levels at which the demand for the commodity is sufficiently reduced. In theory, those buyers who have a willingness-to-pay for the energy commodity below the market price will withdraw from the market. After all, buying a product at a higher price would reduce their welfare, which is not a rational economic decision. Because of scarcity prices, which exceed the marginal costs, both the marginal and inframarginal suppliers realise an operational profit which can be used to compensate for the fixed costs. These profits can also be called scarcity rents.

Hence, in order to make an investment decision, firms have to explore the future development of markets and, in particular, how often and to what extent scarcity prices will occur. When future scarcity is expected, firms have an incentive to invest in expanding their capacity when the expected scarcity rents are sufficiently high.

Market prices may, however, not fully capture the risks regarding the future availability of the commodity and, hence, they may underestimate the value of having capacity. As a result, market parties do not invest sufficiently from a social welfare perspective. This may be the case, as will be discussed in Chap. 3, when market parties overestimate the magnitude of natural resources, which is a problem of imperfect information. Another reason could be that market parties cannot fully capture the benefits of having sufficient capacity, which is a problem of positive externalities. The latter may, for instance, happen when governments do not allow (for political reasons) market prices to rise to (very high) price levels which are needed to clear the market. As a result, the scarcity revenues that producers can realise are restricted, which reduces the incentive for them to invest in sufficient capacity. Another factor why the market process may fail to trigger sufficient investment in production capacity is that equilibrium prices which depend on scarcity, may coincide with greater uncertainty about the level of the prices and, hence, profits.[28]

[28] This may, for instance, happen when the market share of renewable energy, with low marginal costs, increases. As a result, investments can only be profitable when market prices often exceed the marginal costs of the marginal, price-setting producer. In such circumstances, the market prices are set by the marginal willingness-to-pay, which is more difficult to predict than the marginal costs of a production unit. See further on this issue, Section 4.6

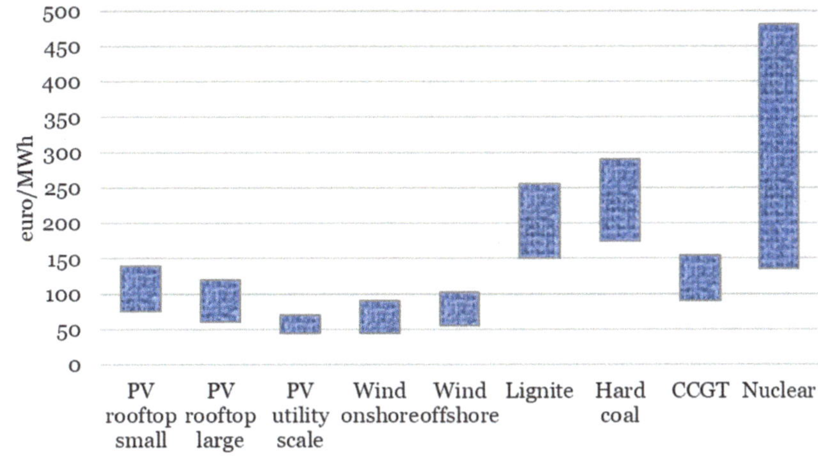

Fig. 2.19 Range of estimations for the Levelised Costs of Electricity (LCOE) of various electricity-generating technologies at locations in Germany in 2024 (Source: Fraunhofer Institute for Solar Energy Systems ISE (2024). Note: CCGT stands for Combined-Cycle Gas Turbine, which uses both gas and electricity turbines to generate electricity)

2.5.4 Understanding Investments in Renewable Electricity

When economic agents pursue their own objectives by making choices among alternatives, they may also choose for renewable energy when this is beneficial for themselves. When a company wants to invest in, for instance, electricity-generation capacity, it will consider the total costs over the lifetime of that capacity and compare them with the total revenues which can be realised. For a profitable investment, the latter should at least be equal to the former. When the revenues of different technologies are equal, one can base the decision for a particular technology on the lowest costs. As was discussed in Box 2.5, the metric Levelised Costs of Energy (LCOE) can be used for this. In Fig. 2.9, we saw that the values of the LCOE of renewable technologies as solar panels and wind turbines have starkly dropped over the past decades. Looking at the current values of the LCOE of renewable electricity-generation technologies in comparison to those of fossil fuel and nuclear plants, we see that the former appear to be significantly below the latter (see Fig. 2.19). In this figure, we also see that there is quite a range of uncertainty in particular for the fossil fuel power plants and even more for the nuclear power plants. In the case of fossil fuel plants, the uncertainty about the LCOE is primarily related to uncertainty about the future fossil-energy prices, while for nuclear power plants, the uncertainty is related to uncertainty about the magnitude of investment expenditures and the duration of the construction period.[29]

[29] A factor which may affect the future costs of both fossil fuel and nuclear power plants is the availability of cooling water, which is crucial for these technologies. Renewables such as wind turbines and solar PV do not have that dependence. As climate change results in more periods of droughts, the availability of cooling water may become a limiting factor for investments in fossil fuel power and nuclear plants.

When only using this information on the lifetime costs per unit of product, an economic agent that wants to minimise its costs of electricity generation will likely choose to invest in utility-scale PV installations or onshore wind turbines. For the realisation of such investments in renewable energy, no financial governmental support seem to be necessary given the relatively low life-time costs. Of course, one has to acknowledge that the current relatively low costs of renewables partly result from government support in the past. After all, the historical policy measures to support renewables contributed to technological developments and efficiency improvements resulting from learning-by-doing. Hence, in the past, policy support was needed, but this may not be the case any more.

For the decision to invest in new generation plants, however, not only the costs are relevant, but also the revenues. Here two factors are relevant, both related to the price-formation process in electricity markets. The first factor refers to the general phenomenon of peak-load pricing and its relevance for investments. The other factor refers to the revenues a particular technology is able to capture given its supply characteristics.

A general characteristic of electricity markets where the electricity price is based on so-called peak-load pricing, like in European nodal electricity markets, is that the electricity market only gives incentives for investments when there are many hours of scarcity of generation capacity. Only in these hours, the electricity price can be significantly above the marginal generation costs, and, hence, result in profits which are needed to recoup investment costs. How does the price-formation process in these markets actually work?

In hours when the available generation capacity exceeds the demand, the electricity price is determined by the marginal costs of the marginal (price-setting) power plant. This situation is reflected by the Demand curve 1 in Fig. 2.20, with p_1 and q_1 being the equilibrium price and quantity, respectively. In this situation, for plant type B (i.e. the price-setting technology), the market price is equal to its marginal costs, which means that this plant does not make any operational profits which can be used to recoup the fixed costs of investments.[30] Plant type A, which is the so-called inframarginal supplier, does make some inframarginal profits,[31] but this may be insufficient to recoup its fixed costs of the investments. Hence, in a situation of a relatively low demand, electricity suppliers are not incentivised to invest in

[30] When the marginal supply in an electricity market comes from a gas-fired power plant, the marginal costs are related to the price of gas (and also the price of carbon allowances when there is a carbon-pricing mechanism) and the conversion efficiency. When a gas-fired power with a conversion efficiency of 50% plant is the price-setting plant, the gas price is 40 euro/MWh and the carbon price is 80 euro/ton, the electricity price will be equal to 112 euro/MWh (i.e. 40 euro/MWh/50% + 0.2 × 80 euro/ton/50%). Note that the carbon content of natural gas is 0.2 ton/MWh. See Appendix A.

[31] Note that these profits are just operational profits, being the difference between the revenues from operation, e.g. the electricity price, and the operational costs, such as fuel costs. These profits can be used to compensate for the fixed costs, consisting of the costs of capital and the depreciation. The term 'inframarginal' refers to the fact that these operational profits are realised by suppliers having lower marginal costs than the so-called marginal or price-setting supplier.

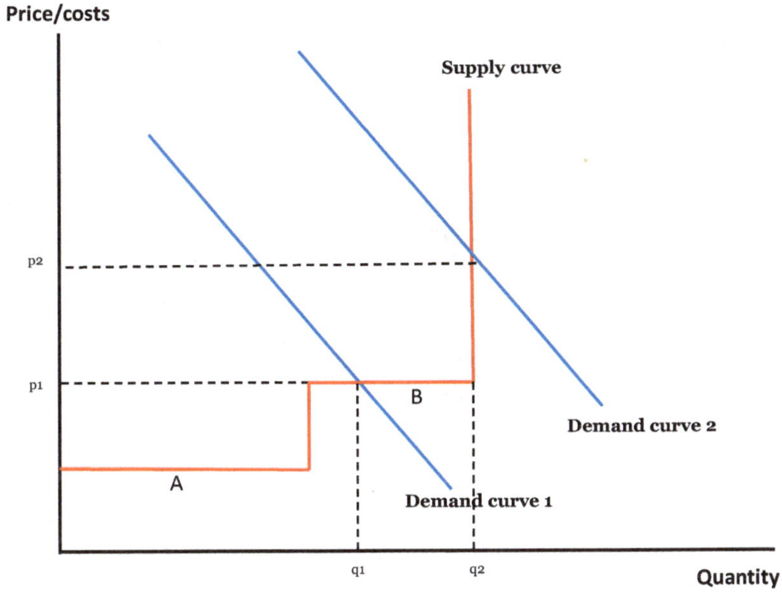

Fig. 2.20 Market outcomes in two different situations of demand versus available production capacity

additional capacity. In order to have such an incentive, the market situation should be tight, which means that the demand exceeds the available production capacity. This situation is reflected by Demand curve 2, with p_2 and q_2 being the equilibrium price and quantity, respectively. Here, both production technologies A and B are making operational profits. If firms expect this situation to happen frequently, investments in additional generation capacity can be profitable.

The expectations regarding the future market parties are not only related to the outlook for the supply and demand conditions in the electricity market, but also to how governments may intervene in these markets. For instance, if market parties are afraid that governments may intervene when electricity prices become too high, this will negatively affect their expected profits and, hence, the incentive to invest in new generation capacity. The expected profits are also reduced when there is more uncertainty about the future availability of generation capacity, such as in the case of weather-dependent renewables (i.e. wind turbines and solar panels). This implies that investing in power plants, as any other type of investment, occurs within uncertainty, and this uncertainty is included in the economic decision-making, by for example including an additional risk premium in the costs of capital. When the impact of this uncertainty on investments is considered too large, additional regulatory measures may be needed, such as the introduction of a capacity mechanism (see Box 2.10).

Box 2.10 Capacity Remuneration Mechanisms to Incentive Investments

When market prices are not able to fully reflect the true value of capacity, i.e. when the market is subject to a fundamental shortcoming, government intervention may improve the overall welfare. An example of such a policy measure is the introduction of a capacity remuneration mechanisms which gives a revenue for simply having available capacity. Such a mechanism can take on different forms, such as public procurement of strategic reserves, the implementation of market-wide capacity auctions, the introduction of reserve obligations on a particular group of market parties, or advance payments for new builds (Guidehouse and Frontier Economics, 2026). The general idea)behind these mechanisms is that payments for capacity (i.e. per MW) contribute to the reliability of energy supply, as markets where only the supply of energy is paid for (i.e. per MWh) may not be sufficient.

Capacity mechanisms are not easy to implement as (regulatory) choices have to be made regarding the amount of capacity that is needed, and which types of technologies and which market parties are allowed to participate. In addition, such mechanisms may have a number of caveats. One of the risks is the crowding out of commercial investments. Other caveats are the transaction costs required to implement such schemes as well as the risks of windfall profits (i.e. capacity payments which are too generous) and too high costs for energy users (see e.g. Holmberg & Tangerås, 2023; Teirilä & Ritz, 2019). These risks may in particular occur when capacities, which are rewarded through such a mechanism, are also used to make revenues to sell energy in the commodity market. When such mechanisms are introduced, the expectations regarding the occurrence of future scarcity prices are affected. After all, the presence of capacity payments may increase the availability of production capacity, which reduces the likelihood of tight market circumstances as well as commodity prices. As a result, the expected profitability of investments decrease.

Consequently, such capacity mechanisms may distort market-based incentives for investments. This is called the moral-hazard effect of capacity mechanisms, which is similar to the change in the risk attitudes of economic agents that have taken an insurance. In case of insurance, agents face less risk (i.e. they are less exposed to the adverse consequences of events) and may, therefore, be inclined to take more risk. The other potential downside of such capacity mechanisms is that they may result in supranormal profits. This occurs when firms offer existing capacity, which results in extra revenues for them without investing in new capacity, while the prices in the commodity market may hardly be reduced by the presence of capacity payments to existing capacities.

What does the presence of this price-formation mechanism mean for the relevance of the LCOE as a metric to determine whether financial support is needed to stimulate investments in renewables? The answer is that in case of excess generation capacity, firms do not have any incentive to extend the generation capacity as the expected future revenues are below the total costs. Even if a technology, like utility-scale solar PV, has the lowest LCOE of all technologies, it is not profitable to invest in such a technology as the market does not value investments. When there is excess generation capacity, this effect is even strengthened by the fact that the use of existing power plants is lower than it technically could be, which raises the costs per unit of production (i.e. the LCOE).[32] Hence, if a government wants to stimulate investments in a technology in such a situation, financial support is needed.

The other factor which is relevant for the revenues of investments in generation capacity are the prices which can be captured by a particular technology. This factor is in particular relevant for technologies which availabilities are strongly influenced by external circumstances. Wind turbines can only produce electricity when the wind blows, while solar PV can only produce when the sun shines. In an electricity system with a large amount of wind and solar capacities, these technologies may be the price-setting technologies when there is a lot of wind and sunshine. As these technologies have low marginal costs, the electricity price becomes close to zero when wind or solar is price-setting. In hours when there is hardly any wind or sunshine, other technologies, like gas turbines, may be the price-setting technologies, resulting in much higher prices as their marginal costs are generally much higher. The changing availability of wind and solar capacity cause the supply curve to shift horizontally, resulting in volatile prices. This is the so-called merit-order effect of renewable electricity. This effect is shown in Fig. 2.21, where Supply curve 2 shows the supply when technology A has a larger availability compared to Supply curve 1, resulting in a lower equilibrium price.

A consequence of the merit-order effect is that the prices which can be realised by renewable technologies can be significantly below the prices of other technologies, such as gas turbines.[33] After all, when the external circumstances are favourable for wind turbines (i.e. much wind) and solar panels (i.e. much sunshine), these technologies have a high production, but also a low electricity price. When the

[32] This also holds for wind turbines and solar panels, as operators of these technologies that sell the generated electricity on a market will reduce their supply in case the market prices becomes negative. After all, producing electricity against negative market prices would be economically irrational. This does occur, however, in real markets, but that is due to the design of support schemes. When firms receive a fixed fee per unit of electricity, such as in Feed-in-Tariffs schemes, they do not face any market incentive to adapt their production patterns (see Sect. 4.6.3). In such circumstances, the production of renewable technologies is only based on environmental and technical factors, not on the situation in the electricity market.

[33] This difference in revenues for the same type of commodity, shows that electricity is not a homogenous good from an economic perspective, although it is in physical terms. The heterogenous character of electricity in economic terms is related to the fact that the electricity grid needs to always be in balance, while electricity cannot be stored as such (only through conversion into other energy carriers). As a result, the economic value of electricity can vary from one moment to the next, depending on the market situation.

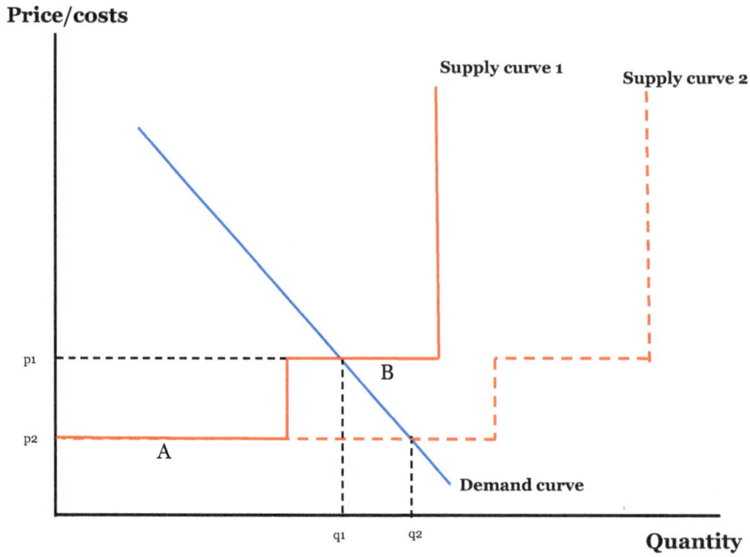

Fig. 2.21 Illustration of the merit-order effect in electricity markets

external circumstances are less favourable for them, their production is much lower, but the market prices are higher. As a result, the average annual price these technologies realise can be much below the average annual price realised by, for instance, gas turbines. The price a particular type of power plant realises during a period (such as a year) is called the capture price. This price for a particular technology i is calculated by weighing the hourly electricity prices with the hourly generation, where p stands for electricity price, G for electricity generation and t is the index for hours:

$$\text{captureprice}_{\text{i}} = \frac{\sum_t p_t * G_i t}{\sum_t G_i t} \tag{2.6}$$

It appears that this capture price for renewable technologies like wind turbines and solar PV can be significantly below the hourly weighted average electricity price. The higher the market share of these technologies, the lower their capture price and, hence, the lower the so-called market-value factor (see Fig. 2.20).[34] This factor is defined as the ratio between the capture price realised by a technology and the average hourly weighted electricity price in a period, where T is the number of hours in a period (e.g. 8760 in a normal year):

[34] Note that when the demand for electricity strongly increases, the capture price of renewable technologies can be less negatively affected by increasing shares of renewables.

$$\text{market}-\text{valuefactor}_{\text{i}} = \frac{\dfrac{\sum_t (p_t * G_i t)}{\sum_t G_i t}}{\dfrac{\sum_t p_t}{T}} \tag{2.7}$$

The market value of renewables declines the higher the share of renewables in a system, their profitability also decreases. This is another argument for why only looking at the LCOE is insufficient to determine to what extent market forces sufficiently incentivise investments in renewables. The higher their market share, the more problematic the economic feasibility for such investments becomes if the rest remains the same1 Consequently, there is bigger need for financial support if a government wants to have higher shares of renewables in its electricity system.

2.6 Theoretical Economic Concepts to Evaluate Energy-Transition Policies

2.6.1 Introduction

Above, we have shown that economic agents respond to market signals, and other incentives, which results in changes in economic systems. In the case of agents active in energy systems, this results in all kinds of changes within these systems, such as lower energy intensity and investments in generation capacities. Such changes belong to the natural characteristics of energy systems. Letting economic agents in energy systems make other decisions than what they otherwise would do is what we define as energy transition.

In order to assess effective policies to realise such a transition, a number of theoretical economic concepts are relevant. These concepts help to formulate recommendations for governments to intervene in energy systems. In this section, we will distinguish two different ways governments can intervene in decisions of economic agents: (a) by changing the circumstances in which economic agents make their choices regarding the use of energy carriers and (b) by influencing the way economic agents assess the various choice options, or, to say it in formal economic terms, by changing their objective functions.

2.6.2 Economic Agents Responding to Changing Circumstances

In the previous section, we have seen that economic agents respond to changing circumstances. Higher oil prices in the 1970s triggered all kinds of measures to reduce their oil dependency, and during the more recent energy crises of 2022 and 2026, we saw that (extremely) high prices for natural gas and oil similarly led to a reduction in the use of these fossil fuels and the substitution to other energy carriers.

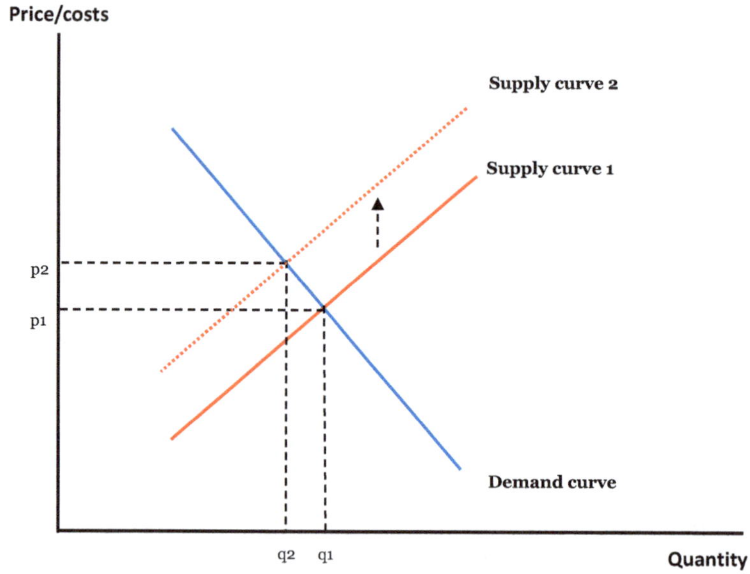

Fig. 2.22 Change in market-equilibrium outcome when demand responds to increasing costs

Hence, economic agents changed their choices regarding the use of oil and natural gas, respectively, as changing prices resulted in different optimal decisions. Apparently, higher oil and gas prices may mean that the value an agent places on consuming a particular good that requires the use of oil or gas (such as driving a car or heating a house) is insufficient to compensate for all the costs, including, in this example, the price of gasoline or heating oil. Hence, it is a rational decision of an agent not to consume that good anymore or to consume less.

In theoretical economic terms, the effect of higher costs can be represented as a movement along the demand curve due to an upward shift of the supply curve (see Fig. 2.22). If the costs of suppliers increase, the supply curve shifts upwards (from 1 to 2), resulting in a higher equilibrium price (p_2) and lower equilibrium quantity (q_2). This new market outcome shows that some consumers (i.e. those representing the shift from q_1 to q_2) reduced their demand, as the market price exceeds their willingness-to-pay (WTP).[35] In case of a rising market price, consumers with a

[35] Remember that the demand curve ranks all the consumers according to their willingness-to-pay for a commodity, from the highest WTP to the lowest. At least, this holds for most commodities. In some, exceptional cases, the demand curve is not downward sloping, but upwards. An upward-sloping demand curve occurs in case of so-called Giffen goods. An example of such goods are staple food (i.e. basic food that has a large share in the food provision, like rice or potatoes). When the price of this food increases, poor people may not have sufficient income any more for other food products, like meat, and therefore, consume more of the staple food to replace the more expensive alternatives. An upward demand curve also occurs in the case of so-called Veblen goods. This refers to luxury goods, which obtain a higher status when their price increases, and as a result, their demand increases.

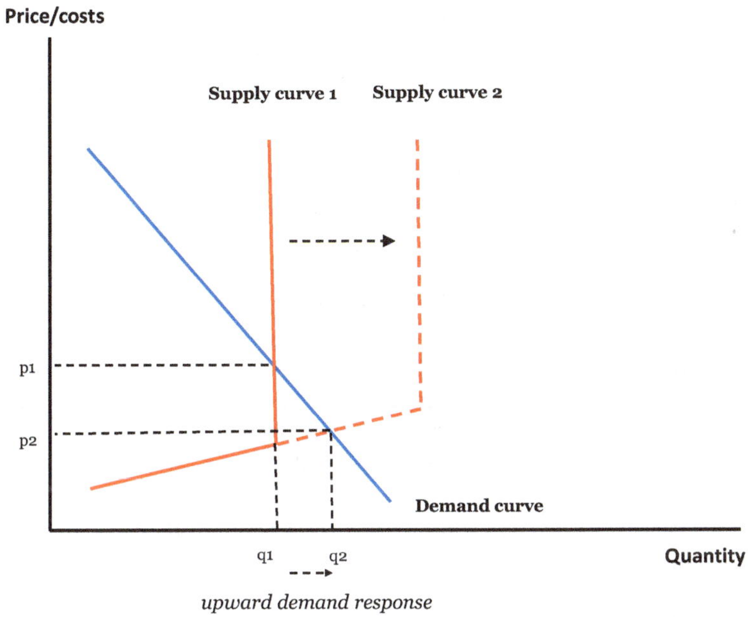

Fig. 2.23 Change in market-equilibrium outcome when demand responds to increasing availability of supply

WTP below the new market price are no longer buying the product. At least, when we assume that their behaviour is economically rational.

Changing circumstances for consumers may also entail a change in the availability of a commodity. The costs for suppliers may remain the same, but they may face the introduction of new supply-side constraints or just the relaxing of existing constraints, which affects the amount they can offer to their customers. These changes in external constraints can be due to natural circumstances, but also governmental policy measures. An example of the former is the impact of changing weather conditions on the available supply of renewable electricity generated through solar panels or wind turbines. Changing weather circumstances influence the amount the operators of these renewable technologies can offer to the market. A strong change in the weather circumstances may result in a large change in the renewable electricity available to consumers.

When there is, for instance, hardly any wind or sunshine, there may be insufficient electricity to supply all consumers given the initial market prices and demand. As a result, market prices will have to rise in order to stimulate consumers to buy less, which is reflected by price level p_1 in Fig. 2.23. So, when there is a scarcity in the supply of a commodity, the market prices have to rise to stimulate consumers to respond. When the weather circumstances, however, become more favourable for electricity generation by solar panels or wind turbines, there may be an oversupply: the total amount that can be produced exceeds the existing demand. In such a situation, consumers respond by moving along the demand cure, but now going downwards until the market price (p_2) is equal to the marginal costs of the producers. This is the new market equilibrium. This increase in demand is beneficial for consumers having a WTP that exceeds the new market price, as they will now also obtain the electricity. The resulting decrease in the market price is also beneficial for all other consumers, as they can now buy electricity at a lower price. As a result of this demand response, the equilibrium volume increases from q_1 to q_2.

In the above examples, we saw how consumers respond to changing circumstances on the supply side. These changing supply-side conditions referred to changing costs and changing availability. The supply curve may also change due to other factors, such as technological improvements which reduces the costs of producers, resulting in a downward shift of the supply curve, or changes in the intensity of competition among suppliers. To elaborate on the latter, if the overall number of suppliers decreases, suppliers may face less competitive pressure from each other. This may enable them to behave strategically, meaning they could ask higher prices for their products or offer less products to create more scarcity, which causes the prices to rise.[36] As a consequence of such strategic behaviour, the supply curve moves to the left or upwards, resulting in a higher equilibrium price, which triggers some consumers to reduce their consumption.

To what extent consumers respond to changing conditions on the supply side depends on their price sensitivity. If consumers are very price sensitive, a small change in the costs of producers, the availability of the product or the behaviour of suppliers may trigger a large response in consumption. In such cases, the demand is said to be price elastic, reflected by a relatively flat demand curve. When consumers, however, are hardly responsive to changing conditions on the supply side, they want to continue consuming no matter what the market price is. In such cases, the demand is said to be price inelastic, which is reflected by a steep demand curve.

Figure 2.24 shows two demand curves which differ in their price sensitivity: Demand curve 2 is, at the same price or quantity levels, more price elastic as it is less steep than Demand curve 1.[37] We also see two supply curves, with Supply curve 2 resulting from an increase in the marginal costs compared to those in Supply curve 1. Consumers on Demand curve 1 respond less strongly to the increase in costs, as they are less price sensitive than the consumers on Demand curve 2. Hence, in the case of Demand curve 1, the market-equilibrium price changes more when the supply curve shifts upwards (i.e. $p_3 > p_2$), while the new equilibrium volume is also higher (i.e. $q_3 > q_2$), although lower of course than in the situation without the cost increase (i.e. q_1). This implies that when the demand curve is less price sensitive, an increase in the required prices (i.e. the marginal costs) by suppliers has a relatively strong impact on the market-equilibrium price, and a relatively weak impact on the volume of consumption.

[36] The former behaviour by firms having market power is called economic withholding (i.e. asking higher prices) and the latter physical withholding (i.e. reducing supply to the market).

[37] Note the price elasticity is not constant for linear demand curves, as is discussed further in Appendix C.

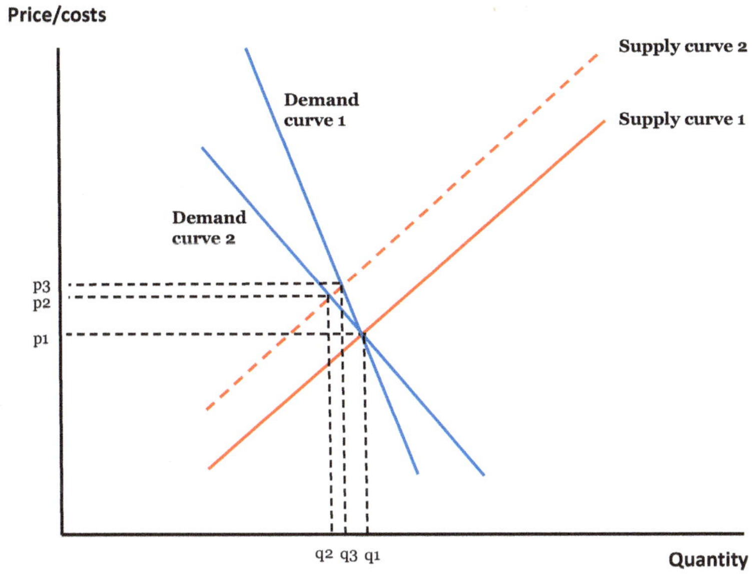

Fig. 2.24 Response of consumers to changes in supply depends on their price sensitivity

Market circumstances can also change due to developments on the demand side. If the number of consumers or their average income increases, the demand for a product can increase. If the price sensitivity of individual consumers remains the same, but the number of consumers or their income increases, the demand curve shifts to the right (see Fig. 2.25).[38] A shift of the demand curve to the right results in a higher market price (from p_1 to p_2) if other circumstances remain the same. Hence, now we see that there is a movement of suppliers along the supply curve, resulting in a higher equilibrium output (from q_1 to q_2).

The extent to which the price increases when the demand increases depends on the responsiveness of the supply curve. If the supply is very responsive to price changes, the supply will change strongly, resulting in a relatively small change in the market price. This is reflected by Supply curve 1 in Fig. 2.26, while Supply curve 2 shows the situation in which the supply side of the market is not very able to extend its offers to the market at quite similar costs, resulting in a relatively strong increase in the market price (to p_3) and only a small increase in the quantity consumed (to q_3). In this latter example, an increase in the demand does not result as much in bigger consumption, but rather in higher prices to be paid to producers.

[38] Mathematically, this is expressed through a higher value for the parameter a in formulas C.1 (in case of a linear demand curve) and formula C.9 (in case of a demand curve with a constant elasticity) (see Appendix C).

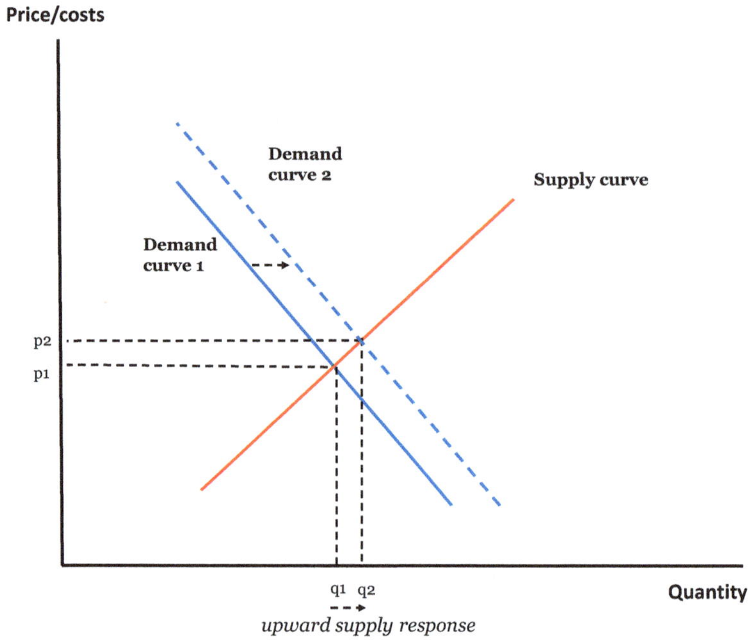

Fig. 2.25 Change in market-equilibrium outcome when supply responds to increase in demand

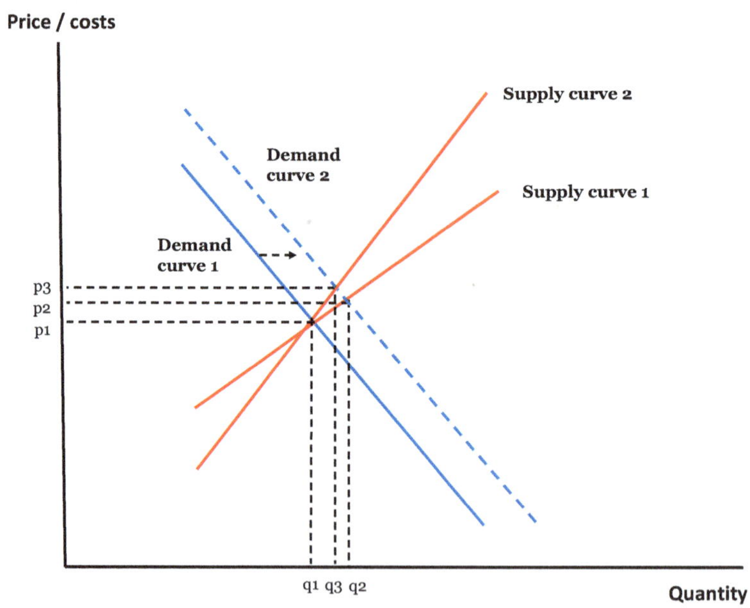

Fig. 2.26 Response of supply to change in demand depends on the slope of the supply curve

Box 2.11 Factors that Move Supply and Demand in Electricity Markets

Supply curves change because of changing input prices, technological developments, innovating behaviour of firms and changes in the competitive process, while demand-curve changes result from factors like changes in population density, economic growth and consumer preferences. In case of electricity systems, for instance, the supply is affected by the prices of the inputs for generation, the installed generation capacity and the conversion efficiency of the generators, while the demand is related to the size of an economy, its degree of electrification of an economy and external factors, like outside temperature.

Electricity markets belong to the most complex markets as the commodity electricity cannot be stored as such, only through conversion, and the electricity system has continuously to be balanced. Because of these characteristics, every time unit has its own market. In most systems, this time unit is an hour, a quarter of an hour or 5 min, which means that the market is cleared every single hour, quarter or 5 min. In addition to that, there are also various future time frames for which the markets are cleared, from the long term (years) to very close (5 min) before real time, while in many countries there are also real-time (balancing markets). The short-term markets, varying from the day-ahead market to the intraday market, are called spot markets. The supply and demand curves in these markets depend on the short-term availability of generation capacity, their generation costs, the flexibility of demand and the use of flexibility assets like batteries.

2.6.3 Behavioural Responses by Economic Agents Are Reflected in Price Sensitivities

Information on the factors that move supply and demand curves is crucial to understanding how real markets develop and how economic agents may respond to changing market circumstances. In Box 2.10, this is briefly discussed for the electricity market.

The degree by which consumers and producers respond depends on their price sensitivity, which is measured through their price elasticity.[39] The price elasticity is defined as the percentage change in demand (or supply) in relation to a percentage change in the price.[40] In case of energy systems, the price elasticity of demand generally is not high: the energy demand is known to be price inelastic, as the price elasticities are generally less than −1. This holds in particular for the short term, as consumers do not have many options to respond to changing prices (see Table 2.1).

[39] Note that this is a simplistic presentation of real economies, as more economic agents play a role here, such as traders, retailers and storage operators. Note as well that these behavioural adaptations occur on a micro-level, with individual economic agents making other choices, but they are translated to the market level resulting from the aggregate of all individual choices.

[40] See Appendix C for a discussion of linear demand curves with a non-constant price elasticity and demand curves with a constant price elasticity.

Table 2.1 Price elasticities of the demand for various energy carriers, short and long term

Energy carrier	Short-term price elasticity	Long-term price elasticity
Electricity	−0.126	−0.365
Natural gas	−0.180	−0.684
Gasoline	−0.293	−0.773
Diesel	−0.153	−0.443
Heating oil	−0.017	−0.185

Source: Labandeire et al. (2017)

When, for instance, the price of natural gas increases, consumers who use gas for heating cannot do much to respond to these higher prices, except for accepting lower temperatures in their premises. In the longer term, however, they can also respond by, for instance, taking insulation measures.

2.6.4 Choices of Economic Agents Are Based on Preferences

We have seen in the previous section that economic agents may respond to changes in all kinds of factors that affect their utility or production functions, including the (relative) prices of goods, the availability of these goods, and their personal or corporate income. The degree to which they respond to changes in these factors can be expressed through various types of elasticities, such as the price elasticity, the cross-price elasticity and the income elasticity.[41] Although economic agents are assumed to respond to changing circumstances when these affect their optimal choice, in this analysis one aspect is assumed to be constant. This aspect refers to the preferences and objective functions of economic agents.

Economics is about the choices economic agents make, assuming that everyone pursues her/his own objectives. To what extent these objectives are right is not part of the economic analysis. This follows from the fundamental principle in economic analysis that no one can determine what is truly important to someone else. This principle is called the theorem of the impossibility of interpersonal-utility comparisons. After all, as humans we cannot read other peoples' minds and, hence, we cannot determine which decisions someone else should make to raise her/his own utility. A consequence of this basic economic principle for policymaking is that in order to maximise welfare, economic agents should be completely free to choose their own objectives.[42] Intervening in the decisions economic agents make can, therefore, only raise welfare when there are fundamental shortcomings in the organisation of markets, so-called market failures (see Sect. 4.2).

[41] The cross-price elasticity measures the degree by which the demand for good X is affected by a change in the price of good Y, while the income elasticity measures the degree by which the demand for a good changes as a result of a change in income.

[42] This consequence is related to the so-called Arrow's Impossibility Theorem, which says that it is impossible to formulate a group-decision-making mechanism to determine the choice which maximises the welfare of all individuals. For more information on this theorem, see, for instance: https://plato.stanford.edu/entries/arrows-theorem/.

Box 2.12 Factors Behind the Willingness-to-Pay for Renewable Energy Systems

The preferences of individuals for particular goods can be estimated through various methods, such as the conjoined choice experiment. In this method, a survey is conducted among a group of respondents who are asked to make a series of choices among sets of alternatives. These alternatives are described through a number of so-called attributes, including at least one financial attribute, typically the price of the good. The preference of the respondents for the various non-financial attributes of a good can be estimated by analysing their choices. These preferences are expressed as their so-called willingness-to-pay (WTP) by determining the amount of one of the financial attributes which respondents are willing to give up in order to have an extra unit of one of the other attributes. This estimation method results in a WTP for each individual. As economic agents generally have different preferences, this results in a distribution of WTP estimates. Figure 2.27 shows the distribution of WTP estimates of Dutch households for various attributes of heating systems, based on Rekker et al. (2024). It appears, among others, that Dutch households on average want to have a discount of about 30% on their monthly energy bill in case of a district-heating system compared to decentralised gas-boiler based system. When the heating system would be based on electricity instead of natural gas, on average, they are willing to pay about 30% extra (Rekker et al., 2024).

The differences among respondents can be explained using econometric techniques. In this study, it was found that people in the northern part of the Netherlands have the highest WTP for low-carbon heating systems, which may be related to the fact that in this region, where the famous Groningen gas field was located, there was more attention for energy transition then in other parts of the Netherlands. This shows that public attention for a topic may have an influence on the preferences and objective functions of economic agents.

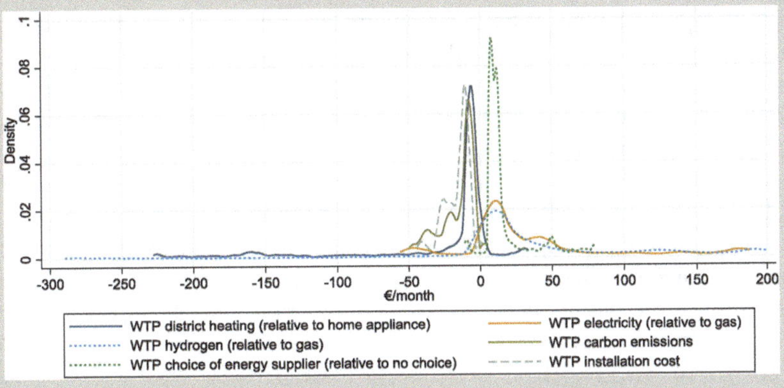

Fig. 2.27 Distribution of willingness-to-pay of Dutch households for characteristics of heating systems (Source: Rekker et al. (2024))

Sometimes, however, it is said that societies or governments should try to convince individuals and firms to change their objectives. For instance, some believe that firms should not focus on shareholder value, but on contributing to societal objectives, such as reducing global climate change. Others state that individuals should not be interested in a higher income and more spending, but in realising a sustainable way of living. In the same sense, some people say that societies should not pursue economic growth, but realise degrowth.

The question, however, is to what extent it makes sense from an economic point of view to try and influence the objective functions of other economic agents. By this, we mean to ask to what extent societal welfare is increased by fostering individual economic agents to change their objective functions. In general, when economic agents have all the relevant information and are able to consider the various choice options, any intervention in the individual choices would be disturbing, i.e. result in suboptimal decisions. Because of the theorem of the impossibility of interpersonal-utility comparisons, one cannot determine what the best decision would be for other economic agents.

It is, however, conceivable that an economic agent is not able to digest all the relevant information and, as a result, (s)he makes decisions which (s)he would not make when not facing that information-processing problem.[43] In such a situation of imperfect decision-making, the problem remains however that intervening can make things even worse. For instance, if residential households have difficulties comparing various offers in retail energy markets, they may feel uncomfortable making a decision regarding the choice of retailer or contract type. Governments could step in by stimulating them to take a particular type of contract, such as a fixed-tariff contract, but there is a chance that a particular household prefers to have a variable-tariff contract, but is not able to find the one that suits him/her the most. Instead of stimulating economic agents to make a particular choice, it is therefore more efficient to help them make more-informed decisions, for instance by making markets more transparent.

In case of commercial firms, governments can require firms to pay attention to other aspects than only financial profits. This occurs, for instance, through Environmental, Social and Governance (ESG) regulations, which requires firms to report on their actions related to environmental, social and governance aspects. Although some firms may state they voluntarily comply with such rules, regulations are needed to make sure firms really comply with them, as complying may not be in their direct own interest. The ESG criteria can be used by investors to determine to what extent particular companies or investments meet sustainability, ethics or good governance standards. By enforcing reporting on the ESG criteria, economic agents can be better informed about other aspects than only financial aspects and, consequently, may make other decisions.

[43] As an example, in an empirical analysis on residential energy consumers in the United Kingdom, Wilson and Waddams Price (2010) showed that almost 1/5 of all consumers made a decision to switch from an energy contract which made them worse off in financial terms.

From this follows that although preferences and objective functions of economic agents cannot be assessed by others, they can be influenced to some extent. For that, it is also useful to know what the driving factors are behind particular types of behaviour. Through various methods, more information on these motivations can be obtained. As both characteristics and preferences of people differ a lot, by analysing the relationship between the two, one may be able to estimate what the underlying factors behind preferences are. An example of a crucial factor behind preferences of individual economic agents is education. When people become more educated, they learn about other aspects of society, other people and how things are related. This increased knowledge affects the way people value things, which translates into other preferences. From empirical research, it is for instance known that people with a higher level of education tend to have a higher willingness-to-pay for energy transition or are more supportive of climate policy.[44] In Box 2.12, a study shows that the value people attach to particular types of renewable energy may be affected by the available information on the topic in the local media.

2.6.5 An Economic Framework for Choosing Effective Policy Measures

All this information on the price sensitivity of economic agents is very relevant for governments that want to intervene in energy systems. Using insights on the underlying microeconomic mechanisms, they can define the required policy measures to realise a particular objective (see Table 2.2). The general principle is that changing supply curves leads consumers to respond by buying more or less, while changing demand curves leads producers to respond by offering more or less of various types of products. Depending on their objectives, governments can take several types of policy measures to make use of specific mechanisms in markets.

When governments impose, for instance, a carbon tax on the use of fossil energy, economic agents who use these energy carriers may reduce their use by operating more efficiently or switching to another energy carrier. This results in a downward shift of the demand curve for fossil energy. When the tax is imposed on producers, their break-even prices are increased, resulting in an upward shift of the supply curve. Governments can promote the production of particular types of products by lowering the marginal costs for producers, for instance by providing a subsidy per unit of product, or by lowering their fixed costs by providing investment support which may result in a shift to the right of the supply curve. As supply and demand curves interact, the ultimate effect of a policy measure is less straightforward since indirect effects may partly neutralise the direct effect of, for instance, a tax or subsidy.

[44] The correlation between level of education and willingness-to-pay for energy transition and climate policy does, of course, not necessarily indicate causation, although education may play a role in awareness of the climate-change problem.

Table 2.2 Defining policy measures to realise policy objectives through market mechanisms

Objective of intervention	Microeconomic mechanism	Policy measure
Less consumption	Upward shift of supply curve	Raising marginal costs for suppliers by imposing a tax
	Shift of supply curve to the left	Imposing constraints on supply side
	Downward shift of demand curve	Taxing consumers or influencing their preferences through educational programs
	Shift of the demand curve to the left	Subsidising the consumption of alternatives
More production	Downward shift of supply curve	Subsidising marginal costs for suppliers
	Shift of the supply curve to the right	Subsidising fixed costs for suppliers (i.e. giving them investment support)
	Upward shift of demand curve	Subsidising consumers
	Shift of demand cure to the right	Subsidising fixed costs for consumers (i.e. giving them investment support)
More welfare for both consumers and producers	Constructing demand and supply curves which reflect all relevant information	Improving transparency on market process
More consumer welfare	Downward shift of supply curve	Regulatory oversight on monopolistic supplier
More producer welfare	Shift of demand curve to the right	Imposing consumption obligations

From these examples, it appears that governments can intervene in energy systems by changing the circumstances which affect the optimal choices of agents, such as prices of inputs or outputs, availability of technologies or access to markets. As intervening in the decisions of agents can also result in indirect effects, such as influencing the international competitiveness of industries, these effects have to be included in the overall (economic) assessment. Note that economic agents are also influenced by other types of factors (see Box 2.13). In Chap. 4, we will discuss the economics of the various types of policy measures.

2.7 Conclusions

The widely adopted definition of energy transition is formulated in terms of particular changes within energy systems, such as lower energy intensity or a higher share of renewables. In the economic definition, however, energy transition is defined in terms of interventions by governments in the decisions of economic agents regarding the supply or use of energy. These interventions have as their objective that agents should make other decisions than the ones they would make without

Box 2.13 Rational Economic Behaviour Amidst Social and Psychological Influences

People are also influenced by what is happening in their own neighbourhood. This is called spatial contagion. This influence is partly the result of social interaction, in the same physical space or online environment. As such, this influence is not intended. For another part, however, the influence is intended. This occurs, for instance, when commercial firms want to influence customers' decisions through their marketing actions. In their campaigns, advertisers make use of smart psychological insights in order to attract peoples' attention and influence their thinking and decision-making. As a result of such marketing actions, consumers may make decisions which are not favourable for themselves. Therefore, in many countries governments have implemented regulatory measures to protect customers, in particular against misinformation and forced fast decision-making (see e.g. Huisman et al., 2026).

In all these cases, consumers are still viewed as economically rational agents. This does not mean that it is assumed that consumers always make cost-benefit calculations before making a decision, but rather that their decisions are consistent with their own preferences. After all, because of the impossibility of interpersonal-utility comparison, which is one of the underlying assumptions in economic analysis, no one else can decide for them whether their own decisions are beneficial to themselves.

government intervention. By using this economic definition, one can account for the fact that energy systems are constantly changing.

As we have seen in this chapter, energy systems have changed in many different ways over the past decades and centuries. The current energy mix is very different from the ones of a century, a few decades, or even a few years ago, while the magnitude of total energy use is (much) higher. In addition, energy systems used to be quite regional, but are now strongly internationally integrated. This holds in particular for coal, oil and natural gas, but also electricity is traded and transported on a large international scale. Hydrogen will likely also become an energy carrier that is traded on a global scale. Only heat systems are still mainly operating on a local scale, which is due to the high transport costs and energy losses during transport. In addition, the way energy systems operate has also changed. In the past, gas and electricity systems were more centrally managed by vertically integrated utilities, based on an engineering perspective. In many countries these systems are currently more decentrally organised with the options and incentives for individual economic agents to respond to changing circumstances, while marketplaces have become more international. Moreover, supply chains have changed strongly as well, which is an ongoing process. New firms enter to benefit from opportunities resulting from technological and economic developments, existing firms change the scope of their activities by becoming more specialised or increasing the scope of their activities. In Chap. 5, we will discuss the transitions which may occur on the level of individual agents.

The observation that energy systems are constantly changing is related to the fact that economic agents are constantly responding to changing external circumstances, such as developments in production technologies and prices of inputs and outputs. For example, the energy intensity of economies is changing not only because of technical energy-efficiency improvements, but also because of structural changes within economies. Therefore, energy transition should be defined in such a way that it refers to changes in energy systems on top of the autonomous changes caused by many other factors.

This economic approach also entails that energy transition cannot be defined only in terms of the technical measures which are taken by economic agents, as their relation with macroeconomic changes or changes in energy systems has to be taken on board as well. In this chapter, we have shown that it is important to have an integrated view of economic developments and that one should not focus only on actions which are (or can be) taken on an individual level. Such an analysis should also be completed by looking at changes withineconomic structures, both nationally and internationally.

For the definition of energy transition, it does not matter what the government's public objectives are when they try to intervene in the decisions of economic agents regarding their use of energy carriers. The motivations to implement such interventions can be related to environmental objectives, such as decreasing carbon emissions by reducing the use of fossil energy, but these motivations can also be related to other types of policy objectives, such as raising the security of the energy supply, reducing the energy costs for vulnerable consumers, or reducing the dependence on (international) market forces in the supply of energy. In fact, governments may have various motives to intervene in the decisions of economic agents regarding the use of energy carriers. In practice, these motivations not only differ among countries, but they also change as governments respond to changing circumstances, while governments also change as a result of political and societal events, such as elections.

Although the motivations for governments to pursue energy transition are not relevant for the (above) definition of energy transition, these motivations are relevant to assess whether such policy measures are effective or efficient. Motives to intervene in energy systems may be based on a misunderstanding of how these systems actually work and contribute to welfare, and, as a result, policy interventions may not be efficient. Even when the motivation to intervene is related to a real shortcoming in energy systems, policy measures can be ineffective. If a government wants, for instance, that households use less natural gas in order to reduce overall carbon emissions, policy measures are not effective when these households shift to the use of oil or to the use of electricity which is generated through gas-fired power plants. In Chap. 3, we will further discuss the various motivations governments can have to intervene, using an economic perspective, while in Chap. 4, we will go into how these interventions can be implemented in an efficient and effective manner.

Exercises

1. Explain why the widely adopted interpretation of energy transition may not be so helpful to determine the effectiveness of policies.
2. How can behavioural economic insights be useful for the realisation of energy transition?
3. What are the factors behind changes in the energy intensity of economies?
4. Why is the price elasticity of energy demand a crucial metric to understand changes in energy systems?
5. What does it mean if energy supply is price inelastic?

References

Agora. (2026). *State of the energy transition in Germany: annual review 2025*. https://www.agora-energiewende.org/publications/state-of-the-energy-transition-in-germany-annual-review-2025#c1920

Bolderdijk, J. W., & Steg, L. (2014). Promoting sustainable consumption: The risks of using financial incentives. In *Handbook of research in sustainable consumption* (pp. 328–341). Edward Elgar Publishing. https://doi.org/10.4337/9781783471270.00033

Carrol, J., Aravena, C., Boeri, M., & Denny, E. (2022). "Show me the energy costs": Short and long-term energy cost disclosure effects on willingness-to-pay for residential energy efficiency. *The Energy Journal, 43*(2). https://doi.org/10.5547/01956574.43.2.jcar

CREA, Centre for Research on Energy and Clean Air. (2025). *China's climate transition: Outlook 2025*.

Croner, D., & Frankovic, I. (2018). A structural decomposition analysis of global and national energy intensity trends. *The Energy Journal, 39*(March 2018), 103–122.

Dijkstra, P. T. (2020). Gedragseconomische valkuilen bij de energietransitie; Hoe te zorgen voor een gedragsverandering in het kader van verduurzaming en energieverbruik? *Mens & Maatschappij, 95*(3). https://doi.org/10.5117/MEM2020.3.004.DIJK

Energy Institute. (2026). *Statistical review of world energy*. EI Statistical Review of World Energy. https://www.energyinst.org/

European Commission. (2023). *Press release: Commission welcomes completion of key 'Fit for 55' legislation, putting EU on track to exceed 2030 targets*. https://ec.europa.eu/commission/presscorner/detail/en/ip_23_4754

European Court of Auditors. (2023). *Internal electricity market integration, special report 03*.

European Environmental Agency. (2025). *Total net greenhouse gas emission trends and projections in Europe*. https://www.eea.europa.eu/en/analysis/indicators/total-greenhouse-gas-emission-trends

Fraunhofer Institute for Solar Energy Systems ISE. (2024). *Levelized cost of electricity renewable energy technologies*.

Fressoz, J.-B. (2025). *More and more and more; an all-consuming history*. Penquin.

Gorus, M. S., & Karagol, E. T. (2022). Reactions of energy intensity, energy efficiency, and activity indexes to income and energy price changes: The panel data evidence from OECD countries. *Energy, 254*, 124281.

Gregory, P. R., & Stuart, R. C. (1981). *Soviet economic structure and performance* (2nd ed.). Harper & Row Publishers.

Guidehouse and Frontier Economics. (2026). *Study on capacity remuneration mechanisms for the Netherlands*.

Holmberg, P., & Tangerås, T. (2023). A survey of capacity mechanisms: Lessors for the Swedish electricity market. *The Energy Journal, 44*, 6.

Huisman, H. M., de Haan, E., Mulder, M., & Wieringa, J. E. (2026). The impact of energy retailers' loyalty programmes on the effectiveness of regulation of retail energy markets. *Journal of Regulatory Economics, 69*(7). https://doi.org/10.1007/s11149-025-09505-9
IEA. (2025). *The implications of oil and gas field decline rates.* International Energy Agency.
IEA/NEA. (2020). *Projected costs of generating electricity.* International Energy Agency/Nuclear Energy Agency.
IRENA. (2025). The energy transition in Brazil.
Jacobsen, G. D., & Stewart, J. I. (2022). How do consumers respond to price complexity? Experimental evidence from the power sector. *Journal of Environmental Economics and Management, 116*, 102716. https://doi.org/10.1016/j.jeem.2022.102716
Jain, M. (2025). Energy savings from efficiency improvements in past three decades: estimates from 144 countries. Applied Energy, 381: 125129.
Kahneman, D. (2013). *Thinking, fast and slow.*
Keller, J. T., Kuper, G. H., & Mulder, M. (2022). Challenging natural monopolies: assessing market power of gas transmission system operators for cross-border capacity. *Energy Policy, 170*, 113228.
Keynes, J.M. (1936). The General Theory of Employment, Interest and Money, The Royal Economic Society.
Labandeire, X., Labeaga, J. M., & López-Otero, X. (2017). A meta-analysis on the price elasticity of energy demand. *Energy Policy, 102*, 549–568.
Meletiou, A., Cambini, C., & Masera, M. (2018). Regulatory and ownership determinants of unbundling regime choice for European electricity transmission operators. *Utilities Policy, 50*, 13–25. https://doi.org/10.1016/j.jup.2018.01.006
Mulder, M. (2023). Regulation of Energy Markets: Economic Mechanisms and Policy Evaluation. Springer, 2nd edition.
Pepermans, G., J. Morbee, M. Ovaere, and S. Proost (2023). Energy economics, Leuven, acco learn.
Petit, V. (2017). *The energy transition; an overview of the true challenge of the 21st century.* Springer International Publishing.
Rekker, L., Hulshof, D., Kesina, M., & Mulder, M. (2024). Willingness-to-pay for low-carbon residential heating systems: A discrete choice experiment among Dutch households. *Energy and Buildings, 323*(2024), 114712.
Rumpf, J. (2020). Congestion displacement in European electricity transmission systems: Finally getting a grip on it? Revised safequards in the clean energy package and the European network codes. *Journal of Energy & Natural Resources Law, 38*(4), 409–436. https://doi.org/10.1080/02646811.2019.1707441
Teirilä, J., & Ritz, R. A. (2019). Strategic behaviour in a capacity market? The new Irish electricity market design. *The Energy Journal, 40*(SI1), 105–126.
UCTE (2010). The 50 year success story – evolution of a European interconnected grid.
UNIDO. (2015). Structural decomposition of energy consumption, energy intensity, emissions and emission intensity; a sectoral perspective: Empirical evidence from WIOD over 1995 to 2009. Inclusive and sustainable industrial development working paper series WP11.
Unnerstall, T. (2017). *The German energy transition; design, implementation, costs and lessons.* Springer.
Varian, H. R. (2003). *Intermediate microeconomics; a modern approach.* W.W. Norton & Company.
Veenstra, A. T., Li, X., & Mulder, M. (2026). Economic assessment of the role of nuclear and renewables in future decarbonized electricity markets. *The Energy Journal.*
Wilson, C. M., & Waddams Price, C. (2010). Do consumers switch to the best supplier? *Oxford Economic Papers, 62*(4). https://doi.org/10.1093/oep/gpq006
Yergin, D., P. Orszag and A. Arya (2025), The troubled energy transition; How to find a pragmatic path forward. Foreign Affairs, March/April.
Zweifel, P., Praktiknjo, A., & Erdmann, G. (2017). *Energy economics; theory and applications.* Springer.

3 Economic Arguments for Energy Transition

3.1 Introduction

In the previous chapter, we have seen that energy transition entails that governments intervene in the optimisation decisions of economic agents. Without such interventions, at least when these are effective, economic agents would make other decisions. Departing from the theoretical assumption that the behaviour of these agents is rational and, hence, directed at maximising their objectives, it follows that an intervention in their choices results in suboptimal choices from the perspective of the agents. Hence, governments should have good arguments for such interventions, otherwise the interventions lower the overall welfare. This implies that governments should only intervene in markets when there are fundamental shortcomings in the coordination of the activities of the individual economic agents. In this chapter, we will first discuss the theoretical benchmark of well-functioning markets and the presence of market failures as reason for government intervention. Afterwards, we go into various arguments which are used to argue for energy transition. This chapter concludes by giving an overview of the assessment of the economic validity of these arguments as justifications for governments and societies to pursue a transition of energy systems.

3.2 Economic Theoretical Framework

3.2.1 Conditions for Well-Functioning Markets

In order to analyse the functioning of real markets, economists use the concept of well-functioning markets as a benchmark. This concept is not used to describe actual markets, but to have a benchmark for assessing those markets. In order to be a well-functioning market, a number of conditions have to be fulfilled. Basically, these conditions are that all market participants have complete information on the

M. Mulder, *Economics of Energy Transition*, Studies in Energy, Resource and Environmental Economics, https://doi.org/10.1007/978-3-032-29010-6_3

product characteristics as well as the price-formation process, that no one is able to influence the market outcomes and that there are no externalities. When the conditions for such a market are met, any intervention (by governments) reduces welfare, as the economic agents can make the best choices for themselves. Hence, only when there is a clear shortcoming in the coordination mechanism, i.e. when one or more of the above conditions are not met, should market intervention take place. In such cases, without any intervention the market process results in suboptimal outcomes. Such shortcomings are called market failures. Hence, a market failure exists when a condition for a well-functioning market is not satisfied, as is the case with a lack of information, the presence of externalities, the use of market power or the presence of entry barriers. In this section, we discuss each of these conditions in detail.

3.2.2 Complete Information

It is crucial for agents to have full information regarding the market to make choices which maximise their objectives. Without complete information, they will make suboptimal decisions. For instance, an agent that cannot oversee all the characteristics of an offer by another agent may be hesitant to accept the offer, or as an opposite effect, accept it at a higher price than (s)he would do in case of complete information. Given the importance of having complete information, economic agents in principle have an incentive to collect or to provide the relevant information, but sometimes it may be very costly or even impossible to do so.

The required information refers to the product characteristics as well as the characteristics of the contracts regarding the exchange of a product. In a retail electricity market, for instance, the buyers of electricity, i.e. residential households, may want to know how the electricity will be produced, for example, by a fossil-fuel power plant or a wind turbine. As this cannot be inferred from the electricity that will be supplied to them, the consumers face a so-called information asymmetry compared to the producers. Producers have more information on how they generate the electricity than their customers. As a result of this information asymmetry, consumers may not be willing to pay a premium for renewable electricity, as they are uncertain to what extent they will really receive that type of electricity. When a producer of renewable electricity makes more costs than the producer of grey (fossil-energy-based) electricity, the former producer may not be able to sell its product at a higher price. This is the so-called adverse-selection effect of information asymmetry regarding product characteristics. This effect entails that high-quality products that require a higher price cannot easily be sold, as the customers are uncertain they will really receive that product in return for a higher price. As a result, the market will be dominated by low-quality products, since suppliers of more expensive, higher quality products will not be able to realise a positive business case.

The asymmetric position regarding the available information may not only refer to the product characteristics, but also to the characteristics of the contracts. For instance, if households are considering to buy electricity from retailers, but retailers do not tell what the price will be in the future, the households may face too much uncertainty about the future costs. Other aspects regarding contracts are the duration and the conditions for cancelling a contract during the contract duration. When such uncertainties exist, consumers may be hesitant to conclude contracts, and, consequently, they may buy and consume less or other products than what they would in case of complete information. So, this will result in a suboptimal level of consumption causing a loss of welfare (which is called deadweight loss) compared to the situation with perfect information, which is depicted by the blue triangle in Fig. 3.1.

The opposite situation may also occur, in which consumers overestimate the true qualities of an offer by suppliers and, therefore, are willing to pay more than they would do in case of perfect information. This also results in loss of welfare (i.e. the red triangle in Fig. 3.1). Hence, uncertainty about product characteristics may hinder economic agents to make the best decisions for themselves.

These types of information problems have been addressed in energy markets in most countries, as without appropriate market regulation, these markets would not be able to develop. In order to address information asymmetry regarding product characteristics, for instance, governments in various countries have introduced certificate schemes which provide consumers with information on the product characteristics. In addition, some energy regulators prescribe that all retailers should present all the information regarding their products in a standardised way to enable consumers to make the best decisions for themselves.

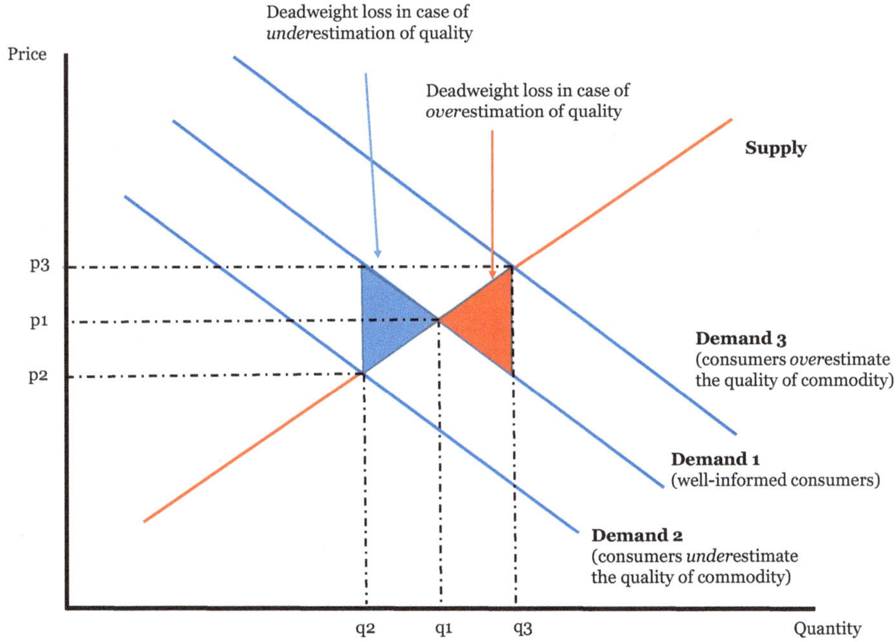

Fig. 3.1 Effects of the presence of information asymmetry on market outcomes and welfare

3.2.3 Ineffectiveness of Strategic Behaviour

Another crucial aspect of a well-functioning market is that the process of coordinating demand and supply needs to be trusted by all agents. Not only the information on products and contract characteristics should be correct and complete, but economic agents also have to be sure that the offers from other agents are reasonable and fair. Agents should not be able to behave strategically, which means they are unable to succesfully adapt their offers to influence market outcomes. Such strategic behaviour is only possible when firms do have some market power, which enables them to determine their offers in such a way that it maximises their profits, without (much) responses by competitors or consumers.[1]

When a firm has market power, it may, for instance, tell potential buyers of its product that it can offer only a limited amount, while in reality it could offer way more, in order to create artificial scarcity resulting in higher prices. Because of the resulting artificially high prices, consumers will consume less. This reduced consumption is a loss of welfare, as the value the consumers attach to the missed consumption exceeds the real marginal costs of producing the products. As a result, the overall social welfare is reduced because of this strategic behaviour. This loss of welfare or deadweight loss of market power is depicted by the triangle in Fig. 3.2. In this figure, the supply curve based on the bids of suppliers lies above the supply curve which is based on the actual marginal costs. As a result, the equilibrium price (p_1) is higher than the competitive price (p_2), while the equilibrium volume (q_1) is lower than it would be without abuse of market power (q_2).

When a market is characterised by firms having the ability and incentive to behave strategically, this may not only result in higher prices for consumers, but also in a lower productive efficiency and less innovation, i.e. dynamic efficiency. After all, in such circumstances firms have fewer incentives to become more productive and to innovate, as they can already make profits by charging higher prices. Next to this effect on the firm level, there is also an effect on the industry level. In a competitive environment, firms can only survive when they distinguish themselves from competitors through lower costs and/or higher quality. Firms that have relatively high costs and/or offer products of lower quality will not be able to survive in such an environment. However, in a market where the competition is less fierce, these high-cost or low-quality firms may be able to continue their business. As a

[1] In a competitive market environment, firms are not able to do so. In such an environment, firms can only raise their profit by becoming more efficient (than competitors) and/or raising the quality of the products they sell. Sources of market power are inflexibility of consumers and/or competitors. When a firm uses its powerful position in a market to raise its profits, this can be called abuse of market power, at least in an economic sense. In legal terms, it is more difficult to conclude that a firm has market power and is abusing it, as one (i.e. the competition authority) has to prove that the firm has the ability and incentive to use its position and its actual behaviour (e.g. selling at prices that are too high) harms consumers.

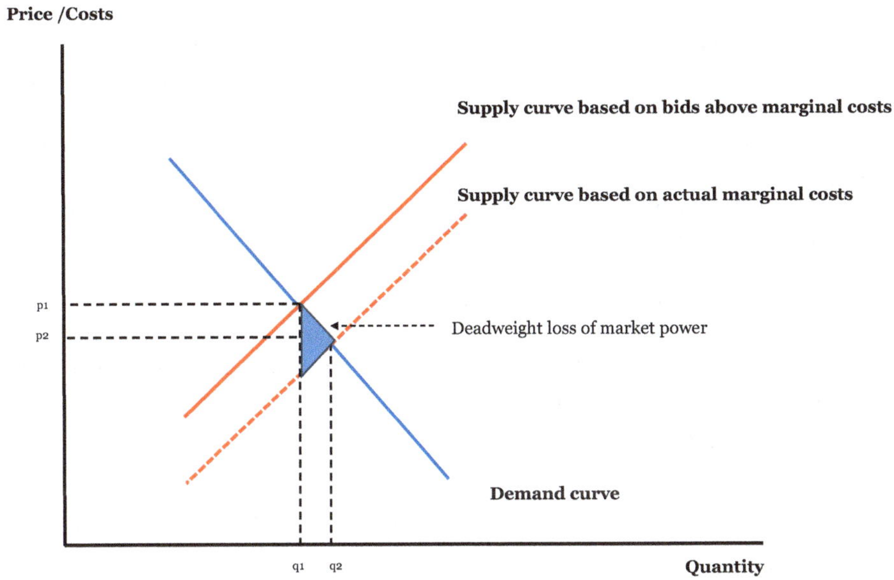

Fig. 3.2 Effects of the presence of market power on market outcomes and welfare

result, the average productive efficiency and quality of the products is lower than in a market with fierce competition.[2]

In a well-functioning competitive market, however, no supplier is able to successfully influence market outcomes. If a supplier tries to create scarcity in a market, other suppliers step in or consumers choose other products, and as a result that kind of strategic behaviour is not a profitable strategy for the supplier. If a firm would try to do so, it results in lower sales while the price remains the same. Hence, suppliers do not have an incentive to behave in this way. Even if a firm has the possibility to influence market outcomes to some extent, it will not do so when it harms its own profits. When assessing the degree of competition of a market, competition authorities, therefore, analyse both the ability firms have to influence market outcomes, and when that ability exists, to what extent firms also have the incentive to do so.

In energy markets, the condition that firms are not able to influence market outcomes is often not met. This is due to the presence of all kinds of constraints on economic agents' ability to adapt their production or consumption profiles. In particular, at certain hours or days in electricity markets, the available generation capacity may be really scarce, while electricity consumers are generally not really

[2] Note, however, that the competition should also not be too strong. Otherwise, firms may not be able to recoup the fixed costs of innovation. Therefore, competition should not be not too fierce in industries where firms have to invest significant amounts in research and development or in infrastructure. Or stated differently, in a market with fierce competition, firms may have fewer incentives to invest in innovation, as it can be unlikely to recoup the investments in innovation.

price sensitive (see Sect. 2.6.3). The latter means that they are not able or willing to strongly adapt their consumption profile in the short term. In such situations, the suppliers may be able to raise the electricity price by either reducing their own supply a bit (which is called capacity withholding) or asking a much higher price (which is called economic withholding). The high prices resulting from this kind of strategic behaviour may, however, form an incentive for other producers to invest in more generation capacity or for other agents to invest in storage capacity (e.g. batteries) or in demand flexibility to respond to high prices in the long term.

In order to prevent the loss of welfare resulting from such strategic behaviour, governments may intervene through the implementation of sector-specific regulation or general competition policies. An example of the former type of regulation is the removal of cross-border transportation bottlenecks, with the aim of increasing the size of the market. That increase may reduce the market power of individual players, as in a larger market more options (e.g. technologies and firms) are available to respond to higher prices. In Sect. 2.4.5, we have seen that these enlargements of electricity market through reduction of cross-border transmission bottlenecks have been quite successful, although there still exist several remaining bottlenecks. Moreover, within the EU, electricity firms also need to disclose the availability of their power plants[3] to make the market more transparent. This information may raise the trust of market parties in the well-functioning of the market process, as well as reduce the risk of capacity withholding. In addition to such sector-specific regulatory measures, all firms in all industries are subject to general competition laws in many countries. Based on these laws, firms are not allowed to collude with each other, i.e. form cartels, at the expense of consumers, by for example increasing the product prices or lowering the quality of the products. The same holds for companies with a dominant market position, which are not allowed to abuse that position.

3.2.4 No Externalities

Another condition for a well-functioning market is that economic agents are incentivised to take all effects of their choices into consideration. If an economic agent does not have an incentive to look at costs caused by his/her decision, we are talking about a negative externality. This externality typically occurs when someone does not need to pay for the costs or does not experience the consequences of the costs. Hence, the costs are underestimated and, as a result, the use is higher than what would be socially optimal. When the external costs are ignored, the supply curve is below the one which would occur when these external costs would be taken on board (in the so-called social supply curve, see Fig. 3.3). Consequently, the market-equilibrium quantity is higher (q_1 instead of q_2), while the equilibrium price is lower

[3] This is the so-called REMIT regulation, which stands for the EU Regulation on wholesale Energy Market Integrity and Transparency. For more information, see the website of the European agency for the cooperation between energy regulators, ACER: https://www.acer.europa.eu/remit/about-remit.

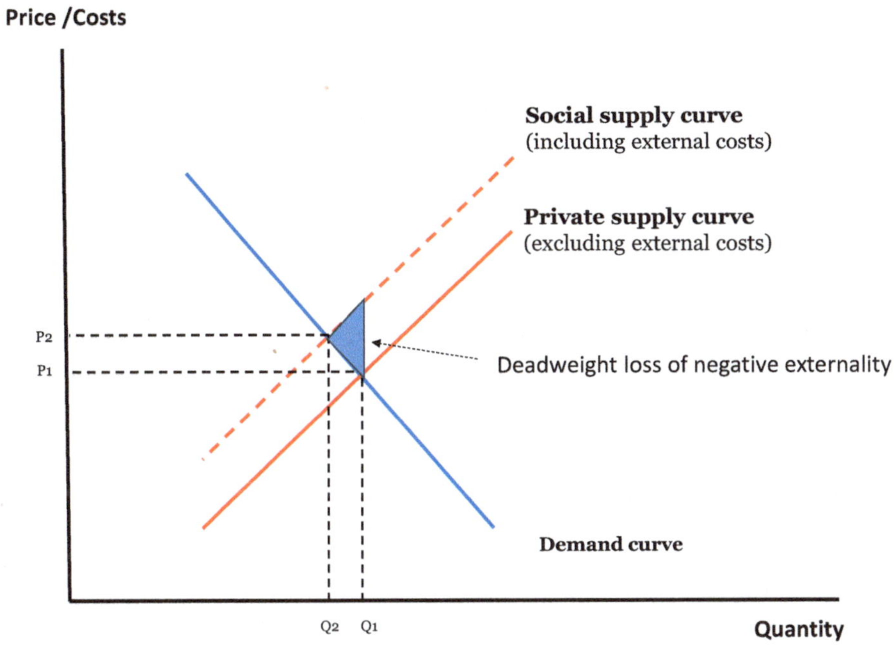

Fig. 3.3 Effects of the presence of negative externality on market outcomes and welfare

(p_1 instead of p_2). The presence of a negative externality results in a so-called deadweight loss. This is a loss of welfare because the consumption above the social equilibrium quantity (q_1-q_2) has marginal costs which exceed the marginal value. In the figure, this loss of welfare is depicted by the blue triangle. You can also formulate this loss of welfare in a different way: if these consumers would be asked to pay the full marginal costs (reflected by the social supply curve) they would not buy the product. When this negative externality occurs, economic agents consume more than in the situation where all costs are taken into account. The result is, therefore, overconsumption from a social welfare perspective. This kind of market failure can be addressed through regulatory measures, such as taxes, subsidies or regulatory constraints, which internalise the externality.

A special type of negative externality are so-called common-pool problems. This refers to commodities that can be used by everyone (i.e. the pool) and as a result, no one has the incentive to take care of it. This market failure is also called the tragedy of the commons. After all, when one makes costs and efforts to invest in such a pool or to do some maintenance work, everyone in the pool can freely benefit from these costs and efforts, without being forced to pay for it. Therefore, the exploitation of common pools necessitates the development of a kind of collective arrangement to make sure the necessary investments and maintenance works will be done and the exploitation of the pool is done in a way that is most beneficial for society.[4]

On the other hand, economic agents may also lack an incentive to include all potential benefits of their actions. This is called a positive externality. This externality occurs when an economic agent is not able to capture the benefits which are caused by his/her actions, for instance, because others can freely enjoy these benefits without being forced to pay for it. An example of such an externality is innovation directed at energy production technologies, which result in spillover effects to other economic agents. The consequence of positive externalities is that economic agents are under-providing the commodity from a social welfare perspective. Rational economic agents only supply the amount which maximises their own net benefits, ignoring the benefits which are only enjoyed by others. This kind of market failure can be addressed by, for instance, subsidising suppliers in order to stimulate them to supply more, up to the socially optimal amount.

A special type of positive externality is public goods, which are goods characterised by non-excludability and non-rivalry. The former characteristic means that once such goods exist, no one can be excluded from benefiting from them, while the latter characteristic means that the use by one agent does not affect the availability for others. The classical example of such goods are dikes, which protect everyone living in its neighbourhood, no matter if agents have contributed to it or not, as is also discussed in Sect. 2.3.3. Because of its non-excludability and non-rivalry characteristics, public goods will not be supplied by market parties. After all, agents who take care of a public good like a dike have to make the costs of realising the good, but are not able to make the good only available to those agents who really contribute or pay for it. Therefore, for the realisation of public goods, public arrangements are required.

3.2.5 No Hold-Up

When economic agents interact with each other, they also become dependent on each other. In simple interactions, agents may just exchange a commodity for another commodity or financial assets (i.e. money), without any further commitments for the future. More complex interactions include promises and commitments regarding future deliveries of commodities and/or financial assets. When there is a gap between the timing of the commitment made by one agent and the timing of the execution of the commitments (such as the actual usage of an infrastructure) by others, this may create uncertainty for the first one. For instance, assume an agent is considering to make an investment in an asset, such as a heat-transport

[4] If the exploitation of an oil resource, for instance, would not be coordinated, but left to individual agents, everyone would have the incentive to speed up the exploitation in order to maximise its own profits, assuming the increased production does not affect the market price. Such a fast exploitation, however, may be detrimental for the aggregated production of a resource when it negatively affects the geological characteristics of the resource (see Sect. 4.3.4).

infrastructure, in return for regular payments by the users of that asset, such as heat users, during a future period. The investing agent will want to have certainty regarding the future payments before (s)he makes the decision to invest. Without such certainty, the investment can be very risky.

A crucial aspect here is to what extent the asset can only be used by a specific group of users. If the asset can be easily redirected to another type of use or another groups of users, i.e. when the asset specificity is low, the risk regarding the future use of the asset is limited. On the contrary, in case of a high asset specificity, investors want to have certainty regarding the future use. That certainty can be arranged through contracts in which the future users commit to paying for the future use. Without such contracts providing the required certainty, investors may hold up on their investment decision. A consequence might be that socially efficient investments are not implemented. When such a situation occurs, governments may step in to reduce the risk for one or all parties involved in the development of the infrastructure. This can, for instance, be achieved by offering revenue guarantees to those investing in the infrastructure or by providing subsidies to the future users of the infrastructure, which reduces their risk of being committed to future use and payments.

Government policy may also create uncertainty for investors, resulting in hold-up situations. If, for instance, a government cannot provide security on future regulation of an infrastructure or the precise content of climate-policy measures, such as support schemes or carbon taxes, economic agents may be hesitant to make upfront costs. Consequently, they may not be interested in investing in decarbonisation measures.

3.2.6 Conclusion and Application to Arguments for Energy Transition

The above brief theoretical framework of well-functioning markets and market failures summarises the economic lens used to looking at real economic systems and the need for government intervention. In this book, we use this lens to look at policies to pursue energy transition. As was mentioned in Chap. 1, governments and societies refer to various types of arguments to pursue an energy transition, but to what extent are these arguments related to the presence of market failures? This question will be answered in the remainder of this chapter by discussing a number of arguments that are related to (one or more of) the three core elements of energy policy: security of supply, affordability and sustainability.[5] These arguments are (a) that fossil-energy resources will be exhausted at some point in time, (b) that fossil-energy consumption increases the import dependence of some countries, (c) that fossil-energy consumption has negative effects on the affordability of energy and

[5] On top of these three main pillars of energy policy, some countries have specific targets, such as in Germany where the phasing out of nuclear energy was also part of the so-called *energiewende* (see Box 2.1).

Table 3.1 Four common arguments for energy transition

Topic of energy policy	Arguments for energy transition	Discussed in section
Security of supply	Fossil-energy resources will be exhausted at some point of time in the future and, therefore, governments should implement measures to conserve resources	3.3
Security of supply	Use of fossil energy raises the import dependence and, therefore, governments should promote the supply of domestic renewable energy	3.4
Affordability	Use of fossil energy negatively affects the affordability of energy, and, therefore, governments should promote the usage of renewable energy	3.5
Sustainability	Use of fossil energy results in the emissions of greenhouse gases and, therefore, governments should take measures to reduce these emissions by promoting energy efficiency, renewable energy, and capture and storage of emissions	3.6

(d) that fossil-energy consumption results in the emissions of carbon which is a major factor behind climate change (see Table 3.1). Using both theoretical reasoning and results from empirical evidence, we will discuss to what extent each of these arguments refers to the presence of fundamental shortcomings in the organisation of energy systems, which legitimates, from an economic perspective, the implementation of specific policy measures. While this question will be answered in the remainder of this chapter, the next chapter will focus on the type of policy measures that are most effective and efficient to address particular failures in energy markets.

3.3 Energy Transition in Response to the Depletion of Natural Resources

3.3.1 The Argument

The first argument for energy transition that we analyse in more detail is related to the fact that the natural resources of fossil-energy carriers, such as coal, oil and natural gas, are limited. These resources are, therefore, called non-renewable. As a result of this characteristic, the exploitation of these resources results automatically in a reduced number of remaining resources. This may have as a consequence that in the future, mankind may not have sufficient energy to sustain current levels of economic development, let alone for expanding its economic development. In order to prevent this, governments should intervene in energy systems to make sure that the energy resources are more carefully exploited and that sufficient alternative energy carriers are developed. The underlying argument is that economic agents are seen as myopic, which means that they do not sufficiently value the long-term consequences of their current behaviour, and as a result governments should intervene.

This argumentation is used by various governments to implement natural-resource policies that are directed at managing the timing of the depletion of natural

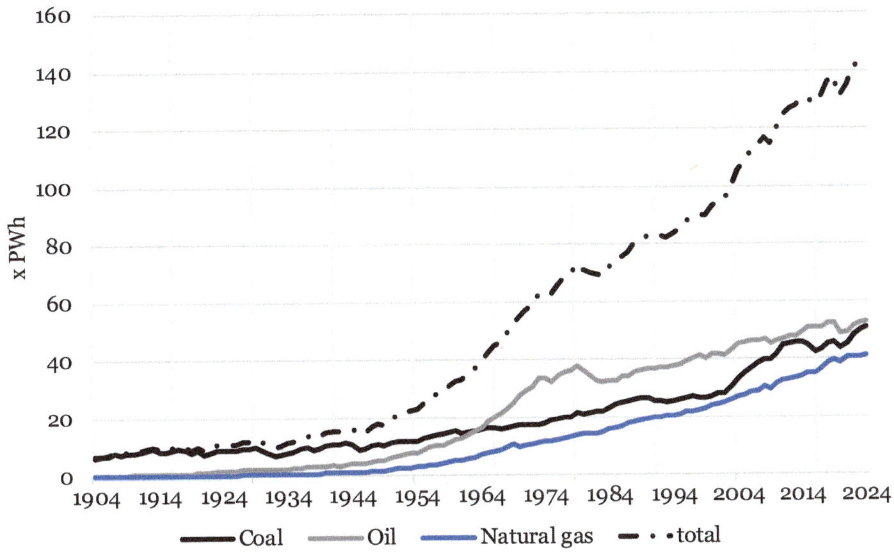

Fig. 3.4 Annual global fossil-energy production, in total and per energy carrier, 1904–2024 (in PWh) (Source: Our World in Data)

resources. In some countries the governments restrict the production of natural gas from the domestic resources to preserve gas for later generations. Such policies may also be motivated by reference to the objective of reducing dependence on energy imports from other countries, which will be discussed in Sect. 3.4.

3.3.2 The Basic Facts

As we have seen in the previous chapter, the production of fossil-energy carriers has increased exponentially since the start of the industrial revolution in the midst of the nineteenth century. Initially, this only referred to the production of coal. Around 1900, the global production of fossil energy mainly consisted of the production of coal and was equal to about 6 PWh of energy.[6] This production level remained fairly stable until WO II. Afterwards, the global production of fossil energy increased strongly, not only the production of coal, but also the production of oil and natural gas. In 2024, the total global production of both coal and oil were about 50 PWh, while the global production of natural gas was about 40 PWh, resulting in a total global production of these three fossil-energy resources of 145 PWh per year (see Fig. 3.4).

This increase in production can be attributed to a strong growth in the demand, caused by two factors: a growing global population (from less than 2 billion around 1900 to slighly above 8 billion in 2024) and a higher production per capita (from

[6] PWh stands for petawatt-hour, which is equal to a billion MWh. See Appendix A.

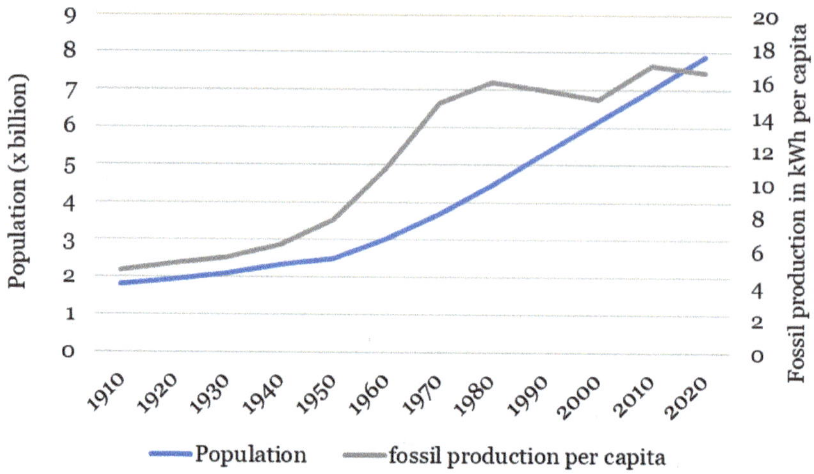

Fig. 3.5 Average annual global fossil-energy production, per capita and global population size, 1910–2020 (in kWh) (Source: Our World in Data)

about 4 kWh per capita around 1900 to about 16 kWh per capita in 2024) (see Fig. 3.5). The latter indicates a strong increase in the energy consumption per person, which is related to the strong increase in income per person. The production per capacity grew in particular in the first decades after WO II, but since then the growth has been moderate. This is another sign that the global economies have become less energy-intensive, as we already saw in Chap. 2. The other factor contributing to this declining growth in the use of fossil energy per person is the growth in the production of renewable energy.

The growth in coal, oil and gas production has resulted in a high cumulative production. The cumulative fossil-energy production over the period 1904 up until and including 2023 equals to 6000 PWh of energy (see Fig. 3.6). This amount of fossil energy was extracted from the Earth's crust.

Despite this strong increase in the annual global production and cumulative production since the start of the exploitation of the fossil-energy resources, the level of (proven) reserves[7] is still increasing (see Fig. 3.7). While in 1980, the global reserve level of oil was about 700 billion barrels, in 2020 this had risen to approximately 1700 billion barrels. For natural gas, the reserves increased from about 70 to 190 TCM (trillion cubic metre).

Hence, the rising production levels coincided with increasing reserve levels. Since both increased roughly to the same extent, the so-called Reserve/Production ratio has been fairly stable over the past decades (see Fig. 3.8). For both oil and natural gas, the current level of reserves is sufficient for about 50 years of global production at current levels.

[7] Throughout this book, whenever reference is made to 'reserves', it refers to the proven reserves. See Table 4.2 for the definition of the various categories of reserves and resources.

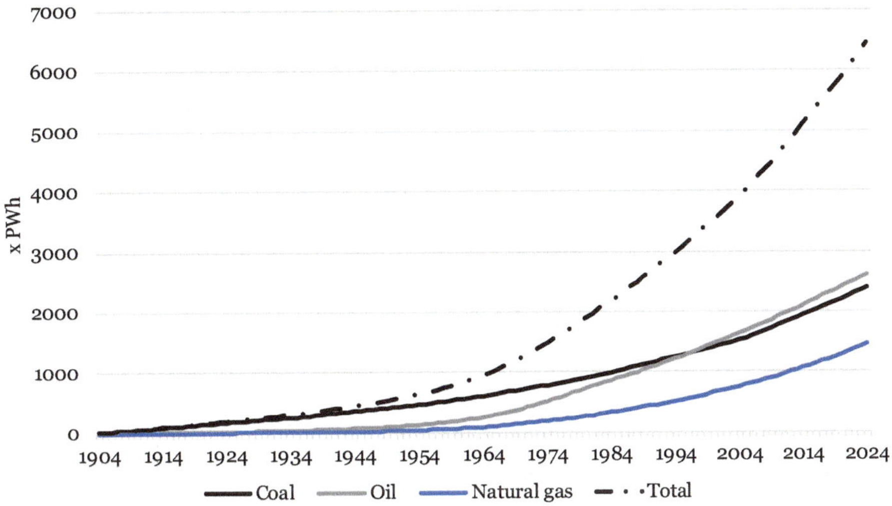

Fig. 3.6 Cumulative global fossil-energy production, in total and per energy carrier, 1904–2024 (in PWh) (Source: Our World in Data)

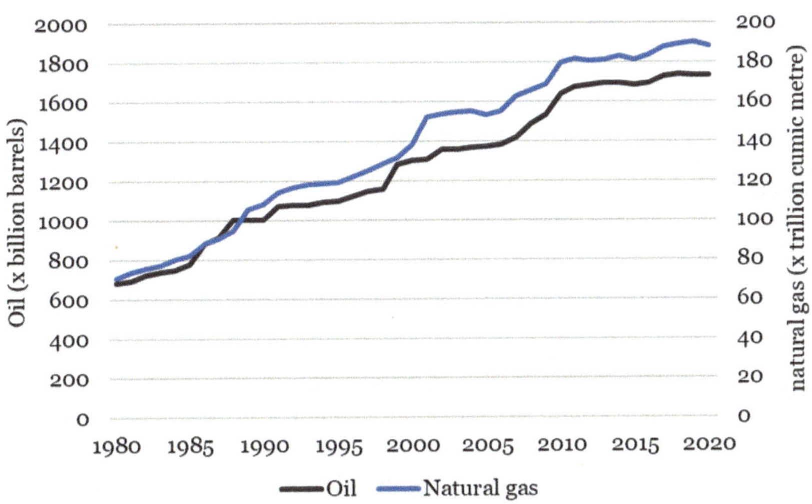

Fig. 3.7 Global reserves of oil and natural gas, 1980–2020 (Source: BP (2022))

From these facts, one can conclude that reserves is a different concept than the Earth's resources. After all, the resources do not change when we produce more. The reserves here refer to the so-called proven reserves, which are that part of the resources which have a high geological certainty and which can be produced with a high economic feasibility. Next to this category, there are other categories of reserves which are less certain and/or less economically feasible. These categories are called probable reserves, possible reserves and prospective resources (see Table 3.2)

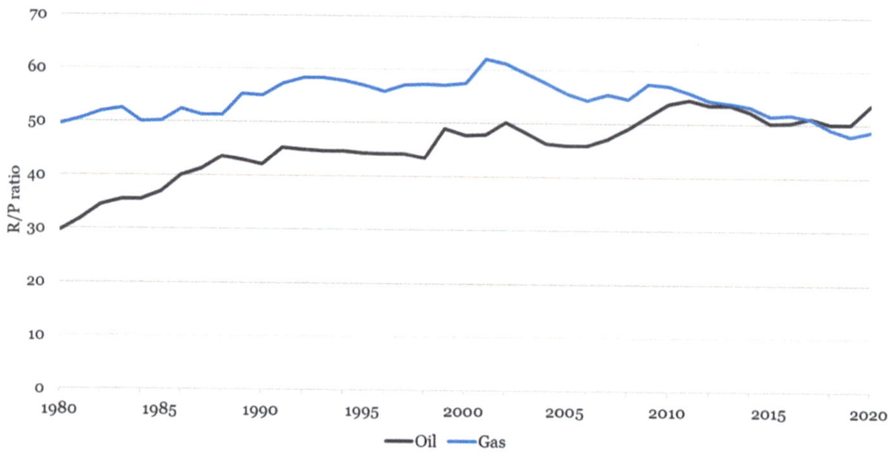

Fig. 3.8 Global reserve/production (R/P) ratios for oil and gas, 1980–2020 (Source: BP (2022))

Table 3.2 McKelvey diagram: classification of resources on the basis of geological certainty and economic feasibility

	Geological certainty				
		High		Low	
Economic feasibility	High	Proven reserves	Probable reserves	Possible reserves	Prospective resources
	Low	Conditional resources			

Note: for more information on this diagram, see for instance: https://energyeducation.ca/encyclopedia/McKelvey_box#cite_note-3

Hence, the proven reserves form that part of the resources which have been discovered with high certainty and which can be produced in an economically efficient way given current technologies and market prices. This implies that the number of proven reserves is related to exploration activities. The more firms search for resources, the more they are likely to find, which in turn has an upward effect on the level of reserves. The incentives for firms to search for more reserves are positively affected when production costs decline or the price of energy carriers (e.g. oil or gas) rises, as this increases their economic feasibility.

Successful exploration activities have an upward effect on the level of reserves, as they provide greater certainty about the magnitude of resources that can be exploited in an economically feasible manner. Despite this positive effect on the level of reserves, one cannot deny the knowledge that the remaining amount of the aggregated geological resources is decreasing. Hence, the resources become scarcer in a physical sense. To what extent that will also be the case in economic sense, depends on the demand for the resources. The indicator for economic scarcity is the price of the commodity. Looking at the prices of fossil energy, it appears that these prices have been volatile over the past decades, in particular the prices for oil, but overall, these prices have not risen in real terms since the mid 1970s. In real terms,

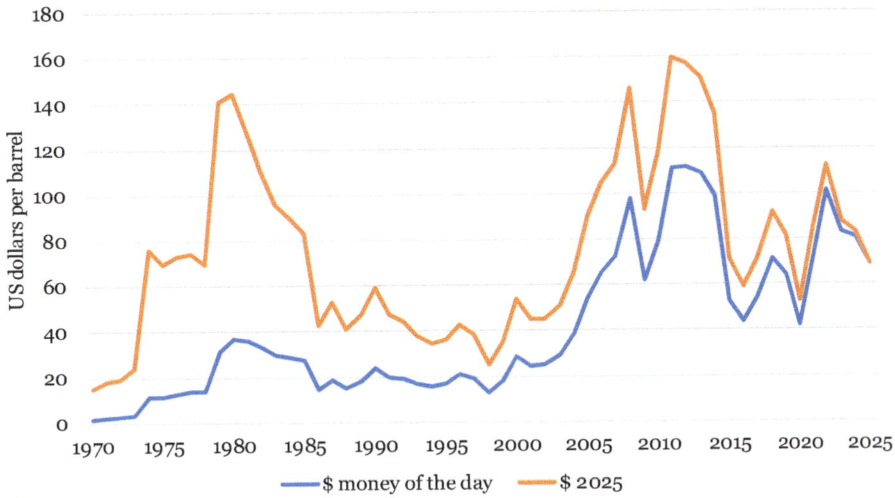

Fig. 3.9 Average annual spot crude oil prices, 1970–2025, in nominal terms (i.e. money of the day) as well as real terms (in dollars of 2025) (Source: Statistical Review of Energy (2026), 75st edition)

the oil price was lower in 2025 than at the end of the 1970s (see Fig. 3.9). The real oil price was also lower than the price 160 years ago, as we have seen in Fig. 2.6. Hence, the level of the oil prices does not indicate that the oil resources have become scarcer from an economic perspective.

3.3.3 Economic Mechanisms

The fact that natural resources are non-renewable, which means that any exploitation reduces the remaining amount, makes that economic agents have to deal with the so-called intertemporal consequences of their decisions. The exploitation of a natural resource today implies that less of that resource will be available in the future. Hence, the opportunity costs of producing a natural resource consist of the missed benefits of producing it in the future. A rational economic agent takes these opportunity costs into account when determining the best way of exploiting a resource. When an agent does not have any information on the future prices of the commodity and can therefore ignore any impact of its actions on the future price, then the optimal intertemporal exploitation of the resource is to do this as soon as possible. After all, any delay in production results in a delay in the profits of the exploitation. The costs of this delay are related to the costs of capital, i.e. the discount rate.[8] Postponing production, when the nominal value of marginal revenues

[8] The discount rate influences what the present value is of a future income (or costs). The present value of x which will be received in year t from now is equal to $\frac{x}{(1+r)^t}$, where r is the discount rate.

and costs remains the same, results in a lower discounted value of the net revenues (NPV), at least when the discount rate is positive. This follows from the following formula, where *p* stands for the price of the commodity, *q* for the quantity produced, *mc* for the marginal costs, *r* for the discount rate and *t* for time in years:

$$\mathrm{NPV} = \sum_{t} \frac{(p_t - mc_t) * q_t}{(1+r)^t} \tag{3.1}$$

If an economic agent, however, expects that the prices will increase in the future, while the marginal costs will remain the same, the optimal decision may be to postpone production. If prices are expected to increase annually by a percentage *x*, it is optimal to postpone production as long as the discount rate *r* is below this rate of increase. After all, the future revenues in that case increase more than the discount rate reduces the present value of the revenues. When the discount rate equals the expected annual percentage increase in the net revenues (i.e. $r=x$), a rational economic agent is indifferent to the depletion path (see Fig. 3.10). No matter what the depletion strategy is (e.g. as soon as possible, a gradual annual depletion path or postpone to the future), the discounted value of the revenues remains the same. When the discount rate, however, exceeds the expected price increase (i.e. $r>x$), the most profitable strategy is to produce as fast as possible.

This decision rule holds, of course, only when the economic agent does not have any impact on market prices. If many economic agents, however, would decide to postpone their production expecting that future prices will increase at a faster pace than the level of the discount rate, the market outcomes are affected. If many

Fig. 3.10 Numerical example of impact of discount rate and expected price increase on Net Present Value of depletion path. (Note: *r* stands for discount rate and *x* for the expected price increase. If we assume a period of 10 years, a net price of 10 and a resource amount of 10 units; *Now* means everything is produced in year 1, while *Later* means that everything is produced in year 10)

producers postpone their production, the current supply drops, making the market tighter and, hence, raising the current market price. In addition, agents will expect there to be more supply in the future, which reduces the expected future price. Consequently, the expected price will increase less, which impacts the optimal depletion decision.

This adaptive behaviour of economic agents and their joint impact on market prices, both now and in the future, makes that the expected future development of the market prices is related to the discount rate. This mechanism is called Hotelling's rule, which says that the net revenues (i.e. price minus the marginal costs) of non-renewable resource increases with the time value of money, i.e. the discount rate (r):

$$100\% * \frac{(p_{t+1} - mc_{t+1}) - (p_t - mc_t)}{(p_t - mc_t)} = r \tag{3.2}$$

As we have seen above, if the discount rate is higher than the expected price increase of the commodity, it is more profitable to produce the resources as soon as possible and invest the revenues in, for instance, stocks or government bonds. These investments generate dividends and interests which are related to the discount rate.

In addition, the price of non-renewable resources is related to the expected price of alternative energy carriers. The latter is referred to as the backstop technology, such as renewables. The optimal supply of the non-renewable resource is such that the total resource can be exploited before the backstop technology becomes more competitive. If the costs of the backstop are expected to be lower than the costs of producing the non-renewable resource in, for instance, 10 years from now, a depletion path will be chosen that maximises the profits[9] during this period. This mechanism also creates an incentive for exploiters of the non-renewable resource to bring forward production when the (expected) costs of the backdrop technology fall. This, in turn, lowers current prices of the non-renewable resource[10].

From this analysis of the theoretical prediction for the development of the prices of non-renewable resources, we can conclude that economic agents have an incentive to form expectations about future revenues when deciding on their resource depletion policy. If an economic agent expects that the commodity will become economically scarce and that, hence, the market prices will increase, it affects their decision about how much to produce today. Hence, this theory states that economic agents evaluate the future availability of non-renewable resources, as they have an incentive to do so. If a resource will likely become more valuable in the future, it is efficient to conserve it instead of using it now. Conserving a resource can be done

---

[9] The profit of the exploitation is determined by the difference between the market price and the marginal costs, which is called the resource rent. So, these rents are the profits due to the expected scarcity of the commodity. Note that this theorem assumes that the marginal costs of producing will remain constant. When the marginal costs increase, the future price of the resource will raise with a lower percentage than the discount rate.

[10] This mechanisme is called the green paradox, since (policy) measures reducing the (future) costs of renewables incentivises fossil-fuel producers to advance their production, which lowers the fossil-fuel price, making renewables less competitive.

by postponing the consumption of the energy carriers, through for example energy-efficiency measures, or by looking for alternatives which can replace them, such as developing renewable-energy sources.

The above theoretical mechanism, of course, only works when all conditions for well-functioning markets are met. This means that (a) economic agents are well-informed, (b) they have an incentive to take all effects of their decisions into account, (c) they can capture the future benefits of their investments and (d) they cannot distort the allocation process by behaving strategically. When these conditions hold, markets for non-renewable resources can appropriately manage the declining number of geological resources due to exploitation. The question now is whether all these conditions are met, i.e. whether there are no market failures. When market failures exist, the economic agents may not optimally deal with the increasing resource scarcity.

If economic agents do not have the same level and quality of information about geological expectations regarding prospective resources or possible or proven reserves, their decisions about the use of non-renewable resources are differently affected. This information asymmetry can result in an inefficient depletion path. If some agents, for instance, believe there are many reserves, while others know the amount is much lower, the latter may have a stronger incentive to explore new resources than the former group. From a social welfare perspective, the exploration activities of the former group, that overestimates the current reserves, are too low.

Note that the absence of information asymmetry does not mean that economic agents have perfect foresight and complete information about the current situation. No matter how economies are organised, the future remains uncertain. Consequently, a fundamental characteristic of economies is that economic agents have to make decisions under uncertainty. In the case of the exploitation of non-renewable resources, they do not have perfect information on the precise size of these resources, while the characteristics of non-renewable resources are also unknown. The issue at hand is that in a well-functioning market, all existing information is potentially available to all economic agents. In these circumstances, it is up to them how they assess the information and how they deal with the accompanying uncertainty.

Uncertainty regarding the precise characteristics of a field of non-renewable resources can be addressed by making various scenarios and/or by making more costs for explorative research. A market failure, resulting from information asymmetry, would mean that some (types of) economic agents would not be able to access crucial information available to others. If, for instance, new entrants are unable to access information on remaining geological resources, they will conduct less exploration than they otherwise would.

Another market failure could arise when economic agents do not sufficiently consider the consequences of their decisions regarding the use of non-renewable resources for other economic agents, including those working in the same resource base and future generations. When individual agents do not fully acknowledge the impact of their depletion activities on the potential aggregated revenues of the whole industry in that region, there might be a common-pool problem. In order to maximise the total revenues from a particular resource, the pace of exploitation should not be too high, as otherwise the technical characteristics of that resource (such as pressure) are adversely affected. Therefore, uncoordinated exploitation of natural resources may have an adverse effect on the aggregated revenues from a field.

The concept of discount rate is relevant when we look at the attention of economic agents for the impact of their depletion activities on future revenues. Suppose that economic agents do not make any difference between their net revenues today or in the long-term future, then their discount rate is zero. The optimal depletion strategy in that case would be to flatten the annual production, at least when the impact of the depletion path on market prices is taken into account. After all, if the producers would advance the production, current prices would drop, while future prices would increase. This would lower their total net revenues, as the low prices are realised when production volumes are high, and high prices when production volumes are low.[11] The consequence of a flat production profile is that future consumers will see the same amount of production and price levels as at present (of course, assuming everything else remains equal). However, when economic agents are not indifferent to when they receive their revenues, i.e. when their discount rate is positive, they have an incentive to advance the production, at least when this discount rate exceeds the expected increase in the price of the resource. The consequence of advancing the production is that future generations will see less production and higher prices.

Crucial here is to what extent the discount rate used by economic agents deviates from the socially optimal one. When an economy is in a dynamic equilibrium, the social discount rate is equal to the private discount rate based on the price of capital in capital markets (Tol, 2023a). After all, if the private interest rate would be higher than the costs of capital, economic agents would consume less and save more which reduces the private interest rate, and the other way around. So, when the market functions perfectly, the private discount rate adapts itself in order to reflect the social discount rates. Capital markets can, however, be imperfect as a result of, for instance, not taking into account all effects of investments or the presence of uncertainty about future conditions, which can result in a structural deviation between the private and socially optimal discount rate. The crucial factor here is the parameter for the pure rate of time preference: what should this factor be when looking at long-term effects (see Box 3.1)?

When the discount rate of (private) economic agents exceeds the socially optimal one, economic agents are said to be myopic, which means that they overvalue the short-term effects and undervalue the longer-term effects. The consequence of such

[11] This is similar to what happens to the revenues of solar-power producers. They produce the most when their competing solar producers generate electricity, because of their dependence on the common resource: sunshine. Because of this correlation in production, solar producers realise a low electricity price when they produce the most, while they have low production levels when the electricity price is high. As a result, their so-called capture price is low. This mechanism is called the market-value effect of renewables, as is explained in Sect. 2.5.4.

myopic behaviour is that the depletion of non-renewable resources occurs too rapidly from a social welfare point of view.

Box 3.1 What Should be the Social Discount Rate?
The social discount rate can be based on the Ramsey rule, according to which it depends on three components: the pure rate of time preference (δ), the expected future income level (g) and the elasticity of the marginal utility of consumption (η) (Schoenmaker & Schramade, 2024):

$$r = \delta + \eta g \tag{3.3}$$

The key parameter in the debate on the social discount rate, is the pure rate of time preference. In the literature, there are opposing viewpoints regarding the true value of this rate. On the one hand, there is Nordhaus (1998) who states that the time preference can be based on the market interest rates, and on the other hand, Stern (2004) who states that the time preference parameter should be based on ethical considerations (Schoenmaker & Schramade, 2024). This debate refers to two completely different approaches. The former approach states that one can infer the time preference from the actual behaviour of economic agents which is reflected in the price they ask when investing capital in capital markets, i.e. the market interest rates. The latter approach is of a normative nature, as it does not focus on what the actual discount rate is, but what it should be, based on ethical reasoning. Both approaches are relevant for societal debates on energy-transition policies, as they provide alternative views on how to deal with the future consequences of current decisions.

Economic agents may also choose to advance the exploitation of their non-renewable resources when they are uncertain about their ability to exploit them in the future (Zweifel et al., 2017). If they are uncertain to what extent societies and governments will allow them to exploit these resources in the (long-term) future, they have an incentive to produce more quickly than what would be socially optimal.

Another potential market failure in the exploitation of non-renewable resources is that some economic agents distort the allocation process by influencing market outcomes. In a competitive environment, all producers of the resource take the market prices as exogenous, hence they are so-called price takers. As a result, their depletion path is based on the intertemporal optimisation as discussed above. When some producers, however, can behave like price setters, the optimal depletion path changes. By supplying less of the commodity to the market, the market becomes tighter and prices higher. This might be a profitable strategy for them when the additional profits because of the higher prices exceed the loss of producing less. Note, however, that the reduced production is not so much a loss, but the postponement of production. After all, in case of non-renewable resources, a reduction in production implies that more can be produced later on. The welfare consequences of such a distortion of the allocation process are that current consumers are paying more for the commodity, and that a later generation may pay a lower price. Given the effect of the use of market power on the depletion path of non-renewable resources, it is said that the monopolist is the environmentalist's best friend (Perman et al., 1999).

3.3.4 Evidence from Research

The key empirical question here is to what extent actual markets for non-renewable resources are able to deal with the geological fact that the remaining amount of these resources is diminishing and that this may result in a loss of welfare in the future which is not taken into account by the current economic agents. What evidence do we have that market prices adequately reflect the increasing geological scarcity? Moreover, to what extent is the allocation process in the markets for non-renewable resources distorted by information problems or by economic agents who insufficiently consider the interests of future generations?

In order to analyse to what extent market prices of non-renewable resources reflect information on geological scarcity, we can look at studies into the impact of the availability of resources on exploration, production as well as market prices. It appears that information on the potential of new reserves has a negative impact on current market prices. If firms see that there will be more resources available in the future, they expect that future prices will be lower, which gives them an incentive to advance production, which in turn lowers current market prices.

From various studies, it appears that the exploration and production activities are related to current and forward market prices. Dahl and Duggan (1998) find clear evidence that exploration activities for oil are positively related to the oil price with a long-term oil-price elasticity larger than 1, which means that a 1% increase in the oil price raises drilling activities by more than 1%. Widyastuti (2022) also find a positive impact of oil prices on exploration activities, namely that higher oil prices trigger firms to search for so-called frontier oil fields which have a relatively larger size compared to the existing fields. Also, Boyce and Nøstbakken (2010) find, based on an empirical analysis of exploration and development of US oil and gas fields over the period 1955–2002, that expected future prices affect both scarcity rents of assets and decisions of operators regarding exploitation and drilling.

Regarding the impact of information on exploration activities, Reynolds (2001) relates the volatility in the oil discovery in the USA in the twentieth century to the availability of information on resources. He concludes that, initially, the information on resources in the USA was scarce and, therefore, exploration costs were high and with a low probability of success. As a result, exploration activity remained limited. When the availability of information on the presence of resources improved, the exploration activity increased.

Regarding the level of the discount rate, there is an intense discussion in the economic literature on what the social discount rate should be and to what extent it deviates from the private discount rates (Schoenmaker & Schramade, 2024). A few economists (following Nordhaus, 1998) state that the pure rate of time preference can be based on interest rates, resulting in a value of 3%. Others (following Stern, 2004) argue that this rate of time preference should be set equal to 0% because of ethical considerations. According to the latter approach, the discount rates used by economic agents are too high, which implies that current production of non-renewable resources is too high.

If the latter is true, one would expect governments to restrict private companies in their exploration and production activities. This is, however, not really apparent. Most countries having non-renewable-energy resources do their best to exploit their resources and motivate commercial parties to conduct exploration, development and production. The UK government, for instance, recently offered about 30 new licences to operators to develop and produce oil and gas in the North Sea region,[12] while the Norwegian government issued more than 50 new licences for the production of oil and gas on the Norwegian Continental shelf.[13]

3.3.5 Conclusion

In their decisions regarding the use of non-renewable resources, economic agents take the consequences of the future availability of these resources and potential alternatives into account. When the resource is expected to become more scarce in the future, the current price increases because of the scarcity rents. These scarcity rents are an incentive for future exploration and development of non-renewable resources, but also for the development of the so-called backstop technologies. Energy markets do, however, not function perfectly, since there appear to be several shortcomings.

Information on resources may not be available to all agents, which raises the exploration costs, and as a result less exploration activities occur than would be socially optimal. This failure in the organisation of energy systems is not necessarily an indication of market failure, as it may also result from a regulatory failure, in the sense that governments are not transparent regarding the available resources in their country. If the amount of resources (or proven reserves) is underestimated by market parties, they overestimate the resource rent and, as a result, it is optimal for them to produce less of the resource than would be socially optimal. Hence, the consequence of this failure is a too low level of exploitation, not a too high level, which means this cannot be a reason to pursue a transition away from fossil fuels. Instead, improving the transparency about resources would be a more appropriate policy measure to address a shortcoming in the markets.

Uncertainty about the future ability to capture the revenues of exploiting a non-renewable resource gives economic agents an incentive to advance the exploitation compared to the socially optimal scheme. Therefore, giving these agents certainty about the rights to exploit in the future removes this incentive. This can be done by

[12] See https://oeuk.org.uk/new-oil-and-gas-licences-strengthen-every-sector-of-the-uk/.

[13] See https://www.regjeringen.no/en/whats-new/57-new-production-licenses-awarded/id3145952/.

an appropriate legal framework regarding exploration and production licences. When this legal certainty is provided, the risk of too fast exploitation is addressed.

When market parties are myopic in their decisions regarding the use of non-renewable resources, the consequence is that the exploitation of the resources is too fast from a social welfare perspective. Myopic behaviour here may also mean that economic agents insufficiently pay attention to the consequences for other agents in the future. In that case, this indicates a kind of negative externality, which is a market failure. This can be an economic reason for a transition towards other energy carriers. Governments may step in to change the exploration and production decisions. Such an intervention may be directed at measures which stimulate the use of renewable resources in order to conserve the non-renewable resources for future generations. The problem here is, however, that governments also show myopic behaviour, which implies that myopic behaviour is not only a market failure, but it can also be a regulatory failure. In Chap. 4, we will further discuss the effectiveness and efficiency of such policy measures.

3.4 Energy Transition in Order to Reduce Import Dependency

3.4.1 The Argument

Another argument for implementing energy-transition policies is that they may help reduce the import dependence of countries with little or no domestic fossil-energy resources. Fossil-energy resources are unequally distributed among countries and regions. Because of this, many countries need to import fossil-energy carriers from other countries to meet their domestic demand. Since energy is crucial for economic and societal activities, this import dependency may weaken the position of importing countries in relation to the exporting countries. After all, import dependency may give exporting countries a stronger negotiation position, which may adversely affect importing counties' welfare when exporting countries (ab)use this position. This relationship between geography and international affairs is actually the topic of geopolitics (Overland, 2019). The basic idea of geopolitics is that countries that own and control resources and/or have access to the transport routes possess power in the international political system.

In order to reduce the risk of exporting countries abusing their strong position in energy markets for geopolitical purposes, it is sometimes said that governments of fossil-energy importing countries should stimulate economic agents to import less fossil energy and make the domestic energy system more self-reliant. The latter can, for instance, be realised by increasing the share of domestically produced renewables, by promoting the use of storage facilities or the stimulation of energy-efficiency measures. The fundamental economic question, however, is to what extent import dependence must be seen as a fundamental shortcoming of energy markets which requires government intervention.

3.4.2 The Basic Facts

Fossil-energy resources are indeed unevenly distributed over the globe. More than half of the global oil reserves are concentrated in the Middle East, while about one-fifth is located in Venezuela (see Fig. 3.11). The remaining quarter of the global oil resources is mainly located in countries like Russia, Libya, Nigeria and the USA.

Because of their huge reserves, the Middle East and Latin America (i.e. Venezuela) have high Reserve/Production ratios. This ratio, which is defined as the value of the reserves over the aggregated level of annual production, indicates how many years the current level of production can be sustained with the existing level of reserves. From Fig. 3.12, it appears clearly that, for instance, the OECD America and OECD Europe can only continue the current production levels for a rather limited number of years.

To obtain more information on the import dependence of countries and regions, one should look at the ratio between the domestic production and domestic consumption. From Fig. 3.13, it is clear that several regions, in particular Europe and Asia Pacific, as well as various countries, such as China and India, strongly depend on imports of crude oil, while others, in particular the Middle East and the CIS region (i.e. Russia and other former members of the Soviet Union), produce significantly more crude oil than they consume. In this figure, we also see that the aggregated crude-oil production is globally more or less equal to the aggregated consumption levels, but small differences typically occur which gaps (i.e. too much or too less annual production compared to annual consumption) are addressed through the use of storage facilities.

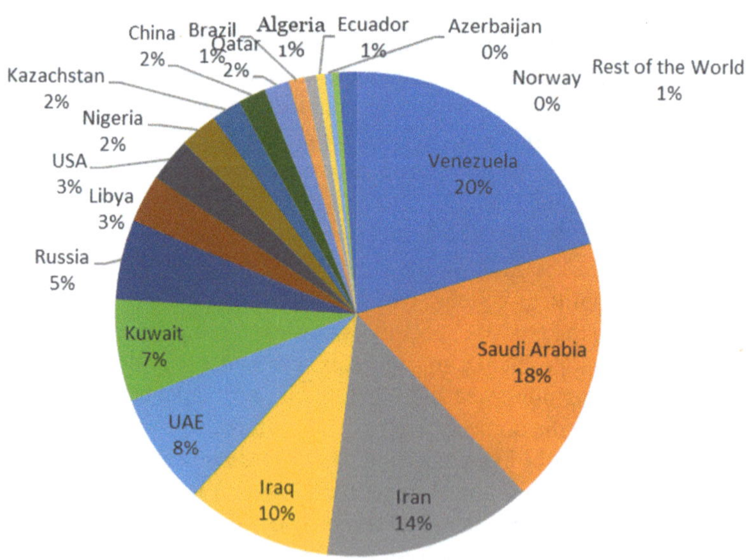

Fig. 3.11 Global distribution of oil reserves, 2024 (Source: World Population Review https://worldpopulationreview.com/country-rankings/oil-reserves-by-country)

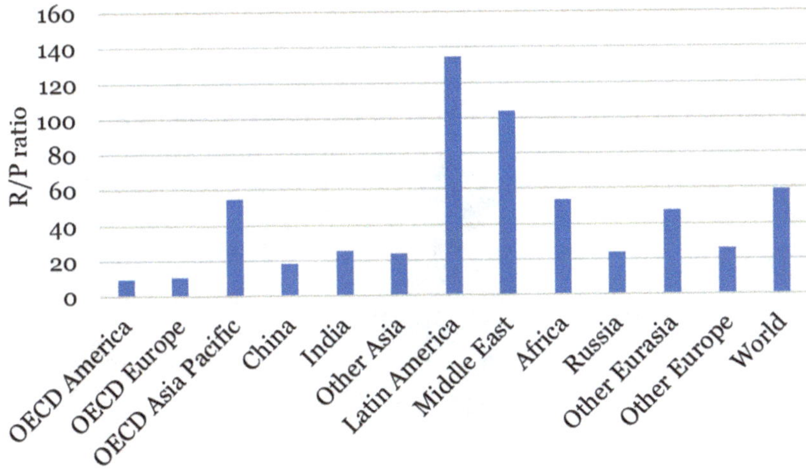

Fig. 3.12 Reserve/production (R/P) ratio for crude oil, per global region, 2024 (Source: OPEC (2025). Note: 'Other Europe' refers to non-OECD members such as Albania, Serbia, Ukraine and Moldova)

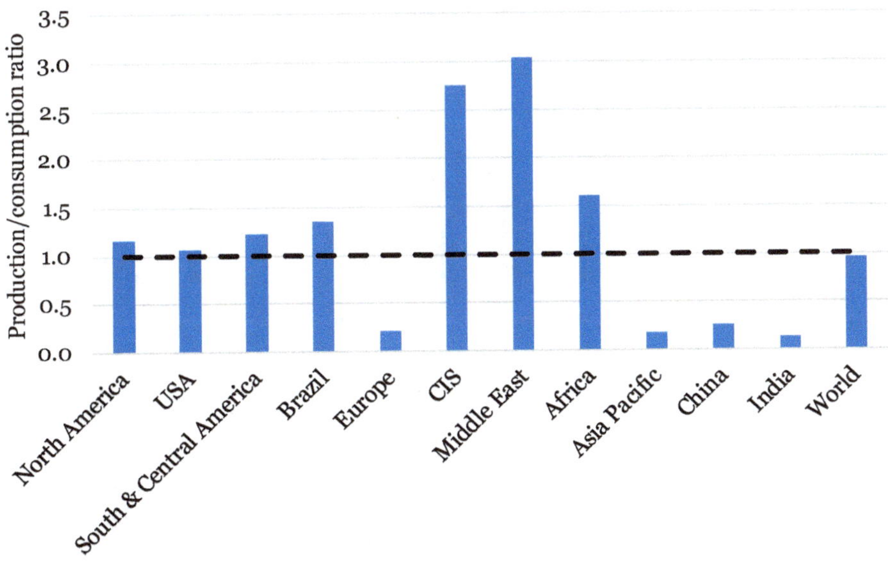

Fig. 3.13 Ratio between production and consumption of crude oil, per global region, 2025. (Source: Energy Institute https://www.energyinst.org. Notes: CIS stands for the Commonwealth of Independent States, consisting of Russia and former Soviet Union states; the dashed line refers to the situation when domestic production equals domestic consumption)

Regarding natural gas, more than 50% of the proven reserves are located in three countries (Russia, Iran and Qatar), but the other reserves are spread over a large number of countries (see Fig. 3.14).

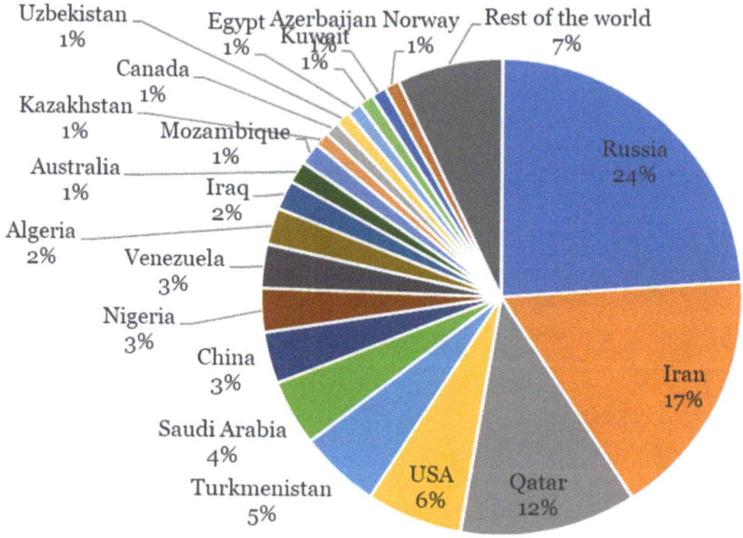

Fig. 3.14 Global distribution of natural-gas reserves, 2025 (Source: GlobalFirepower (2025) https://www.globalfirepower.com/proven-natural-gas-reserves-by-country.php)

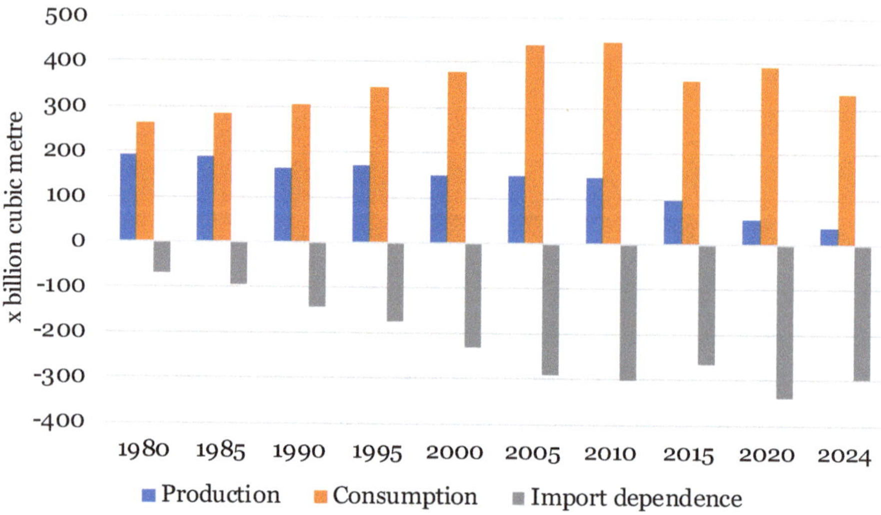

Fig. 3.15 Production, consumption and import dependence of natural gas in the European Union 27, 1980-2024 (in bcm) (Source: Our World in Data. Note: Import dependence is defined as domestic production minus domestic consumption)

The uneven distribution of natural gas-resources contributes to the significant differences between domestic production and consumption. This holds in particular for the European Union, where the domestic natural-gas demand is much higher than domestic production, as is depicted by Fig. 3.15. Since both EU consumption

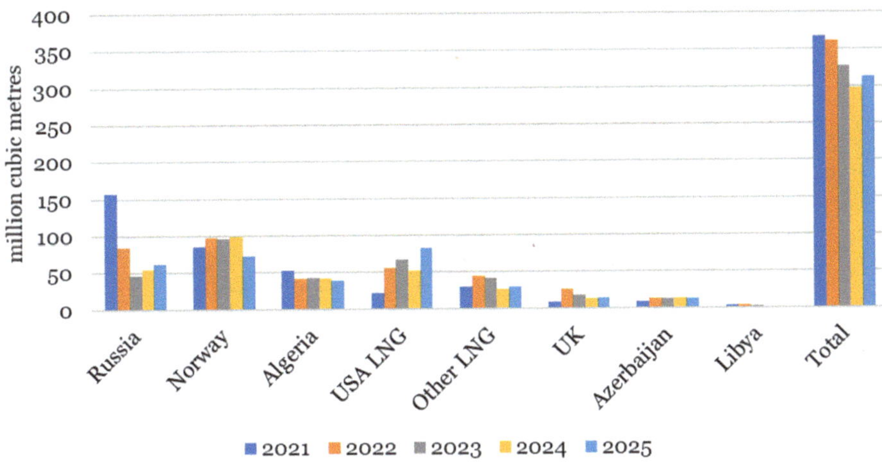

Fig. 3.16 Import of natural gas in the EU, by country of origin, 2021-2025 (Source: Bruegel https://www.bruegel.org/dataset/european-natural-gas-imports)

and production of natural gas have declined over the past years, the import dependence remains high.

As natural gas in Europe is mostly transported through pipeline systems, this import dependence is related to the dependence on a particular transport mode. In the short term, the ability to replace the import of natural gas through pipelines by import of Liquefied Natural Gas (LNG) is limited. This limitation is due to the required physical infrastructure, such as liquefaction and (re)gasification installations, terminals and LNG tankers.[14] After Russia's invasion of Ukraine in 2022, European countries significantly reduced their imports of pipeline gas from Russia, but it took some time before these imports could be replaced by LNG import from countries like the USA and Qatar. During this period, the gas prices in Europe surged to unprecedentedly high levels. Since the investments in the LNG infrastructure have been made, the European import of LNG has strongly increased (see Fig. 3.16).

Although the European Union is also strongly dependent on the import of crude oil, the import dependence does not coincide with a dependence on a particular transport system as, for many countries, in the case of natural gas. The transport of oil is mostly done by ship, which gives importing countries more flexibility to change the country they import the oil from. Although also here, there are some technical constraints, for example, crude oil has a different quality depending on the field where it is produced and users, such as refineries and chemical industries, need particular types of quality. These technical constraints are, however, of a limited nature and do not result in large price differences among the various types of oil, as was already shown in Fig. 2.10.

[14] See Appendix A for the characteristics of LNG.

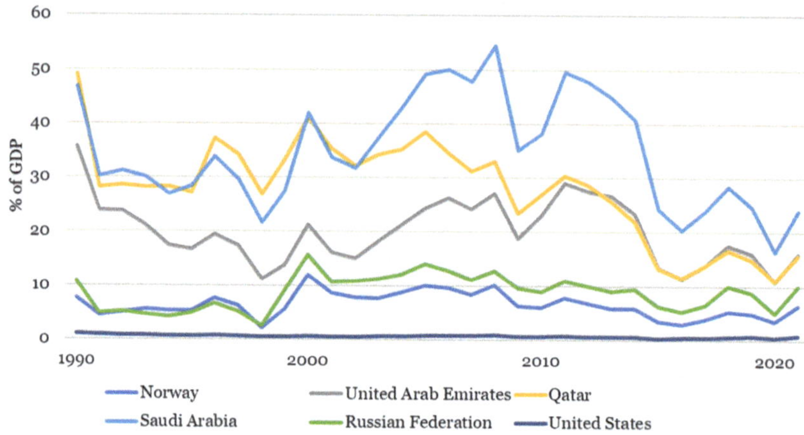

Fig. 3.17 Rents from exploitation of oil and gas resources as percentage of GDP for a number of oil-producing countries, 1990–2021 (Source: Worldbank, World Development Indicators. *Note by the Worldbank*: 'The estimates of natural resources rents are calculated as the difference between the price of a commodity and the average cost of producing it. This is done by estimating the price of units of specific commodities and subtracting estimates of average unit costs of extraction or harvesting costs. These unit rents are then multiplied by the physical quantities countries extract or harvest to determine the rents for each commodity as a share of gross domestic product (GDP)')

Because oil and gas are still crucial commodities for most economies, while the resources are concentrated in only a few countries, the producers of these energy carriers have a strong market position. This position is even strengthened through mutual collaborations among producers, like we have seen with the OPEC in the oil market. This cartel enables the oil-producing countries to manage their supply to the market and raise and maintain the price above competitive levels. This results in high market prices which significantly exceed the marginal costs of production. Consequently, the oil-producing countries are able to realise huge resource rents (see Box 3.2 and Fig. 3.17). In Saudi Arabia, for instance, the rents from exploiting their oil and gas resources are responsible for more than 20% of the total GDP. In Norway, the largest oil and gas producer and exporter in Europe, this share is significantly lower, notable about 5%. This lower share of rents from the exploitation of oil resources is due to basically two factors: first, the costs of producing oil and gas in Norway are much higher than in Saudi Arabia, and, second, the Norwegian economy is more diverse.

The importance of revenues from fossil-fuel exploitation in countries like Saudi Arabia and the Russian Federation means that their economies and societies are heavily dependent on this activity. So, not only the importing countries can be dependent on the exporting countries for their natural resources, but the exporting countries can also be dependent on the revenues from export. Actually, this idea of mutual dependence was the key argument to believe that the Russian Federation would not use its gas exports as a political instrument, but 2022 has shown that this was a misperception, held not only by business but also by governments.

Box 3.2 What Are Rents and How Can They Be Realised?

Rent is a particular type of profit which does not result from an effort, such as investing capital or entrepreneurial activity, but from possessing unique characteristics. For instance, a farmer that owns a very productive piece of land can make more profit compared to farmers having less productive land when they sell their products to the same marketplace. The production costs per unit of output of the former farmer are lower than those of the competitor, but they may receive the same price. The resulting extra profit was for the first time called rent by the economist Ricardo and is, therefore, also known as Ricardian rent.

Rents are also called economic profits or supranormal profits. These profits can also be defined as profits that are not needed to compensate for the cost of capital or the risk a firm takes. This implies that economic profits can be seen as a subsample of the so-called accounting profits. The latter are defined as the difference between the revenues of a company (or project) and the operational costs, plus the depreciation of the fixed assets. When the accounting profits are below the costs of capital, one can conclude that a firm (or project), from an economic perspective, is making a loss. When the accounting profits exceed the costs of capital, economic profits or rents are realised.

Economic profits can only be realised in case of constraints on the supply side, while the demand side is not flexible to respond. After all, only then the market price can be structurally above the price needed to compensate for all the costs. In the example of a farmer having a high-productive parcel of land, that farmer is (only) able to realise economic profits, when other farmers are not able to obtain parcels of land with a similarly high productivity. When the other farmers would be able to do so, the market prices of the commodities would go down, and no farmer would make an economic profit. Hence, rents do not occur in a competitive market environment where firms can easily enter the market and consumers can switch to other producers or products.

Import dependence does not only have financial and economic consequences for a country, in the form of a negative trade balance, but it may also have political consequences. The recent history with the energy crisis in Europe and Asia has shown that being dependent on the import of an energy carrier, like natural gas, can seriously weaken countries' geopolitical strength. In 2022, Russia used its strong position in the gas supply to reduce its supply to Europe. Russia could do this, because the importing countries hardly had other options to replace the reduced import of Russian gas, not only because of their dependence on gas, but also their dependence on the pipeline transport infrastructure. Consequently, gas prices in Europe surged.

The high prices resulting from the supply shock, together with the policy response aimed at increasing gas demand to fill storage, led to a significant loss of welfare on the side of importing countries. After all, gas consumers were forced to pay way more for their gas, and these increased expenditures flowed to Russia and other gas-exporting countries.[15] The surge in gas prices caused other prices to increase as well, since gas is part of the primary commodities that fuel the economy. Higher prices for natural gas, therefore, translated into higher prices in the rest of the economy. So, the gas crisis resulted in high inflation, and through the response of central banks directed at managing the inflation, in higher interest rates. All this economic damage would not have been, if Europe had not been strongly dependent on gas coming from Russia.

The gas crisis of 2022 also showed, however, how markets can respond to sudden shortages in supply. Triggered by the extremely high gas prices, consumers started reducing their consumption, while traders started looking for other sources of gas, which gave rise to a strong increase of import of liquefied gas from the USA and Qatar.

3.4.3 Economic Mechanisms

The fact that a country depends on the import of fossil energy from other countries is not necessarily a market failure, as economic agents may pay attention to the economic consequences of such import dependence. They will do so when the import dependence affects the certainty of the future availability and the volatility and level of prices of the energy carriers. If economic agents expect that exporting countries might abuse their position as major suppliers of a commodity in the future, leading to supply disruptions and higher prices, then they may have an incentive to protect themselves against this risk. They can reduce this risk, for instance, by diversifying their import sources, by storing energy or by reducing their energy consumption. The existence of these risks may also be an incentive for other agents, such as storage operators or operators of alternative transport technologies, to offer products that enable others to reduce their risks. All these measures are related to changes in the use of energy, but economic agents can also take financial measures, such as concluding long-term contracts with fixed prices, or by concluding insurance contracts that provide compensation for interrupted supply or high prices. Hence, insofar economic agents foresee the risks of supply interruptions because of import dependence, they might take appropriate risk-mitigating measures. In that case, this risk is internalised within market processes, which means market parties take action to deal with the risk. Consequently, there is no fundamental shortcoming in the market and no need for government intervention.

There may, however, be a remaining risk which is not internalised by markets. Namely, the risk that an exporting country may use its strong position in the

[15] Actually, all producers of gas benefitted from the high gas prices, including internationally operating companies producing gas in other regions, such as the North Sea and the Gulf of Mexico. In addition, as electricity prices are closely related to the price of natural gas in many countires, also producers of electricity benefitted from the high gas prices, including producers of renewable electricity.

supply of fossil energy as leverage to realise other types of political objectives which may not be seen by market parties. If that is the case, economic agents may not take sufficient measures, such as reducing their consumption, resulting in a too high import dependence. If such remaining risk exists, it can be considered a negative externality of the use of (fossil) energy, which may call for government intervention.

3.4.4 Evidence from Research

There is not much evidence on how the degree of import dependence influences the behaviour of economic agents in energy markets, but the relationship to geopolitical risks has been analysed by a number of authors. Sweidon (2021), for instance, tested the hypothesis that geopolitical risk results in a higher uncertainty about the flow of fossil energy to the developed economies. This uncertainty motivates importing countries to become less dependent on import, for instance, by developing domestic renewable-energy projects. In this paper, the geopolitical risk was measured through the Geopolitical Risk Indicator (GRI) developed by Caldara and Iacoviello (2022). This indicator uses electronic archives of a number of leading English-language newspapers to collect information related to geopolitical risks, which was defined as 'the risk[s] associated with wars, terrorism, and tensions among states that affect the normal course of international relations'. Sweidon (2021) finds a positive impact of the GRI on the development of renewable energy, measured as the share of renewable energy in total primary energy consumption, in the USA. Although this empirical result can be seen as an indication that economies and energy systems adapt to geopolitical risks, it does not exclude the possibility that energy markets alone fail to realise this result. After all, the increase in the deployment of renewables can also be due to changes in policy measures.

In order to assess to what extent geopolitical risks are captured by markets, one can look at the impact on market prices. Several authors find that measures for geopolitical risks, such as the GRI, positively affect the volatility in oil futures, i.e. the long-term contract prices for oil (see e.g. Mei et al., 2020). Analysing global energy markets over the period from 1990 to 2018, Qin et al. (2020) conclude that geopolitical risks affected the returns of trade in oil in particular, while the return on trade in gas was less affected. This different effect for these two fossil-energy carriers is related to their different price patterns during the period of analysis. During this period, the oil market had a global character and was subject to several strong variations, while the gas market was primarily of a regional nature and less based on market forces, as there were hardly any liquid gas markets. The latter has changed strongly over the past decade, as gas markets have become more liquid and, in addition, became increasingly interconnected on a global scale with prices resulting from global demand and supply conditions. As a result, gas prices are also becoming more sensitive to geopolitical risks, as we have experienced during the most recent energy crises.

The above empirical studies show that market parties are aware that geopolitical circumstances may change and have an impact on their business opportunities. Evidence from theoretical or model-based studies shows that political risks have an impact on the optimal decisions of economic agents. Egging and Holz (2016), for instance, show it would be an economically rational decision for market parties to invest in facilities, such as LNG terminals, to reverse the gas flow in Europe. This would help navigate the risk of disruptions in the East-West transit flows.

In spite of these studies that suggest markets deal with the risk of import dependence and the resulting increase in geopolitical risks, there are also several scholars who state that markets fail to sufficiently incentivise economic agents to invest in security of supply. For example, Codognet and Glachant (2008) argue that investments in gas storage require huge investments and, given the uncertainty about the future revenues, commercial parties may not be willing to realise these investments. Therefore, these authors conclude, governments should give regulatory guarantees to address this market failure. Others, such as Stern (2004), however, state that liberalised markets are the best guarantee to assure security of supply. As import and supply risks are translated into price risks, economic agents are incentivised to take action, like investing in storage or improving energy efficiency.

3.4.5 Conclusion

It is a fact that some countries strongly depend on the import of fossil energy, and that this import dependence may have negative economic consequences in case of supply shocks. This is particularly the case when the dependence on import for meeting domestic consumption is enhanced by a dependence on a particular transport infrastructure, as was the case for the European import of pipeline gas. It is, however, less clear to what extent such import dependence must be seen as a fundamental shortcoming of energy markets. The simple reason to question such a statement is that market parties face the financial risks of events, such as supply shocks. Consequently, they also have an incentive to take risk-mitigation measures, like investing in storages, diversification in import channels or becoming less energy intensive.

There may, however, be some risks related to import dependence which cannot be overseen or addressed by market parties. An example of such a risk is the political dependence of a country that arises from strong dependence on the import from a particular country or group of countries (such as OPEC). Market parties may not be able to fully notice and assess this political risk, and as a result import more from that country or group of countries than would be socially optimal. When this is the case, governmental measures to reduce the import dependence can be welfare improving.

3.5 Energy Transition in Order to Reduce Vulnerability to High Energy Prices

3.5.1 The Argument

Another argument that is often mentioned to implement energy transition is that this may help reduce the vulnerability of societies to high and volatile energy prices. After all, prices of fossil energy can be very volatile from time to time and reach high levels. This characteristic of fossil-energy markets was in particular visible during the energy crisis of 2022, with extremely high gas prices in Europe and Asia, while the European electricity prices surged as well. Also in Spring 2026, gas and in particular oil prices reached very high levels due to significant supply disruptions in the Middle East. Such high price levels have dramatic effects on the affordability of energy for both industrial and residential consumers, while, on the other hand, some producers of energy, in particular those which did not face the high costs (such as renewable and nuclear power plants) may realise very high profits, resulting in distributional effects which can be considered as unfair. In addition to these distributional effects, the high prices of fossil energy may also have strong negative macroeconomic effects, such as inflation and loss of competitiveness of major industries.

When a country is less dependent on the use of fossil-energy carriers, economies and societies are less vulnerable to the price volatility in these markets. This argument was used by the European Commission in response to the outbreak of the energy crisis in 2022. The European Commission initiated the REPowerEU plan, meant to reduce the dependence on Russian fossil fuels by, amongst others, boosting the production of renewable energy within the EU.[16] Other measures the European Commission implemented to reach this goal were directed at reducing energy demand and increasing the filling degree of gas storages. Moreover, it was discussed to change the way electricity prices were set, making them less related to the price of natural gas.

Hence, because of these risks of high and volatile fossil-energy prices, it is said that governments should intervene in markets to reduce both the price volatility itself and the vulnerability of economic agents to such high and volatile prices. Reducing the price volatility can be done by intervening in the price-formation system, by for example capping energy prices, in particular in retail energy markets, or by changing the way wholesale markets function. The vulnerability to high prices can be reduced by stimulating economic agents to reduce their energy consumption, to stimulate them to invest in storage, such as gas storage or batteries or to diversify their energy portfolio. Governments can also help economic agents diversify their energy purchases, for instance by investing in infrastructure, such as LNG terminals and cross-border transport capacity. This would enable economic participants to obtain energy from other sources or to exchange it regionally. Before we start discussing the effectiveness and efficiency of such policy measures, we first have to determine to what extent vulnerability to high and volatile energy prices is a fundamental shortcoming of energy markets.

---

[16] European Council/Council of the European Union, https://www.consilium.europa.eu/en/policies/energy-prices-and-security-of-supply/.

3.5.2 The Basic Facts

In the past, prices for fossil-energy carriers were very volatile during several periods, reaching sometimes extreme values. This happened, for instance, during the 2022 energy crisis in which the gas price in Europe reached levels of about 400 euros/MWh, while the normal levels range from 10 to 20 euros/MWh. The gas prices in Europe reached their peak levels of about 400 euros/MWh in August 2022. In that month, the average monthly day-ahead price was 235 euros/MWh (see Fig. 3.18). These extremely high gas prices spilled over to the European electricity market, as gas-fired power plants were the price-setting power plants during many hours in a year. As a result, the electricity prices also surged to extremely high levels. The average of the day-ahead electricity prices in August 2022 was almost 450 euros/MWh.

While prior to the 2022 energy crisis, the electricity price on the day-ahead market used to be within the range of 40–60 euros, during this energy crisis the electricity prices in several European countries reached levels above 600 euros/MWh. In the Dutch power market, the day-ahead electricity price reached levels above 850 euros/MWh (see Fig. 3.19). These extremely high prices during a relatively long time period would not have occurred if the electricity system had been less reliant on natural gas. This energy crisis was caused by the sudden and strong reduction in the supply of natural gas from Russia to Europe. There was, however, also another factor that contributed to the extreme energy price peaks, namely the European policy to force gas-storage operators to reach minimum filling grades before the

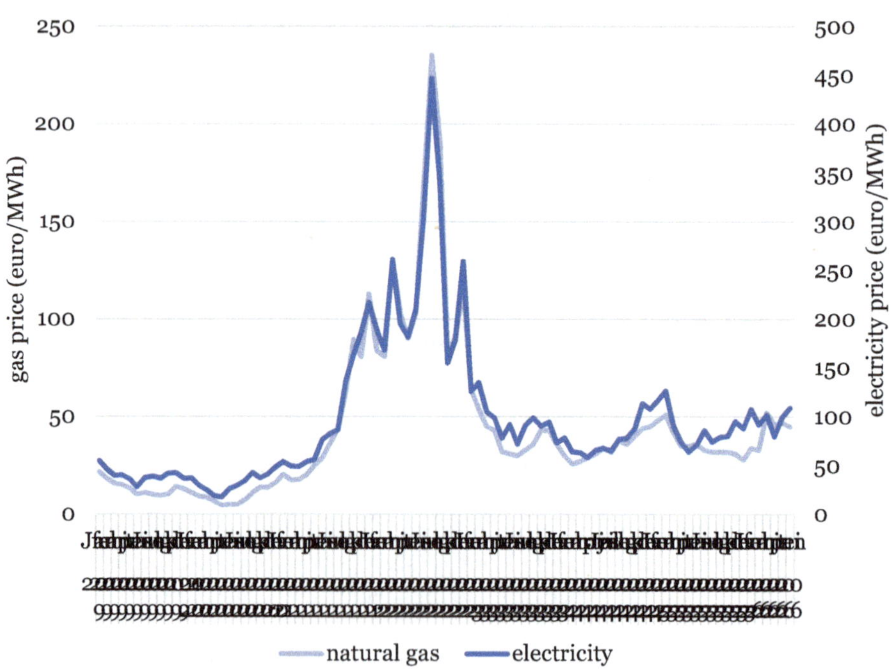

Fig. 3.18 Average monthly day-ahead electricity price and natural-gas price in the Dutch market, January 2019– June 2026 (Sources: gas prices: Elexys; electricity prices: ENTSOE Transparency Platform)

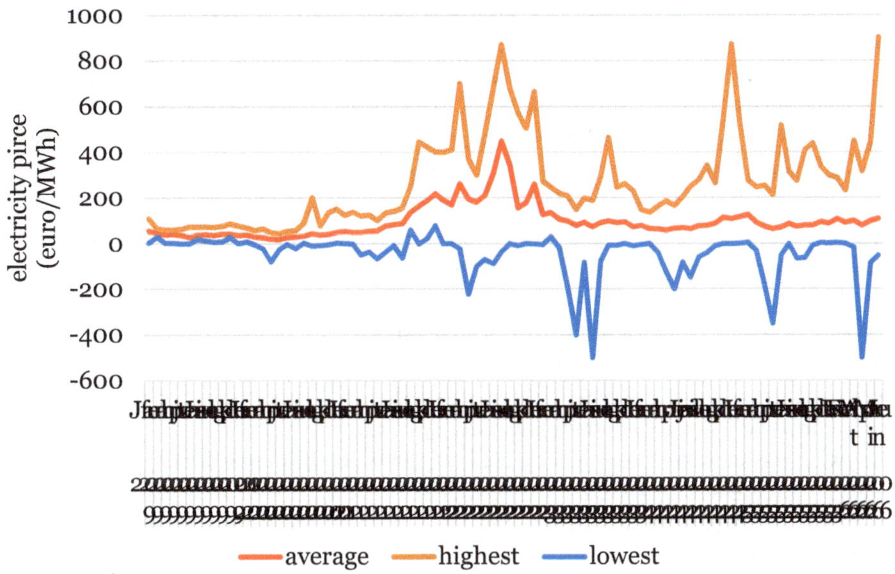

Fig. 3.19 Day-ahead electricity price in the Dutch electricity market, average per month and highest and lowest monthly values, January 2019–June 2026 (Source: ENTSOE Transparency Platform)

start of autumn 2022. As a result of that policy, the demand for gas increased which in combination with the strong reduction of supply coming from Russia raised the scarcity in the market. This event shows that price movements typically result from a mixture of factors (see Box 3.3).

Volatile and extremely high energy prices can also result from factors which are not related to events in fossil-energy markets. The high electricity prices which occurred in 2024, for instance, were not due to high gas prices, but scarcity within the electricity market. In Western European markets in December 2024, there were a number of days in which there was hardly any production by renewable sources, because of a lack of both wind and sunshine, while the demand for electricity was high. In order to clear the markets, high prices were needed to incentivise consumers to consume less electricity. A similar event happend in June 2026 when extremely high temperatures during a heat wave in Western Europe strongly raised the electricity demand for cooling, while in the evenings of those days the production by solar PV was low and there was hardly production by wind turbines due to little wind. These high prices occurred, however, only during a few hours on one or a few days, which is a huge difference with the price peaks two years earlier when the high price levels were persistent for many months.[17] This episode shows that reducing the role of natural gas does not automatically imply that the price volatility diminishes, but rather that in energy systems dominated by renewables, prices can still be very volatile.

[17] The day-ahead electricity prices peaked in the Dutch power market on 12 December 2024 from 7 am to 9 am.

The extremely high gas prices triggered users of gas to consume less gas. This reduction in demand was substantial in both an absolute and a relative sense. Despite the reduction of several tens of percentage points, the price remained in line with what we know about the magnitude of price elasticity of energy demand, as discussed in Chap. 2. After all, if the gas price increases from 20 to 200 euros/MWh, which is an increase of 900%, and the gas consumption decreases by 30%, the price elasticity is −0.03.[18] This elasticity is even quite low compared to the numbers we presented in Sect. 2.5. This is partly due to the fact that in the really short term, consumption cannot be easily adapted, such as by insulating houses or switching to another energy carriers. For some users, the substitution possibilities are larger than for others. In the electricity sector, for instance, power producers with a diverse portfolio of power plants raised the use of their nuclear and coal-fired power plants, while the use of gas-fired power plants was reduced. This substitution was restricted by the installed capacity and the availability of nuclear and coal-fired power plants. Anyway, the substitution of gas by coal, triggered by high gas prices, consequently raised the coal price. As coal has a higher carbon content than natural gas, the demand for carbon allowances in the EU ETS also increased, which resulted in higher carbon prices.

Box 3.3 Supply and Demand Factors Behind Surge in Gas Prices

The surge in the European natural-gas price in 2022 and 2023 was initiated by the sharp reduction in the supply of gas coming from Russia, but it cannot be fully attributed to that supply shock. Generally, supply shocks are followed by price increases, which trigger consumers to consume less. During the European energy crisis, this also occurred, but a specific policy response strengthened the impact of the supply shock. The European Commission imposed a regulatory standard requiring minimum filling levels for European gas storage facilities. These storage facilities had to be filled by 90% by the end of August in 2022 (Oxford Institute for Energy Studies (OIES), 2025). The purpose of this regulation was to make sure that Europe would have sufficient gas supplies for the upcoming winter and prevent Russia from further disrupting the European economy. Because of this regulation to quickly fill the storages, the demand for natural gas increased very strongly. Normally during summer, the demand for gas is relatively low, but this particular year, the demand was very high, contributing to the tightness of the European gas market and the surge in gas prices.

[18] Relative price increase is (200–20)/20 = 180/20 = 900%; price elasticity = −30%/900% = −0.03. Note, however, that end-users respond to their end-user prices, which are not only based on the wholesale market prices, but also on retail margins and governmental taxes. As a result, the percentage change in the end-user price was much lower, which implies that the (absolute value of the) actual price elasticity of gas consumption was larger than this number.

Another reason why the short-term consumer responses to changes in wholesale prices are limited is that residential users are generally not directly exposed to wholesale prices, but rather to retail prices. Prices in retail energy contracts are in most of the cases not related to the daily wholesale prices, but are fixed for a period of time, such as months or even years. On top of that, retail prices are based on more components, such as the margin for the retailer and energy taxes, which mitigate the impact of volatility in wholesale prices.

An earlier period of very high fossil-energy prices was between 2004 and 2008, when the oil price exceeded 100 dollar per barrel, while the price levels previously were in the range of 20–40 dollars (see Fig. 2.10). This surge in the oil price was caused by a stark increase in the demand in emerging countries, in particular China, while the production capacity in most oil-producing countries was not able to increase at the same pace. Hence, this price increase was caused by the combination of a strongly growing demand and constraints on the supply side. High oil prices were needed to clear the markets. Similar price levels in nominal terms occurred in the energy crisis following the US-Israeli attack on Iran in March 2026. The blockade of the Street of Hormuz by both the US and Iran reduced the global oil supply by about 15 billion barrels per day, which was about 15% of the daily global oil supply. When the blockade was lifted after a few months, the oil prices declined quickly to about 70 dollar/barrel by the end of June 2026. The high prices during the crisis can be attributed to a so-called convenience yield, which means that market parties assign a high value to have oil in stock because of the large uncertainty regarding the future developments in the oil market.

The first episode of very high fossil-energy prices was in the 1970s. After a period of strong economic growth, the demand for oil in the developed economies had risen firmly, in particular for transport. The supply of oil came mainly from countries in the Middle East, which gave these countries the ability to influence market outcomes. Together with geopolitical events in the Middle East, in particular the relationship between Israel, neighbouring countries and the Palestinian people, the oil-producing countries formed a cartel which was called OPEC (i.e. Organisation of Petroleum Exporting Countries). This cartel enabled them to control the oil price by reducing their supply to the market.[19] This resulted in a number of oil-price crises which caused a severe economic downturn in many oil-importing countries, resulting in loss of employment. Only in the mid-1980s the economies recovered and started to grow again.

Several episodes of extremely high energy prices showed they can have severe economic impacts such as the loss of economic growth, unemployment and households experiencing loss of welfare. The higher energy costs triggered firms and

[19] That the OPEC was successful in influencing the price, was due to the fact that there were hardly any alternatives for oil consumers, while the oil demand was also relatively inflexible. The costs for OPEC resulting from the reduced production were more than compensated by the higher profits realised on the remaining production. This event shows that a cartel (or any other firm with market power) not only needs to have the power to influence market outcomes, but also the incentive to do so.

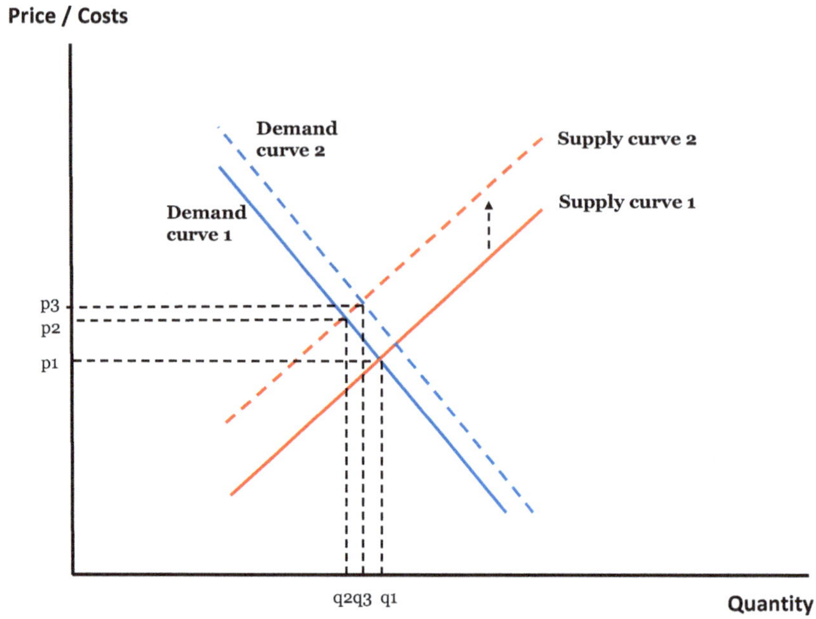

Fig. 3.20 Changes in prices as a result of changes in supply and demand curves

consumers to reduce their energy consumption, also by becoming more energy efficient. As was discussed in Chap. 2, the energy intensity of economies fell sharply over the past decades as a result (see Fig. 2.17).

3.5.3 Economic Mechanisms

The question here is to what extent the high volatility of (fossil-energy) prices is a valid argument to intervene in energy systems. This is not only a question about what the volatility would be when the share of fossil energy is smaller or when energy markets have a different design, but first of all whether there exist some fundamental shortcomings causing the high price volatility. In order to answer that question, one should first look into the economic mechanisms behind price volatility and to what extent there are any fundamental shortcomings in this mechanism. Next, if there is no sign of market failures, other kinds of arguments for intervention should be explored, in particular in relation to distributional policy objectives.

In theory, price volatility results from changes in demand and supply. When the (marginal) costs of suppliers increase, the supply curve shifts upwards (in Fig. 3.20 from Supply curve 1 to Supply curve 2) and, as a result, the equilibrium price increases (from p_1 to p_2). The same occurs when the demand increases, for instance, because the number of consumers increases or consumers are willing to pay a higher price for the same commodity. The latter may happen when their income has grown or the price of an alternative commodity has increased.[20] If the Demand curve 1 shifts to Demand curve 2, the new equilibrium price becomes p_3. Although this price exceeds the price from before the demand increase, the equilibrium quantity is also higher, which is due to the increase in the demand.

From this graphic presentation, it appears that the magnitude of the resulting price changes does not only depend on the size of the changes in demand and supply, but also on the price responsiveness of both, as was already discussed in Sect. 2.6.3. The higher the price sensitivity, the less a change in demand or supply affects equilibrium prices. The price sensitivity is related to the ability of economic agents to adapt their behaviour, e.g. by changing their production or consumption levels or by being able to make use of storage. When consumers, for instance, are not able or willing to quickly change the consumption of a commodity, such as electricity, an increase in the costs of producers may strongly increase the equilibrium price. Hence, a low sensitivity to prices may coincide with a high price volatility, while a high sensitivity reduces the volatility of prices.

The ability to respond to higher prices of an energy carrier is also related to the ability to substitute that energy carrier with another one. This ability sometimes occurs on plant level, such as in the case of dual-fired power plants, which have the option to use both gas and coal. Firms with a portfolio of different types of power plants can adapt to changing relative prices by changing the intensity with which they use the different types of power plants. All these changes are deliberately realised as economic agents switch to other energy carriers in order to minimise their costs. In addition to these firm-level effects, demand responses and substitution also occur on an industry level. Firms facing higher costs as a result of changes in energy prices experience a deterioration of their competitive position in relation to firms using other technologies. As a result, the latter types of firms may be able to increase their market share at the expense of the former. Consequently, changes occur within the industrial structure. The industry as a whole has reduced the use of the energy carrier that has become more expensive. Note, however, that this only holds when all firms face the same (end-user) price. In practice, this condition is often not fulfilled, in particular for firms operating in an international context, where energy wholesale prices can differ per country, while countries can also impose different tax levels or different kinds of financial arrangements for the industry.

The degree of price volatility is not only related to the price sensitivity of economic agents, but also to the magnitude of changes in demand and supply conditions. The impact on prices is modest when changes in demand and supply are also fairly modest. However, when the demand and/or supply conditions fluctuate strongly, the price volatility can be high. Hence, the volatility of prices depends on two fundamental factors: the price sensitivity of economic agents and the degree of changes in demand and supply conditions. This implies that prices will be particularly volatile in markets where economic agents do not strongly respond to prices, for whatever reason, while the supply or demand conditions fluctuate strongly. This is particularly the case for electricity markets, as electricity is a basic commodity for

[20] Note that this refers to the cross-price elasticity of demand, as is discussed in Sect. 2.6.

various types of consumers (both residential and industrial), while the production capacity is fixed in the short term.[21] When the capacity of market players to adapt their production or consumption profiles is restricted, the activity of providing flexibility to the system may be valuable (see Box 3.4).

Box 3.4 Price Volatility, Constraints and the Value of Flexible Capacity

Volatility of market prices forms an indication of the ability of supply and demand to adapt to changing circumstances. The more supply and demand are flexible in changing their production and consumption patterns, respectively, the flatter prices will be. After all, a small change in prices due to a change in a part of the supply function, for instance, may be quickly followed by a change in other parts of the supply function or in the demand function. If, however, supply and demand hardly have the ability to change, an external shock to the system may result in large price changes. Such large price changes are needed to rebalance the system.

Figure 3.21 shows a situation with perfectly flexible supply, which means that capacity can be expended immediately at zero costs (left-hand panel) when the demand increases (from the solid to the dashed line), while the other

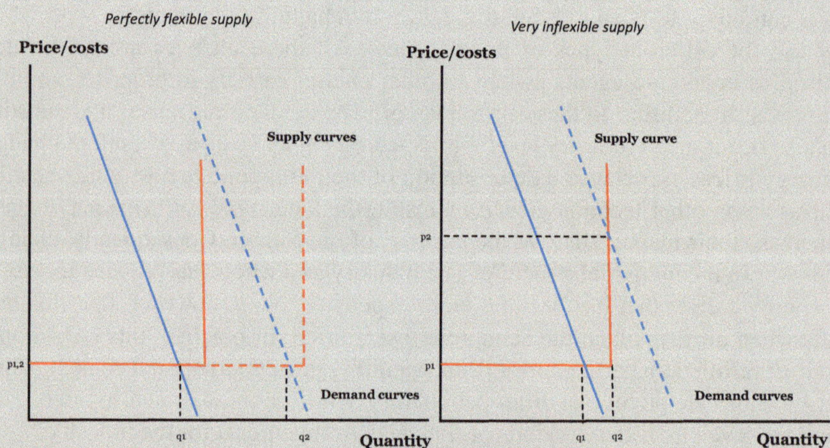

Fig. 3.21 Market outcomes in case of perfectly flexible supply and very inflexible supply (Note: in case of the perfectly flexible supply curve, the capacity increases without higher marginal costs, while in the case of inflexible supply, the capacity remains the same when the demand increases)

(continued)

[21] In general, price volatility is higher the closer trade occurs to real time, i.e. the actual exchange of a commodity. In the short term, there are typically fewer options for market parties to respond. Consequently, a change in a market condition, such as changing weather conditions, requires stronger economic incentives (i.e. larger changes in equilibrium prices) to stimulate (some) market participants to change their behaviour (i.e. changing supply or demand).

Box 3.4 (continued)

situation shows a situation with very limited flexibility on the supply side (right-hand panel). The high prices during the latter situation can also be understood as the so-called shadow price of the constraint, which means this price is also the value of relieving the constraint by one unit. Hence, the high prices during moments of tightness in a market can be understood as the value of providing flexibility. Those agents able to provide flexibility can earn this value. The magnitude of this value acts as an incentive for those agents to enter the market.

This phenomenon can be clearly seen in electricity markets. In the short term, both supply and demand used to be quite inflexible, which resulted in a relatively large price volatility. This process is strengthened by the increase of weather dependent generation technologies (e.g. wind turbines and solar PV), which adds more constraints to the system. The resulting price volatility created an incentive for new technologies that can add flexibility, such as batteries and enhanced demand responses enabled by smart meters. Price volatility is, for instance, also an incentive for hydrogen production through electrolysis when the number of hours with low electricity prices strongly increases.

These factors affecting price volatility can occur in competitive, well-functioning markets, which implies that price volatility is not necessarily an indication of a fundamental shortcoming, but can belong to the nature of particular markets. In these markets, fluctuating prices have a role in finding equilibria between supply and demand. After all, changes in prices inform economic agents about the scarcity of a product and trigger them to make efficient choices regarding the supply or use of that product. When prices are high, consumers will buy less of the product, while producers have an incentive to supply more to the market, which results in lower prices.[22] In addition to these responses to volatile and high prices, economic agents can also respond by concluding (financial) contracts to mitigate the exposure to such kind of risks (see Box 3.5).

Box 3.5 Contracts to Mitigate Consequences of Price Volatility

Market parties can also protect themselves against price volatility by concluding contracts with each other. A producer of electricity from wind turbines, for instance, can conclude a so-called Power Purchasing Agreement (PPA), under which the electricity is sold for several years in advance at an agreed price. Such a contract shifts the price risk to the counterparty in the contract, which can be a retailer or large electricity firm. In return, the counterparty

(continued)

[22] When economic agents have access to storage, they can reduce their vulnerability to high prices by buying (or producing) energy when prices are low and storing the energy for moments when market prices are high. In well-developed energy markets, this reduction in vulnerability can also be realised by concluding supply contracts at fixed prices (during a period) with other agents.

Box 3.5 (continued)

typically wants to receive a discount on the price, which is called the forward premium.

Another example of contracts, concluded to reduce price risk, are the fixed-price contracts in retail energy markets. Through such contracts, residential users do not face any price uncertainty during the contract period and, hence, are protected against any price shock in the wholesale market. As such contracts give retailers the obligation to supply the energy against the agreed price, they may want to mitigate the risk related to the wholesale price at which they buy the energy. They can do this by concluding long-term contracts with a wholesale counterparty, such as a trader or an electricity producer. This kind of risk-mitigation strategy is called hedging and can be defined as the strategy economic agents can use to reducing its risk on one market (in this example in the retail market) by taking a position in another market (in this case the wholesale market).

Note that hedging contracts do not reduce the risk in general, but rather shift the risk from one market party to another in return for a compensation (i.e. the risk premium). From these examples, it becomes clear that market parties have various options to deal with price risk.

Because of these responses of market parties, markets can solve the problem of high prices themselves. Suppressing such price changes would, therefore, distort the market process and, hence, result in a less efficient allocation of commodities (for more on this topic see Sect. 4.6). This does not mean that governments should never intervene when prices fluctuate strongly in well-functioning markets, as some groups of economic agents may be more severely affected than others. Because of distributional concerns, governments may wish to intervene in market outcomes, for instance, by supporting particular groups negatively affected by high prices or by taxing economic agents (i.e. a particular group of producers) who strongly benefit from high prices.

Next to the abovementioned factors affecting price volatility, there may also be flaws in the functioning of the market which cause volatility. If one market player or a group of players possesses market power, they have the possibility to raise market prices by reducing their supply to the market or asking higher prices. The first action is called physical withholding and the second one economic withholding. Hence, market players possessing market power may strategically intervene in markets, leading to a sharp increase in prices. When high prices are due to abuse of market power, there is a clear reason for government intervention which is called competition policy (see Sect. 3.2.3).

3.5.4 Evidence from Research

The history of energy markets provides many cases of volatile prices. These events have been extensively analysed by researchers, trying to determine the factors behind price volatility and how this volatility caused behavioural responses by market parties. Here, we discuss only a few examples from the oil, natural gas and electricity markets.

The oil markets have experienced periods of low prices, followed by periods in which prices rose to very high levels, as we have seen in Chap. 2. In all cases, the high prices triggered market parties to respond. The oil crises of the 1970s stimulated energy users to raise the efficiency of energy use, while the industrial structure of economies also became much less energy-intensive (see e.g. Nasseh & Elyasiani, 1984). Consequently, the energy intensity of many countries decreased significantly, as was shown in Fig. 2.17.

Next to these demand responses, there were also several responses on the supply side. The strong increase in the oil price made the exploitation of other oil resources profitable, such as the so-called Brent oil originating from the North Sea in Northwest Europe.[23] The exploitation costs of this oil are significantly higher than the costs of the oil coming from fields in the Middle East, but after the oil-price surge following the 1970s, the North Sea oil became profitable. A similar type of supply response occurred at the end of the first century of this decade, when the oil prices skyrocketed again, which was the result of the strong growing demand from a number of emerging countries, in particular China. The very high prices at the time made the commercial exploitation of shale-oil resources in the USA possible, resulting in a strong increase in the US oil production (see e.g. Thorbecke, 2019). In turn, this increase in supply from outside the OPEC region, contributed to the strong decline in the oil prices, although the decline also resulted from the reduction in oil demand caused by the international financial crisis. These episodes show that the oil prices used to reflect the international macroeconomic conditions which affected the tightness in the oil market, but also that the oil price triggered responses.

The impact of the oil price on economies in the past was higher than it is now, not only because the oil-intensity of economies is significantly lower than a few decades ago, but also because the prices of other energy carriers are less linked to the price of oil. This holds in particular for the price of natural gas. This energy carrier used to be a kind of side product from the exploitation of oil fields, but it gradually became one of the primary energy carriers. This is also reflected by the fact that in the past, the price of natural gas was based on the price of oil, but since the development of natural-gas markets, the price of this commodity is less connected to what happens in the oil market (Oxford Institute for Energy Studies (OIES), 2020). The 2022 gas-price crisis resulted from the reduction of supply from Russia to the European market, combined with the European policies to raise the filling grade of gas storage facilities. The extremely high gas price in the second half of 2022 gave

[23] Brent oil was originally the name of the oil coming from the Brent oil field close to the Shetland Islands, but it is now used as the name of oil coming from different locations in the North Sea.

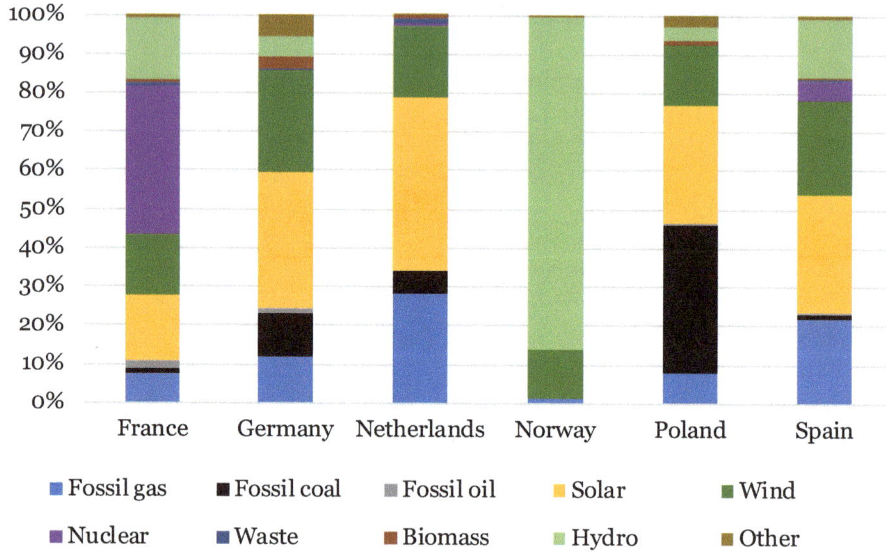

Fig. 3.22 Composition of installed generation capacity in a number of European countries, 2026 (Source: ENTSOE Transparency Platform; own calculations)

an impulse to gas users to reduce their consumption (see e.g. Bagheri et al., 2024). Industries and residential consumers took measures to improve the efficiency of their gas use, but some just consumed less given their inability to pay the high costs. Overall, the gas consumption in Europe decreased by about 30%.

In the past, the natural-gas market was subject to other supply shocks. In January 2009 and February 2022, the supply of gas to Germany was reduced significantly as a result of a dispute between Russia and Ukraine about the financial compensation for using the transport pipelines through the latter country (Artelet & Mulder, 2020). The supply disruption happened during a cold-winter spell and resulted immediately in surging gas prices in the German gas market. In turn, these high prices triggered gas flows from neighbouring countries, such as the Netherlands and the UK, towards Germany, raising the spot prices in these countries as well. These events showed that as a result of the integration of European gas markets through interconnected gas infrastructure systems, market parties were quickly able to respond to changing prices.

As electricity systems differ strongly among countries, it may also be insightful to look at the price volatility in countries that have a different composition of electricity generation. In some countries, like the Netherlands and Poland, the generation is (still) more based on fossil fuels than in some others like France and Norway (see Fig. 3.22). Although significant investments were made in renewable technologies such as wind turbines and solar panels, in 2026 about 40%–50% of the installed capacity in these countries still consisted of coal- or natural-gas-fired power plants.

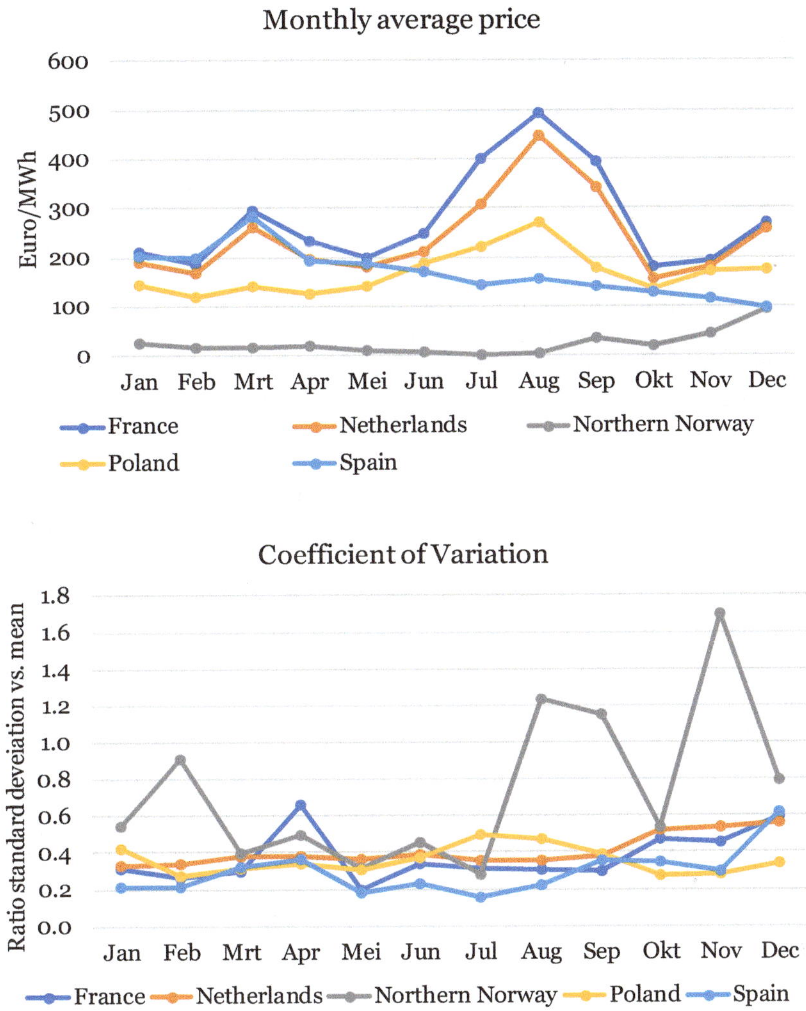

Fig. 3.23 Average monthly day-ahead electricity prices and coefficient of variation in a number of European electricity markets, 2022 (Source: ENTSOE Transparency Platform; own calculations)

One may wonder whether countries that rely on nuclear power plants, such as France, or hydropower plants, like Norway, may have experienced less economic effects from the rise of gas prices in 2022 than countries that are more reliant on fossil energy, such as the Netherlands and Poland. Figure 3.18 indeed shows that in the Netherlands, the average monthly day-ahead electricity price rose starkly in 2022 in response to the surging natural-gas price. However, in France the electricity price also increased significantly, even though the generation mix in this country is to a large extent based on nuclear power plants (see Fig. 3.23). The French electricity price rose because of two factors. One factor was its integration with the electricity markets in other Northwest European markets. Because the electricity price in, amongst others, the Dutch market, increased significantly, traders had an incentive to buy electricity in France and export it to the Netherlands. This raised the French electricity prices. The other factor behind the increase in French electricity prices in 2022 was the scarcity of nuclear power capacity (Astier, 2025). Due to maintenance works, technical problems and cooling restrictions because of low water levels in rivers, a number of power plants were not or less available, and, consequently, market prices needed to rise in order to balance demand and supply in the French electricity market. As a result, there were moments during which the French wholesale electricity price reached very high levels, resulting in a large spread between the maximum and the minimum price during a month. Hence, this volatility in the French electricity market is not only the result of its relation (through international trade) to markets based on more volatile fossil-energy prices, but it results also from the availability constraints within the French nuclear fleet.

Compared to France and the Netherlands, the electricity prices in Spain and the north of Norway[24] were much lower during the summer of 2022. The latter markets are much less connected to the Northwest European electricity market, while the prices in these markets are also less related to the gas price. In Spain, apparently, it has become rare for gas-fired power plants to become the price-setting power plants as a result of the strong growth in wind and solar capacity.[25] In addition to this, the gas price in Spain was less affected by the European gas crisis, as gas in this country is mainly coming from the global LNG market (see Fig. 3.23). On top of that, the Spanish government subsidised the use of gas by power plants in order to stabilise the electricity prices.[26]

In the north of Norway, the electricity market has limited connections to other parts of Norway, while the supply is mainly based on hydropower. Despite the much lower prices in Norway, the price volatility was relatively large. This is revealed by the coefficient of variation.[27] Looking at the mean price level in the last months of 2022, it appears that the price in this part of Norway rose from a very low level to a level of about 100 euros. Hence, despite this market having a much lower average electricity price than other European countries, the (relative) volatility was much higher in this period.

From these examples, it appears that high electricity prices do not automatically imply high volatility. It also reveals that both high electricity prices and high price volatility can occur in markets which are not dominated by fossil-fuel power plants.

[24] The electricity market in Norway is divided into five bidding zones, where the market is cleared within each zone while taking the transport capacity between the zones and the connected countries (i.e. Sweden, Denmark, Germany and The Netherlands) into account.

[25] From all large European countries, Spain has been the most successful in decoupling the electricity price from the gas price (Rosslowe & Petrovich, 2025). In 2019, gas-fired power plants were price setting in 75% of all hours, while in 2025 this share was reduced to only 19%.

[26] See the following news item on the matter: https://www.enerdata.net/publications/daily-energy-news/spain-and-portugal-extends-gas-price-cap-power-production-end-2023.html.

[27] The coefficient of variation is calculated as the standard deviation divided by the mean. Hence, a high (low) coefficient of variation means that the fluctuations are high (low) in comparison to the mean.

3.5.5 Conclusion

Energy prices can be very volatile and reach very high levels from time to time. This characteristic of energy prices, however, does not appear to be an indication of a shortcoming of energy markets, as the movements in energy prices result from changes in demand and/or supply conditions. The role of prices is to bring balance between demand and supply by incentivising market parties to adapt their behaviour regarding using or supplying a commodity. The lower the ability of market parties to adapt, the higher the price volatility can be. This is in particular the case in electricity markets, where in the short term the supply is constrained by the amount of installed generation capacity, the consumption of electricity is fairly price inelastic, while it is impossible to store the commodity without converting it into another energy carrier.

Markets offer options to economic agents to protect themselves against the risk of volatile prices through all kinds of financial contracts, such as forward contracts in the wholesale market, Power Purchasing Agreements (PPAs) between producers and counterparties, and fixed-price contracts in retail energy markets. Such contracts also protect market parties against high prices in the short term. At some point, however, high energy prices in international wholesale markets do translate into higher prices for users, for instance, when retail contracts are renewed.

Price volatility resulting in high prices may affect some groups in society more strongly than others, which can be a reason for governments to intervene when they want to protect vulnerable households or local industries which are more strongly affected by high energy prices than their international competitors. Instead of intervening in the prices they have to pay, it is more efficient to implement measures which directly provide this support. Residential households can, for instance, be supported by subsidising technical measures to insulate their houses, while industries can be supported by facilitating the transition to other energy carriers.

3.6 Energy Transition in Order to Reduce Carbon Emissions

3.6.1 The Argument

The most common argument used by governments and societies to pursue energy transition is related to climate change. The intensive use of fossil energy results in a strong increase in the emissions of carbon dioxide and other greenhouse gases, which disturbs the global physical balance of carbon. The natural capacity of oceans, land, plants and trees to absorb carbon dioxide (the so-called sink capacity) is not big enough to cope with the increasing levels of greenhouse gas emissions, contributing to an increase in the atmospheric concentration of greenhouse gases. This increased concentration contributes to fundamental changes in the climate, negatively affecting the living conditions for all living organisms, including mankind. Therefore, the argument goes that in order to prevent these negative effects, governments should intervene in the energy sector to reduce the emissions of greenhouse gases. This intervention should mainly be directed at reducing the consumption of fossil energy

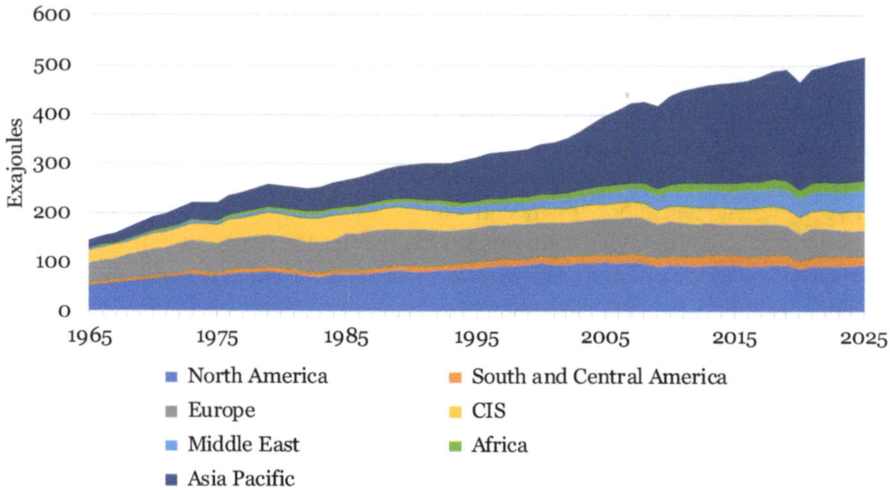

Fig. 3.24 Global fossil-energy consumption, per region, 1965–2025 (Source: Energy Institute Statistical Review of World Energy. Note: CIS stands for the Commonwealth of Independent States, consisting of Russia and former Soviet Union states)

by fostering energy-efficiency measures and promoting renewable energy. Hence, energy transition is seen as a crucial component of climate policy.

3.6.2 The Basic Facts

The consumption of fossil-energy carriers has strongly increased over the past decades. In 1965, the aggregate global consumption of coal, oil and natural gas was 145 exajoules, which has grown by more than 300%, reaching a level of above 500 exajoules in 2025 (see Fig. 3.24).[28] This growth in fossil-energy consumption was the strongest in the Middle East and Asia Pacific, where the average annual growth rate since 1965 was 28% and 18%, respectively. In North America, the increase in fossil-energy consumption was the lowest, with an annual rate of less than 1%. These differences are, of course, related to the fact that the initial levels of fossil consumption were already relatively high in the latter region.

Until World War II, the fossil-energy consumption mainly consisted of the use of coal (see Fig. 2.5), but after the end of the war, the use of oil rose significantly, which was related to, amongst others, the rapid growth in transport and the further industrialisation of in particular the industrialised economies. Although at a slower pace, the consumption of oil continued to grow since the oil-price crises of the 1970s. The current global annual oil consumption is approximately 200 exajoules, which is equal to about 95 million barrels per day. The global natural-gas consumption was relatively low until the 1960s, but since then it has risen from a global level

[28] See Appendix A for the definitions of the various metrics and how they are related to each other.

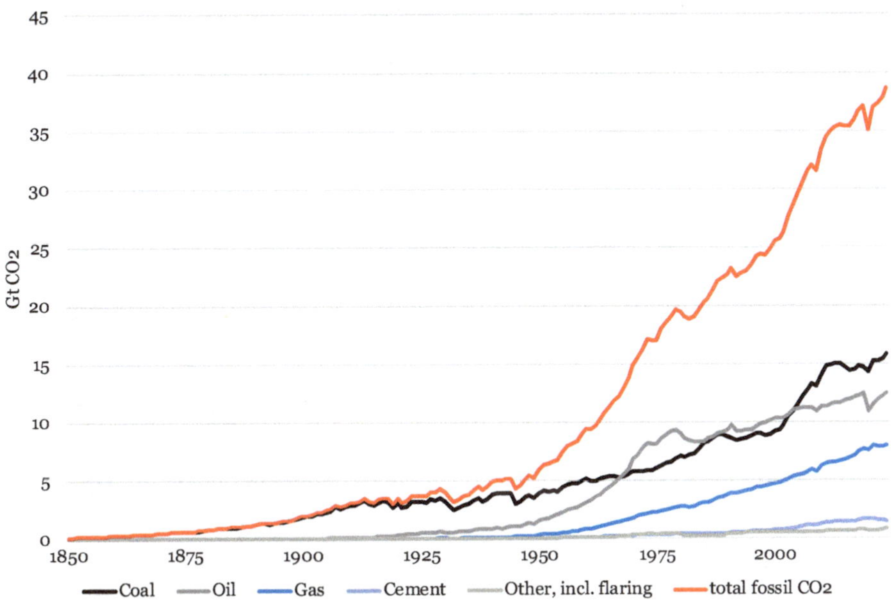

Fig. 3.25 Global fossil CO_2-emissions, total and per type of energy carrier, 18505–2024 (Sources: Friedlingstein et al. (2025); Global Carbon Project 2025)

of about 20 exajoules per annum to about 140 exajoules currently, which is equal to about 4000 bcm. Global consumption of coal increased gradually until the beginning of the current century, but since then it has risen to about 165 exajoules in 2025. This increase was related to, amongst others, the industrialisation of emerging countries, in particular China.

The continuing increase in the use of coal, oil and natural gas coincides with a continuing increase in the emissions of carbon dioxide, which can be seen in Fig. 3.25. While in 1965, the use of these three fossil fuels produced in total approximately 10 Gt in carbon dioxide emissions, it has risen to about 38 Gt in 2025. Since coal has a higher carbon content than oil and, in particular, natural gas,[29] its use contributes significantly to global emissions.

The continuing increase in carbon dioxide emissions, together with the ongoing albeit slightly decreasing emissions from land-use changes (e.g. deforestation or forest fires), contribute to the increase in the concentration of greenhouse gases in the atmosphere. The increase in atmospheric concentration occurred because the natural sinks through oceans (e.g. uptake by ocean algae) and land use (e.g. planting trees or expanding forests) were unable to increase their rate of absorption to the

[29] Because natural gas and oil have a lower carbon content than coal (see Appendix A), more oxygen is needed to burn them, which results in higher amounts of water vapour per unit of CO_2. Burning natural gas and oil, therefore, results in less environmental effects, but the downside is that it is more complicated and expensive to capture the CO_2 from the exhaust gasses than is the case when you burn coal.

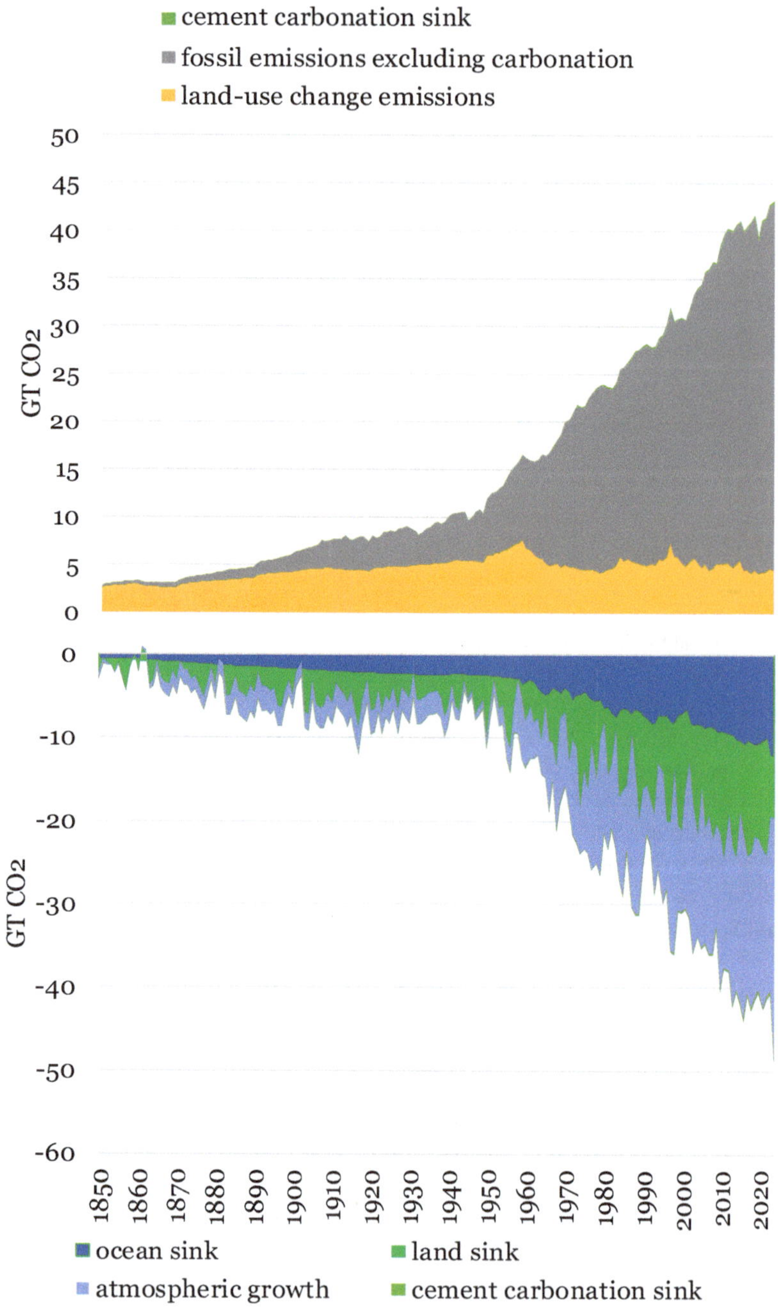

Fig. 3.26 Global physical balance of CO_2, 1850–2024 (Source: https://globalcarbonbudgetdata.org/data-archive.html)

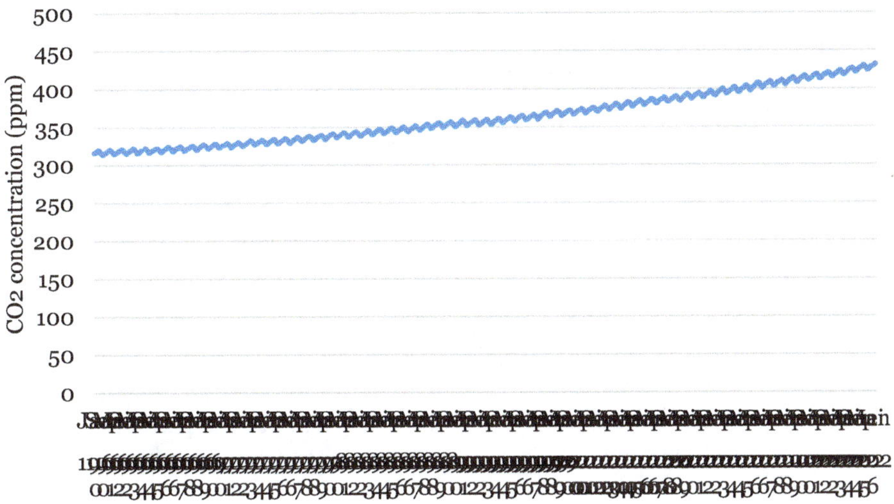

Fig. 3.27 CO_2-concentration in atmosphere at Mauna Loa Observatory, average per month, Januay 1960– May2026 (Source: https://keelingcurve.ucsd.edu/)

same extent as the emissions (see Fig. 3.26). Although the absorption by sinks increased because of the higher carbon dioxide concentration in the atmosphere, it was not enough.

As the natural, physical carbon balance became distorted, the atmospheric concentration of carbon dioxide increased from year to year, as can be seen from the so-called Keeling curve (see Fig. 3.27). In 1960, the concentration was a bit more than 310 ppm and in May 2026 it has risen to above 430 ppm.[30]

A reason for this steep increase in the carbon dioxide concentration is that the molecules in the atmosphere have an average lifetime of about 100 years. Some molecules may be absorbed by land sinks or ocean sinks quite quickly, while for others it may take decades or even centuries. When they are not absorbed, they will break down and change into other types of molecules, but this process can take years. This implies that even if emissions would be fully halted, the atmospheric concentration will remain high for a long period of time.

Besides CO_2, other gases contribute to the increase in the concentration of greenhouse gas emissions in the atmosphere. These gases, including methane (CH_4) and nitrous oxide (N_2O), have different chemical characteristics and, therefore, have a different global warming effect (see Box 3.6).

[30] Ppm stands for parts per million. Hence, 430 ppm means that there are 430 carbon-dioxide molecules per one million of molecules in the atmosphere. In percentages, this boils down to 0,043 percent. The fact that the concentration of CO_2 is so low explains, for instance, why the capture of CO_2 from the atmosphere through Direct Air Capture technologies requires a lot of energy, which makes it an expensive technology.

Box 3.6 Greenhouse Gases and Carbon-Dioxide Equivalents

The use of fossil energy does not only result in the emissions of carbon dioxide, but also of other greenhouse gases, in particular methane. Methane emissions, for instance, result from leaks during the transport of natural gas, flaring at oil or gas extraction fields and in industrial processes. Next to the greenhouse gases caused by the use of fossil energy, there are also other causes for the emission of these gases, such the production of cement, dairy farming and deforestation. The various greenhouse gases differ in their impact on climate change. The impact of methane molecules on global warming is much stronger than the impact of carbon dioxide molecules, but the methane molecules have a much shorter lifetime in the atmosphere (i.e. only a few years).

Based on these differences in impact on global warming and lifetime, the so-called global warming potential (GWP) of the various greenhouses is determined. The benchmark for these potentials is the GWP of carbon dioxide over a period of 100 years. This GWP is defined as 1. The GWP of methane is 25, which means that the overall impact on climate of 1 ton of methane is 25 times that of a tonne of carbon dioxide. For nitrous oxide, another greenhouse gas, there appears to be some confusion on the GWP: Eurostat uses the number of 298 as the GWP, while the European regulation uses the number 265. Anyway, by using the GWP of the different greenhouse gases, the emissions of the various gases can be expressed in a single metric which is called carbon dioxide equivalents (CO_2-eq). This is done by using the following formula: million metric tonnes of CO_2 equivalents= $\sum_i$ million metric tonnes of $gas_i * GWP_i$

Sources

Eurostat:https://ec.europa.eu/eurostat/statistics-explained/index.phptitle=Glossary:Carbon_dioxide_equivalent

EU regulation: https://eur-lex.europa.eu/legal-content/EN/TXT/PDF/?uri=CELEX:32020R1044

The key metric to measure the global warming effects is the change in the average temperature on Earth. On average, the global temperature has risen with almost 2 °C compared to pre-industrial levels (see Fig. 3.28).

A change in the average global temperature is an indicator of much larger changes in living conditions, as it coincides with increased likelihood of extreme weather events. The relationship between a (small) change in the average and the probability of extreme events is depicted in Fig. 3.29.

Even if the distribution of all observations remains the same, a small change in the average value may coincide with significantly higher changes of extreme values. A small increase in the average temperature, therefore, may have severe consequences for life on Earth as it coincides with a much higher likelihood of extreme weather circumstances, such as rainfall, droughts, storms and temperatures. This effect is even stronger when the distribution of observations also changes, in

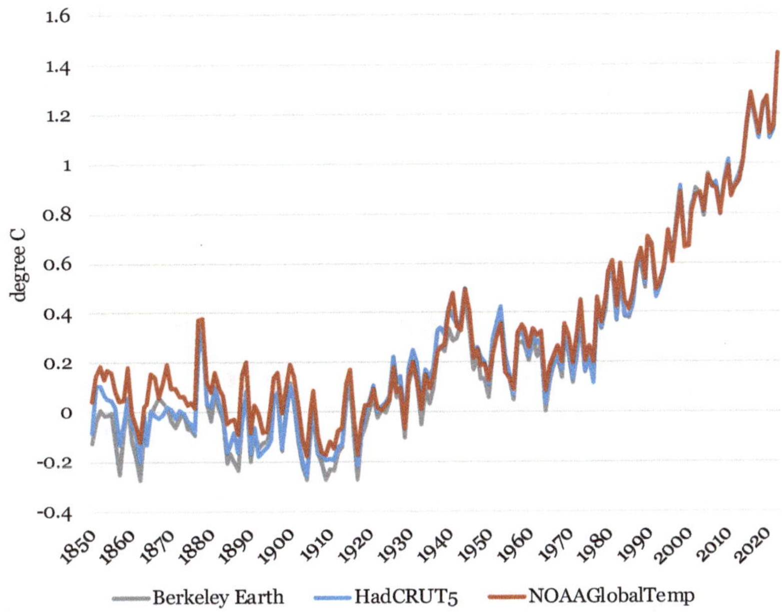

Fig. 3.28 Change in global average temperature relative to 1850–1900 reference level, based on various data sets, 1850-2023 (Source: Copernicus program of EU https://climate.copernicus.eu/esotc/2023/surface-air-temperature/)

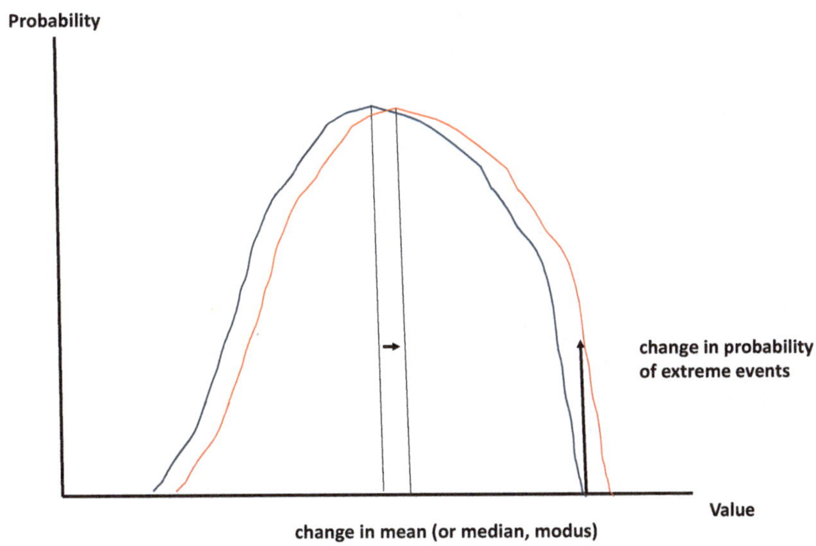

Fig. 3.29 Relationship between change in average value of a distribution and change in probability of extreme values of that distribution

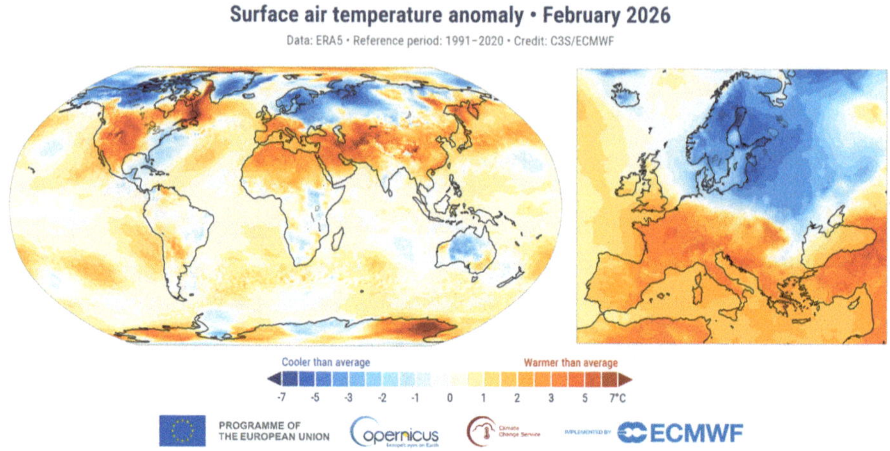

Fig. 3.30 Spatial distribution in average temperature in February 2026 in comparison to the temperature in the reference period 1991–2020 (Source: Copernicus: https://climate.copernicus.eu/surface-air-temperature-february-2026)

particular when it becomes skewed on the right side, which means that it is characterised by a long tail for the large numbers.

On top of this increased likelihood of extreme weather events when the average global temperature increases, there is also a large spatial distribution around the global average. Figure 3.30 shows the spatial distribution of the average surface air temperature in 2023 in comparison to the reference period 1991–2020. It appears that in some regions the average temperature was more than 3 °C higher than in the reference period, while in other regions the average temperature was lower than in the reference period.

3.6.3 Economic Mechanisms

It is generally well known, also outside the economics discipline, that the negative consequences of emissions of greenhouse gases resulting from the use of fossil energy must be considered a negative externality. Economic agents do not (sufficiently) take the negative climate consequences into account when making decisions regarding the use of fossil energy. The problem is that, without any regulation, these consequences do not have any direct impact on those who are responsible for the emissions, besides effects through other emissions, such as small particles.[31] Individual users of fossil energy, however, do not directly experience the climate

[31] When economic agents experience other types of negative effects of the use of fossil energy, they may have an incentive to change their use. For instance, citizens may experience a deterioration of air quality because of flue gases resulting from the use of coal in coal-fired power plants or steel factories. Because of that, societies have a direct interest to install filters or even replace coal by other energy carriers.

consequences of emitting these gases when there is no price for it or when they do not need to make any other sacrifice to compensate for the consequences of emissions. This also implies that individual economic agents do not see the benefits of reducing the emission of greenhouse gases, while they do experience the costs of realising that transition. This is due to the fact that climate change is both a global and a long-term issue.

Although everyone will experience the consequences of global warming sooner or later, the marginal effect on climate change by individuals reducing their emissions is negligible. Climate change is a global issue, as for the effects of global-warming, it does not matter where on Earth the emissions take place. Any emission contributes to the global concentration in the atmosphere.[32] This implies that everyone on Earth will also benefit when someone somewhere reduces their emissions. Hence, the key problem is that when agents are making efforts to reduce their emissions, they have to bear the costs of this effort themselves, while the benefits for the climate are shared with all global citizens.

This problem of the uneven distribution of costs and benefits of mitigation efforts is extended by the fact that the carbon dioxide molecules remain in the atmosphere for, on average, a century. This implies that the benefits of emissions reduction have to be shared not only with all those living on Earth now, but also with those living in the next one hundred years or so.

Because climate change is a global, long-term issue, it can be understood as a tragedy of the commons or common-pool problem, as was discussed in Sect. 3.2. In these types of market failures, individual agents do not have an incentive to care for the common good, while it would be in the common interest if all did. When these kinds of problems occur, individual agents consume more than socially optimal according to their individual strategy to maximise their own objective (i.e. utility or profit). To address this market failure, coordination of the individual activities of economic agents is needed (see Box 3.7).

This common-pool problem is relevant when talking about incentives for individual economic agents to mitigate their impact on the climate by reducing their emissions. This kind of market failure, however, is much less of an issue in the case of adapting to climate change. For efforts of agents to adapt to climate change, this common-pool problem is much less relevant. After all, when individual households invest in retrofitting their houses in order to protect them against hot summer spells, they alone will benefit from these investments. The same holds for farmers who invest in new types of crops which can better deal with extreme rainfall or periods of drought, as the benefits of these investments are directly going to the farmers themselves, since these measures may result in higher revenues.

From an economic perspective, this implies that the problem of mitigating climate change and adapting to climate change are different types of problems. In the first category, there is clearly a shortcoming in markets and, therefore, a need for government intervention, while in the latter category, the presence of market failures is less clear and, hence, it is less straightforward what kind of policy measures should be taken.

---

[32] There are, of course, regional differences in the way societies are affected by climate change, as is shown by Fig. 3.30.

Box 3.7 International Efforts to Address Climate Change

The fact that climate change is caused by human activities and that addressing this requires coordination because of the common-pool problem, is widely accepted. As a result of this, several international organisations have been established. The IPCC, the Intergovernmental Panel on Climate Change, is a UN organisation with the objective to provide governments with the most relevant and recent information on the various aspects of climate change. This information consists of monitoring reports regarding the current situation of climate change, explanations for climate change based on findings on the emissions of greenhouse gases and changes in atmospheric concentration, and the consequences of climate change for living conditions on Earth. For the latter, they develop scenarios regarding technical and socio-economic pathways.

After the publication of the first assessment report by the IPCC in 1990, the UN established the United Nations Framework Convention on Climate Change (UNFCC), which provides the legal basis for the international climate negotiations. The negotiations take place during the annual conferences which are called the Conferences of Parties (COP), the first one of which took place in Berlin in 1995. The first crucial international agreement was concluded in Kyoto in 1997 (the so-called Kyoto protocol) and another important agreement was made in Paris in 2015 (the so-called Paris Agreement). This last agreement is a legally binding international treaty on climate change, with the overarching objective to hold 'the increase in the global average temperature to well below 2 °C above pre-industrial levels' and pursue efforts 'to limit the temperature increase to 1.5 °C above pre-industrial levels' (United Nations Climate Change: https://unfccc.int/process-and-meetings/the-paris-agreement).

These international climate agreements have resulted in the implementation of various types of policy measures, internationally, regionally, nationally and locally. Examples are the Clean Development Mechanisms, the EU Emissions Trading System, national support schemes and local energy-transition projects.

3.6.4 Evidence from Research

The impact of the use of fossil energy on the living conditions on Earth, for both humans and other organisms, can be expressed in terms of cost per tonne of carbon dioxide emissions. There are many empirical and model studies that estimate the size of these costs. This is not an easy exercise, since the costs of emitting here and now extend to all places on Earth and, on average, one century into the future. First of all, one has to explore possible future developments in emissions, which can be done through scenario analysis (see Fig. 3.31). Next, the emissions have to be translated into changes in the atmospheric concentration and how that affects the climate, for which climate models are needed. Then, the consequences of changes in the climate for living conditions on Earth have to be estimated. This is done through so-called damage functions.

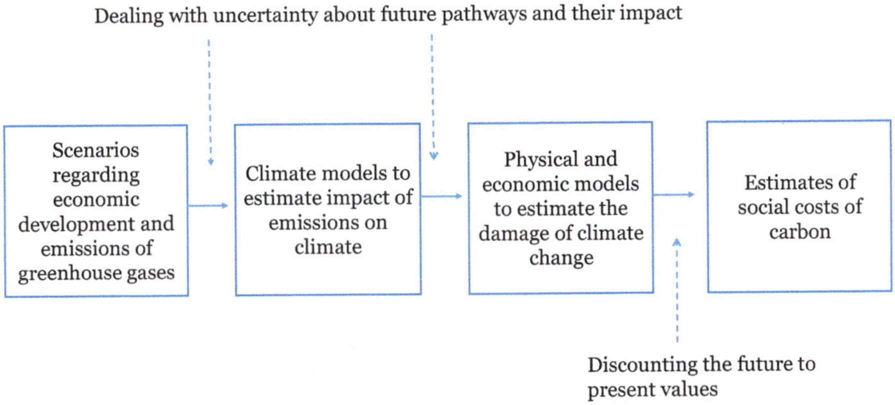

Fig. 3.31 Elements in the process of determining the social cost of carbon (Source: https://climatechangefork.blog.brooklyn.edu/2021/08/31/calculating-social-cost-carbon-already-spending/)

Because of the effects of emissions occurring in the future, the choice of the discount rate is a crucial one, as discussed in Sect. 3.3. When a high discount rate is chosen, the future costs of climate change do not really count for decisions today, which results in much lower social costs of carbon than when a low discount rate is used. From a meta-analysis of a number of studies estimating the social cost of carbon, Tol (2023b) concludes that the estimates are in a range between about 50 dollars per tCO_2 and more than 500 dollars per tCO_2.

3.6.5 Conclusion

Using fossil energy results in the emissions of greenhouse gases, in particular carbon dioxide, which raises not only the average temperature on Earth, but also the likelihood of extreme weather events regarding rainfall, drought, temperatures and storms. These changes have severe consequences for the living conditions on Earth, both for humans and other living organisms. These costs for using fossil energy are, without governmental intervention, not taken into account by economic agents. This has to do with the global and long-term nature of these effects. Because of this tragedy of the commons, economic agents use more of fossil-energy carriers (without capturing emissions) than would be socially optimal. The key problem is that the benefits of mitigation measures, i.e. reducing the emissions or capturing carbon from the atmosphere, are enjoyed by everyone on Earth, both now and in the future, while the costs of such measures are only incurred by those who take them. Consequently, without adequate policy measures, markets will fail to address the problem of climate change.

These kinds of problems can only be addressed through cooperation. Since the mid-1990s, the international collaboration on climate policy intensified, resulting in the implementation of various types of policy measures on various levels of government. The policy measures also address the energy sector, as the use of fossil energy is a major contributor to the global carbon emissions. Hence, intervening in the energy sector in order to reduce the emissions of greenhouse gases has a clear argumentation grounded in the presence of market failures.

3.7 Conclusions

In this chapter, we have discussed a number of arguments which are used to plea for active policy intervention in energy systems, i.e. to pursue a transition of these systems. Using the economic lens of market failures, some arguments, however, are clearer than others (see Table 3.3). When an argument is less convincing, in the sense

Table 3.3 Economic assessment of arguments for energy transition

Topic	Which arguments for energy transition are used in the societal debate?	Which evidence exists about the presence of market failures?	Concluding: which types of market failures appear to be relevant?
Security of supply: resource depletion	Economic agents are myopic: they do not sufficiently pay attention to the consequences of fast depletion	No evidence that private agents are more myopic than governments	Negative externality, not only as market failure, but also as a regulatory failure
	Economic agents do not have access to all information on resources and proven reserves	Depletion is mainly internalised by market parties, but available resources may not be fully transparent, resulting in a too low level of exploration	Information asymmetry
Security of supply: import dependence	Economic agents do not fully acknowledge the geopolitical consequences of import dependency	Both market parties and governments cannot fully oversee the future geopolitical consequences of import	Negative externality
Affordability: high and volatile energy prices	Market forces may result in high prices, negatively affecting vulnerable consumers	No strong evidence of market failure, although abuse of market power can be an underlying factor. However, distributional consequences can be reason enough for intervention	Use of market power Distributional effects
Sustainability: climate change	Climate is a common pool, which implies that consequences of carbon emissions for the climate are hardly taken into account by economic agents	Climate change resulting from carbon emissions is a clear example of a negative externality, with sharply rising emissions related to the use of energy	Negative externality

that it does not refer to a clear market failure, policy measures based thereon may not be beneficial for welfare. This holds in particular for the argument that energy transition is needed to reduce price peaks and price volatility. As government measures to intervene in energy systems result in a cost for society, there need to be other types of benefits. These benefits may be related to distributional aspects, such as protecting vulnerable households against high prices. In such cases, the challenge is to realise these benefits, without adversely impacting the functioning of energy markets.

Other arguments for energy transition are more straightforward. This holds in particular for the argument that using fossil energy contributes to climate change, and that the costs of these consequences are not taken into account by economic agents in the absence of governmental intervention. Intervening in energy systems in order to incentivise economic agents to reduce fossil energy or to capture emissions can, therefore, be welfare improving.

An intermediate position is taken by the arguments related to resource depletion and import dependence. Both aspects do have consequences in markets as market parties notice that a resource may become depleted or that the supply of a resource may become vulnerable to international risks. As such, these aspects are internalised in economic optimisation by market parties. However, to some extent, market parties may fail to incorporate all effects of their decisions on resource depletion or the consequences of increased import dependence. In so far this is the case, energy markets show a fundamental shortcoming which may call for government intervention.

Exercises

1. Explain why transparency is one of the crucial conditions for well-functioning markets.
2. What are the characteristics of a public good, and why are market parties not able to take care of them when there is no proper coordination or governmental regulation?
3. It is clear that the amount of fossil-energy resources is limited, but why is that fact in itself not a sufficient reason for government intervention in energy systems?
4. What is the market failure related to high shares of import dependence?
5. To what extent is price volatility a unique characteristic of energy markets which are based on the use of fossil energy?

References

Artelet, H., & Mulder, M. (2020). Natural gas markets in the European Union: Testing resilience. *Economics of Energy & Environmental Policy, 9*(1), 185–206.

Astier, N. (2025). French market design in practice: Some lessons from the 2020 energy crisis. *The Electricity Journal, 38*, 107483.

Bagheri, M., Kochański, M., Kranzl, L., Korczak, K., Mayrhofer, L., Müller, A., Öcer, E., & Rao, S. (2024). Reduction of gas demand through changes in heating behaviour in households: Novel insights from modelling and empirical evidence. *Energy & Buildings, 318*, 114257.

BP (2022). Statistical Review of World Energy, 70st edition.

Boyce and Nøstbakken (2010). Exploration and development of U.S. oil and gas fields, 1955–2002. *Journal of Economic Dynamics & Control*, 35(891–908).

Caldara, D., & Iacoviello, M. (2022). Measuring geopolitical risk. *American Economic Review, 112*(4), 1194–1225.

Codognet, M.-K., & Glachant, J.-M. (2008). *Weak investment incentives in new gas storage in the United Kingdom?* European University Institute.

Dahl, C., & Duggan, T. E. (1998). Survey of price elasticities from economic exploration models of US oil and gas supply. *Journal of Energy Finance & Development, 3*(2), 129–169.

Reynolds, D.B. (2001). Oil exploration game with incomplete information: An experimental study. *Energy Sources, 23*(6), 571–578.

Egging, R., & Holz, F. (2016). Risks in global natural gas markets: Investments, hedging and trade. *Energy Policy, 94*, 468–479.

Friedlingstein, P., et al. (2025). Global Carbon Budget 2025. Earth System Science Data, 15(12).https://essd.copernicus.org/articles/18/3211/2026/

Mei, D., Ma, F., Liao, Y., & Wang, L. (2020). Geopolitical risk uncertainty and oil future volatility; evidence from MIDAS models. *Energy Economics, 86*, 104624.

Nasseh, A. R., & Elyasiani, E. (1984). Energy price shocks in the 1970s; impact on industrialized economies. *Energy Economics, 6*, 231–244.

Nordhaus, W. (1998).

OPEC (Ed.). (2025). *Annual statistical bulletin* (60th ed.). OPEC.

Overland, I. (2019). The geopolitics of renewable energy: debunking four emerging myths. Energy Research & Social Science, 49(36–40). https://doi.org/10.1016/j.erss.2018.10.018.

Oxford Institute for Energy Studies (OIES). (2020). A comparative history of oil and gas markets and prices: Is 2020 just an extreme cyclical event or an acceleration of the energy transition? April.

Oxford Institute for Energy Studies (OIES). (2025). EU gas storage regulation; a journey from crisis-induced rigidity to increased flexibility. November.

Perman, R., Ma, Y., McGilvray, J., & Common, M. (1999). *Natural resource & environmental economics* (2nd ed.). Prentice Hall.

Qin, Y., Hong, K., Chen, J., & Zhang, Z. (2020). Asymmetric effects of geopolitical risks on energy returns and volatility under different market conditions. *Energy Economics, 90*(2020), 104851.

Rosslowe, C., & Petrovich, B. (2025). *Decoupled: how Spain cut the link between gas and power prices using renewables*. EMBER.

Schoenmaker, D., & Schramade, W. (2024). Which discount rate for sustainability. *Journal of Sustainable Finance and Accounting, 3*, 100010.

Stern, J. (2004). UK gas security: Time to get serious. *Energy Policy, 32*(2004), 1967–1979.

Sweidon, O.D. (2021). Is the geopolitical risk and incentive or obstacle to renewable energy deployment? Evidence from a panel analysis. Renewable Energy, 178(377–384), https://doi.org/10.1016/j.renene.2021.06.089.

Thorbecke, W. (2019). Oil prices and the U.S. economy: Evidence from the stock market. *Journal of Macroeconomics, 61*, 103137.

Tol, R. S. J. (2023a). *Climate economics: Economic analysis of climate, climate change and climate policy* (3rd ed.). Edward Elgar.

Tol, R. S. J. (2023b). Social costs of carbon have increased over time. *Nature Climate Change, 13*, 532–536. https://www.nature.com/articles/s41558-023-01680-x#MOESM6

Widyastuti, E. T. (2022). The relationship between crude oil price, exploration, production and uncertainty. School of Economics, Finance and Property, University of Aberdeen (PhD thesis).

Zweifel, P., Praktiknjo, A., & Erdmann, G. (2017). *Energy economics: Theory and applications*. Springer.

4 Realising Energy Transition in an Efficient Way

4.1 Introduction

From an economic perspective directed at social welfare, governments should only intervene in energy markets in case of fundamental shortcomings in the way markets function, as we have seen in Chap. 3. When such shortcomings are absent, any governmental intervention results in a lower welfare, as such interventions encourage economic agents to make decisions which deviate from their optimal choices. The fact that market failures are the only economic argument for government intervention implies that the mere existence of a policy objective is not a sufficient economic argument.

Realising a policy objective can increase welfare, when it is clear that without any intervention, markets are not able to achieve the optimal outcome. There is one exception to this economic principle, which is related to societal preferences regarding the distribution of welfare. When fundamental shortcomings are lacking, government intervention may, therefore, have net societal benefits when that intervention changes the distribution of the welfare in such a way that it is more appreciated within society.

The presence of a fundamental shortcoming in a market does not automatically imply that a policy measure will be successful in realising public objectives in an effective and efficient way. When a fundamental shortcoming is present, one has to determine whether an effective and efficient measure could be introduced. In theory, governments have many different options to intervene in energy systems, which not only differ in the way economic agents and markets are affected by a policy measure, but also in their effectiveness and efficiency in improving the functioning of the markets. In Sect. 4.2, we will first discuss the general economic framework for determining the type of policy measures that may be helpful to effectively and efficiently realise objectives regarding the energy system. Here, we also discuss the general types of market interventions that governments can implement to stir the functioning of the market process and address market failures. In the following sections, we dive into various types of specific measures directed at fundamental shortcomings in energy markets related to arguments for energy transition, as discussed in Chap. 3.

M. Mulder, *Economics of Energy Transition*, Studies in Energy, Resource and Environmental Economics, https://doi.org/10.1007/978-3-032-29010-6_4

4.2 Economic Framework: Market Failures and Policy Measures

4.2.1 Introduction

The fundamental economic principle is that governments should only intervene in economic systems when markets show fundamental shortcomings, so-called market failures. A market failure exists when a condition for well-functioning markets is not met, as was discussed in Sect. 3.2. These conditions can be used to formulate four categories of market failures: asymmetric information, strategic behaviour by one or more agents, externalities, and hold-up. In addition to these market failures, the distributional outcomes of the market process can be seen as a reason for government intervention (see Table 4.1). The government interventions can also be distinguished into a number of types. A common distinction is made between regulatory obligations, financial instruments, behavioural measures and public participation. For each type of market failure, several types of policy instruments can be considered. The category of regulatory obligations includes a large number of different types of measures, varying from rules on information disclosure in marketplaces, merger control, rules regarding the use of a common pool, legal frameworks to provide certainty to investors and rules regarding price formation. Although the category of regulatory obligations can be widely applied, this does not mean that these types of measures are also the most efficient type of intervention. In some cases, it is more efficient to use financial instruments, such as taxes or subsidies. In other cases, it may be more efficient for a government to financially and operationally participate in a particular project instead of prescribing what other economic agents should do.

In this chapter, we will first have a general discussion on the effectiveness and efficiency of the various types of policy measures. By effectiveness, we refer to the degree to which the objectives are realised, without looking at the costs of the policy measures. As economics is about analysing trade-offs between costs and benefits, efficiency is a key metric to assess policy measures. The concept of efficiency refers to various aspects of the relationship between costs and benefits. Productive efficiency concerns the costs made per unit of output, allocative efficiency refers to how well a product is produced using the low-cost technologies and supplied to those who appreciate it the most, and dynamic efficiency refers to the long-term impact on costs and benefits. We will use these various aspects of efficiency to evaluate different types of policy measures.

Government interventions in energy markets can be separated into two categories. One category consists of policy measures which are directed at improving the functioning of markets in general, without any specific objective regarding the outcomes of these markets. These general characteristics of markets refer to the information position of market players, the dominant position of some market parties and the ownership of assets and firms. The other category of government interventions consists of policy measures directed at realising particular policy objectives, such as those related to energy transition. Below, we will first briefly discuss policy

Table 4.1 Examples of government interventions per type of market failure and type of policy measure

	Type of policy measure			
Type of market failure	Regulatory constraints	Financial measures	Behavioural measures	Public participation
Asymmetric information	Rules for marketplaces regarding information disclosure	Fines for providing misleading information	Supporting consumers to process retail information	Public provision of information
Market power	Competition rules, for example, regarding mergers Regulation of natural monopolies Removing bottlenecks for international integration of markets	Fines for abuse of market power	Naming and shaming of firms abusing market power	Public ownership of crucial infrastructure
Externalities	Rules for using common pool Implementation of capacity market	Tax or emissions trading scheme for negative externality Subsidy for positive externality	Information campaigns to reduce consumption of goods with negative externality	Investments in reserve capacity in case of negative externalities
Hold up	Legal frameworks to reduce risks for investors	Public financial guarantees for investments		Public participation in infrastructure to reduce risks for private parties
Uneven distributional outcomes	Rules regarding price formation	Tax on supranormal profits Subsidies for low-income groups		Social welfare arrangements

measures belonging to the first category, but the focus in this book is on policy measures of the second category. In the next sections, therefore, we will extensively discuss how the various types of policy measures may be useful for realising various types of objectives related to energy transition. Note that governments may also intervene in energy systems without any economic need to improve the allocation process, but to promote certain interests (see Box 4.1).

4.2.2 Regulatory Constraints

Regulatory constraints can be applied to address various types of market failures. In the case of information asymmetry among economic agents, these constraints can be used to make markets more transparent. Economic processes can result in optimal decisions only when economic agents have accurate information about the current situation and what can be expected in the relevant future. Without this information, economic decisions can be distorted and result, for example, in adverse selection. As an example, in case the quality is not easily observable by consumers, high-quality, but more expensive products cannot compete with less expensive, lower quality products (see Sect. 3.2.2). When markets are not able to improve their transparency, governments may step in, for instance, by organising certificate schemes or by imposing rules on market parties regarding the disclosure of information.

Regulatory obligations are also a commonly used policy tool to make markets more competitive. In competitive markets, economic agents can only maximise their profits by operating as efficiently as possible or by improving the quality of their products so that they can charge higher prices. In such a market, economic agents cannot behave strategically, which means that they try to influence the market prices by reducing their supply to the market or by asking prices above their marginal costs. In a competitive market, such behaviour cannot be successful as competitors can easily outcompete a firm that behaves strategically, by increasing their supply or by charging lower prices. Because of this competitive behaviour, prices for consumers are not higher than needed to compensate for the real costs. However, when a market is not so competitive, firms can have both the ability and the incentive to behave strategically, which can result in higher prices for consumers. In addition, in less competitive markets, firms do not have strong incentives to operate more efficiently and reduce their costs, at the expense of consumers.

Hence, when governments want to improve the position of consumers in markets subject to market power, they may intervene in these markets by making them more competitive. The general form of market intervention to enhance competition is called competition policy. This policy consists of two types, notably merger control and antitrust. The former, which sets constraints on the extent to which economic agents can merge, is meant to prevent firms from becoming too large compared to the market size, which would enable them to obtain market power. The latter type of competition policy imposes constraints on the behaviour of firms with market power. This type of competition policy is meant to prevent anticompetitive behaviour by firms with market power or groups of firms that collude to influence market outcomes.

Regulatory obligations are also commonly used to restrict the behaviour of operators of natural monopolies. Such monopolies are present in, for instance, the markets for electricity, natural gas, hydrogen and heat, as they are based on the presence of physical infrastructure for the transport of energy, as was discussed in Sect. 2.4.4. Without a grid, it is impossible to have an electricity system and market. For natural gas, hydrogen and heat systems and markets, a grid is not a necessary condition, but its presence makes the exchange of these energy carriers way more efficient. In the case of these energy carriers, transport can be carried out in alternative ways, such as by trucks and ships, but this is generally much more expensive.

Box 4.1 Government Interventions in Energy Systems May Also Reduce Welfare
In this book, the central approach is that markets may suffer from fundamental shortcomings which call for government interventions. Without such interventions, the allocation process in energy markets results in loss of welfare, such as the deadweight loss of market power or negative externalities. By taking appropriate measures, such as antitrust policies, taxing fossil fuels or providing subsidies for renewables, this loss of welfare may be mitigated. Even when governments are focused on raising the overall welfare, defining the appropriate measures is complicated, for instance, because the government also suffers from information asymmetry.

This idea of governments striving to promote the overall welfare is applied in many countries, but there are also countries where governments have different objectives. Some governments are more directed at pursuing the interests of the politicians themselves or those closely related to them. As a result, they may take measures to protect particular incumbent industries, for instance, by imposing high import tariffs or constraints on the products of foreign competitors. Such measures result in higher costs for consumers and, hence, lower consumer welfare, but the profits of the protected industries may be protected for a while. In the long term, such protectionist measures have a negative effect on the dynamic efficiency of an economy, as the incumbent industries have fewer incentives to innovate because of the protection against foreign competition. Governments may also heavily subsidise the domestic energy industry in order to promote their exports, but this also results in a lower overall welfare, because cheaper products from elsewhere face a competitive disadvantage. Governments may also have different views on what the market failures are, and consequently take different policy measures which may counteract each other. If the government of one country imposes carbon taxes to reduce the use of fossil energy, because of the impact on climate change, but the government of another country provides subsidies to fossil-energy producers, the overall (international) effect may be that the latter country raises its export of fossil energy resulting in a higher level of consumption and carbon emissions. For global problems, such as climate change, international exchange of ideas and coordination of policies is, therefore, crucial to raise the effectiveness and efficiency of policy measures.

As the grids are subject to strong economies of scale, it is not efficient to have multiple infrastructures in the same region. Hence, the operators of these infrastructures do have so-called natural monopolies. A consequence of being a natural monopoly is that there is no competitive pressure to operate efficiently or to reduce the costs for grid users. Through regulation of natural monopolies, such as the operators of electricity grids, governments can ensure that the tariffs for grid users are not higher than what is needed to compensate for the grid costs. Such regulation helps to prevent grid users from paying too much and grid operators from making too much profit, i.e. profits which exceed the level necessary for a reasonable return on their investments.

When determining the reasonable tariff levels, governments (represented by regulators) face the problem of information asymmetry. The regulator generally does not know exactly what the characteristics of the regulated company, i.e. the grid operator, are, while it also cannot really observe the actual behaviour of that company. The characteristics refer to aspects like the actual costs of operating a grid and the technological options to become more efficient, while the behaviour of the grid operator refers to the extent the operator does its best to become more efficient and improve the quality of its services to grid users. Because of these information problems, two types of risks occur: adverse selection and moral hazard. The former risk entails that the regulator makes incorrect assumptions regarding the true costs of the grid operator, resulting in tariff levels which are either too high or too low. Moral hazard is that the regulated company has less incentive to do its best if it knows that the regulator will allow the reimbursement of all its costs. To address these information problems, a regulator can apply so-called incentive regulation, which basically means that the regulator lets the agent benefit from realising its objectives.[1]

Regulatory obligations are also used to design marketplaces. Markets are devices to allocate scarce commodities. This allocation can be achieved in several ways. The most basic way is a bilateral commodity exchange without the support of any intermediate party. Such an allocation method may be efficient in case of a low number of market parties, but when this number is larger, it may be efficient to have the help of intermediate parties, such as brokers. The role of these parties is to bring different parties together in order to maximise the benefits of the exchange of commodities. The efficiency of this allocation process can be further fostered through standardisation, which occurs in the case of exchanges. Which allocation process is chosen can often be left to the market parties themselves, but governmental regulation is required to set the proper legal frameworks. Sometimes market parties are unable to develop a well-functioning allocation system. This, for instance, occurs in the case of allocating available capacity of transport infrastructure over potential users. When the owner of the infrastructure does not face (sufficient) competitive pressure, e.g. from price-elastic consumers, it may allocate the transport capacity to users with whom it has close relationships, for instance, through vertical relationships in one holding company. In order to improve the efficiency of the allocation of this capacity, governments may step in by requiring another type of allocation, such as through an auction mechanism.

In the case of common-pool problems, collective arrangements are needed to address that market failure. This can be done with the use of regulatory obligations

[1] See Mulder et al. (2023) for an extensive discussion of how incentive regulation can be applied to set the tariffs of grid operators.

that organise the use of the common pool. An example of this is the creation of a cap-and-trade design of emissions-trading schemes, where a number of firms are legally made subject to the collective constraint, which is the cap on emissions. This will be further discussed in more detail in Sect. 4.6. Another example of a regulatory constraint to address negative externalities is the obligation for economic agents to use less of a particular type of input (e.g. fossil energy) or to use a minimum amount of another type of input (e.g. renewable energy).

Regulatory obligations can also be useful to address problems of hold-up, which means that some market parties are not willing to commit to something (e.g. investing in a new infrastructure) because of uncertainty about the future use. By imposing obligations on the potential users,[2] this uncertainty can be reduced.

Finally, regulatory obligations can be used to address adverse distributional effects of market processes. For instance, if the process of exchanging a particular commodity is viewed as unfair for some groups, the government can impose rules on the price formation. An example of this is that energy retailers are forbidden to sell energy to residential households by phone, as this makes the latter vulnerable, because of psychological factors, to unfavourable decisions (see Box 2.4).

4.2.3 Financial Policy Measures

While regulatory constraints directly influence economic agents' margin of manoeuvre, financial policy measures do this indirectly by affecting the economic incentives. This category of policy measures consists of different types of measures, notably subsidisation, taxing and providing financial guarantees. The former two types of financial measures are particularly used in case of externalities, when market parties do not sufficiently pay attention to the (marginal) costs and benefits of their actions. By changing the costs or benefits they experience, this market failure can be addressed.

When the externality refers to costs which are not taken into account, imposing a tax can be an effective tool to address this market failure. A condition for this is that it is possible to determine the size of the negative externality to choose the right tax rate. After all, when the tax rate deviates from the marginal social cost caused by the externality, it may create another inefficiency in the market process. Either the costs of market parties are raised too much, resulting in a deadweight loss of a sub-optimal level of energy use, or they are raised too little, resulting in a continuation of a, from a societal perspective, too high level of consumption. An alternative for imposing a tax on consumption that causes a negative externality is combining a financial instrument with a regulatory constraint. This combined use of two types of instruments is done in, for instance, emissions-trading schemes. In such schemes, a constraint on the amount of emissions is combined with the option to trade in allowances, which result in a price to emit. In Sect. 4.6, we will discuss this type of measure more in depth.

[2] Such as households in a particular region who are obliged to connect to a district-heating system in order to assure that there is sufficient utilisation of that system.

Instead of financially raising the costs of an activity causing a negative externality, one could also use subsidies to promote actions which counteract the negative externality. A clear example in the case of negative externalities resulting from the use of fossil energy is giving financial support for renewable-energy or energy-efficiency measures. A caveat of providing subsidies, however, is that this instrument may trigger a rebound effect, which reduces the effectiveness of the measure. Subsidies for energy saving, for instance, make the use of appliances which use energy less expensive, and, hence, may encourage, for instance, lighting homes also on the outside. Another risk of providing subsidies is that it results in windfall profits, which means that too much subsidy is given, at the expense of those (e.g. the general taxpayer) who contribute to the financing of these subsidies.

These caveats, i.e. rebound effects and windfall profits, do not occur when taxes are introduced and because of that, economists generally prefer taxes to subsidies. This is, in particular, the case when economic agents have several options to respond to raising costs, such as investing in various types of renewables or taking energy-efficiency measures. As economic agents generally have more information than the government about which of these options is the best choice for them, it is more efficient to give them the freedom to make their own choices. This positive effect on efficiency does not occur in case of subsidies for particular technologies, as the government has to choose which technologies or actions should be subsidised. Therefore, subsidies may result in productive inefficiencies when the most efficient technologies are not subsidised.[3]

Financial policy instruments can also be used to address adverse distributional effects. When, for instance, some firms realise extraordinary profits because of external circumstances, so-called windfall profits, governments can tax such profits in order to allocate them to other agents in society. The downside of such policy measures, however, is that they may have adverse effects on the incentives for economic agents to invest. For instance, if electricity-generating firms are making exceptional profits during a number of years because of high fuel costs of the price-setting technologies or due to exceptional tightness in the market, taxing these profits may reduce the incentive for these firms to invest in more generation technologies. This implies that measures to address distributional concerns should take into account possible adverse effects on the efficiency of markets. In general, it is therefore preferred, from an economic perspective, to take distributional measures that do not affect the functioning of the market process. An example of such a measure is subsidising vulnerable (i.e. low-income) households with subsidies for insulating their houses instead of intervening in the prices they have to pay for energy.

[3] The same inefficiency would result in the case of taxes, when these are only charged on specific energy uses or on particular groups of agents.

4.2.4 Behavioural Policy Measures

While regulatory constraints directly restrict the behavioural options for economic agents and financial-policy measures influence the economic incentives for agents, behavioural policy measures are used to influence the decisions made by the agents in a different way. The objective of this type of measure is to influence the decision-making process. This can, for instance, be done through naming and shaming of firms that do not comply with regulatory constraints. If a firm does not comply with a regulatory standard, for example, regarding the quality of the product or the production process, a government can make the non-compliance transparent to other economic agents. This is sometimes, for instance, done by energy regulators who want regulated grid operators to comply with quality standards. Instead of, or next to, confronting non-compliant operators with financial consequences, regulators can also make the names of these operators known to grid users. Although grid users may not be able to switch to another grid operator, due to the natural-monopoly character of grids, the operators may not like it when their non-compliance is made public. Consequently, regulators may hope that the grid operators will change their behaviour and comply with the regulatory quality standards. From this, it becomes already clear that the effectiveness of behavioural measures can be quite uncertain.

Another example of a behavioural measure to affect the behaviour of economic agents consists of providing information. The underlying idea is that economic agents may not be well-informed about the characteristics of a particular technical measure, such as the costs of various options for insulation of houses. By making this type of information more transparent, governments may hope that more economic agents take appropriate actions, such as in this case insulating their houses. Also, in this example, the effectiveness is fairly uncertain.

4.2.5 Public Participation

A more direct way of intervening in market processes is through public ownership. An argument for this can be that firms operating in competitive markets can still make high profits and benefit from high prices. Consequently, some argue that firms active in the provision of basic commodities like energy should be publicly owned. Sometimes, people refer to other types of economic systems, such as the one in China, where governments have a much higher direct stake in all kinds of activities and transitions seem to be realised much faster (see Box 4.2).

Public ownership may be helpful to foster investments in, for instance, infrastructure which is needed to realise the energy transition. Investments in such infrastructure may suffer from the hold-up problem, given the fact that market parties face the risk that once the investment has been made, the counterparties, i.e. the potential users of the infrastructure, have a strong position to (re)negotiate a lower use tariff. In addition, such infrastructure may suffer from coordination problems, for example, between future developments in the supply of an energy commodity and its use by other parties. In case of a lack of coordination, market parties may be hesitant to invest, which may call for public participation. Moreover, public participation is sometimes seen as a method to ensure the development and operation of an infrastructure, for example, regarding the reliability of supply, is not distorted by commercial objectives of the operator and owner. The latter argument is used by several countries, such as the Netherlands, to keep essential infrastructures, including energy grids, in public hands.[4] In several other countries, however, energy grids are privately owned or partially publicly and privately owned. Globally, about ¾ of all electricity distribution grids are publicly owned, about 20% privately owned, while the rest have mixed ownership (Pollitt et al., 2025).

Public ownership may also be helpful to prevent commercial firms from making (high) profits at the expense of consumers. The high profits may result from, for instance, high commodity prices caused by large interruptions in supply or stark increases in demand. The question is, however, to what extent public ownership is effective to address such societal problems. After all, high prices must also be seen as signs of the presence of market tightness, regardless of the type of ownership (see Sect. 3.5). Even when publicly owned firms operate in such a market, the market-equilibrium price is high in case total demand exceeds the total available capacity. In such circumstances, high scarcity prices are needed to find a market equilibrium, resulting in high profits for companies. This mechanism does, however, not change when the suppliers, e.g. energy companies, are publicly owned.

It is conceivable that publicly owned companies do not want to maximise their profits and offer their products at a price only linked to their costs. However, state-owned companies may also act as commercial players just as privately owned companies (see Chap. 5). The consequence of offering commodities at a relatively low price can be that demand remains higher than the available capacity. In order to clear the market, another allocation mechanism is needed, such as first-come-first served or an allocation based on prioritisation of particular groups. The result of such alternative allocation mechanisms is that there are still consumers who are not able to consume the product because of the scarcity, but those who have received the commodity do not need to pay a higher price. Such mechanisms may, therefore, be good for affordability as it prevents high scarcity prices.

There are, however, a few downsides to such alternative allocation mechanisms. One downside is that the allocation may not be efficient, by which is meant that some consumers who do not really value the product may receive it, while others who greatly value the product will have bad luck as they will not receive it. Another downside is that the suppliers do not have an incentive to extend their capacity, as these incentives only occur when the market prices generate sufficient revenues to compensate for all costs, including the costs of capital. When a publicly owned company caps end-user prices while it has to pay high itself on international

[4] In this respect, it is interesting to see that the Dutch electricity grids suffer from severe congestion problems due to lack of investments in grid capacity, while they are fully publicly owned (IEA, 2024b). Hence, public ownership is not a guarantee for sufficient and timely investments. This may also indicate that the type of ownership may not be so important for the functioning of grid operators.

markets, then it actually subsidises those users. These subsidies have to be paid, in one way or the other, which implies that the price cap only redistributes the costs of the scarcity, while it does not mitigate the scarcity itself.[5] Hence, public ownership in itself does not solve the problem of scarcity, but can be societally preferred to allocate scarce commodities in a fairer way.

Box 4.2 Role of Governments in the Energy Transition: The Case of China
In discussions on the (lack of) pace of energy transition, China is often mentioned as the example of a country that is really successful in quickly realising large amounts of investments. This high pace is often attributed to the way the Chinese government intervenes in its society. China is now indeed leading the investments in wind turbines, solar panels, electrolysers, batteries and electric vehicles. It invests more in renewable capacity than the rest of the world together (see Fig. 4.1).

China is, however, also leading the investments in fossil-fuel capacity. In 2025, almost all global investments in unabated (i.e. without capturing the carbon) coal-fired power plants were realised in China. These numbers show that the investments in renewables are not completely related to a transition from a fossil-fuel based economy to a renewable-based economy, but that these investments play a role in meeting the growing demand for energy. In this respect, one can state that renewables add energy to the system, instead of replacing fossils (see Yergin et al., 2025). Apparently, in China, investing in

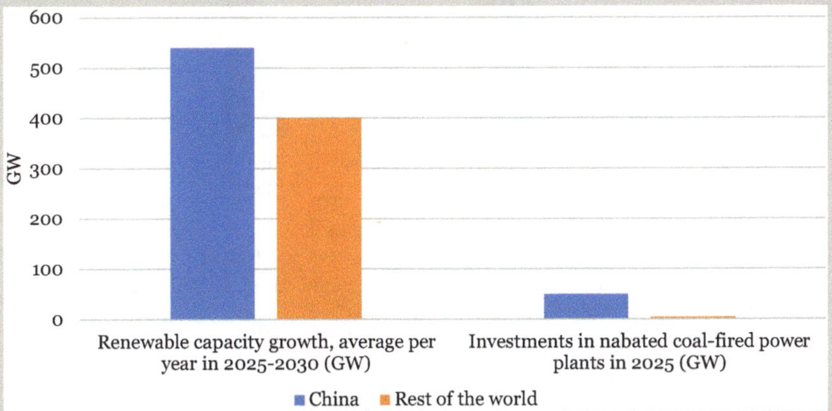

Fig. 4.1 Investments in renewable-energy capacity (2025-2030) and unabated coal-fired power plants (2025), in China and rest of the world (Source: IEA (2024a, 2025))

(continued)

[5] Something similar occurs when a government reduces taxes on gasoline in order to compensate car drivers for increased fuel costs. Such a measure means that the burden of the higher fuel costs shift to the general tax payer.

Box 4.2 (continued)

renewables has become an economically attractive option to expand the production capacity. That the strong increase in renewable investments does not indicate a move towards to a low-carbon energy system also follows from the fact that the total carbon emissions in China are still rising (since 2000 by 2.6% per year), while emissions are declining in other regions, such as Europe (since 2000 by 2.7% per year).

When one looks at China's performance in transitioning to a renewable-based economy, China is not at all outperforming other countries. Many countries, in particular in Europe, currently have a higher share of renewables in their power production than China. It is expected that this will still be the case by 2030 (see Fig. 4.2). In many European countries, the share of renewables in the total electricity generation will exceed 50% by 2030, while that share in China is expected to be less than 40%. These facts show that also in decentralised economies with much less direct governmental influence, it is possible to successfully realise an energy transition.

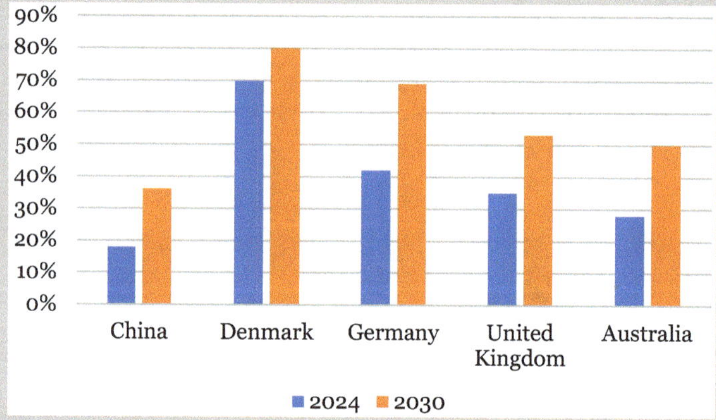

Fig. 4.2 Share of renewables in total electricity generation, in a number of countries, in 2024 and 2030 (Source: IEA (2025))

Another argument against public ownership is that it may negatively affect the incentives to operate more efficiently, as there is no pressure from capital markets. A company that is privately owned has to go to the capital market, for equity and loans, when it wants to finance investments and its own financial resources are not sufficient to do so without external capital. Investors and banks, however, only want to invest or provide loans when there is the prospect of adequate return and repayment of loans with interest. Because of this mechanism, a privately owned firm has to operate efficiently and supply products which are valued by its customers.

Because of these downsides, public ownership together with non-market-based allocation methods is not really an appropriate measure to deal with the issue of scarcity in markets. High prices in such circumstances do not need to result from strategic behaviour by firms, but may be needed to clear markets. In case firms are abusing tight market circumstances by artificially raising the scarcity, general competition policy measures can be used. In order to protect consumers against very high prices during scarcity circumstances, other types of measures seem to be more effective, such as social-income support, as will be discussed in Sect. 4.5.

4.2.6 Conclusions

Even without any objective regarding the particular outcomes of markets, governments can have reasons to intervene. These reasons refer to the basic conditions for a well-functioning allocation process. Sometimes, market parties are not able to organise transparency, which prevents market parties from maximising their objectives. Government policies that facilitate information exchange can be helpful to raise the efficiency of markets. Markets may also suffer from a lack of competition, as some players have a dominant position or collude with each other to obtain such a position. General competition policy is helpful to improve the competitive process. Moreover, market parties may also pay insufficient attention to all the effects of their decisions, which results in (negative or positive) externalities. By taxing negative externalities or subsidising positive ones, these shortcomings in the allocation process may be reduced. Sometimes, the owner of the scarce resource, like a transport infrastructure, may not be willing to facilitate an efficient allocation process. Then, governments may be required to improve the design of the allocation process. Finally, governments can also be active in market processes through ownership, for instance, to make sure rents are captured by society as a whole, instead of private parties.

After this general introduction in the various types of policy measures governments can use to improve the functioning of markets, we will now analyse which types of measures governments could take to realise their energy-policy objectives which are related to market failures. For each of the four topics analysed in Chap. 3, we will first summarise the market failures and then discuss the effectiveness and efficiency of appropriate policy measures.

4.3 Policy Measures to Deal with Depletion of Resources

4.3.1 Introduction: Summarising the Market Failures

As we have seen in Chap. 3, the depletion of natural resources may be subject to a number of fundamental shortcomings. Consequently, market forces may result in suboptimal depletion paths of natural resources when no additional specific regulations are implemented. This problem is not bound to fossil-energy carriers, but in principle extends to all kinds of natural resources, including those which are crucial to realise a transition to renewable energy, such as the so-called critical minerals, lithium, cobalt and copper (see Box 4.3). We can use the societally optimal depletion path in which the marginal societal costs of depletion are equal to the marginal societal benefits as the benchmark for analysis. The marginal benefits (mb) consist of the marginal value that the current economic agents attach to the use of these resources, while the marginal costs include not only the marginal costs of production (mc_p), but also the opportunity costs (mc_{op}) determined by the missed benefits resulting from the inability to consume the resource later. This results in the following condition for optimal depletion:

$$mb = mc_p + mc_{op} \tag{4.1}$$

In an optimally working system, the exploitation of a natural resource will continue until the marginal costs equal the marginal benefits. A deviation from the optimal depletion path can be caused by a lack of information on the magnitude of remaining resources, which makes economic agents overestimate the remaining resources. As a result, they underestimate the opportunity costs of exploiting the resource and, consequently, produce too much, notably until the marginal benefits equals the (underestimated) marginal costs.

A suboptimal depletion path can also result from the presence of negative externalities, as economic agents may not sufficiently pay attention to the availability of resources for later generations. This can also be framed as economic agents not being concerned with the consequences of their use of non-renewable resources for future agents. This latter market failure is equal to saying that economic agents are myopic, as they use a discount rate that, from a societal perspective, is too high.

A suboptimal level of depletion may also result from a lack of coordination among the depletion activities of various economic agents in a particular resource base. This so-called tragedy of the commons results from the fact that every individual agent maximises its own profits, while a joint optimisation of the profits would result in a different depletion path.

Suboptimal depletion of natural resources can also occur due to a lack of competition. This market failure, however, results in lower production levels than would be socially optimal. The presence of this failure may partly neutralise the other market failures which result in too high levels of production. The above market failures can be addressed by policies fostering transparency, measures that result in the internalisation of negative externalities, policy measures that foster the coordination of exploitation activities and policies improving the degree of competition.

Even in the absence of market failures, the exploitation of natural resources may have adverse distributional consequences when the exploitation results in large supranormal profits, which are enjoyed by a limited group of economic agents. In such cases, governments may intervene in order to change the distribution of the exploitation benefits.

Box 4.3 Availability of Critical Materials for Electrification

As part of the energy transition, countries promote the electrification of transport, heating as well as industrial processes. Next to this induced move towards higher electricity use, the latter is also increasing because of innovation and market forces. In particular, the strong growth in the role of Artificial Intelligence and data centers contribute to a surge in the electricity consumption. The resulting electrification of economies has as a consequence that the demand for so-called critical materials increases as well. In the recent past, the global consumption of materials like lithium, nickel, cobalt and copper grew significantly (IEA, 2025). These materials are not only needed for the generation of renewable electricity, but also for equipment for storage (e.g. batteries) and transport (i.e. extension of electricity grids) as well as appliances consuming electricity.

The strong increase in the demand for these materials contributes to the rise in prices, followed by significant increases in the supply. The global supply of both lithium and cobalt, for instance, more than doubled in the period 2021–2024. The strong increase in the supply in recent years decreased the prices of essential materials for the electrification after an initial strong increase until 2023 (IEA, 2025). This shows that market forces in the supply of critical materials seem to be rather capable to respond to changing requirements from the energy systems. Nevertheless, the market responses may not fully account for the risk of increasing dependence on a small number of supplying countries, which may call for additional governmental measures promoting diversification, just as in the case of fossil-energy markets (see Sect. 4.4).

4.3.2 Information Policies

When firms explore the Earth's crust to find new natural resources, they obtain information on their precise characteristics, which enables them to estimate the location and magnitude of the resources. As we have seen in Section 3.3.1, these resources are usually divided in a number of categories, depending on the geological certainty and economic feasibility: conditional, prospective, possible, probable and proven. A lack of information on the geological certainty and economic feasibility may have negative effects on the incentives for economic agents to adequately explore undeveloped natural resources and manage these resources. This kind of information is, therefore, valuable to the firm as it can be used to define potential profitable investment options. In principle, firms do not have an incentive to make this information public, as that would also enable competitors to make better forecasts of the future market circumstances. If firms are not transparent about the information they have secured, other agents are not well-informed about the existing proven reserves or geological resources, and, consequently, may overestimate the resource rents. In other words, they overestimate the opportunity costs of producing a non-renewable resource. This results in a too low pace of producing (and consuming) these resources.

Within a market setting, there is pressure on firms to be transparent about the reserves they have discovered. In particular investors, both shareholders and providers of debt, want to have this information as it affects the value of the firm and, therefore, the value of their stocks or loans. Because of this, financial regulations generally require companies to publish their information resulting from exploration through, for instance, their regular financial reports.

On top of that, national governments that have issued licences for exploration, generally require the publication of the results of exploration activities. The reason for this is that this information not only helps them in their natural-resource policy, but it also helps other firms that want to be active in the same resource base. The rules for information disclosure can be included in the licensing procedures, which is an effective way to make sure that all newly generated information regarding the characteristics and scale of natural resources is shared with the government administration.

When governments have information on natural resources, they can decide to share this with market parties to help other firms, which may be interested in the field, to formulate more accurate expectations surrounding the potential production volumes. When this information is published by public authorities, economic agents might trust this more than when individual, commercial firms publish their information directly. Figure 4.3 shows an example of the information provided by the Norwegian government on the current activities surrounding the oil and gas resources in the Norwegian Continental Shelf (NCS). Visitors of the website can search for field-level information, such as the discovery year, remaining reserves of oil, gas and condensate per field, the operators of the field, type of licence and status of production.

As natural resources, like coal, oil and natural gas, but also materials like lithium and copper, are traded in international or even global markets, economic agents need to have information on all relevant countries worldwide to make good estimations of the future supply and other relevant factors in these markets. Therefore, collaboration among governments, for instance, through international institutions, is needed to realise this. The problem, however, here is that governments may also have an interest not to be transparent about the magnitude and production costs of natural resources in their country, just as individual, commercial firms may have the incentive not to be transparent. In many countries, as said above, commercial firms are forced by financial regulators to publish their information on the characteristics of the fields they have explored or for which they have a licence to produce. In some other countries, however, in particular those where the natural resources are produced by state-owned companies, this regulation is less developed.

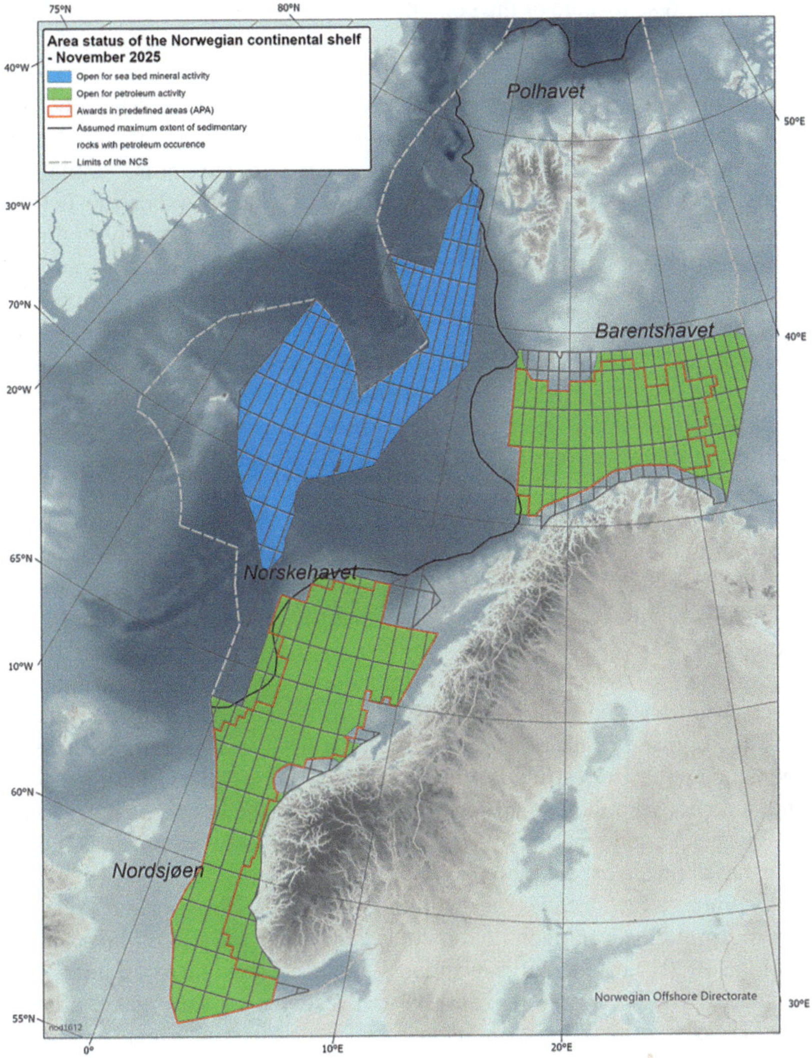

Fig. 4.3 Online information provided by Norwegian government on oil and gas resources and activities by the upstream industry (Source: https://www.norskpetroleum.no/en/interactive-map-quick-downloads/interactive-map/ retrieved on 10 November 2025)

4.3.3 Policy Measures to Address Negative Externalities Related to Depletion

The depletion of a non-renewable resource suffers from a negative externality when economic agents do not fully acknowledge the impact of the depletion on other agents. This in particular refers to the consequence of current depletion on future availability. The latter is reflected by opportunity costs of current production, which is equal to the present value of the benefits which can be enjoyed later. Hence, these opportunity costs depend on the discount rate that is used to determine the present value of future benefits.

The discount rate that is used by private economic agents is determined by the costs of capital resulting from the interaction between agents on capital markets. These agents may underestimate the risks related to the future availability of resources, and may also have a higher time value of money[6]. When this is the case, the discount rate used by private agents is higher than the socially optimal rate, resulting in a too rapid depletion path. Determining the social discount rate is, however, not easy as follows from the fact that it is heavily debated in economic literature (see Box 3.1).

Governments have different policy options to address the overexploitation of non-renewable resources. One category of policy measures concerns making exploitation for private economic agents more expensive. Raising the costs of exploitation can be done through resource taxation which is directed at the marginal (most expensive) units, so not on the inframarginal profits,[7] as that would not change the optimal decisions of economic agents (see Sect. 4.3.6 for that kind of tax). Such a measure raises the marginal costs, which reduces the production level, as a new equilibrium will be found where marginal costs are equal to the marginal benefits. After all, utilisations with relatively low marginal benefits will not be served any more.

Another type of policy measure is directed at restricting the availability of resources which can be exploited. This can be done by limiting the number of licences or imposing restrictions on the use of a licence. An example of the latter was the Dutch policy to restrict the annual production from the Groningen gas field. The initial depletion policy regarding this field, one of the largest onshore gas fields on the European continent discovered around 1960, was to exploit it as quickly as possible, based on the expectation that nuclear energy would be the dominant source of energy within a few decades (see Mulder & Perey, 2018). As a consequence, the production from the Groningen field increased exponentially (see Fig. 4.4). The oil crises of the 1970s caused a large awareness about the relevance of natural gas and, hence, that it would be wise to conserve the reserves for later generations. This awareness was translated into a number of consecutive policy measures. A major element of this policy was the so-called small-fields policy. According to this policy, the incumbent operator of the gas system (called Gasunie), which was responsible for selling the gas from the Groningen gas field as well as the operation of the high-pressure gas-transport grid, was asked to give a preferential treatment to gas that was produced by operators of the so-called small fields, both onshore and offshore. These fields had relatively high production costs, and would not be produced

[6] By using a higher discount rate, the estimate of the present value of future production is lower. As a result, it is optimal to have a faster depletion rate than when the discount rate would be lower.

[7] The inframarginal profits refer to the profits on production units which do not have the highest marginal costs. When taxing such units does not make their costs rise above the costs of the marginal units, the optimal production decision of a firm is not affected.

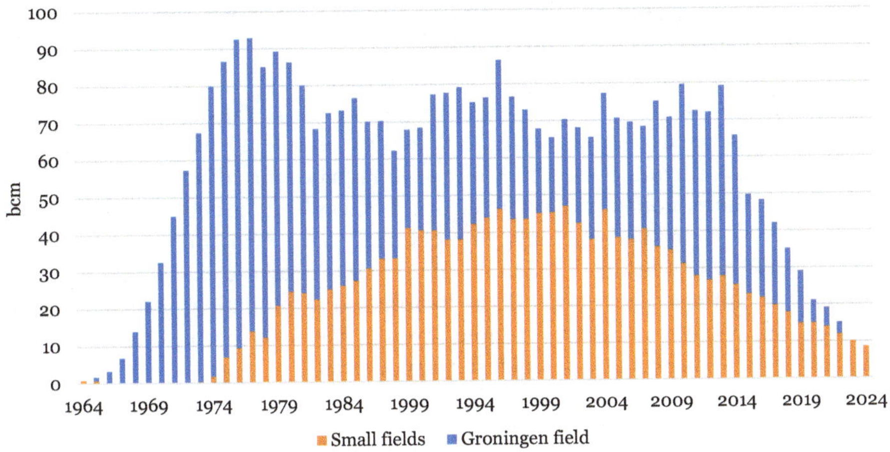

Fig. 4.4 Production of natural gas from the so-called small fields and the Groningen gas field, Netherlands, 1964–2024 (Source: TNO (2025))

without such a preferential treatment. After the introduction of this small-fields policy, the production from these fields increased, while the production from the huge Groningen gas field decreased and remained rather constant (on an annual basis) for several decades. From day to day and from season to season, however, the Groningen field showed a large variability as it was used as a so-called swing-supplier (enabled by its physical characteristics such as high pressure) providing flexibility to the gas system and market in Northwest Europe.

This process continued until the early 2000s, after which the production from the small fields declined because of a gradual depletion. In order to prevent a too intense exploitation of the Groningen gas field, the Dutch government introduced a cap on its production levels. Initially, the government introduced a cap on the Groningen gas production, which was equal to 80 bcm per year minus the production from the small fields. Around 2005, it imposed a cap on the average production level from the Groningen field over a period of 10 years.[8] After a number of earthquakes in the Groningen region, followed by fierce societal debates, this production cap was even further reduced to end in a complete ending of the Groningen gas production in 2023. Although the Groningen gas field still possessed about 400 bcm of gas (with a commercial value, using conservative values for costs and gas prices, of about 40 billion euros),[9] the Dutch government believed that the damages of the ongoing earthquakes made the exploitation of the Groningen gas field societally and politically unacceptable.

---

[8] The production cap was 425 bcm over a period of 10 years.

[9] The production costs of the Groningen gas field were about 0.10 euro/m^3, and assuming a gas price of 0.25 euro/m^3, an annual production level of 40 bcm, and a discount rate of 7%, the Net Present Value of the net revenues are 44 billion euros.

4.3.4 Policy Measures Directed at Lack of Coordination in Depleting a Resource Base

Because of the technical characteristics of a resource base, the depletion pace must be carefully managed to prevent that it deteriorates too quickly, which makes further depletion more difficult. Such a lack of coordination occurred, for instance, in the early days of the exploitation of oil fields in Texas, USA, at the end of the nineteenth century. Many individuals, mainly farmers, started to drill for oil in the same resource base, which resulted in a rapid decline of the reserve levels (see Fig. 4.5). In order to mitigate the effect of uncoordinated exploitation, management is required; this could be done, for example, through licensing schemes. Through such schemes, a state can allocate the rights for exploitation to a limited number of agents.

4.3.5 Policy Measures Directed at Lack of Competition in Depletion

The depletion of a natural resource can also deviate from the societally optimal depletion path if economic agents are able to make use of market power. When economic agents having market power reduce the production compared to the socially optimal level, which is called physical withholding, they may be able to

Fig. 4.5 Rigs on oil fields at Sour Lake #45 in Texas, USA, around 1900 (Source: East Texas photograph collection, di_01294, The Dolph Briscoe Center for American History, The University of Texas at Austin)

raise the market price and, hence, increase their profits. A consequence of this is that the natural resources are underexploited compared to a situation of perfect competition in which there would be more production and consumption and less conservation of fossil resources for the future. Because of this effect, it is also said that the 'monopolist is the environmentalist's friend' (Perman et al., 1999).

As the presence of market power (partly) neutralises the effects of information problems and negative externalities on the depletion path, one may believe that governments should facilitate the absence of competition in the exploitation of natural resources in order to overcome the other problems. Although this may be an effective policy to reduce the risk of a too rapid exploitation, it is not an efficient approach, as introducing targeted measures to address the other market failures is paired with less adverse effects. After all, having a monopoly has a number of downsides. First of all, the higher prices for the commodity which the monopolist realises implies a transfer of welfare from consumers to the monopolist. Even when the monopolist is a state-owned company, this does not guarantee that profits will be used for societal objectives. Therefore, fossil-fuel systems, like the gas system, have been liberalised in many regions, such as in Europe (see Box 4.4).

Box 4.4 Introduction of Competition in the European Gas System

Until the early 2000s, the supply side of European gas systems was dominated by mainly national incumbents, which were responsible for the operation of the transportation, distribution grid and the sales of gas. The trade in gas mainly took place through bilateral contracts between these suppliers and gas users. These contracts did not give much freedom to the users because of take-or-pay conditions, which implied that users needed to pay for the contracted gas, regardless of using it or not. In addition, the prices in these contracts did not result from the interaction of demand and supply, but were set by the suppliers maximising their profits. For instance, the gas from the Netherlands, which was one of the major gas-producing countries in Europe, was sold on the basis of the so-called market-value principle. This principle entailed that the gas price was set just below the level of alternatives for the various types of users, such as fuel oil for residential households. Because of this price-setting rule, the end-users had no economic incentive to shift to alternatives, while the profits of the supplier were maximised. To strengthen the position of the suppliers, users were not able to resell their contracted gas.

Initiated by the European Commission, the European gas systems have been liberalised by enabling users to choose alternative suppliers and resell their contracted gas on marketplaces. In addition, the incumbent gas suppliers were forced to unbundle the operation of the transportation and distribution grids from any commercial activities. Although the incumbent players tried to resist this transformation of the gas system into a competitive gas market, the latter now already exists for many years, as was discussed in Chap. 2. The liberalisation and introduction of competition promoted the exploitation of gas resources since new entrants now can easily access the market to sell their gas, without facing the competitive disadvantage towards the incumbent players.

Another reason for the liberalisation of the gas (and electricity) markets was that monopolists have fewer incentives to innovate and reduce the costs of exploitation than firms operating in a competitive environment. Innovation does require effort and expenditures by the monopolist, while it does not necessarily result in more revenues. If a monopolist develops a new type of product which is more appreciated by its customers, the sales of the new product may just replace the sales of the old product. This effect is called the replacement or Arrow effect of a monopoly on innovation.

Moreover, a firm that has a monopoly on the exploitation of a natural resource may also have the ability to influence the political process. This is in particular the case when the natural resource itself or the realised revenues are important for a society and government. As a result, the government may be sensitive to the wishes of the monopolist. In such circumstances, it is also likely that the private interest of the monopolist of maximising its profits is directly in line with the government's interest of maximising the revenues from the monopolistic firm. Because of these interdependences, this may result in additional suboptimal governmental decisions, which is another example of government policies which result in a lower welfare (for more on this issue see Box 4.1).

Hence, even when the actual production is above the socially optimal path, because of problems related to a lack of available information or the presence of negative externalities, it makes more sense to foster competition in the depletion than to use lack of competition as an indirect tool to slow down the exploitation.

4.3.6 Implementing Efficient Distributional Policy Measures

As natural resources can be perceived as gifts from nature, it is generally considered fair that the net revenues resulting from the exploitation should be enjoyed by society as a whole and not only by particular stakeholders. If the latter is the case, these stakeholders would receive so-called windfall profits, which are profits which are not due to their efforts or risk-taking activities, but to external circumstances. According to ethical principles, this is not fair because these stakeholders do not deserve the (extra) revenues. Insofar stakeholders, such as upstream energy companies, are making costs to explore new resources and develop and produce them, an appropriate reward is not only fair, but also efficient. After all, without the prospect of such a reward, commercial parties are not prepared to make any effort in this business (see Martén et al., 2014).

The challenge, therefore, for governments is to develop mechanisms that, on the one hand, incentivise economic agents to become active in the depletion of the natural resources of a country, while, on the other hand, the net revenues are shared with the public society (i.e. the state). Generally, there are three options to deal with this issue: designing smart tax systems, auctioning licences for exploration and exploitation, and public ownership.

Through a resource tax, governments can force commercial agents to transfer a part of their net revenues to the state. A crucial element here refers to the determination of the net revenues, which are defined as the gross revenues minus the costs for the stakeholder to explore, develop and produce resources. When these costs not only include the operational costs, but also the costs of capital, the transfer of profits to the government is not at the expense of the compensation for the costs of equity and costs of debt.[10] As a result, commercial stakeholders may have an incentive to become active in the upstream business in a particular country, while the society does receive a share in the net revenues of the natural resource. The level of this share can be part of profit-sharing agreements between a government and commercial parties. In practice, however, developing a fair tax scheme that does not distort incentives for commercial parties appears to be complicated, as can be seen from the experience in Norway, where the resource tax system seems to have a negative impact on investment incentives (Ahi et al., 2025).

Another option to align the incentives for commercial agents with a fair distribution of the net revenues is to make use of auctions of licences to operate in the upstream business. In this approach, commercial parties are asked to become active in the business in a country by submitting a bid on a license. In order to formulate such a bid, stakeholders will explore the business potential of a particular natural-resource area and based on that determine the amount they are willing to pay for the licence. When there are several firms (or consortia) participating in such auctions, i.e. when the auction is competitive, they will be forced to submit competitive bids. This means that their bids will be close to the maximum price they can afford to pay to the state for the licence while the project is at least break even. As a consequence, the state can also maximise its share in the net revenues coming from the exploitation of the natural resource, while the commercial firms still have an incentive to become active in this business. In order to prevent the winners curse, i.e. that the winning bid is based on a too optimistic view of the profitability of a field, the government that organises the auction can base the fee for the licence on, for instance, the second-best bid.

Instead of using financial instruments to align the incentives for exploitation with a fair distribution of the net resources, a government can also choose to make use of state-owned enterprises to conduct the activities. This approach enables the government to decide which part of the revenues should be transferred to the public budget and which part can be used to compensate for the costs of the exploitation. Although this seems a straightforward approach to make sure that the government (and society) benefits from the exploitation of a natural resource, the downside is that state-owned companies have fewer incentives to operate efficiently. In order to address this risk, the state-owned company can make use of commercial parties as subcontractors, giving them incentives to operate as efficiently as possible.

---

[10] Note that the commercial agents generally have to pay corporate-income tax on their profits,

4.3.7 Conclusion

The exploration, development and production of natural resources is one of the key activities in energy systems. Economic agents do have incentives to be(come) active in these activities, but without any government intervention they may not operate at the societally optimal level. This is due to a number of market failures, related to information asymmetry, market power, negative externalities and unequal distribution of resource rents. In order to address these market failures, governments can intervene in energy systems, making use of various types of energy-transition measures. These measures boil down to fostering the distribution of information regarding the characteristics of natural resources, promoting competition in the upstream business, internalising the externality of a too rapid depletion through financial or regulatory measures, and redistributing the resource rents through financial measures or public ownership.

4.4 Policy Measures to Reduce Import Dependence

4.4.1 Introduction: Summarising the Market Failures

Because of international differences in the availability of natural resources, production circumstances as well as energy needs of industries and preferences of consumers, energy carriers are internationally traded. This international trade, in principle, results in welfare benefits for all participating countries. After all, the overall welfare in all countries increases as the importing countries realise higher consumption levels at lower prices, while the exporting countries realise higher production levels at higher prices, compared to the situation without international trade. However, there are always distributional effects within each of the countries. In importing countries, there may be a loss of welfare for the domestic producers, as the international competition can result in both lower production volumes and lower prices for them. The consumers in this country, however, can consume more at lower prices. The opposite is the case in the exporting countries, where consumers have to pay higher prices and, as a result, will consume less. Although such distributional effects of international trade cannot be considered market failures, the consequences can prompt governments to mitigate them.

International trade may also result in import and export dependencies for some countries. This means that some countries (i.e. net-importing countries) depend on imports to meet their total domestic demand, while other countries (net-exporting countries) need the exports as offtake for the domestic production. This dependence may create risks related to the reliability of supply in case of the net-importing countries or risks related to the offtake in case of the net-exporting countries. These risks may lead to uncertainty about the future availability, use and prices of commodities. As long as these risks are reflected in price movements, market participants can respond to them, and one can say that the markets internalise the underlying risks. Assessing risks and taking appropriate measures to mitigate them belong to the normal activities of market parties, and, hence, the uncertainty related to future availability and prices cannot be considered a market failure.

Some risks, however, may not be fully perceived by market parties and, as a result, are not incorporated in market outcomes. These risks may relate to geopolitical events. There is some evidence that markets indeed do not fully deal with such risks, which can be considered a market failure. This particularly refers to the impact of import on international (geopolitical) relationships. In order to address this market failure, governments may want to intervene to reduce the dependence on supply from other countries. This intervention can be accomplished by promoting domestic production, reducing domestic consumption, making import less attractive for economic agents or raising the resilience of an economy against supply shocks.

4.4.2 Promoting Domestic Production

At first glance, the most obvious measure to reduce import dependence is to promote domestic production. After all, by raising the domestic production in a country, there is less need to import a commodity. Promoting domestic production can, for instance, be achieved by providing domestic producers with financial support. This support may improve their international competitiveness when it is used to lower the production costs or increase the quality of the products.

In the second instance, however, this policy may be less obvious as one has to first analyse what makes domestic production less competitive in comparison to foreign suppliers. There can be various factors contributing to this. A country may not have the natural endowments to supply a particular commodity, for instance, in the case of natural gas or oil resources. As we have seen in Chap. 2, the global distribution of these resources is rather unequal. If economic agents in a country lacking such endowments want to use that commodity, it has to be imported, which automatically results in an import dependence. It could also be the case that the economic agents in a country prefer the quality of the products supplied by foreign agents over the domestically produced ones. For most energy carriers, there exist various types of qualities as they are products of nature. This holds for coal, oil and gas. For the production of steel, for instance, another type of coal is needed than for the generation of electricity. This heterogeneity in product qualities is a key factor behind international trade. Both factors imply that it may not always be possible to fully replace import by domestically produced products without any adverse effect on the domestic supply.

When a product of the preferred quality can be produced domestically, its promotion does not necessarily reduce import dependence. Reducing the costs of domestic production, for instance, by providing investment or production subsidies, may raise the total supply to the market and, hence, result in lower commodity prices which encourages economic agents to consume more. At the end of the day, the import dependence may not be changed when the higher domestic production is translated into higher domestic consumption. In addition, production subsidies may not result in higher domestic production when constraints exist. In particular in the short term, production extension has a relatively high likelihood of being hindered by limits on the available production capacity. For instance, power plants have a limited generation capacity and when they are fully utilised, the power producers are not able to further expand their production as they first have to invest in expansion of their generation capacity.

When domestic production is not hindered by capacity constraints, however, it may be possible to achieve a higher market share with the use of received subsidies, at the expense of lower imports. Although being effective in reducing the import dependence, this policy may come at a high cost. These costs follow from the difference in the international (import) commodity prices and the domestic production costs. As discussed in Box 4.5, the differences in production circumstances of energy can be quite large.

Box 4.5 International Differences in Production Costs of Energy Carriers

For all energy carriers, it holds that the production costs vary strongly among regions. The average costs of producing oil are the lowest in Saudi Arabia and other countries in the Middle East, where oil can be supplied to the international oil market at costs below ten dollars per barrel. In other countries, both belonging to OPEC, like Nigeria and Venezuela, and non-OPEC countries like the USA and Canada, the average production costs are twice to five times higher.

Also for natural gas, large differences in production costs exist, with relatively low production costs in the shale-gas resources in the USA and the conventional gas fields in the Middle East. In other regions, the costs can be significantly higher. These differences in costs are related to the natural circumstances of the resources.

The costs of producing electricity also show regional differences, which are related to regional differences in fuel prices and natural circumstances. The costs of producing electricity with wind turbines or solar panels are very much related to the utilisation rate of the installation, which depends on the climatological circumstances. The capacity factor of solar panels in Germany, for instance, is about 10%, while this factor is about 25% in Chile. For wind turbines, the capacity factor differs quite a lot between onshore and offshore locations. On the latter type of location, the capacity factor can be close to 50%, while the capacity factor of onshore locations can be 25% or even lower.

In competitive markets with sufficient production capacity, the production costs of the most competitive producers determine the international market price.[11] As a

[11] During periods of tight market circumstances, when all production capacity is fully utilised, the market prices are determined by the willingness-to-pay of the marginal buyers (see Sect. 2.6).

result, these prices can be significantly lower than the domestic production costs, as these only depend on the domestic circumstances. If the domestic costs are artificially lowered through subsidies, consumers pay similar or even lower prices than for imported products, but the societal costs consist of the subsidies needed to overcome the difference between domestic and foreign production costs.

Hence, promoting domestic production can be an expensive policy measure to address the issue of import dependence. These high costs result from the fact that production circumstances and technologies can be quite different internationally, which makes international trade an attractive option. Restricting market parties to making use of this option comes, therefore, at a high price. From a welfare-economic point of view, these costs should be compared to the societal benefits of reducing the import dependence. In order to determine to what extent these benefits exceed the costs of the policy measures, a social cost-benefit analysis should be conducted (see Box 4.6).

Box 4.6 Social Cost-Benefit Analysis to Assess Policy Measures from a Societal Perspective

In order to determine whether a particular policy measure is beneficial for society, one can conduct a so-called social cost-benefit analysis (SCBA). In this type of analysis, all costs and benefits caused by the given policy measure are taken into account. In principle, it does not matter whether the costs and benefits are in monetary terms. Expressing all effects into monetary units makes it easier to compare all effects and determine the overall (net) effect, but theoretically the unit of measurement of the separate effects is not relevant. The crucial point of a SCBA is that it departs from the economic concept of welfare, which is related to the concept of utility that economic agents derive from particular types of uses of scarce commodities. If economic agents, for instance, attach value to being less dependent on energy imports from other countries, reducing import dependence results in a benefit to them. When the size of this value cannot be immediately measured through market prices, this means one should try to determine a good estimate of this value. In economics, there are several estimation methods for this, such as the hedonic pricing method and conjoint-choice experiments (see Box 2.12).

Another essential component of an SBCA, is that it treats subsidies and taxes as internal monetary transfers, unless the subsidies are received from parties outside a country, such as an international institution. These subsidies and taxes are paid and received within a country (or other region of analysis), and as a result, do not form net benefits or costs for that country or region.

In order to determine the (future) social cost and benefits of a policy measure, one needs to determine in which (economic) environment the policy measure will be implemented. Hence, one has to formulate scenarios regarding future economic conditions, like international energy prices, interest rates and the degree of international exchange of commodities. Against the

(continued)

Box 4.6 (continued)

background of such scenarios, one can estimate how a particular measure, such as a tax on gas consumption, may affect the dependence of a country on, for instance, natural gas.

Since both the costs and the benefits of the policy measure typically extend to a number of years, one has to discount the future values, using an appropriate discount rate (see Box 3.1 on the social discount rate).

Finally, it is important to realise that the objective of conducting a SBCA is not only to determine the overall welfare effect, but also to receive information on the distributional effects. Generally, policy measures affect economic agents in different ways: some will benefit, others will lose. For a proper societal debate on both the efficiency and fairness of policy measures, the distributional effects are just as important as the aggregated welfare effect.

4.4.3 Reducing Domestic Consumption

As fostering domestic production of a commodity may not be really effective, while it can also be rather expensive, governments may consider another approach to reduce import dependence, such as reducing domestic consumption of that commodity. When a government wants economic agents to consume less natural gas, for instance, it can make this energy carrier more expensive by imposing an end-user tax. Such a policy measure does not directly reduce the welfare of a country, as it in principle only shifts income from a particular group of economic agents, in this case consumers of natural gas, to the government. Hence, such a tax only results in the redistribution of welfare, not a reduction of welfare. The societal costs of introducing a tax may, however, include the transaction costs for the organisation of the tax, but these can be fairly small when the tax scheme is efficiently designed. There is another cost caused by taxation, which results from the impact of the choices economic agents make. As a result of an end-user tax, (some) consumers will make a different choice. In the case of, for instance, a tax on natural gas, some economic agents may decide to replace natural gas by another energy carrier, such as heating oil or electricity, which would be more expensive without the tax measure. Such a substitution implies that in society, more costs are made for the same purpose, such as heating houses.

Another financial measure to make domestic consumption of a particular commodity less attractive for economic agents is making an alternative commodity cheaper, for instance, through providing subsidies to the producers of that commodity or by subsidising its consumption. Such a policy, however, is not necessarily effective in reducing import dependence, as can be seen from the example of subsidies for hydrogen (see Box 4.7).

Box 4.7 Subsidies for Hydrogen to Reduce Dependence on Import of Natural Gas

In order to reduce the dependence on the import of natural gas, a country can consider promoting the use of hydrogen as an alternative energy carrier. Hydrogen can be used for heating, in industrial processes as a feedstock, in transport as a fuel, as well as in electricity generation, which means that it has a similar wide array of potential applications as natural gas. Promoting the use of hydrogen, however, does not automatically imply that the dependence on natural gas or on imports will be reduced.

When a government provides subsidies for consumers to switch from natural gas to hydrogen, several effects may occur (Li et al., 2026). When a country does not have (sufficient) domestic hydrogen production, the hydrogen has to be imported, which may create another import dependence. To what extent that is an issue depends on the competitiveness of the international hydrogen market and the presence of alternative transport routes. Currently, this market is not really mature, which implies that there are not many options to choose from. Another factor is that the import of hydrogen may maintain dependence on gas, depending on how the hydrogen is produced in the exporting country. When that country mainly uses natural gas to make hydrogen through Steam Methane Reforming (SMR), stimulating domestic hydrogen demand does not really help to reduce the import of natural gas. After all, in SMR, natural-gas molecules, which include methane (CH_4), are needed to produce hydrogen. This latter aspect is also relevant when a country does have sufficient domestic SMR capacity. Replacing natural-gas demand by hydrogen demand does not necessarily reduce the dependence on natural gas, but, on the contrary, raises that dependence. This is due to the energy losses in the SMR processes, which implies that more natural gas is needed to produce the same amount (in energy terms) of hydrogen.

Hence, in order to reduce the dependence on natural gas, hydrogen needs to be produced through electrolysis. In this process, water molecules (H_2O) are split into hydrogen (H_2) and oxygen (O_2) molecules through the use of electricity. Although natural gas is not directly involved in this process, it may play a role in the generation of electricity. When an electricity system has limited amounts of renewable-generation capacity, an increase in the demand for electricity, resulting from the promotion of hydrogen demand, may result in a higher gas demand from gas-fired power plants. This implies that the promotion of hydrogen to reduce a dependence on the import of natural gas only makes sense when the share of renewable generation within the electricity system also increases. Only then can the hydrogen produced through electrolysis be called renewable hydrogen.

To make things even more complicated: raising the domestic renewable-electricity capacity also means that more wind turbines and solar panels have to be installed, while the electricity grid has to be expanded as well. For all these investments, use has to be made of other commodities, such as copper and silver, which can also be scarce, potentially resulting in a less secure supply (see Box 4.3).

The theoretical assumption used here is that economic agents use a commodity up to the point where the marginal benefits of the use are equal to the marginal costs. When the marginal costs increase, for instance, because of the tax, consumers with relatively low marginal benefits will not consume the commodity any more, which results in less consumption (and, hence, a loss of consumer surplus) or the use of another more expensive alternative. The reduction in the consumption of the taxed commodity automatically results in less import and a lower import dependence. In principle, the benefits of this decreased import dependence should be compared to the increased societal costs. Such a comparison of the societal costs and societal benefits of a particular policy measure can be done, again, through the use of the social cost-benefit analysis (see Box 4.6).

When the societal benefits of introducing a tax to reduce import dependence exceed the societal costs, it makes sense to continue exploring the design of the tax. One of the potential design issues refers to the tariff level. How high should it be? As the tax is meant to address the negative externality of import dependence, the tariff should be related to the value of that externality. If the tax tariff is below that value, there consequently remains a societally suboptimal import of the commodity. On the other hand, when the tariff exceeds that value, the costs of the reduction in the consumption are higher than the benefits of a reduced import dependence. Although this theoretical approach for determining the optimal tax design is quite straightforward, the practical application is a lot more difficult as the value of the externality is difficult to estimate. After all, the underlying challenge is to determine the damage for a country if it becomes more dependent on the import of a specific commodity. In the process of determining the tax level, one also needs to control for the fact that the risk of geopolitical incidents may already partly be internalised in current market prices. This means that market prices have already changed to some extent, calling for less correction to control for the externality. In order to determine to what extent this is the case, one can use empirical evidence on the relationship between import dependence and the occurrence of geopolitical incidents with macroeconomic adverse effects. However, no one knows to what extent the historical evidence is representative for the future, as was discussed in Sect. 3.4.

4.4.4 Making Imports less Attractive

Instead of subsidising domestic production of a commodity or subsidising the consumption of alternative commodities, governments could also make imports more expensive through import tariffs to encourage the competitive position of domestic producers. This policy does not have adverse (rebound) effects on consumption as occur in the case of production subsidies, since a tax on import results in higher consumer prices which stimulates consumers to consume less. Imposing import tariffs raises the costs for domestic users which, depending on the price elasticity of demand, reduces consumption levels to a larger or smaller extent.

The increase in price levels is also affected by the difference in (marginal) production costs between the foreign and domestic producers. When this difference is smaller than the import tariffs, the domestic producers may become price-setters, as the product prices of domestic producers are lower than the product prices including import tariffs of foreign suppliers.[12] Hence, the impact of import tariffs on consumption prices is restricted by the difference in production costs of domestic versus foreign suppliers. When, however, a product is not domestically produced, the increase in the product prices is determined by the foreign (or international) product prices plus the degree by which suppliers include the import tariff in their product prices. Depending on the intensity of international competition and the price elasticity of demand, the suppliers (both exporting and importing companies) may be able and willing to reduce their product prices at the expense of a smaller margin. When foreign suppliers reduce their product prices, the impact of import tariffs is reduced. All these mechanisms show that imposing a tariff on import may not be so effective to reduce the import of a particular commodity.

A more effective policy to reduce import dependence may be the introduction of a cap or ban on the import of particular types of products. Such a measure can be used to incentivise domestic producers to look for alternative inputs in their production processes. If a government, for instance, limits the import of natural gas, some users of this energy carrier may decide to use alternative energy carriers or technologies. In the electricity industry, a cap on the available natural gas may subject the generation of electricity to a constraint, as some gas-fired power plants may not be able to generate electricity anymore. This could result in more scarce prices in the electricity market, which triggers investments in other types of generation, such as renewable sources. In the longer term, these responses by producers will mitigate the scarcity, in turn reducing the electricity prices again. In the short term, however, other types of responses may occur, for example, the higher electricity prices might encourage more efficient use of electricity. These responses by energy users also happen directly as the higher gas prices trigger more efficient use of gas in the short term, as well as investments in alternatives for gas, such as biogas, in the longer term. Hence, introducing regulatory constraints on the availability of imports of particular commodities may be an effective measure to reduce the volume of its imports.

Such regulatory constraints on the import of a particular commodity seem to be more effective in reducing import dependence than the above-discussed financial policy measures, as they are directly focused on the import quantities. A crucial condition for such regulatory constraints is, of course, the presence of an effective regulatory oversight to prevent market parties from finding other (illegal) routes to import the commodity, which would make the regulatory rule ineffective. This risk exists in particular for those commodities that can be exported through various types of transport modes, such as natural gas that can be transported as LNG by vessels and in gaseous form through pipelines. This occurred during the energy crisis in Europe after the Russian invasion of Ukraine, when the import of Russian gas was significantly reduced and rather quickly partly replaced by higher imports of LNG, which was

---

[12] If such a situation occurs, the suppliers (both exporting and importing companies) may increase their product prices less than the import tariffs, which means they pay a part of these tariffs themselves, in order to protect their competitive position.

facilitated by the fast development of LNG infrastructures in a number of countries (see Sect. 3.4.2). For a commodity where the transport is restricted to a physical infrastructure, such as electricity, regulatory constraints can be more effectively implemented. If a country wants to limit the import of electricity, the grid operator can easily limit the technical availability of the cross-border transport capacity, although that may make maintaining system reliability more challenging.

4.4.5 Raising the Resilience of an Economy

A quite different approach to make a country less vulnerable to geopolitical risks is to increase the resilience of the economy. This means that the ability of an economy to respond to supply shocks is increased. This can be achieved with several types of measures. One of these measures is promoting the diversification of import. Instead of reducing the import, a government can also facilitate the import from alternative exporting countries. After all, a more diversified import portfolio implies that an importing country is less vulnerable to a supply shock in one of the exporting countries. This approach is, for instance, applied by countries that want to foster the import of hydrogen by concluding import contracts with a number of countries in various global regions.

The resilience of a country can also be fostered by increasing the ability of economic agents to respond to changing market situations. When economic agents have access to alternative energy carriers and alternative infrastructures, they are less vulnerable to shocks related to one type of energy carrier and infrastructure. Next to having the ability to respond to changing market circumstances, economic agents should also have the incentive to do so. In this respect, it also helps when energy contracts of residential consumers are related to recent developments in wholesale markets, as that gives them incentives to adapt the levels and profiles of their consumption. As a result, when electricity wholesale prices rise due to higher gas prices, residential consumers may not only change their consumption of gas, but also their use of electricity.

The resilience of economic agents to adverse effects in energy markets is also improved when they are less dependent on the use of energy. When consumers need less energy to heat their houses, for instance, they are less adversely affected when the prices of energy increase. Supporting households taking measures that improve the efficiency of their energy use, therefore, also raises the ability of an economy (and society) to deal with shocks in energy systems.

On a national scale, governments can further increase the resilience of the economy by promoting the development of cross-border infrastructures that facilitate the import from various countries. Of course, the abilities of a country to do so depend on its natural circumstances. A country that is geographically only connected to one other country, like Canada,[13] can only increase its resilience by facilitating imports from overseas or increasing domestic production facilities, while a country that

[13] Although Canada also shares a land border with Greenland on the Hans Island, which is a small island between Greenland and Canada that is divided by these two countries.

does not have any seaports as it is surrounded by other countries, like Austria, may also invest in storages to improve its resilience against negative shocks in particular supply routes (see Box 4.8). Hence, depending on its natural circumstances, countries have different options to increase the resilience of its economies.

Box 4.8 Holding Energy Stocks in Order to Reduce Vulnerability to Supply Shocks

Since the oil crises of the 1970s, many countries invest in strategic oil stocks. Members of the International Energy Agency (IEA) have as policy that they have oil in stock for at least 90 days of net oil imports. For natural gas, such an international policy does not (yet) exist, but several countries do have national policies for strategic gas reserves. One of these countries is Austria that was previously heavily dependent on the import of gas from Russia. This country has significantly more gas in storage than many other countries, which resulted from the Austrian policy to reduce the risk of the high dependence on Russian gas imports. Figure 4.6 shows that the storage levels in Germany and Italy, but in particular the United Kingdom are much lower, which is related to the fact that these countries have more options to secure their gas supply through various import channels. During the 2022 gas crisis, however, the gas storage facilities were not sufficient to cope with the strong reduction in gas imports from Russia.

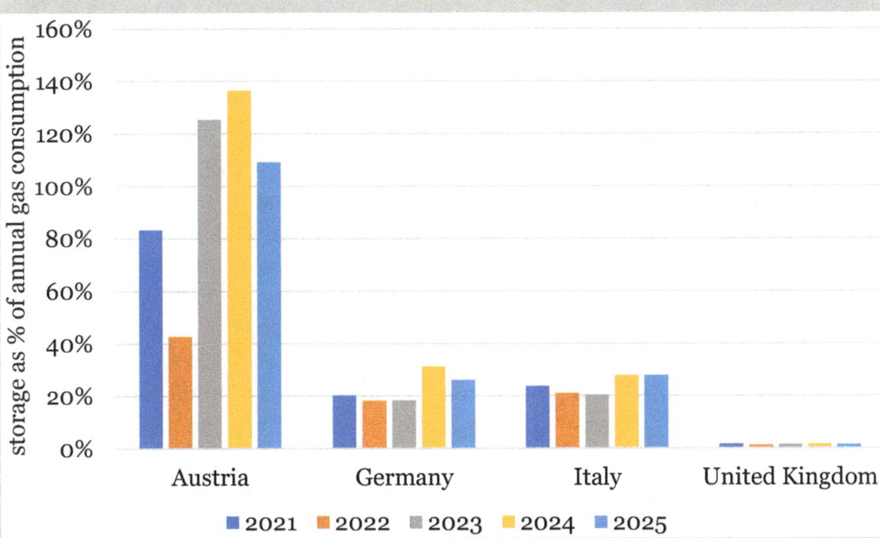

Fig. 4.6 Storage levels per 1 January as percentage of annual gas consumption, in a number of European countries, 2021–2025 (Sources: gas consumption: Energy Institute Statistical Review of World Energy 2026, https://www.energyinst.org/statistical-review/home; gas in storage: ENTSOG Transparency Platform https://gasdashboard.entsog.eu/)

4.4.6 Conclusions

Regional differences in production circumstances, industrial structure as well as consumer preferences result in the international exchange of commodities, which automatically leads to import dependencies. Risks related to such dependencies are to some extent reflected in the levels and volatility of future prices. As such, these risks are internalised by markets and, therefore, form no (economic) reason for government intervention. Some risks related to import dependence are, however, not fully captured by market forces, as market parties may not be able to see and evaluate them properly. This in particular refers to geopolitical risks.

In order to address these risks, governments can take several types of policy measures. In this chapter, we have discussed four of them. Subsidising domestic production seems to be the least effective, while imposing regulatory constraints on imports seems to be the most effective, as this measure directly intervenes in the import volume. More efficient policy measures facilitate the resilience of an economy, for instance, by promoting the diversification of import routes and enabling economic agents to flexibly respond to supply shocks.

4.5 Policy Measures to Mitigate High Prices

4.5.1 Introduction: Summarising the Market Failures

When energy carriers are traded on (international) markets, the prices result from market conditions. These market conditions can be divided into the costs of supply, the tightness of a market (i.e. the magnitude of supply in relation to the magnitude of demand), and the intensity of competition. When (marginal) production costs of price-setting technologies increase, this raises market prices. Moreover, when the magnitude of supply is not sufficient to meet the magnitude of demand, i.e. when the market is tight and the commodity is scarce in the common-sense understanding of this term, the market prices need to rise in order to realise a market equilibrium. Finally, when there is not much competition among suppliers, they may be able to behave strategically and raise market prices. In all these circumstances, prices for energy carriers can be relatively high for a shorter or longer period.

In the case of abuse of market power, high prices may result from a fundamental shortcoming in the allocation process, which can be a reason for government intervention. This type of government intervention includes merger control and antitrust measures, as was discussed in Sect. 4.2. In the other cases, i.e. high production costs or tightness of supply, the high prices can be needed to clear the markets in an efficient way. Despite the lack of a fundamental shortcoming in the market processes, high prices can be a reason for government intervention. This holds in particular for energy commodities, as energy is seen as essential for many activities of economic agents, and therefore governments may want to protect them against too high prices, not to correct a market failure, but because of concerns with affordability of energy. Such protection can, for instance, be achieved by intervening in the price-formation process, either by directly influencing the prices economic agents have to pay, or indirectly through changing the tightness in markets. Another option to protect users is by supporting them in dealing with the consequences of high prices.

4.5.2 Direct Intervention in Price-Formation Processes in Wholesale Markets

When energy prices are perceived as too high, politicians may want to intervene in the price-formation process to reduce them. This can, for instance, be done by imposing a cap on the market price or the price that is charged to residential consumers. The latter happened in various European countries during the 2022/2023 gas crisis (see Sect. 2.5). In that period, the European gas prices reached extremely high levels, resulting from the Russian invasion of Ukraine and the subsequent regulatory measures taken by the European Commission and EU member states. The exceptionally high gas prices in the international wholesale market raised the end-user prices of gas and, indirectly, electricity for both industrial and residential users. The surge in electricity prices was due to the strong increase in the costs of gas-fired power plants.

In this respect, it makes sense to distinguish between two types of price increases: one through higher costs and the other through scarcity. This is illustrated by Fig. 4.7. In the left-side panel, the marginal costs of production technology B are increased and since this technology is price-setting, also the equilibrium price increases. In the right-side panel, the marginal costs of both technologies remain the same, but now the available capacity of technology A is reduced, shifting the supply curve to the left. That results in a very tight market situation in which the market can only be cleared when the equilibrium price increases significantly above the marginal costs of technology B. Note that in both cases, the change in equilibrium volumes depends on the price elasticity of the demand.

The increase in the gas price during the energy crises in 2022 and 2026 resulted from a sudden increase in the scarcity in the gas market. This increase in scarcity in 2022 resulted from two mechanisms: on the one hand, a sharp decline in the gas supply from Russia, the major supplier of gas to Europe, and on the other hand, an increase in the European demand for gas because of the EU policy to increase the filling rate of the gas storage facilities during the summer period. Both factors contributed to the increase in scarcity in the gas market, and as a result a surge in gas prices was needed to find a new balance in the gas market. The economic role of these high gas prices was to incentivise the demand side of the market to buy and consume less, also to incentivise suppliers to bring LNG from other regions to the region with high gas prices, in this case Europe.

The surge in electricity prices did not result from scarcity of electricity generation, but from higher generation costs of the marginal, price-setting units. During most of the time in the 2022 crisis, in several European electricity markets, gas-fired power plants were the marginal units needed to clear the markets and, as a result, their marginal costs strongly influenced the electricity prices. A consequence of this

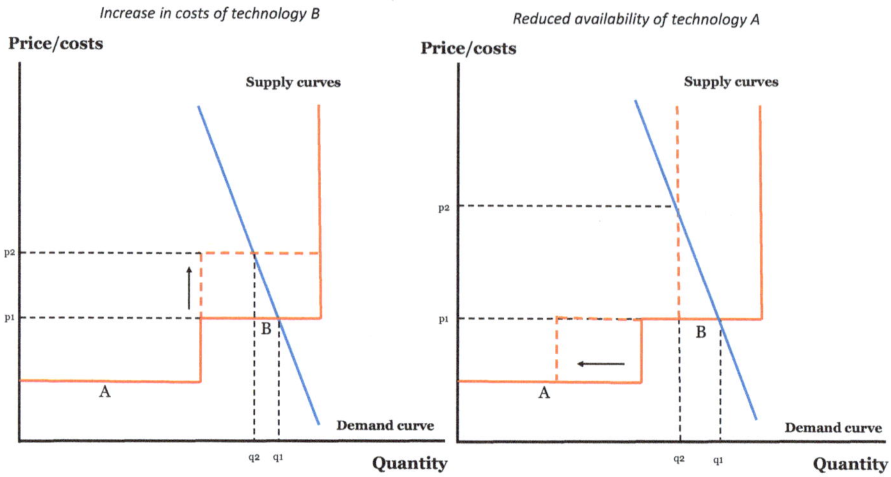

Fig. 4.7 Two types of causes of high prices: cost increase and scarcity

mechanism is that inframarginal units (technology A in Fig. 4.7) realised much higher profits as the equilibrium price increased, while the marginal costs of nuclear and renewable units remained the same.

Because of these exceptionally high profits resulting from the market-clearing mechanism, there were policy proposals to decouple the electricity price from the gas price as if the electricity price was linked to the gas price through regulation (European Parliament, 2023). These proposals, however, did not make much sense as the coupling of electricity prices and gas prices was not the result of regulation, but resulted from the fundamental economic principle that market prices are set by the last unit needed for supply. It is possible to change the rules of price setting, but this does not necessarily result in lower consumer prices. After all, in the current price-setting method in European electricity markets, all market parties know the market price is based on the marginal unit which enables them to make so-called inframarginal profits if their marginal costs (i.e. bid price in the power market) are below the marginal costs of the price-setting unit. These inframarginal profits, which can also be called operational profits, can be used as compensation for the fixed costs, i.e. the costs of capital and depreciation of the assets. The outlook of making such profits determines to what extent firms have an incentive to invest in new generation capacity (see Sect. 2.5.3).

If this market-clearing scheme, which is also called peak-load pricing, is changed into a scheme in which all units are paid according to their bidding price,[14] market parties will raise their prices. Under such a scheme, their bidding prices will no longer be based on their marginal costs, but their total costs, as they also need to have compensation for their investment costs.

[14]The current market-clearing scheme in European electricity markets is called an pay-as-clear scheme, while an alternative scheme would be a pay-as-bid scheme.

Another option that is often mentioned to make electricity prices less sensitive to the prices of natural gas is promoting the share of renewables. If gas-fired power plants are less often the price-setting technology, the electricity price will be less affected by the level and volatility of the natural-gas price. As the marginal costs of renewable technologies like wind turbines and solar panels are close to zero and not volatile, increases in the electricity prices due to surging fuel prices (as shown by the left-side panel of Fig. 4.7) become less likely. However, price volatility due to tightness of the market may become more frequent, since the available production capacity of wind turbines and solar panels is more heavily determined by exogenous (weather) circumstances. As we have seen in Sect. 3.5, also in countries dominated by renewables, electricity prices can be very volatile.

4.5.3 Direct Intervention in Price-Formation Processes in Retail Markets

Instead of changing the price-formation process, governments sometimes also implement measures which cap the prices for particular groups of consumers. During the recent energy crisis, some countries, like the Netherlands, the United Kingdom and Norway, capped retail energy prices in order to protect residential consumers. The Dutch measure was implemented as a governmental guarantee to retailers that the excess in the retail price above a certain threshold would be paid by the government. Hence, this measure did not really intervene in the price-formation mechanism, as retailers could ask a price related to their costs, in particular the wholesale-market prices and the competitive pressure in the retail market, knowing that a part of their invoices would be paid by the government in case a certain threshold was passed. This measure was very effective in protecting consumers against any increase in their prices above the cap during the period of the policy measure.

Capping energy prices for particular groups also has some downsides. First of all, by capping retail prices, consumers face fewer incentives to adapt their energy consumption. Although during the recent energy crisis, many consumers reduced their use of gas and electricity in response to the increase in energy prices, this response could have been even larger if the price cap had not been introduced. The social costs of such responses, including poor households that cannot afford to heat their houses at all, can be seen as too high, and, therefore, may warrant government intervention in the prices for residential consumers during a crisis. In addition, the price increase during the energy crisis of 2022 was so strong in such a short period of time that many consumers were not able to take effective measures to reduce their energy consumption, for instance, through insulating their houses.

A consequence of price-capping measures for particular groups of users, however, is also that other groups of energy users will be incentivised to reduce their consumption more significantly in order to compensate for the limited demand response by residential consumers. After all, when one group of consumers respond less to high prices, others have to respond stronger in order to clear the markets.

Instead of capping the commodity price for particular groups of users, governments can also lower other components of their energy bill to protect them against rising energy prices. In many countries, the energy bill of residential households consists of a relatively large share of taxes. Lowering such taxes for a period of time reduces the end-user price at the expense of the budget of the government, but the latter also occurs when the commodity prices are capped, as discussed above, or when subsidies are provided for, for instance, insulating houses.

A downside of both policy measures to lower the energy price for consumers, either through capping the commodity price or lowering the energy tax, is that in most countries the group of residential consumers is very heterogenous. Consumers having high incomes and/or well-insulated houses may be able to deal with very high energy prices, while other groups hardly have options to do so. Because of such heterogeneity, general measures which are meant to protect all consumers can be quite costly, while many of them do not really need such protection. Therefore, in principle, policy measures to deal with distributional consequences should be differentiated in order to make them more cost-effective. A more cost-effective support mechanism requires much less public-budget consequences than a general measure guaranteeing all households the same level of protection. As such, a differentiated approach is not really possible with measures that intervene in the prices consumers have to pay. It is more appropriate to compensate vulnerable households through dedicated income support, energy tax discounts or insulation subsidies.

4.5.4 Indirect Intervention in Price-Formation Processes

Instead of directly intervening in the process of price formation, governments could take measures that indirectly influence price levels. When high prices result from scarcity, it may help when governments have access to extra reserves, which can be used to put more products on the market. Such kind of strategic reserves already exists in the oil market for many decades (see Box 4.8). These reserves are meant to be used in case of extremely tight market circumstances with the intention to reduce the price of oil. As the oil market is a global market, such a measure can only be effective when many countries take joint action. This is also the case, as the strategic oil reserves are coordinated by the International Energy Agency. In the gas market, such reserves hardly existed until recently, but in response to the recent gas crisis, the European Commission requested from all Member States that their gas reserves reached a minimum filling degree by the start of the heating season.[15] In the electricity market, such reserves exist in the form of generation capacity that can be used to generate electricity in case all other available capacities are utilised (see Box 2.10).

[15] Such a minimum requirement for reserves levels is, however, not the same as implementing strategic reserves. The latter are only used in special circumstances when particular conditions are met, while the use of the former depends on regular commercial considerations by market parties.

Strategic reserves can be organised in several ways. One way is to impose an obligation on market parties to procure reserves. This can, for instance, be done through the introduction of reliability obligations in retail markets. In this approach, the government says to market parties, as retailers, that they have to conduct some tasks, and, hence, are made responsible for realising a particular amount of reserve capacity, such as through reliability contracts of retailers with producers of electricity. A more intermediate way, in terms of sharing responsibility between government and market parties, is that the government asks market parties to submit bids for the delivery of reserves. This involvement of market parties can be organised through auctioning procedures, in which a public agency offers to pay a price for making reserve capacity available. In this approach, the agency determines how much capacity is needed and makes use of competition among market players to organise this in an efficient way. In another approach, the governments take full responsibility for realising the strategic reserves, without the support of market parties. This can be done through the public procurement and operation of strategic reserves.

Through these kinds of measures, governments may make an energy system more resilient against (sudden) supply and demand shocks, with the purpose to prevent energy prices from becoming too high. The definition of 'too high' should result from societal (political) debate. From a purely economic perspective, high prices play a role, both in the short-term market clearing (as discussed above) and in long-term incentives for investments and, hence, high prices can be an efficient outcome of market processes. There can be a tension between the societal and economic perspective, as the implementation of a reserve mechanisms may negatively affect the incentives for market parties to invest. In Sect. 2.5.4, we have seen that the introduction of capacity-remuneration mechanisms in electricity systems may contribute to the reliability of supply, but that there are also risks in terms of crowding out commercial investments and too high costs for consumers resulting in windfall profits of suppliers.

4.5.5 Supporting Industrial Users in Dealing with High Energy Prices

Instead of intervening, directly or indirectly, in the price-formation process to reduce price levels, governments can also help economic agents in dealing with high energy prices, as was already briefly mentioned in Sect. 4.5.3. This can also be relevant for industrial users, in particular when they operate in international markets with competitors who do not face similar increases in energy prices. This unlevel situation occurred during and immediately after the 2022 energy crisis in Europe, where internationally operating energy-intensive industries in Europe faced a strong decline in their global competitive position because of the high energy prices, while energy prices in North America were much lower. In many countries, providing direct support to these companies is subject to strict rules regarding state aid, but governments may have other options to lower energy costs, such as by lowering taxes on energy or providing subsidies to make a transition to other energy carriers, such as hydrogen and electricity. The downside of such measures is that they also reduce the incentive for the industrial companies to reduce their energy use or to change the portfolio of their products.

4.5.6 Supporting Households in Dealing with High Energy Prices

Measures to support residential households in dealing with high energy prices can be divided into measures that result in higher net income and measures that help to reduce the volume of energy use.

Policy measures directed at raising the net income of households increase their ability to deal with high energy costs. Examples of such measures are reductions in energy taxes or income taxes and providing lump-sum subsidies. As such measures can be rather costly for governments when they do not differentiate between different groups, the challenge is to design the measures in such a way that only households who really need support are eligible. Although this principle seems to be straightforward, implementing this in practice is challenging. Energy taxes can, for instance, be charged only on the energy use above a certain threshold to make sure that all basic energy consumption is not charged with a levy, but high-income households also benefit from this discount. In order to prevent that, energy tax tariffs could also be differentiated according to income categories, but such a design may result in high transaction costs. Therefore, it seems most efficient to use only income-support measures to help more vulnerable households and not mix this with other types of taxation, such as one on energy use.

Another approach to help households becoming less vulnerable to energy-price shocks is to support them to lower the volume of their energy use. An example of this type of measure is helping households insulate their house. This support can be given in the form of financial support for materials to be used for insulation, or as technical advice on how households can make their premises more energy efficient. A caveat of the latter type of support is the so-called rebound effect. In case of house insulation, support to make insulation easier or cheaper may result in a higher heat consumption (e.g. raising the in-house temperature), as heating a house has become less expensive. This effect, which is also called the Jevons paradox after the researcher who describes this for the first time, may be quite significant. Empirical literature shows a wide range of results of estimations of the rebound effect, depending on country, sectors and research method, but it is clear that this effect can be very significant up to 50% or even larger (Santarius et al., 2018; Sorrel, 2009).

4.5.7 Conclusions

Energy prices result from the interaction of demand and supply and are affected by developments in production costs, tightness in the market circumstances and competitive conditions. All these factors belong to the normal functioning of markets, making high or volatile prices in principle normal market phenomena and not an economic reason for government intervention. Sometimes, however, market processes can be distorted, for instance through a lack of competition, abuse of market power by one or more suppliers, or lack of transparency which makes it difficult for economic agents to respond efficiently. For these kinds of market problems, governments can use common competition or regulatory measures, making markets more competitive and/or more transparent.

However, even when a market process functions well, it may result in high and volatile prices which are perceived as societally unacceptable. If this is the case, governments can intervene in energy markets in different ways, although they differ in effectiveness and efficiency. Measures which directly intervene in the price-formation process, for instance, changing the rules of market clearing or capping prices, are generally not effective in solving the underlying problem causing high prices, and can be rather costly. The risk of such measures is that they reduce the incentive for economic agents to invest in new assets which may help to reduce high market prices when the underlying problem is scarcity of supply. Measures which support economic agents to deal with high prices can be effective, but can also be very costly for society when the underlying cause of high prices is not addressed. The overall conclusion here is that, from an economic perspective, governments should be hesitant to intervene in energy systems to help economic agents deal with high prices. As far as vulnerable households are concerned, it seems to be more efficient to make use of specific income-related measures or measures directed at reducing their energy use to help them to cope with high and volatile energy prices.

4.6 Policy Measures to Address Climate Change

4.6.1 Introduction: Summarising the Market Failures

The use of fossil energy results in the emissions of greenhouse gases, in particular carbon dioxide and methane, which contribute to climate change. This is a clear example of a negative externality, as these negative consequences are not internalised in market processes in the absence of any regulation. After all, individual economic agents do not have an incentive to reduce their emissions as the costs of the mitigation measures have to be carried individually while the benefits, i.e. the mitigation of climate change, are shared by everyone on the globe, both now and in the next centuries. As a result, the individual costs of mitigation measures exceed the individual benefits. For all economic agents together, however, it would be beneficial to reduce emissions, as the societal costs of the mitigation measures are significantly below the societal benefits of having less damage caused by climate change. This negative externality can also be characterised as a common-pool problem (see Sect. 3.4).

Governments have various options to correct this market failure, i.e. to internalise this negative externality. These options include financial instruments, such as taxation of the negative externality and subsidies for measures reducing that externality (i.e. low-carbon technologies), regulatory standards, and combinations of these two types of measures in the form of emissions-trading schemes. Because of such financial and regulatory measures, economic agents may want to use other types of energy carriers, for which infrastructures have to be developed. In order to facilitate such investments, specific government measures may be needed as well.

4.6.2 Taxation of Fossil Energy and Carbon Emissions

Imposing a tax on the negative externality is from an economic perspective seen as a straightforward way of internalising the negative externality of climate change. The reason for this is that a tax only attaches a price to the emissions, leaving room for economic agents to determine how to respond to that. If their private benefits of, for instance, using fossil energy and, hence, emitting carbon are high, they may be willing to pay the tax without changing their behaviour. In the opposite case, i.e. when their private benefits are below the costs of using fossil energy, they may decide to emit less carbon by reducing their fossil-energy consumption. As a result, those economic agents having a relatively high willingness-to-pay for using the fossil energy will continue consuming it, while others will change their behaviour. This results in a socially efficient outcome which maximises social welfare if the tax level is set on the appropriate level.

This mechanism is illustrated in Fig. 4.8 which shows the changes in the supply curve of fossil energy when the carbon emissions are taxed. Without this internalisation of the negative consequences of carbon emissions, the market process results in the equilibrium A. In this point, the private (marginal) supply curve (i.e. the curve only based on the private costs of economic agents) intersects the demand curve (based on the marginal willingness-to-pay of consumers).[16] Because of the presence of the negative externality resulting from the carbon emissions, this equilibrium results in a deadweight loss, which is depicted by the triangle ABC. This triangle is based on the difference in market equilibrium based on the private supply curve and the one based on the social supply curve. The latter supply curve is based on all costs, both private and external, which in this case refer to climate change. Based on that curve, the market equilibrium would result in market price p_2 and volume q_2,

[16] Here, it is implicitly assumed that there are no market failures disturbing the marginal willingness-to-pay of economic agents, which implies that their preferences reflect the true social preferences.

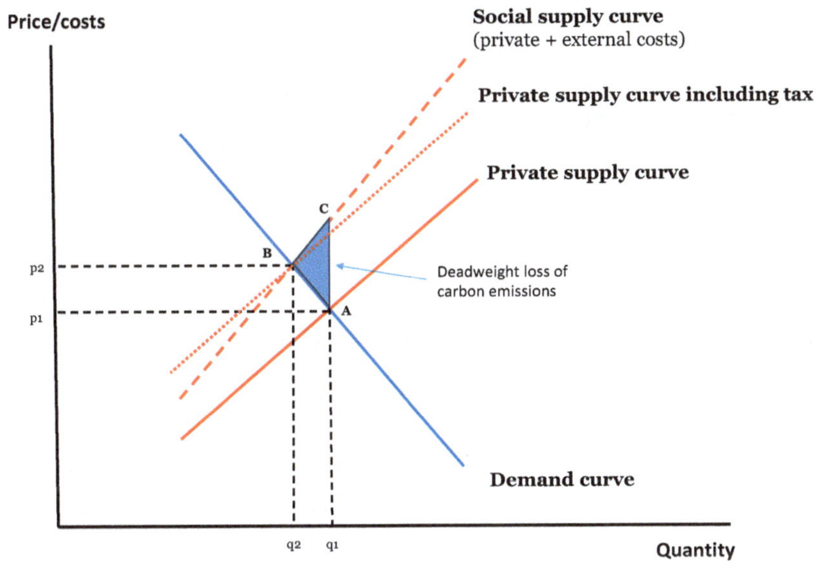

Fig. 4.8 Using a carbon tax to internalise the externality of carbon emissions

while the market equilibrium based on only the private costs consists of market price p_1 and volume q_1. The deadweight loss, that is depicted by the triangle ABC, means that the consumption is too high from a social welfare perspective: the consumption levels between q_1 and q_2 result in marginal social costs which exceed the marginal benefits. After all, the marginal willingness-to-pay for these consumption levels is below the social costs.

Consequently, from a social welfare perspective, it would be better not to have this consumption. This situation can be achieved by raising the costs for suppliers. By raising the costs for the supply of fossil energy, the supply curve shifts upwards, resulting in a different market outcome with a higher equilibrium price and lower equilibrium output. When all supplying economic agents face an equal marginal increase in their costs (i.e. a fixed tax rate per unit of consumption), the new private supply curve including taxes emerges. Theoretically, the tax rate should be set on the level where this new supply curve intersects with both the social supply curve and the demand curve.[17] In that point, the new market equilibrium results in lower output (q_2) and, hence, a lower level of carbon emissions. In this equilibrium, there is no deadweight loss anymore, i.e. no consumption by consumers whose marginal willingness-to-pay is below the marginal social costs.

From this example, we see that it is not necessary to design a tax scheme in which the new supply curve precisely reflects the true social-cost curve, but that it should be equal to the latter in the optimal market equilibrium. The key objective is

[17] This tax level is called the Pigouvian tax rate, which is set equal to the level of the marginal external costs at the efficient level of emissions (see e.g. Zweiffel et al., 2017).

to give incentives to economic agents which result in that equilibrium, i.e. to remove the deadweight loss. This also implies that, from an economic perspective, the objective of taxing carbon emissions is not to bring these emissions completely down to zero. The basic idea behind this is, from a social welfare perspective, to balance the social costs against the social benefits by searching for the point where the marginal social costs equal the marginal social benefits. In the social optimum, there may still be a positive amount of carbon emissions if and only if the societal value of activities resulting in these emissions exceeds the societal costs of the increase in climate change.

Although the theoretical idea behind carbon taxes seems to be quite straightforward, in practice it is challenging to implement as it requires attention for many aspects. The most fundamental one is the height of the carbon tax. Only when the tax rate is set at the appropriate level, the above result of optimum welfare can be achieved. If the tax rate is set at a lower level, there will still be a remaining deadweight loss resulting from the consumption of fossil energy, while a higher level will result in a loss of welfare due to a too strong reduction in the use of fossil energy.

In theory, the tax level should be related to the social costs of carbon, as these costs refer to the impact of climate change on all economic agents. Determining that level is, however, highly complex as it depends on the discounted value of economic and environmental effects all around the globe. The economic literature shows many publications with estimates of the value of the social cost of carbon, but the distribution of results among these publications is large (see Sect. 3.6.4). This implies that there is large uncertainty around the optimal level of the tax rate.

In addition to this, the practical implementation of a carbon tax can also be complex. In theory, it is optimal to implement a carbon tax related to the social costs of carbon at a global level, as all economic agents would face the same costs for emitting carbon. In such a system, an efficient global response is triggered. After all, firms and consumers with a relatively low willingness-to-pay for the use of carbon will decide to reduce their emissions, while others will continue to emit. In practice, however, most taxes are set on a national level, not only environmental ones but also other types of taxes. This results in large differences in carbon taxes implemented around the world. When economic agents are confronted with different carbon tax levels, inefficiencies in mitigation measures arise. After all, in countries with high carbon taxes, agents are incentivised to take relatively expensive measures, while in countries with low carbon taxes, agents only have incentives to take measures which are relatively cheap. Hence, for an efficient response by economic agents to carbon taxes, it is crucial that the tax levels are as harmonised as possible.

The importance of harmonisation of carbon-tax levels does not only hold on an international level, but also a national one. Besides the differences on a global level between countries, there are also often differences within countries. Countries generally differentiate between various types of sectors, such as between the so-called sheltered industries, which are industries that mainly supply to domestic consumers, and the so-called exposed industries, which operate on international markets and, as a result, cannot fully pass their carbon taxes to their customers. Residential households generally also face higher carbon (or energy) taxes than industrial users, which is sometimes referred to as fossil subsidies to the latter group (see Box 4.9). If economic agents face different tax levels, they will also take different types of measures to reduce carbon emissions. In an industry confronted with relatively high carbon taxes, more expensive mitigation measures may be profitable, while in other industries subject to lower carbon taxes only cheaper mitigation measures may be profitable. This unequal situation regarding carbon taxes results in an inefficiency in taking mitigation measures. Therefore, in theory, all economic agents, both internationally and nationally, should face the same carbon tax in order to minimise the societal costs of mitigation measures.

As energy and carbon taxes are set on a national level, this theoretical objective is difficult to realise, also because countries have different economic characteristics, such as energy endowments and industrial structure, as well as different preferences, for example, regarding economic development and their contribution to global climate policy. A country that has a relatively large energy-intensive industry will be more hesitant to implement or raise energy taxes than a country which has an economy that is more based on less energy-intensive activities, like trade and services. Countries with relatively good opportunities to develop renewable-energy resources may also be more supportive towards carbon taxes than countries that do not have these options. Differences in attitude towards the problem of climate change also play a role in the extent to which countries are willing to implement policy measures that make the use of fossil energy more expensive.

Box 4.9 Differences in Energy Taxes as Input for Debates on Fossil Subsidies

Many countries have implemented taxes on the use of energy in order to incentivise economic agents to use energy more efficiently and/or as means for governments to finance their budget. As countries make different decisions regarding the design and importance of energy taxes, the role of energy taxes in total government revenues varies strongly. In some countries like Bulgaria, energy tax revenues contribute to about 15% of total tax revenues, while in other European countries, like Austria and Ireland, this share was about 2.5% in 2023 (European Commission (EC), 2025).

Countries also make different decisions regarding the tariff structure. Since taxes on the use of energy may have adverse effects on the competitive position of businesses, governments generally differentiate the tariffs according to the various types of agents, but in some countries this difference is much larger than in others. Generally, residential households pay higher tariffs on their energy use than industrial users. In the Netherlands in 2026, for instance, residential households pay 0.60 euro/m^3 natural gas, while large industrial

(continued)

Box 4.9 (continued)

users (with a use above ten million m^3), pay no more than 0.05 euro/m^3 (source: https://www.belastingdienst.nl/wps/wcm/connect/bldcontentnl/belastingdienst/zakelijk/overige_belastingen/belastingen_op_milieugrondslag/energiebelasting/)

Sometimes, the difference in energy-tax tariffs between households and other industries is seen as a fossil subsidy. Fossil subsidies can be divided into direct subsidies and indirect subsidies (IMF, n.d.). Direct fossil subsidies occur when the end-user energy price is below the costs of supply, while indirect subsidies occur when end-user prices do not fully include the external costs. Assuming that the tax level for households is the appropriate tax level which reflects the true external costs, that tax level can be used as a benchmark to assess the implied subsidy given to other energy users. In this perspective, the lower tax for other users is seen as a tax exemption or tax rebate. This approach is, however, debatable, as countries apply rather different tax rates for residential households. As a result, using the residential-household rates as a benchmark implies that the true external costs in every country are different, which does not make much sense since climate change is a global problem.

Another reason why one should view calculations on the magnitude of the so-called fossil subsidies with care, is that these calculations do not pay attention to other climate-policy measures. In particular, the relationship with emissions-trading schemes is relevant. As is explained in Sect. 4.6.5, in case of a cap-and-trade design of emissions-trading schemes, the level of carbon taxes does not have an (additional) impact on carbon-emissions reduction since the latter is only determined by the cap on emissions (Mulder, 2023; Mulder et al., 2023).

All these differences in characteristics and preferences make that harmonisation of energy and carbon taxes can only be done by taking the potential effects of taxation into account when designing tax systems. For instance, in order to protect the international competitive position of energy-intensive industries, an energy tax should be designed in such a way that firms only have to pay higher energy prices (resulting from the tax) on their marginal units, leaving the inframarginal use (which is more difficult to adapt) unaffected. Such a design can be implemented by lowering corporate-income tax tariffs when an energy tax is raised, although some firms (i.e. those which hardly pay corporate-income tax) may be less supported by such a design than others.

Another issue related to the design of climate-policy measures which is relevant for most policy measures, but in particular for the design of carbon taxes, is fairness. Economic agents with a high income and/or accumulated wealth can afford to pay a higher price for using products based on fossil energy, while others with a low(er) income may not be able to do so, while they may also have a strong preference to consume these products. This example shows that efficient outcomes are not necessarily fair ones. In order to address this issue, a carbon-tax scheme can be designed that compensates the latter group for the higher costs associated with using fossil energy. This can, for instance, be achieved by giving all households a fixed tax discount per year, which makes that those agents with a relatively low fossil-energy consumption do not need to face any higher costs if a tax per unit of consumption is implemented, while they keep the incentive to reduce their consumption. After all, any reduction in consumption reduces their expenditures, while the tax credit remains the same, as it is designed as a lump-sum amount.

4.6.3 Subsidising Low/Zero-Carbon Technologies

Instead of making fossil energy more expensive by introducing carbon taxes, governments could internalise the negative externality by providing financial support for alternative energy carriers which results in less or no carbon emissions. Theoretically, this measure can also address the problem of the deadweight loss caused by overconsumption of fossil energy. By giving subsidies to producers or consumers of low or zero-carbon energy carriers, these economic agents will reduce their willingness-to-pay for fossil energy.

Suppose that an agent is prepared to pay 100 euros/MWh to use an energy carrier and there are two types of energy carriers (I and II) supplied in the market with a market price of 80 (type I) and 120 euros (type II) per MWh, respectively. Any price that is below 100 euros/MWh, results in a surplus for this agent. In this case, that agent will only be prepared to buy energy carrier I as its costs are lower than his/her willingness-to-pay. Now, suppose the government provides 50 euros/MWh subsidies for the type II energy carrier, lowering its market price for that type of carriers to 70 euros/MWh. As a result, the market prices of both energy carrier are below the willingness-to-pay of the consuming agent, and this agent will choose the one with the lowest price, which is the type II energy carrier. This is equal to saying the demand for energy carrier I decreases as the willingness-to-pay is equal to the price which has to be paid for energy carrier II.

Hence, by providing financial subsidies to, for instance, renewable energy, the demand curve for fossil energy shifts downwards, as is depicted in Fig. 4.9. When the appropriate level of subsidies is provided, the demand curve for fossil energy can be shifted downwards to such a degree that for the new equilibrium in the fossil-energy market, the consumed quantity is on the societally optimal level (q_2). For this equilibrium, the market price of fossil energy is reduced as well (from p_1 to p_2). For this equilibrium, the deadweight loss of the initial situation (i.e. the triangle ABC) is completely gone.

Although both taxes on fossil energy and subsidies for renewables can, in theory, fully remove the deadweight loss of emitting too much carbon, the distributional effects of both policy measures are quite different. In the case of carbon taxes, emitters of carbon (and users of their products) make more costs, while the government receives more revenues. In the case of subsidies for renewables, emitters (and others) receive financial support, which has to be paid by the government. The latter can finance these payments in several ways. They can be paid from the general budget (e.g. income taxes) or levies on energy use. At the end of the day, subsidies for (for instance) renewables have to be paid by economic agents. Besides these

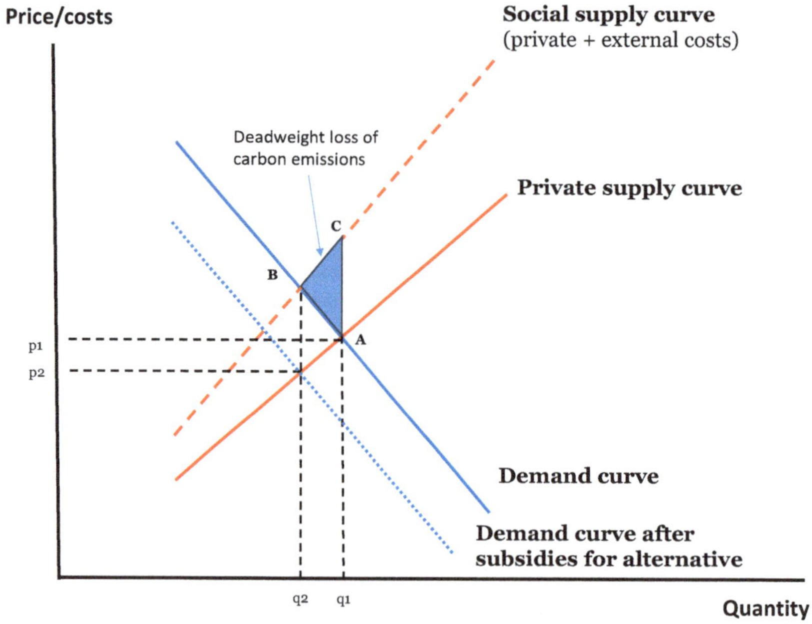

Fig. 4.9 Impact of subsidies for renewables on fossil-energy market outcomes

distributional effects, in particular subsidies result in other types of effects like a rebound effect and free-rider, as will be discussed below.

Of course, this is a fairly basic theoretical exposition of how subsidies for renewables can help internalise the externality caused by the use of fossil energy. The basic idea is that subsidies can be used to reduce the price for consumers of commodities (e.g. renewable energy) having relatively high costs, so they prefer that commodity over others (see Box 4.10).

Box 4.10 Why Giving Subsidies for Renewables When their Costs Go Down?
In the short term, providing subsidies for renewables or other low-carbon technologies is meant to compensate for the excess costs of these technologies compared to the costs or market prices of the conventional (fossil) technologies. In the longer term, subsidies can also be used to reduce the costs of the low-carbon technologies by realising economies of scale advantages or learning-by-doing effects. A consequence of that long-term policy can be that subsidies are no longer needed to compensate for excess costs when the costs of the low-carbon technologies have been (strongly) reduced. This is what has occurred in the case of wind-turbines and solar PV. The levelized costs of energy (LCOE) of these technologies have strongly declined over the past decades (see Sect. 2.4). Governments are, however, still subsidising these technologies, but to what extent is this still needed?

(continued)

Box 4.10 (continued)

The answer to that question is that the required subsidies are not so much determined by the difference in the LCOE, but by the difference between the LCOE of low-carbon technologies and the market price they can realise during the lifetime of their operation. In electricity markets, the price is determined by either the marginal costs of the price-setting technology (in case of abundant generation capacity) or by the marginal willingness-to-pay of the marginal consumer (in case of tight market circumstances). In the first circumstance, the electricity price only covers the marginal costs of, for instance, a gas-fired power plant, and may not be sufficient to recoup investment costs. In order to obtain sufficient revenues for investments in new generation capacity, so-called scarcity prices may be needed. Hence, when an electricity market has a relatively large portfolio of conventional power plants, market forces may not give (sufficient) incentives to invest in new technologies. This means that a relatively low LCOE of low-carbon technology may be not sufficient to trigger investments in that technology.

In addition to this, low-carbon technologies like wind turbines and solar PV may also realise lower prices than conventional power plants because of the so-called market-value factor (see Sect. 2.5.4). The more wind and solar is present in a system, the lower the average prices they realise. This results from the fact that when these technologies are price setting, the electricity price become close to zero as a result of their very low marginal production costs. The financial tragedy for wind and solar PV is that when they produce many units, the aggregated production lowers the electricity price, while when they cannot produce (because of a lack of wind or sunshine) the market prices can be high.

In relation to this, there is another reason why low-carbon generation technologies may still be in need of subsidies in power systems with high shares of renewables, namely they may hardly benefit from any carbon tax (or carbon price resulting from trading mechanism) for fossil-fuel generators. Such a tax (or price) raises the variable costs of these generators and also the electricity price when they are price setting, but in a system with high shares of renewables such an increase in the electricity price only happens when a fossil-energy technology is the marginal, price-setting technology. Otherwise, when renewables are price setting, the electricity price does not change in response to higher carbon taxes or prices, which makes that the renewable technologies do not benefit from higher costs of carbon.

An alternative measure to foster the profitability of investments in renewable technologies is to stimulate the demand for electricity or to promote the use of flexible assets. Both measures move the demand curve, affecting electricity prices. As a result, the market prices will increase during hours in which the renewables are price setting, which raises their profitability (see Veenstra et al., 2026).

Higher electricity prices are of course not beneficial for the electrification of, for instance, industry or transport, and neither for the business case of hydrogen produced through electrolysis. The latter may call for specific subsidies for hydrogen producers (or consumers) to facilitate their business cases (see Li et al, 2026).

In the above analysis, it is implicitly assumed that the suppliers in the fossil-energy market behave like competitive players, only responding to the market price. In reality, however, the fossil-energy market is characterised by a lack of competition, which gives the suppliers the ability to influence market outcomes. When they have the incentive to do so (i.e. by lowering their production, they can raise not only market prices, but also their profits), their supply is not based on their true marginal private costs. This implies that when the demand for their commodity, in this case fossil energy, reduces as a result of subsidies to suppliers of alternatives, the suppliers of fossil energy may respond by increasing their supply or lowering their required price. As a result, the demand for fossil energy will increase. If in the above example, the market price for fossil is reduced from 80 to 60 euros/MWh, the consuming agent will not buy the renewable energy (which costs 70 euros/MWh after the subsidy), but the fossil-energy carrier. The resulting increase in the fossil-energy consumption will reintroduce the deadweight loss as the consumption of fossil energy will rise above the societally optimal level.[18]

Another caveat that must be mentioned regarding the above exposition is that, in practice, there are various types of both fossil and renewable energy, with a different contribution to (the mitigation of) climate change, which makes it complicated to determine the appropriate level of support. In addition to that, support schemes are implemented by national or even local governments and, as a result, show a large variety in their design and support levels. One of the consequences of this is that support schemes can be easily too generous or too modest. A support for renewables is too generous when the support level exceeds what is needed to compensate for the difference between the market prices and the costs of renewables, or that it exceeds the level needed to compensate for the external societal costs of carbon. In the first case, economic agents are receiving public money which they do not need; even with a lower amount of subsidy, they would take the measures. This is called the free-rider effect of subsidies. In the second case, too expensive technologies may be stimulated as their costs exceed the benefits of less damage caused by climate change.

Another caveat of providing financial support to economic agents for particular activities is that this may raise the demand and, hence, reduce the mitigating effect on emissions. For instance, a financial-support scheme for electric vehicles may stimulate households to buy and drive such a car instead of taking the train or metro. Another example refers to the rebound effect of providing support for energy-saving measures. By helping households financially to, for instance, insulate their premises, these households may increase their heating demand as heating becomes less expensive. This is the so-called rebound effect, which was already discussed in Sect. 4.5.6.

---

[18] Note that in the presence of market power, the actual deadweight loss differs from the one shown here, as the private supply curve is not based on the actual marginal costs, but on the strategic choices made by the suppliers. As a result of that behaviour, the consumption is below the societally optimal level. This resulting deadweight loss is, hence, not due to the presence of a negative externality, but due to the presence of market power (see Sect. 3.2). Both deadweight losses can compensate each other, as the one caused by market power results in underconsumption and the one related to negative externalities in overconsumption, which illustrates the saying that a 'monopolist in fossil-energy market is the environmentalist's friend' (see Perman et al., 1999).

Designing support schemes which address the problems of free riders, rebound effects and inefficiency appears to be highly complex. This is partly due to the fact that governments have less information than market parties on, in particular, the costs of new renewable-energy technologies (see Box 4.11). Another factor contributing to the complexity of designing efficient support schemes is that such schemes can be vulnerable to rent-seeking behaviour of economic agents. This means that particular groups lobby to get support that is favourable for their own business, but not necessarily for the rest of society. These groups generally have more information about their technologies than public agencies, which is valuable, but also risky for public agencies as they have to assess that information.[19] In order to reduce the risk of biased decision-making, support schemes can be designed in such a way that all potential recipients of the support have the incentive to reveal their true subsidy requirement. This can, for instance, be done through a system of auctioning in which bidders are asked to submit their required support, knowing that the decision will be based on the lowest bids while the total budget for subsidies is limited.

Box 4.11 Promoting Renewables with Support Schemes and Obligations

In order to promote renewable energy, governments can choose different options. A major distinction is the one between financial support schemes and obligations. In the latter approach, economic agents (e.g. energy retailers) have the obligation to make use of a minimum share of renewables. Because of that obligation, a demand for renewables exists, which results in a market price depending on the magnitude of this demand and the supply characteristics of the supply of renewables (i.e. quantity and costs). In order to facilitate the trade between market parties with the renewable-energy obligation and market parties that can help them to meet that obligation, governments may introduce certificate schemes. These schemes address the information asymmetry between suppliers and buyers, as the latter are generally not able to see the true (renewable) characteristics of an energy product offered to them. These schemes include that the producer of renewable energy receives a certificate from a public agency or grid operator for every unit of energy that is produced in a renewable way. These certificates can be sold to buyers on top of the sales of the energy commodity itself, which results in extra revenue for the suppliers.

The green-certificate schemes can also be useful for the implementation of support schemes. In this case, the suppliers have to hand in their certificates to a public agency in return for financial support per unit of energy. In the past, the support schemes for renewables existed mainly as feed-in-tariff schemes, which means that the producer received a fee for every unit of renewable energy in return for the delivery of the energy to a public agency or grid

(continued)

[19] Stakeholders may present their lobbying actions to promote particular technologies or to obtain government support as part of their perspectives on the long-term development of energy systems (see Sect. 5.1).

Box 4.11 (continued)

operator. The latter sold the renewable energy to other market participants. More and more, this kind of scheme is replaced by feed-in-premium schemes, where the producers sell the energy to other market participants and receive a premium from a public agency to cover the difference between the (benchmark) market price and the average costs of the renewable energy. One of the reasons for the increasing popularity of feed-in-premium schemes compared to feed-in-tariff schemes is that in the former scheme, market participants are stimulated to take market conditions into account, which raises the efficiency of the support mechanism.

The feed-in-premium schemes exist in various forms, with sliding price levels (i.e. where the benchmark price is frequently updated), and as two-sided contract-for-differences (CfD), where the producers not only receive a subsidy when the market price is below the costs of production, but are also required to pay back any excess revenues realised in the market (i.e. when the market price exceeds the production costs). In order to minimise the risk of distorting production decisions, two-sided CfDs should be designed so that the marginal benefits are not affected. This can, for instance, be done by closely relating the reference price to the actual market price (Veenstra & Mulder, 2024).

4.6.4 Imposing Regulatory Standards

Instead of giving economic agents financial incentives to reduce carbon emissions, either through taxing fossil energy or subsidising renewable energy, governments can also impose regulatory standards to realise that objective. Examples of such measures are efficiency standards for cars or homes. Such measures can be highly effective, as they force economic agents to make cars more efficient or to build more energy-efficient homes. The downside of regulatory standards is that they may involve high transaction costs as the standards have to be determined, imposed on economic agents as well as monitored and supervised to make sure they are actually taken into consideration.

Regulatory obligations can be defined in various ways. The fundamental distinction here is between relative and absolute standards. In the case of relative standards, the compliance of participating agents is assessed in comparison to a benchmark, such as energy efficiency (e.g. energy use per house) or carbon intensity (e.g. carbon emissions per unit of energy consumption). In this design, the agents are allowed to use more energy or to emit more when their activities grow (i.e. more houses or higher energy use, respectively), as long as their relative performance does not violate the standard. In the case of absolute standards, however, economic agents have to comply with an absolute limit on their energy use or emissions (in terms of the above example, no matter how many houses they have or how large their energy use is, respectively).

This regulatory-standard approach to stimulate economic agents to reduce their carbon emissions is particularly useful when governments have clear information on what kind of measures agents can take to improve, in the above examples, the efficiency of energy use. The standards should be technically and economically attainable for the respective economic agents, otherwise they would be ineffective. The same effect results when the standards are too lenient, as agents can comply very easily, which might imply that they would have also taken the actions without the regulatory standards. In such a situation, a standard does incur transaction costs, but without much effect.

In addition, it is necessary for the rules of regulatory standards to be fairly efficiently imposed on economic agents, i.e. with low transaction costs. The latter may happen when the rules refer to a limited number of economic agents, such as only industrial companies in the automotive industry or developers of new housing projects. It is less costly for a public agency to monitor compliance with the regulatory standards when less individual agents have to be monitored and take actions in case of non-compliance.

A caveat of regulatory standards is their vulnerability to rent-seeking behaviour of affected economic agents. In the above example, firms in the automotive industry and in the construction business may lobby for less stringent standards to reduce their costs. They may also have an incentive to cheat, i.e. to act as if they comply with the standards while in reality they do not. Regulatory oversight by independent public bodies is, therefore, crucial for an effective application of this type of policy measure.

4.6.5 Regulatory Standards Plus Financial Incentives: Trading Schemes

In the above climate-policy measures, economic agents are stimulated, either through financial instruments or regulatory standards, to reduce their use of (fossil) energy or use more renewable energy. Another type of instrument is a combination of both types. When regulatory standards are supplemented with the option to trade in the degree of compliance with these standards, climate policy may be both more effective and more efficient. A clear example of such a combination is emissions-trading schemes. In such schemes, there is a regulatory standard that economic agents have to comply with, such as the obligation to have an allowance for every unit of emissions, while this obligation is combined with the possibility to buy (or sell) allowances from (to) others. This possibility raises the options for compliance, which can reduce the compliance costs compared to a policy which only consists of regulatory standards. In the latter case, an economic agent that is subject to a standard, such as an energy-efficiency standard for building a new house, can only choose from various technical options to comply with that standard. In the case of an emissions-trading scheme, however, the options to be compliant in an efficient way are fostered by enabling the agent to exchange the regulatory commitments with other agents. This means that an agent is allowed to not (fully) comply with a regulatory standard, if (s)he is able to show that someone else compensates for that.

When each agent has to remain within a (relative or absolute) standard, then his/her only options to comply are related to what they can do themselves. This may not be efficient, as some agents may have a large amount of relatively cheap options, while others can only comply with the standard when they resort to very expensive options. By adding the option to exchange the commitments (i.e. a trade element) to the scheme, the efficiency of regulatory standards can increase starkly. Agents with relatively expensive options can ask agents with relatively cheap options to do more than what is required, and use this overcompliance to compensate for the agent's own undercompliance. This is the basic principle of a trading scheme added to a regulatory standard.

The clearest example of such a scheme is the so-called EU Emissions Trading System (EU ETS), an emissions-trading system based on an absolute emissions cap, introduced by the European Union in 2005. The cap is meant to realise the European climate-policy objective of reducing the emission of greenhouse gases, while the trade option is meant to enable participating agents to realise this reduction as efficiently as possible. By translating the overall cap, formulated at a European level, into allowances, which are auctioned to or allocated for free to the individual participating agents, the latter become subject to a regulatory standard they have to comply with. This standard entails that the agents subject to the scheme are only allowed to emit greenhouse gases when they can hand over the same number of allowances to a public agency (i.e. the national emission authority).[20] Hence, this cap-and-trade mechanism is a combination of a regulatory standard and a financial incentive scheme.

The cap of the EU ETS is related to the European climate-policy objective of reducing the emissions of greenhouse gases. This cap refers to the aggregated annual emissions of CO_2, N_2O and PFCs[21] by economics agents active in electricity and heat generation, industrial manufacturing and aviation (since 2012) and maritime transport (since 2024) in all EU member states, the countries of the European Free Trade Association (Iceland, Liechtenstein and Norway) and Northern Ireland (only for electricity generation).[22] By lowering the annual cap, the aggregated allowed emissions decline over time. The decline in the overall cap is related to the European commitment to the Paris Agreement, which implies that the aggregated greenhouse gas emissions have to be net-zero by 2050. In the current design of the annual reduction percentages, the cap of the EU ETS will already be zero before 2040, although the EU ETS will still release small amounts of allowances for aviation until 2044.[23] In addi-

[20] Legally speaking, the entities participating in the EU ETS are only allowed to emit greenhouse gases if they have obtained a (non-tradable) permit to emit, which they will only receive if their monitoring plan has been approved by the emission authority. This monitoring plan has to describe how the emissions of greenhouse gases will be determined. See, for instance, the website of the Netherlands Emissions Authority, NEa, https://www.emissionsauthority.nl/.

[21] Perfluorocarbons (PFCs) are synthetic compounds consisting of carbon and fluorine atoms. The scope of gases included in the EU ETS is related to the practical feasibility of monitoring and compliance. Including CH_4, for instance, would complicate the scheme significantly as this gas is emitted by, amongst others, cows in the livestock farming.

[22] Participation is mandatory for firms in these industries, but in some industries a minimum scale of operation applies, while countries may also exclude particular small installations if they implement alternative measures to reduce their emissions.

[23] This is related to the fact that the cap for aviation started to decrease later than that for stationary installations (Pahle et al., 2025).

tion, as allowances can be banked, it is expected that there will still be allowances in circulation several years after the allocation of new allowances has stopped.

The calculation of the annual reduction is done separately for the various sectors. Since 2013, there has been an aggregated cap for electricity generation and industrial installations. This cap was reduced by 1.74% in the period until 2020, and in the period 2021–2023 by 2.2%. In the period 2024–2027, the cap is annually reduced by 4.3% and in the period 2028–2030, it will be annually further reduced by 4.4%.[24] The cap for aviation is set separately, as of 2021 it is also subject to an annual reduction factor. In order to have an impact on individual behaviour of participating agents, the caps are translated into allowances which are allocated to them (see Box 4.12).[25]

Box 4.12 Allocation of emission allowances

The allocation of allowances is partly done by giving them for free, initially based on historical emission levels (so-called grandfathering), but for a number of years this process has been based on efficiency benchmarks. Increasingly, however, the allowances are allocated through auctioning, and in the near future, this will hold for all new allowances. The auction is organised by the various countries (i.e. EU Member States and the other four countries) participating in this cap-and-trade scheme, which results in annual auctioning revenues for the respective governments. These governments have to use these revenues to facilitate the energy transition or fund other climate-policy related actions, such as industrial decarbonisation and adaptation to climate change.[26] Each auction is open to buyers from the whole EU ETS region, so from all EU Member States, Norway, Iceland and Liechtenstein as well as Switzerland whose emissions trading scheme has been linked to that of the EU.

The translation of the overall cap into amounts of allowances that can be allocated every year has become a bit less direct and simple since the introduction of backloading in the early period of the EU ETS, and, more recently, the Market-Stability Reserve (MSR). Both components are meant to compensate for too high amounts of available allowances in the system. The MSR automatically reduces, based on predetermined rules, the volume of emission allowances to be auctioned in case of a surplus of allowances in circulation.

---

[24] When maritime transport was brought under the EU ETS in 2024, the aggregated cap was increased by 78.4 million allowances, which was based on the maritime sector's average emissions in 2018 and 2019. Source: https://climate.ec.europa.eu/eu-action/carbon-markets/eu-emissions-trading-system-eu-ets_en.

[25] A small part of the cap is not allocated by the participating countries, but is set aside by the European Commission in order to have a so-called free-allocation buffer, to be used to finance three types of European funds: the Innovation Fund, the Modernization Fund and the Social Climate Fund and to be available for new entrants to the EU ETS. Source: https://climate.ec.europa.eu/eu-action/carbon-markets/eu-emissions-trading-system-eu-ets_en.

[26] Source: European Environment Agency: https://www.eea.europa.eu/en/analysis/indicators/use-of-auctioning-revenues-generated.

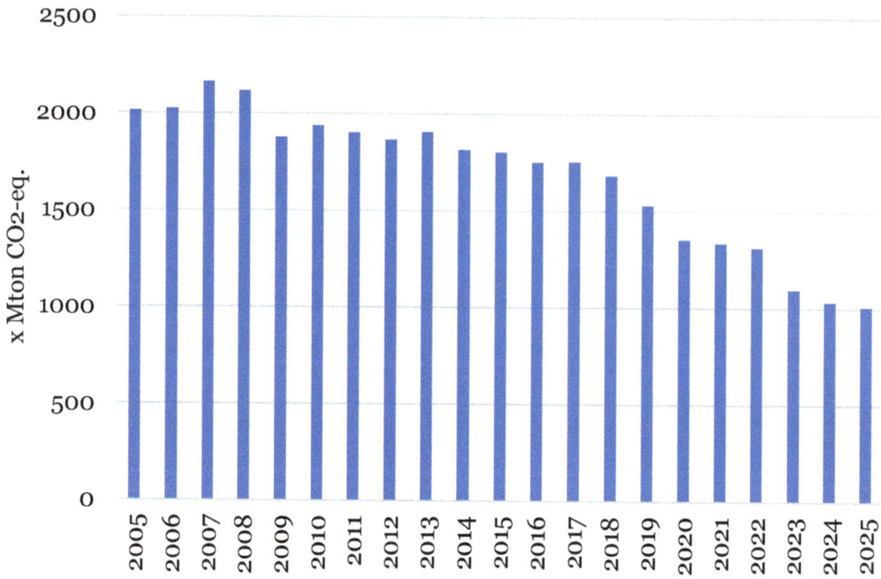

Fig. 4.10 Total verifed annual greenhouse gas emissions within the EU ETS (EU 27, Iceland, Liechtenstein and Norway) in Mton CO_2-eq., 2005–2025 (Source: European Environmental Agency; https://www.eea.europa.eu/en/analysis/maps-and-charts/greenhouse-gases-viewer-data-viewers)

In order to assess the effectiveness of the EU ETS, one should look at the decline in emissions, since the primary objective is to bring these down. Figure 4.10 shows that the total annual greenhouse gas emissions within the EU ETS have been reduced significantly. In 2025, the total emissions were about 50% of the level in 2005, when the trading system started.

The cap-and-trade scheme also results in a price for the emissions of greenhouse gases, both through the initial auctioning and the secondary trading among the participating agents and other market participants, like financial institutions. Although the carbon price is sometimes used as a metric to assess the effectiveness of the EU ETS, that is not correct. The information that can be inferred from this price only refers to the (marginal) costs agents have to make (at system level) to be compliant with the overall target (i.e. the cap). This also indicates a fundamental difference between the carbon price of the trading system and a carbon tax. This difference being that a carbon tax is set exogenously by the government to incentivise economic agents to reduce carbon emissions, while the carbon price in a cap-and-trade scheme results endogenously from the interaction between the participating agents in the scheme.

4.6.6 Interaction between Climate-Policy Measures

As countries typically implement a portfolio of different types of policy measures to reach their climate-policy objectives, the effectiveness and efficiency of these

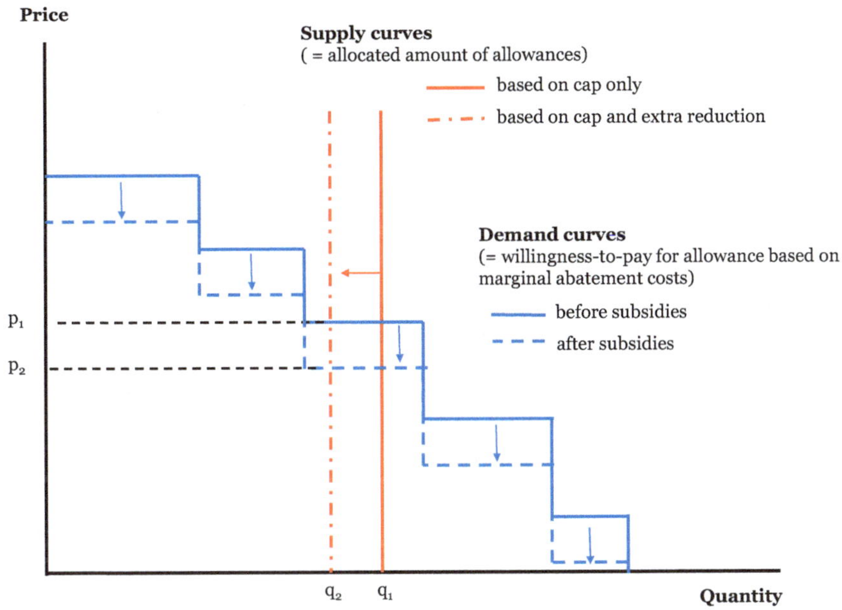

Fig. 4.11 Illustration of impact of subsidies for renewables and extra reduction of emissions cap on outcomes of cap-and-trade carbon market

measures has to be assessed by also paying attention to the interaction effects. This holds in particular for the interaction between, on the one hand, carbon taxes and subsidies for renewables and, on the other hand, a cap-and-trade design of an emissions-trading scheme. As we have seen in the previous section, in such a trading scheme, the environmental effectiveness is only determined by the number of allowances that are allocated to economic agents. When such a system is combined with, for instance, subsidies for low-carbon technologies, like renewable energy, agents' compliance costs are reduced, but the regulatory standard, i.e. the number of allowances, remains the same.

This so-called waterbed effect of a cap-and-trade scheme is illustrated by Fig. 4.11. This figure shows that providing subsidies to participants in a cap-and-trade emissions scheme reduces their willingness-to-pay for carbon allowances, as the subsidies make it less expensive to reduce emissions. Because of the lower willingness-to-pay, the demand curve shifts downwards. When the number of allocated allowances remains the same, the overall magnitude of emissions reduction remains the same as well, while the carbon price is reduced (from p_1 to p_2). There will only be an additional emissions reduction when the allocated number of allowances is tightened even further than foreseen in the initial reduction path, for instance from q_1 to q_2. In order to understand this waterbed effect fully, a so-called classroom experiment can be helpful (see Box 4.13).

Box 4.13 Emissions Trading and Interaction with Subsidies: A Classroom Experiment

In order to better understand complex relationships, classroom experiments can be useful. When applied to the field of economics, participants are asked to make choices within the context of scarcity and the presence of other participants with whom they can collaborate or have to compete with. See for more information on classroom experiments in economics: https://econclass-experiments.com/.

The author of this book has developed a classroom experiment on the interaction between emissions trading and support schemes for particular technologies. Before starting the experiment, the lecturer gives a short lecture on the EU ETS and how it interacts with other policy measures, prior to introducing the experiment. Then, the class is split into two subgroups of (about) equal size. The experiment is conducted in both groups separately. During the experiment, which takes about half an hour, the lecturer only answers technical questions, but (s)he should not be involved in the discussions among group members. After the experiment, the results are discussed, during which participants get deeper insight in the functioning of the EU ETS and its interaction with other policy measures as well as the functioning of markets.

As the introduction to the experiment, the participants receive the following information:

1. The problem is that both groups emit too much carbon. Their initial emissions per person is six tonnes, but this should be reduced by 50%, i.e. to three tons.
2. The good news is that technically, reducing the emissions is possible, but the bad news is that the costs of some options are quite high, while not everyone has access to cheap options. Every participant receives five mitigation options with information on the corresponding costs, which range between one and ten euro/tonne.
3. The two subgroups receive the same reduction options, but in one group the costs of particular technologies (i.e. solar panels and solar parks) are significantly lower than in the other group because that former group received subsidies (without knowing that).
4. In order to enable all participants to benefit from low-cost options within the group, an emissions trading scheme has been implemented, with the objective to reduce overall emissions by 50%. Therefore, all participants receive three allowances, which allows them to emit three tonnes of carbon. Participants can trade in allowances, but not in mitigation options. Participants are not allowed to emit more than the number of allowances they can hand over.
5. Every participant also receives a budget (on paper) of 25 euros, with the remark that they should treat this budget as if it were real money.

(continued)

Box 4.13 (continued)

6. Finally, the lecturer says that (s)he, as representative of the emissions authority, only cares about emissions reduction. It is fully up to the participants what they do, but at the end of the day (the game), everyone should be compliant. If someone does not comply, there are 'serious consequences'.
7. The experiment ends when everyone declares they are compliant with the regulation.

In the discussion following the experiment, attention can be paid to several aspects of the results:

- The effectiveness of the emissions reduction (i.e. to what extent is the reduction target achieved).
- The efficiency of using the cheapest reduction options before more expensive options are used.
- The distributional effects (i.e. remaining capital for each group member).
- The use of the various technologies.
- Whether there are differences in any of these aspects between the group with and the group without subsidies for solar panels and solar parks.

Over the past 10 years, the author of this book played this experiment with numerous groups, varying from BSc, MSc and Executive students to staff members of energy companies, governmental agencies and environmental lobby groups as well as academic colleagues. The smallest group consisted of six participants, the largest had a size of about 50. Depending on the size of the groups, the backgrounds of participants and the openness of communication in the group, the results vary a bit, but there were some results which occurred almost every time. Openness of communication (i.e. market transparency) contributes to a higher efficiency, a high efficiency can be achieved with various distributional consequences, the emissions reduction is for almost 100% determined by the number of allowances, while subsidies for particular technologies lower compliance costs (i.e. lower costs per tonne of emission reduction) and affects the technological choices, but do not affect the magnitude of emissions reduction. Appendix C shows the results of just one application of the experiment, which was conducted with a group of staff members of an energy consultancy.

Within the EU ETS, such an extra reduction in the number of allowances can be realised through the MSR mechanism, but this mechanism is subject to a number of conditions which makes it less clear to what extent reducing the demand for allowances translates into a lower number of allocated allowances. There is also another way by which providing subsidies to low-carbon technologies, in the context of cap-and-trade mechanisms, can have an additional effect on emissions reduction. This route is of a more political nature. Because such subsidies have a downward effect on the carbon price (as is illustrated by Fig. 4.11), they make it politically more feasible to further reduce the cap, and hence, the number of allowances. After all, when the carbon price is relatively high, there will be more societal opposition to further reduction, so keeping the carbon price low can make the political process of lowering the cap easier. The costs of this approach are hidden, as they consist of the extra costs of emissions reduction caused by providing subsidies for technologies which would otherwise not be chosen by the parties subject to the emissions-trading system.

Similar types of interaction effects occur between cap-and-trade systems and other types of policy measures, such as regulatory standards and carbon taxes. When a government imposes a rule on economic agents that limits their ability to use fossil energy, for example, through a ban on coal-fired power plants, the number of emissions declines, which reduces the demand for allowances. As a result, the carbon price declines, which reduces the incentive for other agents to reduce their emissions. At the end of the day, the number of emissions is only determined by the emissions cap, which means that additional emissions reduction can only be realised when the number of allowances is also reduced, in one way or another.

The same applies in case a country abolishes so-called fossil subsidies (see Box 4.9) for activities that are subject to a cap-and-trade system. The abolishment makes the use of fossil energy more expensive, which reduces the demand for carbon allowances, resulting in a lower carbon price. This will only result in lower emissions when the government also reduces the number of allowances.

Another type of interaction may occur, even without the presence of an emissions-trading scheme, when a government sets an emissions reduction target for a sector, which is also crucial for the decarbonisation of other industries. This holds in particular for the electricity sector when it has to greatly increase its output (i.e. generated electricity) to enable other sectors, such as industry and transport, to electrify. When the electricity sector is forced to reach a low amount of carbon emissions, it may be unable to sufficiently raise its output to meet the growing demand. As a result, industry or transport can electrify less and remain more reliant on fossil energy. The resulting level of carbon emissions may exceed those that would occur when the electricity sector was allowed to use natural gas, which has relatively low emissions compared to other fossil-energy carriers (see Appendix A). After all, when an industry that uses coal is able to electrify based on electricity that is generated by gas-fired power plants, the overall level of carbon emissions may reduce.

4.6.7 Facilitating Investments in Infrastructure

When economic agents face financial incentives and/or regulatory pressure to change the way they satisfy their energy demand, investments in alternative infrastructures may be needed as well. Firms will only be able to make the transition to, for instance, hydrogen, residual heat or store carbon through Carbon Capture &

Storage (CCS) projects, when the appropriate infrastructure is available. Investments for the development of such infrastructures can be made by private market parties, but this will only happen when there is the prospect of a profitable investment. That prospect, however, can be problematic when a new industry is in its infant stage. Then, it is not clear how large the demand will be and what the willingness-to-pay of the potential future users will be, while the investments typically have to be made upfront.

This situation of required upfront investments versus uncertain future demand may result in a so-called hold-up problem. This problem entails that if investors do not receive sufficient commitments from users regarding future revenues, they are unwilling to make large upfront investments. In such situations, investors may try to conclude contracts with potential users to secure their commitment to future use of the infrastructure, but these potential users may be hesitant to sign if they are uncertain about their own business case. The problem of realising such an investment may indicate the presence of a market failure, such as insufficient internalisation of the negative external effects of carbon emissions or the presence of a lack of coordination between end-users and developers of the infrastructure. In both cases, the outcome can be that an investment that is profitable from a societal perspective cannot be realised by market parties.

This problem can be addressed by governmental policies in various ways. One option is to give guarantees to the investors regarding the future revenues, taking away the uncertainty about their future revenues. If the future use of the infrastructure does not develop sufficiently, resulting in lower revenues for the investor, the government can make up for the lack of revenues. When, as a result, the investors see a profitable business case, they can realise the investment.

Another policy measure to address the hold-up problem related to investments in infrastructure is providing subsidies to either the investor or the users of the infrastructure. In the former case, the net costs of the investor are reduced, which contributes to the profitability of the investment, even when the future revenues remain uncertain. Subsidies to potential users can be provided through reduction in the tariffs charged by the infrastructure operator. Such subsidies raise the willingness of users to commit to the future use of the infrastructure.

A crucial aspect in all these types of governmental support for infrastructure investments is that they should be based on a societal analysis, for example, a social cost-benefit analysis (CBA), in which the societal value of the investment in a particular infrastructure is explored for a number of scenarios. After all, governmental support should only be given in case a project is beneficial from a societal perspective, but cannot be realised by private investors. The societal analysis can be used to determine the optimal design and size of an investment in an infrastructure, and also the timing of realising it (see Box 4.6). With such an analysis, the government can reduce the risk that the investment (in a particular size, design and timing of realisation) is not beneficial from a societal perspective, and, hence, results in a (too) large burden for the governmental budget.

In theory, the maximum support given to the investor should not be larger than the amount that is needed to make the project (having a positive net societal value) profitable for investors. One of the problems here is determining the amount required to make a project profitable due to the uncertainty about future costs and revenues, as well as information asymmetry between the government and investors. Because of this, it is key to leave some financial risks for the investors, which will incentivise them to make good forecasts and operate efficiently, while the risks for the government budget are mitigated.[27]

4.6.8 Conclusion

Governments have various options to address the negative environmental externalities related to the use of fossil energy. These options include financial instruments, such as taxation of the negative externality and providing subsidies for the low-carbon technologies, regulatory standards and combinations of these two types of measures in the form of emissions-trading schemes. In theory, imposing a carbon tax is a straightforward measure to internalise the externality, but in practice many issues arise, in particular in relation to the economic consequences for industries next to distributional effects. Support schemes can be effective in promoting particular (low-carbon) technologies, but are also subject to a number of caveats, such as free riders, rebound effects and inefficient designs. Regulatory standards can also be effective, but require the government to have a strong information position. Emissions-trading schemes, which combine regulatory obligations with financial incentives, can be both effective and efficient. When such schemes are implemented, interaction with other policy measures, such as carbon taxes, renewable subsidies or regulatory constraints, may reduce the overall efficiency of these policy measures. Because of such financial and regulatory measures, economic agents may want to use other types of energy carriers, for which infrastructures have to be developed, but the development may suffer from hold-up problems. In order to address this, governments can reduce the financial risks for involved stakeholders through support schemes or public participation.

4.7 Conclusions

In order to address fundamental shortcomings in energy markets which may call for energy-transition measures, governments can intervene in energy systems in various ways, depending on the type of problem that is at stake.

Economic agents have economic incentives to be(come) active in exploration, development and production of natural resources because of its commercial value, but without any government intervention they may not operate on the societally optimal level. In order to address the market failures related to information

[27] This was also one of the conclusions of the Netherlands Court of Audit in its analysis of the support given by the Dutch state to an investor (Gasunie) to develop the backbone for the hydrogen infrastructure (Netherlands Court of Audit, 2025).

asymmetry, market power, negative externalities and unequal distribution of resource rents, government can intervene in the upstream part of energy systems. They can do so by fostering the distribution of information regarding the characteristics of natural resources, promoting competition in the upstream business, internalising the externality of a too rapid depletion through financial or regulatory measures and redistributing the resource rents through financial measures or public ownership.

Risks related to import dependencies are, to some extent, reflected in the levels and volatility of future prices, but not completely, particularly with regard to geopolitical risks. In order to address these risks, governments can subsidise domestic production, or impose regulatory constraints on imports. The most efficient policy measures, however, seem to be those that facilitate the resilience of an economy, for instance by promoting the diversification of import routes and enabling economic agents to flexibly respond to supply shocks.

Even when a market process functions well, it may result in high and volatile prices which are perceived as societally unacceptable. If this is the case, governments can intervene in energy markets in different ways. Measures which directly intervene in the price-formation process are generally ineffective and do not solve the underlying problem causing high prices, while they can be rather costly. Measures which support economic agents to deal with high prices can be effective in helping these agents to deal with high prices, but can also be very costly for society if the underlying cause of high prices is not addressed. Therefore, from an economic perspective, governments should be hesitant to intervene in energy systems to help economic agents deal with high prices. As far as vulnerable households are concerned, it seems to be more efficient to make use of specific income-related measures or measures directed at reducing their energy use to help them cope with the consequences of high and volatile energy prices.

Governments have various options to address the negative climate impact caused by the use of fossil energy. In theory, imposing a carbon tax is a straightforward measure to internalise the externality, but in practice many issues arise, in particular in relation to economic consequences for industries and distributional effects. Support schemes can be very effective in promoting particular (low-carbon) technologies, but are also subject to the risk of free riders, rebound effects and inefficient designs. Regulatory standards can also be very effective, but require the government to have a strong information position. Emissions-trading schemes, which combine regulatory obligations with financial incentives, can be both effective and efficient. When such schemes are implemented, interaction with other policy measures, such as carbon taxes, renewable subsidies or regulatory constraints, may reduce the overall efficiency of these policy measures. Because of the policy incentives to make energy systems less reliant on fossil energy, economic agents may want to use low-carbon energy carriers, for which infrastructures have to be developed. When the development of these infrastructures suffer from hold-up problems, governments can reduce the financial risks for involved stakeholders through support schemes or public participation.

Exercises

1. Explain why regulatory constraints can be both effective and inefficient in realising a policy target.
2. How can promoting the transparency about the success of past exploration activities affect how much exploration will be done in the future?
3. By what kind of policy measures can a country enhance the resilience against shocks in international energy markets?
4. To what extent are strategic energy reserves an efficient policy measure to address the societal problem of volatile and high energy prices?
5. Why can it be useful to implement subsidies for particular mitigation measures in case already a cap-and-trade emission scheme exists?

References

Ahi, J. C., Blomgren, A., Guttormsen, A., Misund, B., Tveterås, R., & R. (2025). Investment neutrality in resource rent taxation—Revealed preferences of Norwegian oil & gas companies. *Cogent Business & Management, 12*(1). https://doi.org/10.1080/23311975.2025.2450288

European Commission (EC). (2025). Report from the Commission to the European Parliament, the council, the European economic and social committee and the Committee of the Regions; report on energy prices and costs in Europe. Brussels. COM(2025) 72 final. https://eur-lex.europa.eu/legal-content/EN/TXT/HTML/?uri=CELEX:52025DC0072

European Parliament. (2023). Reforming the EU electricity market. EPRS European Parliamentary Research Service, PE 739.374, March.

IEA. (2024a). World energy investment 2024.

IEA. (2024b). Energy policy review: The Netherlands 2024.

IEA. (2025). Renewables 2025: analysis and forecasts to 2030.

IMF. (n.d.). *Fossil fuel subsidies*. https://www.imf.org/en/topics/climate-change/energy-subsidies

Li, X., & Mulder, M. (2026). Promoting hydrogen through supporting consumers or producers? An international welfare economic analysis. *Climate Policy*, 1–25. https://doi.org/10.1080/14693062.2026.2654964

Martén, I., Whittaker, P., & de Bourio, A. M. (2014). *Government take in upstream oil and gas; framing a more balanced dialogue*. Boston Consulting Group.

Mulder, M. (2023). *Regulation of energy markets: Economic mechanisms and policy evaluation* (2nd ed.). Springer.

Mulder, M., Bollen, J., Cozijnsen, J., Lomme, S., Rooijers, F., van Soest, J. P., & Woerdman, E. (2023). *European emissions system determines meeting the agreed CO_2-targets, fossil subsidies secondary. English translation of 'Europees emissiesysteem bepaalt halen CO_2-doelen, fossiele subsidies secundair'*. Economisch-Statistische Berichten (ESB).

Mulder, M., & Perey, P. (2018). Gas production and earthquakes in Groningen: Reflection on economic and social consequences. Centre for Energy Economics Research, CEER policy papers, no. 3, June.

Netherlands Court of Audit. (2025). *Hydrogen network under severe pressure—Ineffective grant to offset startup losses*. https://english.rekenkamer.nl/documents/2025/12/10/hydrogen-network-under-severe-pressure-ineffective-grant-to-offset-startup-losses

Pahle, M., Quemin, S., Osorio, S., Günther, C., & Pietzcker, R. (2025). The emerging endgame: The EU ETS on the road towards climate neutrality. *Resource and Energy Economics, 81*, 101476.

Perman, R., Ma, Y., McGilvray, J., & Common, M. (1999). *Natural resource & environmental economics* (2nd ed.). Prentice Hall.

Pollitt, M. G., Duma, D., Covatariu, A., & Nillesen, P. (2025). *A global map of electricity and gas distribution network companies*. University of Cambridge, Energy Policy Research Group.

Santarius, T., Walnum, H. J., & Aall, C. (2018). From unidisciplinary to multidisciplinary rebound research: Lessons learned for comprehensive climate energy and climate policies. *Frontiers in Energy Research, 6*, 104.

Sorrel, S. (2009). The rebound effect: Definition and estimation. In J. Evans & L. C. Hunt (Eds.), *International handbook on the economics of energy*. Edwad Elgar.

TNO. (2025). Delfstoffen en aardwarmte in Nederland, Jaarverslag 2024.

Veenstra, A. T., Li, X., & Mulder, M. (2026). Economic assessment of the role of nuclear and renewables in future decarbonized electricity markets. *The Energy Journal, 47*(4). https://journals.sagepub.com/doi/10.1177/01956574261450943

Veenstra, A. T., & Mulder, M. (2024). Impact of contracts for differences for non-carbon electricity generation on efficiency of electricity market. *Energy Economics, 136*, 107674. https://doi.org/10.1016/j.eneco.2024.107674

Yergin, D., P. Orszag, and A. Arya (2025). The troubled energy transition; how to find a pragmatic path forward. Foreign Affairs, March/April.

Zweiffel, P., Praktiknjo, A., & Erdmann, G. (2017). *Energy economics: Theory and applications*. Springer.

Contribution of Stakeholders to Energy Transition

5

5.1 Introduction

In the analysis in the previous chapters, the attention was directed at the functioning of energy systems in general and the economic reasons and options to pursue the transition of these systems in one way or the other. In that analysis, we mainly spoke about economic agents as an abstract concept. In reality, of course, there are many different types of agents active in energy systems. This implies that the governmental measures to intervene in energy systems can only be effective insofar they impact the decisions made by individual agents. Therefore, it is also required to have a good understanding of the variety of stakeholders and how they may be affected by external factors, including policy measures.

In this chapter, we will first explore all the different types of agents that are active in energy systems, which roles they play and what their interests are. Then, we analyse how they may or can respond to changing external factors, like energy prices, macroeconomic circumstances as well as government policies. Finally, we analyse how various types of agents can contribute to an energy transition by looking at a number of examples of agents in various layers of energy supply chains.

5.2 Stakeholders in Energy Systems

5.2.1 Categories of Roles and Alignment of Interests

The developments in energy systems result from activities conducted by many different economic agents, who interact with each other in various ways. These agents can also be called stakeholders as they have an interest (a stake) in the functioning of these systems. The stakeholders operate within societal environments and are subject to all kinds of policy measures as well as market forces. Hence, the

M. Mulder, *Economics of Energy Transition*, Studies in Energy, Resource and Environmental Economics, https://doi.org/10.1007/978-3-032-29010-6_5

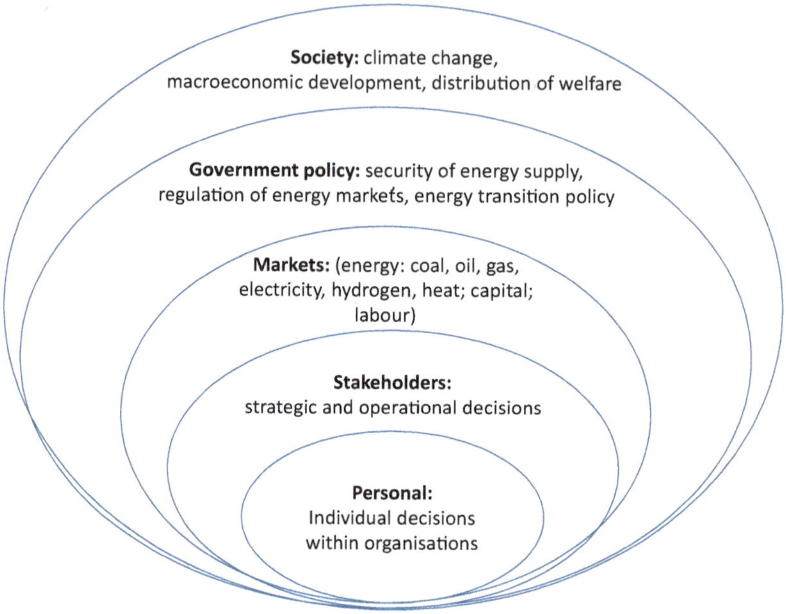

Fig. 5.1 Decisions of economic agents (individuals as well as organisations) in energy systems within the context of markets, policies and societal factors

decisions made by these stakeholders are influenced by the economic, technical, legal, spatial and social environment they operate in (see Fig. 5.1).

Under the influence of external factors, stakeholders pursue their own objectives. By the latter it is meant that these stakeholders have their own interests and that their actions are related to these interests. In economics, such behaviour is called rational, although it is fully acknowledged that often actual behaviour of economic agents is not (fully) consistent with their own interests given the presence of various types of psychological biases (as was discussed in Sect. 2.3). Later in this chapter, we will discuss a number of examples of decisions made by various stakeholders.

First, however, we will introduce the different types of stakeholders. Using the concept of energy supply chains, the stakeholders in energy systems can be split into a number of categories: producers of energy carriers, users of energy carriers, suppliers to both producers and users of energy, intermediate parties facilitating the exchange between producers and users, public agencies directed at public interests related to energy systems, and external parties (see Fig. 5.2). Each type of agent plays a different role in the energy supply chains. Depending on their role, they have different interests and objectives.

5.2.1.1 Energy Producers

The roles of producers differ from each other in the type of energy carrier they are focused on: primary, secondary and tertiary (see Box 1.1). Consequently, producers of energy carriers can be distinguished in (a) agents that explore, develop and

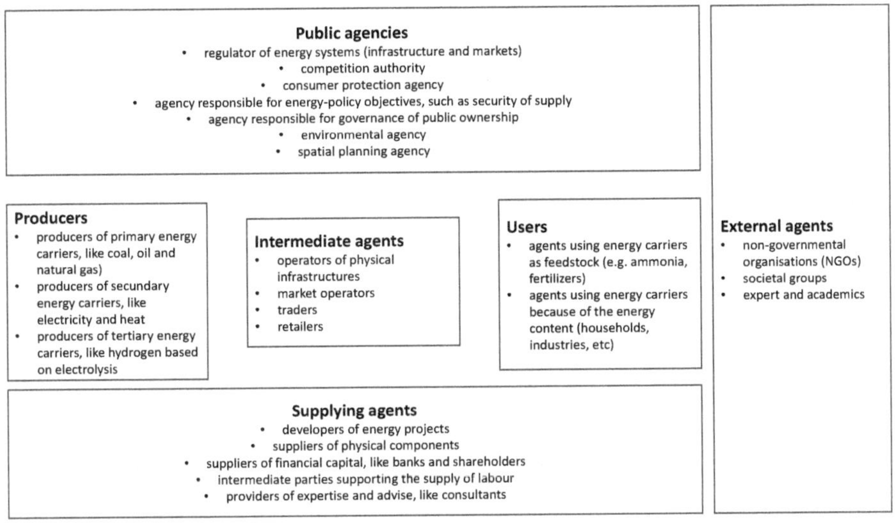

Fig. 5.2 Categories of stakeholder roles in energy systems

produce non-renewable primary energy resources as coal, oil and natural gas, (b) agents that produce secondary energy carriers, in particular electricity and heat and (c) agents that produce tertiary energy carriers, in particular hydrogen.

As secondary and tertiary energy carriers are, by definition, made out of primary and secondary carriers, respectively, these producers have different interests. A producer of gas benefits from higher gas prices as that raises their revenues, but a producer of electricity using a gas-fired power plant has an interest in lower gas prices as that reduces their costs. Similarly, producers of electricity benefit from higher electricity prices, but producers of hydrogen through electrolysis benefit from lower electricity prices as that reduce their costs. This phenomenon of opposing interests among players with a seemingly similar role in energy systems is important to realise when we think about how to change the energy system in a particular way. For instance, promoting the supply of renewable electricity, for instance by a netting measure for residential households (see Sect. 5.4.9), may lead to lower electricity prices which is beneficial to operators of electrolysers, but disadvantageous for the business case of investments in other renewable-energy projects, such as offshore wind farms.

5.2.1.2 Energy Users

The roles of users can be distinguished based on how economic agents use energy carriers. Some economic agents use energy carriers as an intermediate product to produce another commodity. Natural gas, for instance, can be converted, through chemical processes, into products like nitrogen and ammonia, while oil can be converted in many different types of products, such as plastics and cleaning products. This use of energy carriers is called feedstock use, since here the physical content of the energy carriers (i.e. the molecules) is converted into another product. The main type of use of energy carriers, however, refers to the use of these carriers for their energy content. Natural gas and oil, for instance, can be used to generate heat needed for industrial processes, to warm buildings or to generate electricity to power engines and appliances. The objectives of the agents embodying these roles within this category are rather aligned, as they all benefit from lower prices of energy carriers. The users, however, compete with each other as more demand by others may raise the price another user has to pay. Hence, although the preferences of agents can be similar, it does not mean they are inclined to help each other. On the contrary, in the case of scarce resources, it is in the interest of each user that others consume less.

This phenomenon of competition is also relevant for the design of energy-transition policies. After all, attention needs to be paid to the process of allocation of scarce resources. From an economic perspective, this allocation needs to be efficient. Allocative efficiency means that the commodity is allocated to those agents with the highest willingness-to-pay. As a result, the allocation results in the highest societal welfare. In Chap. 3, we have seen that markets can realise such an outcome when all conditions for market well-functioning are fulfilled. For the assessment of the allocation, however, it may also be relevant to look at the distributional consequences and equity considerations. For instance, if the commodity is essential for daily life, it may be fairer that it is allocated to everyone instead of only to those who have the best financial abilities to express a high willingness-to-pay (i.e. priority allocation based on societal preferences). Such considerations can be a reason for governments to intervene in energy markets, as was discussed in Sect. 4.6.

5.2.1.3 Supplying Agents

Both producers and users of energy carriers make use of other agents for the supply of necessary inputs. This supply can refer to physical inputs, such as components for the construction of a gas-fired power plant or wind turbine, financial inputs, such as loans or equity to finance investments in power plants, and other types of inputs, such as legal, technical or economic advice on how to further develop particular activities. This group of agents also includes developers of renewable-energy projects, such as offshore wind parks. The suppliers of inputs to the production or consumption of energy carriers do not directly belong to the supply chain of energy systems, but they are closely related to it. This also implies that these suppliers do not need to be restricted to supplying producers or consumers of energy carriers, as they may be able to provide similar products to producers or consumers in other supply chains. The producers of steel needed for the construction of wind turbines, for instance, may also sell their product to other types of clients, albeit the precise product characteristics may differ among their customers.

The degree to which customers require specific product characteristics affects the degree to which suppliers specialise in serving a particular group of clients. Specialisation could benefit the supplier by realising economies of scale or developing tacit knowledge, which would strengthen its market position relative to potential competitors. Such a strategy may also create a risk for a supplying company, as its business case will be strongly related to the performance of the client's industry.

5.2.1.4 Intermediate Parties

Another category of roles agents can play involves facilitating cooperation and exchange among producers and users. For the producers and consumers of gas, electricity, hydrogen and heat, it is crucial to have an infrastructure for transportation, distribution and storage. That infrastructure should function properly, which implies there is sufficient capacity and the systems are in balance. Hence, managing the operations of these infrastructures is an essential role in these energy systems. Another crucial facility for the cooperation between producers and consumers consists of marketplaces where they can meet and conclude agreements for the exchange of commodities. On these marketplaces, other agents play a role, in particular traders who accommodate the wishes of other market parties including producers and users with each other, as well as retailers who facilitate the exchange of energy carriers between small-scale users, in particular residential users, and producers and traders of these carriers.

5.2.1.5 Public Agencies

All these roles are carried out within a legal societal framework which defines the boundaries of all players' actions. That framework consists of among other things competition law and sector-specific regulatory rules. The legal framework may also define the tasks and responsibilities of public agencies to pursue particular public interests related to energy systems. These public interests can concern the environmental effects of energy production, spatial planning, labour circumstances, consumer protection, market design, regulation of infrastructures, competition and national energy security. In line with this variety of public interests, there is also a wide variety of public agencies involved in the functioning of energy systems. In addition, public agencies can be distinguished according to different regional dimensions. Some agencies only have legally defined tasks at a local (municipal) level, others regional, national or international. Generally, the tasks and responsibility of a public agency at a smaller regional scale (e.g. local or regional) are subject to principles or guidelines formulated at a larger regional scale (e.g. national or international). Public agencies can also be responsible for the public ownership of companies active in energy systems.

5.2.1.6 External Parties

A final category of stakeholder roles comprises agents who do not directly participate in energy systems but seek to influence developments within these systems for various reasons. This category includes non-governmental organisations (NGOs) who pursue societal objectives, such as a low-carbon energy system or a fair energy transition. Other types of agents in this category promote the use of particular technologies, such as hydrogen and nuclear, which may be motivated by concerns about the composition of energy systems or inspired by private interests rooted in relationships with particular types of stakeholders.

Experts, academics, advisory bodies, and others who actively try to influence the societal debate on the direction of energy systems through publications, letters, podcasts and presentations belong to this category as well. Although many of these experts may try to influence the trajectory of energy systems so they benefit society as a whole, their viewpoints and recommendations can be quite different. These differences are related to differences in (academic) perspectives, assumptions, methods and data used, and probably also personal characteristics and preferences. Because of all these differences, it is not reasonable to expect or promote that a society should try to formulate one integrated vision of how the future energy system should develop (see Box 5.1). Differences in perspectives as well as interests will always remain, so the challenge is how to deal with these differences and find a common, shared pathway.

5.2.2 Stakeholders with Various Roles and Differing Objectives

Although the above classification of various types of roles economic agents can play in energy systems is more concrete than talking about economic agents, it is still a bit abstract. In practice, firms, public agencies, residential households and others can play various roles and combine the activities belonging to various types of stakeholders. A producer of natural-gas resources can also be the operator of the gas infrastructure, such as pipelines and storage facilities. A producer of electricity can also act as a retailer and sell electricity to residential households. An operator of a heat-network can also be active as a producer of heat, for instance through the exploitation of geothermal heat installations, as well as a supplier of heat to small businesses. Residential households are, generally, consumers of various types of energy carriers like gas, electricity, gasoline and heat, while they can also be producers when they install, for instance, solar panels on the roofs of their houses.[1]

Box 5.1 Different Approaches to Formulate Visions for the Future of Energy Systems

Energy transition may entail that energy systems have to change quite drastically. As this can only be realised when all the various stakeholders participate, it is sometimes said there is a need for a common view of how these systems should develop. Without such a common view, transitions at an individual stakeholder level may be uncoordinated and, therefore, fail to realise the energy transition at the societal level in an efficient, effective and fair way. As a result of this perceived need for a common view on the future development of the energy systems, several institutes and experts produce visions of the long-term pathways. There exists several types of vision reports.

An example of a forward-looking scenario study is the report by The Copenhagen Infrastructure Partners (CIP), which formulates three scenarios for the European energy system by 2050, which are called Slow Transition, Low Price and Net Zero. In the Slow Transition scenario, European climate

(continued)

[1] In the latter case, they are called prosumers.

Box 5.1 (continued)

policy is weakened and delayed, in the Low-Price scenario, the focus is more on European competitiveness with a modest climate policy, while in the Net-Zero scenario, the European climate objectives for 2050 are reached. Based on these assumptions regarding climate and economic policy, the consequences for the degree of electrification, fossil-fuel dependence and decarbonisation of the energy-intensive industry are analysed. Hence, these kinds of scenarios are examples of studies which use quantitative models to analyse what may happen in an energy system when certain assumptions are made. Depending on the assumptions, the outcomes regarding the future system can be quite different. As was also concluded by Barani et al. (2026) in their analysis of numerous scenario studies on the future energy system, there is no 'uniform picture of how a largely net-zero GHG energy system in Europe could look in 2050 and beyond.'

An alternative approach to explore the future consists of so-called backward-looking scenarios. In this approach, the starting point is a description of the future system, and then it is analysed how such a future situation can be realised. The example of this approach is the Net-Zero Emissions (NZE) scenario made by the IEA. The objective of this NZE scenario is to show how an energy system with net-zero carbon emissions can be realised. As there are more pathways to reach that future than those included in the IEA study, these scenarios are primarily meant to give an indication of how the future system may develop if we want to reach the climate objective.

Both of the above approaches can be seen as technical scenarios, which simply analyse the consequences when certain assumptions are made. The backward-looking approach can also be combined with a normative view on how societies should develop. In the resulting scenarios, it is prescribed what should be done by other stakeholders in order to reach particular societal changes. An example of this approach is the vision published the Climate Action Network (CAN) Europe, which is a coalition of Europe's leading NGOs fighting climate change. In this vision, published in 2020, they formulated that Europe's carbon emissions should be reduced by 65% in 2030 in order to reach net-zero by 2040. As a part of this vision report, they call various types of stakeholders to action in order to realise a strong increase in energy efficiency and a quick and widespread electrification. Hence, this is more a normative approach.

When agents combine various roles, their objectives may be less straightforward. A household that both consumes and produces electricity would like to have low electricity prices as a consumer, but high prices as a producer. Hence, having a portfolio of different activities affects agents' optimal decisions. When a household does not generate its own electricity, it may aim to lower electricity costs by being using electricity more efficiently. However, when it also generates its own electricity, the household may aim to use electricity when its own solar panels are producing. In the first case, the objective is to minimise electricity use, while in the second case the objective is to minimise the net costs of using electricity, which can be realised, for instance, by changing the timing of consumption. During periods of high solar production, these households may want to raise their electricity consumption in order to consume less electricity when there is hardly or no sunshine, and they do not produce their own electricity.

A similar tension in objectives holds for a firm that produces both electricity and hydrogen through electrolysis. As an electricity producer, the firm benefits from high electricity prices, but as a producer of hydrogen it prefers to have low electricity prices. A firm that has the choice to either supply its electricity to the power market or to use the electricity itself in order to produce hydrogen will compare the potential revenues in the electricity market with those in the hydrogen market. As electricity prices tend to be volatile, the optimal strategy of such a firm might be to sell electricity in the power market when electricity prices are high (and, hence, hydrogen production would be expensive) and use the electricity to produce hydrogen when electricity prices are low (and, hence, the revenues in the power markets are low as well).

The fact that many agents conduct various types of activities is relevant for the analysis of the effectiveness of policy measures, since this affects the objective function of these agents. Taxation of electricity use by households has a different effect depending on whether these households also produce electricity through solar panels. If the electricity tax is based on annual electricity consumption, households may have an incentive to become a producer as it reduces the annual net consumption, but this weakens their incentive to reduce their own consumption.

The fact that agents are active in various roles is also relevant for the functioning of systems and the design of policy measures. This holds in particular when agents operate a crucial infrastructure which is also used and needed by other agents. An agent that acts both as grid operator and producer may have an incentive to give its own production plants a preferential treatment over competitors' plants in the electricity market. This would result in an unequal playing field, distorting competition. Because of this mechanism, in the European Union and elsewhere, the operation of the grid has been unbundled from the execution of commercial activities like production, trade and retail. As a result, the operators are not allowed to be active in these activities and have to treat all agents wanting to make use of the infrastructure indiscriminately. With such regulatory measures, governments pursue the well-functioning of energy markets (see Sect. 4.3).

5.2.3 Stakeholders Benefiting from Economies of Scale and Scope

When economic agents combine different types of activities, they enlarge their scope of activities. Variation in the scope of economic agents' activities results in a mixture of different types of economic agents within energy systems. Some agents in energy systems combine many different types of activities, covering many layers of energy supply chains, including the exploration, development and production of oil and gas, international trade and transport of these commodities, refining and chemical activities, sales of the produced products to end-users, while they are also active in developing wind and solar parks as well as the generation and sales of electricity. An example of such a company is Shell, as is further discussed in Sect. 3.4.2. Other agents, however, are highly specialised and are active only in one of these activities, such as specialised wind-park developers or energy retailers.

Both strategies can be profitable. The benefits of a wide scope of closely related activities may refer to the technological, economic or financial advantages of conducting them within one (holding) company. Such a company is less dependent on other market parties and prices resulting from (less competitive) market forces, as the crucial inputs can be acquired at internal cost prices. Instead, such a company may have a strong market position if its customers appreciate that various types of products can be bought from one company, enabling it to realise a higher profit margin. The benefits resulting from combining different types of activities within one company are called economies of scope. This phenomenon is defined as the situation in which the average costs (*C*) of combining various types of activities (such as *x* and *y*) within one company are lower than the average costs of conducting the same of activities in different companies:

$$C(x+y) < (C(x)+C(y)). \tag{5.1}$$

On the other hand, a company that is highly specialised may be able to realise a higher productive efficiency because of its specialisation, next to having the ability to focus more on niche markets where higher profit margins can be realised. When various scope levels have their own pros and cons, we see a combination of these different types of firms.

This variation becomes even bigger when we look at the scale of their activities. The production of electricity, for instance, can be carried out by a small company only operating one solar park, but it can also be carried out by large firms operating a wide portfolio of different types of power plants located in different markets and countries. Both types of companies are only active in the generation of electricity, i.e. they utilise the same scope, but have a very different scale. The benefits related to the scale of operations are called economies of scale, which is defined as the situation in which the average costs of a firm producing more versions of a product (such as x_1 and x_2) are lower than the sum of the average costs of more firms jointly producing the same amount of the product:

$$C(x_1+x_2) < (C(x_1)+C(x_2)) \tag{5.2}$$

Generally, economies-of-scale benefits per unit of activity increase with scale up to a particular point, after which these benefits decrease. This relationship between scale and benefits depends on the (relative) importance of fixed (sunk) costs in the operation and the degree the coordination task (e.g. governance, internal procedures) becomes more challenging when the size of activities increases.

Economies of scale do not only exist at the firm level, but can also occur at the level of installations. Electricity, for instance, can be generated by a large-scale nuclear power unit of 2000 MW and by solar panels of 200 Wp.[2] In the latter case, many units are needed to produce the same amount of electricity, which also requires more coordination and space.

5.2.4 Internal Governance of Stakeholders

Another dimension of economic agents active in energy systems is their internal stakeholder composition and how the collaboration among these stakeholders is governed. In many cases, economic agents consist of various types of stakeholders. Most companies consist of managers, shareholders and employees, while maintaining close relationships with other stakeholders, such as their customers, suppliers and agents operating in their neighbourhood. All those stakeholders may influence what the agent is going to do. Paying attention to the various stakeholders, both internally and externally, and their interests can be seen as a crucial aspect of the strategic management of organisations.[3] Although residential consumers are often seen as one individual stakeholder, they often consist of more than one individual, each having their own objectives and preferences.

Economic agents are also organised in various ways. The type of organisation refers to their ownership type. Many agents in energy systems are privately owned, but there are also many publicly owned companies and companies that are owned by a combination of private and public investors. Both privately and publicly owned companies can operate in markets and behave like commercial players. Both types of agents can conduct activities which are subject to regulatory supervision, such as the operation of electricity grids (see Sect. 4.2.2). This implies that it is important to distinguish the type of ownership from the way companies operate in relation to other agents. There are, for instance, privately owned entities operating a regulated electricity grid, next to publicly owned companies operating as commercial firms in liberalised markets.

When firms want to keep control of related types of activities, they may search for stakes in various layers of the supply chain. As an example, we can look at the grid operator 50 Hz, which is one of the four German Transmission System Operators (TSOs). Besides operating a part of the German high-voltage grid, 50herz is active in offshore grids and connectors, while it also has several financial participations, like in the European Electricity Exchange (EEX). This grid operator is fully owned by Eurogrid Gmbh, which is in turn fully owned by Eurogrid International, which is fully owned by the Elia Group (see Fig. 5.3).

[2] Wp stands for Watt peak, i.e. the peak capacity.

[3] According to Freeman and McVea (2001), stakeholder management is a crucial aspect of strategic management to 'manage and integrate the relationships and interests of shareholders, employees, customers, suppliers, communities, and other groups in a way that ensures the long-term success of the firm'.

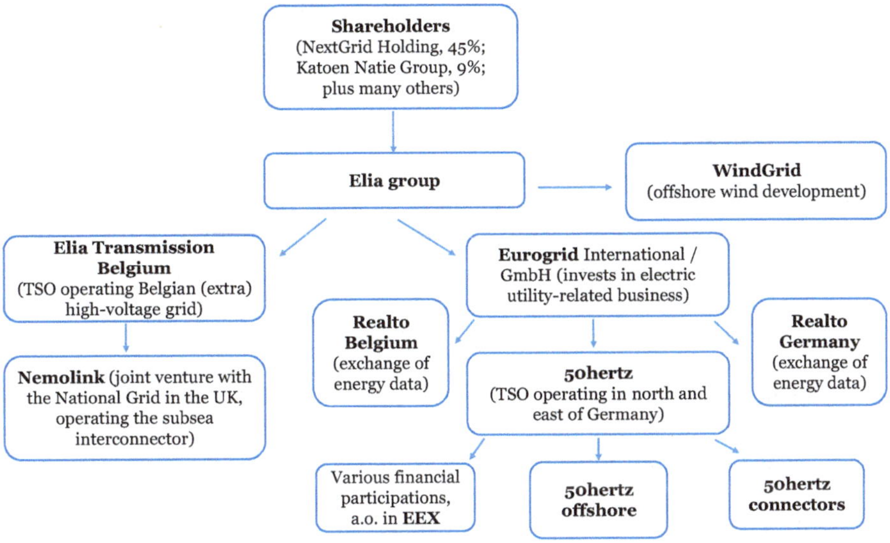

Fig. 5.3 Example of diverse ownership relations among companies: the legal structure of the ELIA group (Source: website Elia retrieved d.d. 30 November 2025)

Eurogrid International also has subsidiaries active in the exchange of energy data (i.e. Realto Belgium and Realto Germany), which is a commercial, non-regulated activity. The Elia group also owns Elia Transmission Belgium, which is the operator of the Belgian (high) voltage grid. This TSO has a joint venture (called Nemolink) with National Grid, which is the TSO in the United Kingdom, to operate the subsea interconnection. The shareholders of Elia Group consist of a variety of investors, both private and public. The shares of this holding can be freely traded. A large part of the shares (45%) is owned by NextGrid Holding, which is controlled by Publi-T. This is an investment vehicle to control the public interest in the electricity grid. This example shows how companies can have influence in various parts of supply chains.

Next to these hybrid private-public entities operating regulated grids, there exist public entities operating in commercial markets, such as Vattenfall, a company owned by the Swedish state which is active in European liberalised electricity wholesale markets and the regulated grid business. The transitions within this company will be further discussed in Sect. 5.4.3.

In contrast to private, public and hybrid private/public ownership, other types of organisations exist, such as cooperatives. In these types of organisations, the ownership is neither private nor public, but in the hands of associations, i.e. group of various (individual) stakeholders (see Sect. 5.4.9). These agents pursue objectives which are formulated by the association, such as the realisation of local renewable-energy projects, like a wind park or district-heating system.

Another hybrid form of ownership is the special-purpose vehicle, which is constructed to realise a particular project, such as an offshore-wind park. Such vehicles are used by equity-providing companies to manage their financial risks related to such investments (see Box 5.5).

5.2.5 Coordination of Stakeholder Activities

Since there are many stakeholders involved in energy systems with various roles and objectives, it is often said there is a need for strong coordination of the behaviour of these stakeholders to fundamentally change the energy system. After all, how would it be possible to change the direction of the energy system, i.e. to realise a system change, if not all stakeholders collaborate and contribute to this change?

It is clear that coordination is needed in one way or another as the activities in supply chains are interrelated. When the installed capacity of renewable-electricity technologies, such as solar panels and wind turbines, in a particular region is expanded, the electricity grid might also need to be extended, otherwise the increase in installed generation capacity cannot be transferred into an increase in renewable-electricity production. Grid operators therefore, need to formulate expectations regarding the future use of the grid and take appropriate measures, like investments in grid extension. It may thus be helpful for the operator to be informed about plans of project developers to install additional renewable capacity, as well as other kinds of plans that may increase or decrease grid usage. Developers of electrolyser projects, for instance, need to know the extent to which sufficient renewable electricity generation will be available, otherwise they cannot be sure that they will be able to produce renewable hydrogen (see Box 4.7). Hence, these developers need to understand the outlook for the development of renewable electricity generation, based on investment plans for renewable capacity and grid availability.

These relationships form just a few examples of dependencies among stakeholders within energy supply chains, which call for coordination and information exchange. Many more examples can be given, such as the interdependence of developing a district-heating transport system and the investments to be made in the production of (renewable or waste) heat and the use of heat in, for instance, residential buildings.

The fundamental question here is what kind of coordination is needed to ensure that individual stakeholders can pursue their objectives, while the overall energy supply chains are efficiently transformed in line with the objectives of an energy transition. The common form of coordination of individual behaviour occurs through markets. Market prices inform stakeholders about the current and future costs and availability of commodities, as well as the preferences of other stakeholders. If the price of electricity, for instance, is high and is expected to remain so, some stakeholders may be incentivised to develop new generation plants, while others may be incentivised to reduce their consumption by investing in more energy-efficient appliances. As a result of this adaptive behaviour in response to the information provided through market prices, energy systems can respond to changing situations in an efficient way. This is one of the reasons why decentralised systems based on markets can take care of the coordination of all the various types of decisions made by stakeholders (see Box 5.2).

The concept of decentralised decision-making should not be confused with systems which operate on a local and small-scale. Even an energy system that consists of large-scale production and consumption units, which are connected to a national transportation infrastructure, can be decentralised when the decisions are made by many individual agents. On the contrary, an energy system consisting of many small-scale production units with a large number of stakeholders active in these units can be a centralised system when the use of these production units is coordinated through a top-down system where from a central point (such as the board of an energy cooperation) instructions are given to all stakeholders on how and when to use the production units.[4] The latter form of organising a system may work on a small scale, but in general, systems with decentralised decision-making function much better.

Coordination of decentralised decisions through markets may not always be the optimal solution. For instance, this coordination system may be unable to realise investments in infrastructure. Such investments may suffer from hold-up problems, as investors face uncertainty about the commitment of potential customers to use the infrastructure. If these customers express interest without making a legally binding long-term commitment, infrastructure investors face too much risk and will likely refrain from investing. Therefore, in such cases more coordination is needed, for instance through so-called open-seasons in which investors sell the new capacity to customers. This is a tool to both explore the future demand for the infrastructure and let customers already commit to using it.

Even when coordination mechanisms such as markets and open-season mechanisms are present, stakeholders together may not fully move into the direction of a societally beneficial energy transition. This can be due to the presence of specific market failures, as was discussed in Chap. 3, which require specific intervention. This intervention can take the form of subsidies for renewables, carbon taxes or emissions-trading schemes, as we have discussed in Chap. 4, but this might not be sufficient. Next to such policy measures, financial guarantees may be needed to reduce the risks for investors infrastructure, as was discussed in Sect. 4.6.7.

[4] Although liberalised electricity systems are based on decentralised decision-making, which means that the economic agents (e.g. producers, traders, consumers) are in principle free to make their own decisions, the physical system of frequency maintenance and allocation of grid capacity is centralised. This also means that even when local communities mutually coordinate their production and use of electricity and make administrative arrangements for the mutual exchange of electricity, technically their local system remains a part of the international electricity system (see Sect. 5.4.4).

Box 5.2 What Are the Benefits and Risks of (De)centralised Energy Systems?

In the societal debate on the organisation of energy transition, the degree of centralisation in decision-making is one of the key issues. Coordination of all the various decisions by stakeholders in energy systems is needed, but should this be carried out by a central agency, or can we rely on market forces based on decentralised decision-making? Often, reference is made to China as the example of a successful centralised energy transition. However, looking at data on the share of renewables in the total energy system, it appears that the decentralised European system is even more successful, as is discussed in Box 4.2.

The economic argument for why a decentralised energy transition is preferred over a more centralised one includes a number of arguments. One of the arguments refers to the presence of information asymmetry within societies, for instance, between governments, firms and consumers. Information asymmetry can be distinguished in two components: lack of information about the characteristics of others, and lack of information on the behaviour of others.

Regarding the information on characteristics, the crucial point is that a centralised agency, such as a government body, cannot possess all the information on all technical possibilities in all circumstances. To gather such information, the agency would need to make huge efforts and costs. A centralised approach requires large-scale centralised administration, data collection and analysis and coordinated decision-making.

Besides the huge costs of organising such a system, there are also a number of other risks. There is the risk that the centralised agency might not make the optimal decision. Since the future is inherently uncertain and decisions, such as investments in energy infrastructure, must be made under this uncertainty, there is always the possibility that an agency will not choose the best choice. The consequences of this could be huge when a decision to invest, for instance, in a particular type of energy network is implemented in many parts of a country. In contrast, if decisions are made by several (decentralised) agents who act independently of each other, the likelihood that one of them will make the optimal decision (such as regarding an innovative idea) is much higher. Hence, decentralising decision-making can also be viewed as a kind of risk diversification.

Another risk of centralised decision-making is that rent-seeking behaviour may become more profitable for economic agents. If an agent can influence the decision of the central authority in a certain direction, this can be highly profitable for that agent. Hence, there is a greater risk that the decisions will not be aligned with the public interest unless appropriate regulatory measures to mitigate this risk are taken. Corruption, therefore, is more widespread in countries with centralised economies than in democratic societies where individual stakeholders have opportunities to participate (see: https://ourworldindata.org/data-insights/democracies-tend-to-have-lower-levels-of-corruption).

(continued)

Box 5.2 (continued)

In addition to these risks associated with centralised decision-making, there is a more fundamental criticism based on what economists call the impossibility of interpersonal utility comparison. It is impossible for us to determine precisely what the preferences of others are, how much value others attach to certain things (see Sect. 2.3). Hence, it is complicated, if not impossible, to determine to what extent the welfare of others is affected by a certain decision. Of course, a central authority can do research, asking firms and consumers about their ideas, but this remains an indirect approach. Therefore, a huge benefit of a decentralised approach is that individual economic agents can make the decision themselves, and make the choices which fit them the best.

The other component of information asymmetry concerns a lack of information on behaviour. The problem with a centralised system, where one central agency makes all the relevant decisions, is that all the other agents lack incentives to do their best. If the central agency decides, for instance, what type of technologies are used to generate electricity and how much they have to produce, at every moment in time, why would a firm with alternative ideas for generating electricity do its best to make that idea happen? Why would firms innovate to reduce costs, if the amount of production and associated revenues are already centrally determined? This is the so-called moral hazard problem of taking away risks and opportunities from agents. A consequence of this is that the agents are less innovative and in general lazier than they would be when seeing the consequences of their behaviour.

5.3 Transitions by Economic Agents in Energy Systems

5.3.1 Stakeholder Choices Resulting in Transitions

In the previous section, it has become clear that energy systems consist of a large variety of agents each with distinct roles, varying scopes and sizes of activities, regional orientation, organisational structures and ownership types, operational contexts, as well as differing preferences and objectives. One may assume that every agent tries to do its best to realise its own objectives, within all the physical, economic, spatial, legal and social constraints, the generally limited available information, limited ability to process all the relevant information and uncertainty about what the future will bring. As agents differ in characteristics, locations, preferences, risk attitudes and information, they make different decisions. Hence, agents are quite heterogenous.[5]

[5] The heterogeneity of agents in energy systems also translates into different roles, tasks and responsibility of stakeholders in different energy systems. Rentier (2025), for instance, shows that public institutions have played a different role in the development of wind and solar PV projects in countries around the North Sea.

From an economic perspective, the behaviour of all these agents can be understood as constant decision-making, as many resources are scarce and can therefore be allocated in alternative ways. In the standard microeconomic approach, it is assumed that these choices are made in a rational way, meaning agents are always making the best decisions for themselves. It is also a fundamental economic insight that when individual agents pursue their own objectives, an optimal social outcome can be realised, provided a number of conditions are met.

In contrast to the standard microeconomic approach, from behavioural economics we have learned that actual decision-making often deviates from what is assumed in theory, as individuals often make decisions which are time-inconsistent and subject to various other biases, as discussed in Sect. 3.2. This holds in particular for human agents like residential consumers, but also to some extent for firms. Although economic agents may believe that their decisions are consistent with their own preferences and objectives, in reality these often deviate from each other. The assumed rationality in economic analysis, however, is not meant to describe actual behaviour of economic agents, but to function as an analytical benchmark to analyse that actual behaviour.

No matter how rational actual behaviour is, for our analysis it is relevant that agents have to make decisions regarding the use of scarce resources in a way that maximises their objectives. The best choices for an agent are affected by external developments, such as societal developments, technological improvements, new policy regulations and changing market conditions (see Fig. 5.1).

In the theoretical economic analysis, it is generally assumed that the objectives for all firms consist of profit-maximisation, while consumers are assumed to pursue maximisation of utility. In reality, economic agents may pursue other objectives. An agent may have the objective to contribute to an energy transition, for instance by focusing on the development and realisation of renewable-energy projects or the provision of support to residential households to increase the energy efficiency of their houses. One of the issues now is how effective individual behaviour is to change the overall system. Crucial here is that individual stakeholders and economic agents (such as an energy company) operate within a society and markets. A change in behaviour by one agent or stakeholders may be counterbalanced by the behaviour of others. There are several examples of energy companies who decided to focus on renewable energy and stop with fossil-energy activities, as we will see in Sect. 5.4, but the question is how effective this is in the overall picture.

Hence, economic agents make their own assessment of the economic, legal and social environment they operate in and choose their objectives. Their objectives can be comprised of various elements: not only shareholder value, but also environmental and social objectives. These objectives may carry different weights, which can also change over time. This was, for instance, the case with Shell, where currently more weight is attached to shareholder value compared to a number of years ago (see Sect. 5.4.2). In order to realise their objectives, agents formulate strategies, in one way or another (see Box 5.3). Some agents will do this only implicitly, but others make extensive analyses of risks and opportunities to choose their strategies. Under the influence of the (strategic) decisions, next to external influences, agents undergo transitions.

Box 5.3 Methods to Formulate Long-Term Strategies

When economic agents have to navigate a complex and volatile environment, it may help to systematically explore what the best strategic options are. There exist a number of methods to do so in a systematic way.

One of the common methods for strategy analysis is the SWOT analysis, which is directed at analysing the Strengths and Weaknesses of an organisation within the context of Opportunities and Threats. The strengths refer to those characteristics of an organisation which give it a strong position compared to similar types of organisations (such as financial position and quality of staff), while the weaknesses refer to characteristics which are less favourable in comparison to others. The opportunities refer to external factors which may be beneficial for the organisation (such as a growth in the demand for the products it offers), while the Threats refer to external factors that may have a negative impact on the organisation (such as new, stricter government regulation). This SWOT framework can be used to systematically explore what the best strategic responses of an organisation could be.

Another common method to analyse the functioning of a company and determine the best way for the future is the so-called McKinsey 7-S model. In this approach, the seven aspects that are perceived to be fundamental for the future development of an organisation are analysed: strategy, structure, systems, shared values, skills, style and staff. The former three aspects are seen as the Hard S's, and the latter four aspects as the Soft S's. The Hard S's refer to the strategy of an organisation to improve its performance, the international organisation of staff and activities, and the formal process used to make the (daily) decisions. The Soft S's refer to values of the staff and organisation, their capabilities, the internal communication and leadership style and the characteristics of the staff.

5.3.2 Types of Transitions at Stakeholder Level

The decisions of economic agents contribute to various types of transitions. These transitions can be related to the various dimensions of the agents, as discussed in the previous section. Firms may decide to expand the scope of their activities, to specialise more, use other types of inputs (e.g. energy carriers) or produce a different portfolio of products. They may also decide to expand the size of their installations and, hence, the company, or to focus on small-scale production. A firm may also decide to going international by starting subsidiaries in other countries, setting up collaborations with companies in the same branch in other countries, or reducing the international dimension of its activities to focus more on local markets. Firms can also decide to change their type of ownership by looking for more private or more public shareholders. Others may decide to establish a new company which is organised differently, such as an energy cooperation or energy community. Firms can also reorganise their business by creating more business units with higher levels

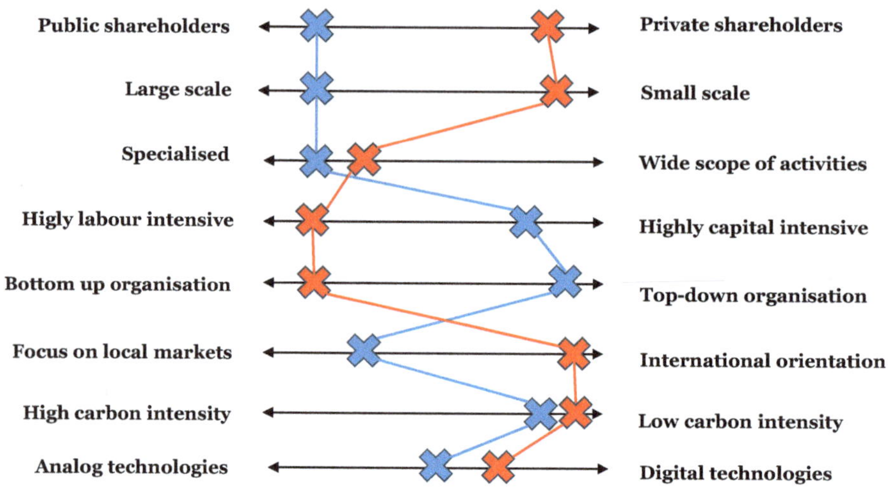

Fig. 5.4 Potential trajectories of transitions at the stakeholder level with two examples of stakeholders: distribution grid operator (in blue) and consultancy (in red)

of responsibility for small groups of employees within the company. All these various types of decisions result in the heterogeneity among the stakeholders in energy systems, as indicated by Fig. 5.4.

Hence, the transitions on micro-level can be distinguished in changes referring to how activities are conducted, the type of activities agents are conducting and changes in the governance of those activities. The former category consists of changes in the intensity of particular types of inputs, the use of a particular type of technology or the location of the activities. Such changes can be measured through, for instance, the intensity of the use of labour, capital or energy per unit of product and the carbon intensity of production processes. The latter category consists of changes in the inputs of the products agents are producing or changes in the type of customers an agent is serving. Such changes can be measured through, for instance, the share of particular types of energy in the total supply of energy.

A problem of using relative measures, such as energy efficiency or carbon intensity, may be that improvements in these metrics do not say anything about the absolute energy consumption or emissions. If an increase in energy efficiency or reduction in the carbon intensity is combined with an increase in the magnitude of output, the total energy use or carbon emissions may increase. A similar caveat holds for measures related to the composition of activities. When a company reduces the share of high-carbon activities in its overall portfolio, not only the carbon intensity, but also the absolute level of emissions may decline, which is reported as a reduction in its so-called Scope 3 emissions (see Appendix B). If, however, a company reduces its emissions by selling high-carbon activities to another company, the latter company will have an increase in its Scope 3 emissions. As a result, at an industry level, there may be no change in the overall level of emissions.

A similar effect may occur when an upstream company active in the exploration, development and production of oil or natural-gas resources decides, for whatever reason, to stop its activities to become more active in low-carbon energy sources. Such a new strategy would result in much less carbon emissions at firm level, but at a system level, the overall level of emissions may remain unchanged when another company expands its upstream fossil activities (see Box 5.4).

5.4 Examples of Transitions at Stakeholder Level

5.4.1 Introduction

To get a better understanding of how diverse the transitions of stakeholders in energy systems are, it is useful to discuss a number of specific examples. These examples refer to (groups of) stakeholders active in various parts of energy supply chains (see Table 5.1). In discussing these examples, we also discuss the relationship between the transitions and external developments in society, markets and/or policies.

5.4.2 Transitions Within Global Energy Companies: The Case of Shell

The group of upstream companies consists of a wide variety of organisational types. Besides state-owned enterprises mainly operating in the domestic fossil-energy resources, there are also globally operating commercial companies that are active in various parts of the supply chain next to privately owned companies that are specialised in upstream activities. A company that belongs to the former group is Shell.

Shell is a globally operating energy company active in various parts of the supply chain related to various energy carriers. It is active worldwide in the upstream business of producing oil and gas, liquefying and transporting gas, refinery and chemical products, distribution and sales of products to end-users and electricity generation

Table 5.1 Stakeholders per layer in energy supply chains discussed in this chapter

Layer in energy supply chain	Types of stakeholders	Examples of stakeholders	Discussed in section
Upstream	Global energy companies	Shell	5.4.2
Production	Electricity companies	E.ON and Vattenfall	5.4.3
Transport	Electricity transmission system operators		5.4.4
Industrial users	European steel industry		5.4.5
Heat users		Dutch horticultural farmers	5.4.6
Suppliers	Financial institutions	Central banks	5.4.7
Retailers		European retailers	5.4.8
Residential users	Households		5.4.9
Local communities	Energy cooperatives		5.4.10

Box 5.4 Effects on Global Carbon Emissions When an Upstream Fossil-Energy Company Reduces Its Activities

Upstream companies in the oil and gas industry are directed at the exploration, development and production of oil and gas resources. When one of these companies reduces its activities, it will reduce its contribution to the supply of fossil energy and, hence, the global carbon emissions. For the overall effect, one should, however, look at what happens with (a) the resources the company was previously operating and (b) the activities of other players in the global markets.

In most countries, the exploitation of natural resources is based on licences which are issued by the national government. When an upstream company reduces its activities, these governments generally withdraw the licence in order to reissue them to another company. After all, national governments are interested in receiving the revenues from the exploitation. When one company is not interested any more to be active in the exploitation, it will be replaced by one that can contribute to realising the government's objectives. Hence, the fact that upstream companies generally operate within a licensing system, a decision by an upstream company to reduce its activities may have no effect on the actual amount that is produced. This may only be the case when the issuing government cannot find another company that is willing to take over the exploitation activities. Given the fact that there are hundreds of companies globally active in the exploration, development and production of oil and gas resources, this is not very likely.

In theory, it is conceivable that the strategic decisions of one company to leave the upstream oil and gas industry may influence the strategic decisions of others, as is stated by advocates of the system-change approach (see Box 1.2). This could be the case when other companies perceive that move as a signal about the risks of being involved in fossil energy. Since the future is uncertain and no one knows precisely how fast an energy transition will take place, stakeholders look around to get more information on what the best strategy is. If this were the case, a government may not be able to find another company to take over the exploitation of the national fossil-energy resources.

It is also conceivable, that a government itself decides that their resources should no longer be exploited due to climate risks. In these cases, and only then, the supply curve of fossil energy will be affected, as is depicted by Fig. 5.5. A new supply curve emerges (Supply curve 2) in which supply coming from resources A is removed. This results in a higher equilibrium price (from p_1 to p_2) and lower equilibrium output (from q_1 to q_2), and, hence, lower emissions. The actual magnitude of these effects depends on the shapes of both the supply and demand curves. Since the demand curve for oil is rather price inelastic (see Sect. 2.6), while the supply curve is fairly price elastic, in particular in the longer term, removing a part of the supply mainly results in a price effect and hardly in a volume effect.

(continued)

Box 5.4 (continued)

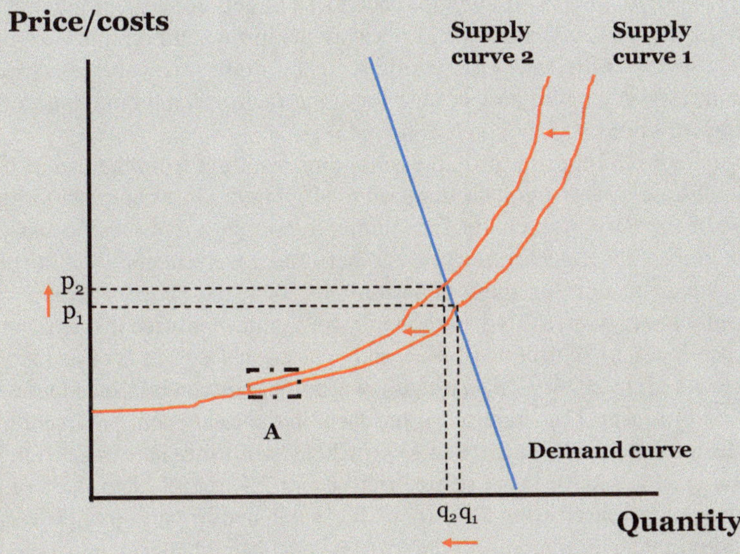

Fig. 5.5 Impact of withdrawal of a particular resource on the market outcomes

and sales. In its 2024 annual report, Shell summarised its mission as creating more value with fewer emissions.[6] This mission is translated into a number of objectives: generating shareholder value, achieving net-zero emissions by 2050, helping customers to decarbonise and providing energy for buildings, industry and transport. Shell wants to realise these objectives through creating a workplace that is inclusive and representative of communities, while also protecting the environment and contributing to biodiversity.

The target for creating shareholder value has been realised according to the metric price-normalised (i.e. controlled for macroeconomic price movements) Free Cash Flow (FCF) per share, which increased by 36% in 3 years' time, while the objective is to realise a 10% annual growth. This growth was due to operational decisions regarding operational efficiencies, portfolio changes, faster decision-making in project development as well as a reduction in the number of shares resulting from share buybacks.

In its 2024 annual report, Shell also states that it is on track to realise its targets regarding emissions. The Scope 1 and 2 emissions (i.e. the emissions resulting from its own operations and use of electricity, respectively) in 2024 were 30% below the level of 2016, the year used as the benchmark year. This reduction is mainly realised

[6] Shell also formulated its strategy in its Energy Transition Strategy 2024: https://www.shell.com/sustainability/climate/shell-energy-transition-strategy.html. See also the website of Shell: https://www.shell.com/what-we-do/our-strategy.html.

by divesting and purchasing renewable electricity. With this reduction, Shell seems to be on track to reach its target of a 50% reduction by 2030 and become a net-zero company by 2050. Shell's strategy to reach these targets consists of making portfolio changes, such as acquisitions and investments in low-carbon intensity projects, improving energy efficiency of operations, using more renewable electricity and developing carbon capture and storage for some facilities and compensate for any remaining emissions by buying carbon credits.

For the Scope 3 emissions (i.e. the emissions resulting from the use of its products), Shell states that there is no standard to align individual company targets with the goals of the Paris Agreement. The annual report says that these emissions can only be reduced in cooperation with customers and governments.[7] Shell does, however, pursue a reduction in these emissions. In 2024, the Scope 3 emissions were significantly lower than in 2016, both in relative terms, measured through the metric Net Carbon Intensity (a decline of 9%), and in absolute terms (a decline from 1.6 Gt in 2016 to 1.1 Gt in 2024). This reduction was mainly driven by the reduction in the sales of oil products. The share of oil products in the total energy delivered to customers declined from 54% in 2016 to 43% in 2024, while the share of LNG increased from 14% to 21% and the share of electricity from 7% to 16%. The share of natural gas, however, decreased from 24% to 19%. As gas and in particular power have a lower carbon intensity than oil products, these portfolio changes contributed to the reduction in the Scope 3 emissions.[8]

These changes are related to Shell's strategy to gradually decarbonise the products it supplies to customers in transport and industry by replacing fossil-fuel products with renewable products, such as synthetic fuels, hydrogen, biofuels and electricity, as well as offering carbon capture and storage services. The motivation to implement this strategy is based on the assessment of risks and opportunities. One category of risks consists of the risk of energy transition resulting in a lower demand for fossil fuels, changing preferences of investors, higher costs resulting from climate policies, as well as risks related to changing expectations in society. The other category of risks consists of climate-related physical risks which may negatively affect the assets and operations of the company. All these events may also offer opportunities, such as a higher expected demand for LNG, biofuels, electrical vehicle charging and CCS.

[7] This statement is related to Shell's response in the court case initiated by environmental organisations against the company. These organisations sought a ruling that Shell should reduce its global Scope 1, 2, and 3 emissions with a net 45% by 2030. Shell's response was that it cannot influence the choices of consumers, that it can only affect the emissions caused by its own activities (i.e. only Scope 1 and 2 emissions). In the first instance, the District Court of The Hague ordered the 45% reduction in all global emissions of Shell, but on appeal, the Court of Appeal of The Hague ruled that Shell cannot be legally compelled to implement these measures. For more information on this court case, see: https://www.stibbe.com/publications-and-insights/no-reduction-order-for-shell-on-appeal-what-does-this-mean. Also, see Box 5.4 for an analysis of the effectiveness of a measure which is directed at only one company.

[8] Although one should acknowledge that LNG transport causes more emissions of methane, which is one of the greenhouse gases, than transport of gas through pipelines.

The recent developments in energy markets resulting in high fossil-fuel prices made the realisation of the decarbonisation strategy more challenging, as there is ongoing pressure from shareholders to realise shareholder value by focusing more on fossil energy instead of renewable energy.

5.4.3 Transitions within Electricity Companies: The Cases of E. ON and Vattenfall

As electricity generation plays a crucial role in energy systems, the companies active in this business have to realise transitions if the energy systems have to change. There are many different types of electricity companies which make different types of strategic decisions. We discuss for a few of them how they have dealt with changing circumstances and developed over the past decades. The examples are E.ON and Vattenfall, both large companies active in (mainly) the European electricity systems, but with quite different histories of transition (see Fig. 5.6).

The German company E.ON[9] was established in 2000 by a merger of two other German companies called VIAG and VEBA. These companies were active in many different branches, including the production of aluminium, electricity and nitrogen, the exploration and production of coal and petroleum, sales of oil products, telecommunications and chemicals. The objective of the merger was to become

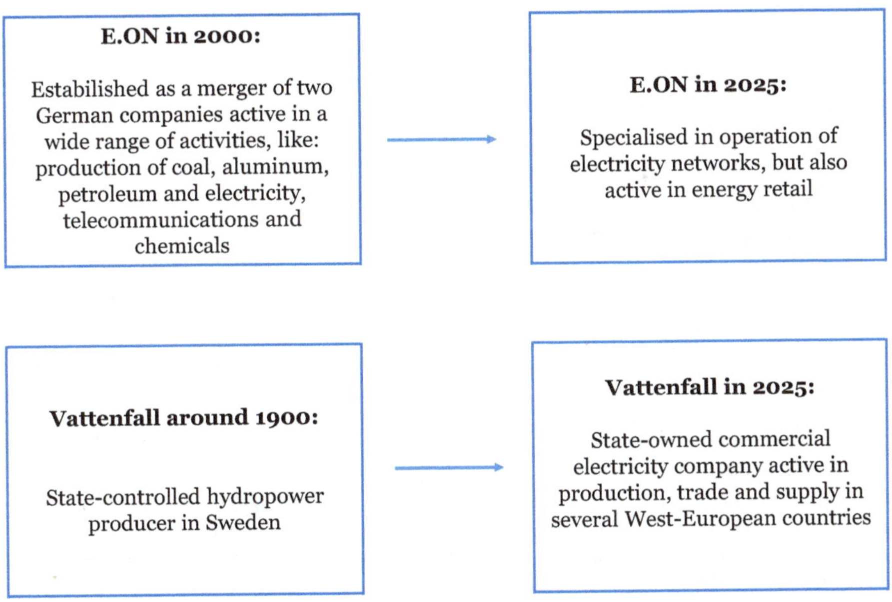

Fig. 5.6 Past transitions of two major European electricity companies: E.ON and Vattenfall

[9] Sources: https://www.company-histories.com/EOn-AG-Company-History.html and homepage E.ON.

more profitable by focusing only on energy and chemicals and become a global player in these activities. Although E.ON initially planned to obtain a position in the US energy markets, it is now strongly focused on energy markets in various European countries. In 2014, E.ON formulated a new strategy, stating that the company will no longer generate energy from fossil fuels and will focus on renewables, grids and customer solutions. Consequently, in 2016, E.ON divested its coal and gas-fired power plants into a new company called Uniper,[10] while its nuclear power plants had to close because of the German phasing out of nuclear power (see Box 2.1). Both transitions within E.ON were directly related to the German energy transition. As a result, E.ON remained mainly active in renewable electricity generation (e.g. hydropower and wind power) and the transport and distribution of gas and electricity. Later on, E.ON sold its renewable-energy activities to RWE, another German energy company, while it acquired grids from RWE. Currently, E.ON is specialised in the operation of energy networks and infrastructures. According to its website, E.ON is the largest distribution-grid operator in Europe, active in nine European countries. In addition, E.ON owns several energy retail companies across Europe with local subsidiary brands, like Essent in the Netherlands, E.ON Next in the United Kingdom and E.ON Energie Deutschland.

The Swedish company Vattenfall[11] originated as a government-owned company responsible for the development and production of hydropower in Sweden at the beginning of the twentieth century. In the first half of the twentieth century, Vattenfall expanded its hydropower production in Sweden in order to meet the growing electricity demand of industrial and residential consumers. In the 1960s, Vattenfall started to develop activities abroad by initiating the Nordic electricity system with the other Nordic countries (Sweden, Denmark, Norway and Finland). This Nordic pool enabled Vattenfall to sell electricity to customers in neighbouring countries.

In the 1970s and 1980s, Sweden built a few nuclear power plants, but after a referendum, the Swedish society decided to gradually phase out nuclear power. Then, Vattenfall started to develop other types of generation, both gas and renewables ((i.e. wind, solar and biomass). As a result, the generation portfolio of Vattenfall became more diverse. Next to electricity generation, Vattenfall is also active in the operation of district-heating systems and electricity-distribution systems. In the 1990s, the corporate structure of Vattenfall changed from a state-controlled company into a commercial company. However, the Swedish state kept all the shares, because it believed the hydro reservoirs should be controlled by the government and not by private players. The new type of governance and the opening

[10] For the supply of gas for its gas-fired power plants, Uniper heavily depended on gas imports from Russia. After the Russian invasion of Ukraine, Uniper was forced to replace the Russian gas supply, based on long-term contracts, by gas from other sources bought on spot markets against extremely high prices. In order to enable Uniper to continue its business (i.e. the production and supply of electricity), the German government nationalised the company. This state intervention needed the approval of the European Commission. See: https://ec.europa.eu/commission/presscorner/detail/es/ip_22_7830.

[11] Sources: https://www.company-histories.com/Vattenfall-AB-Company-History.html and homepage Vattenfall.

of European energy markets triggered the company to become active in more European countries. It acquired subsidiaries in neighbouring European countries. Currently, it is mainly active in Sweden, Germany, Denmark, the UK and the Netherlands. Aggregated across all these countries, in 2024 the share of both nuclear and hydro in its total electricity generation of 100 TWh was a bit more than one third, while the share of wind was 18%. Because of these numbers, Vattenfall says it is one of Europe's largest producers of fossil-free electricity.

5.4.4 Transitions within Grid Operators: The Case of European Transmission-System Operators

Energy carriers have to be transported from the producer to the end-user. For some energy carriers, like coal and oil, transport can be efficiently carried out by ships, which means that no massive investments in infrastructure are required. For other energy carriers, however, these investments are crucial to realise a transport infrastructure that makes it possible to enjoy economies of scale. This holds in particular for the transport of electricity. Given the nature of this energy carrier, it is impossible to store it as such, which implies that electricity systems only function when the total generation always equals the total load. Consequently, the operators of electricity grids play a crucial role in electricity systems and since the use of electricity is expected to increase significantly, this role will become even more important in the near future. With the growing use of electricity and increasing international integration of markets, the grid operators have already had to realise several transitions. These transitions were mainly focused on facilitating the international integration of electricity systems.

One of the technical components that facilitates this integration is physically connecting systems and harmonising the frequency. The Alternating Current (AC) grid[12] of continental Europe is now one physical electricity system with a synchronous frequency of approximately 50 Hertz (Hz), stretching from Denmark in the northwest, Portugal in the southwest, Turkey in the south-east and the Baltic States in the northeast (see Fig. 5.7). On top of this, the grids of North-African countries (Morocco, Algeria and Tunisia) are also synchronised with the continental European

[12] Most of the European grid is based on Alternating Current (AC), but Direct Current (DC) is also important as it is used in many appliances like laptops and solar PV panels. In order to connect those appliances to the grid, one needs converters who convert the AC of the grid to the required DC of a laptop and the other way around for PV panels. An advantage of AC is that it is relatively easy to switch the voltage levels. The latter is important as for long-distance transport a high-voltage level is more efficient, while for the actual use (in, for instance, a laptop) a low voltage is required. In addition, the operation of an AC grid is also more resilient as the electrical energy searches for alternative routes within the grid in case of a disturbance in one component of the grid. In the case of DC, the electrical energy moves only in one direction, which also implies that it can be used to connect different AC grids, as occurs, for instance, between the Norwegian grid and the continental European grid (e.g. the NorNed Line) and between the UK grid and the European grid (i.e. the BritNed line). DC lines are also used to connect AC grids with different frequencies. In those cases, converter stations are required to convert the AC into DC and vice versa.

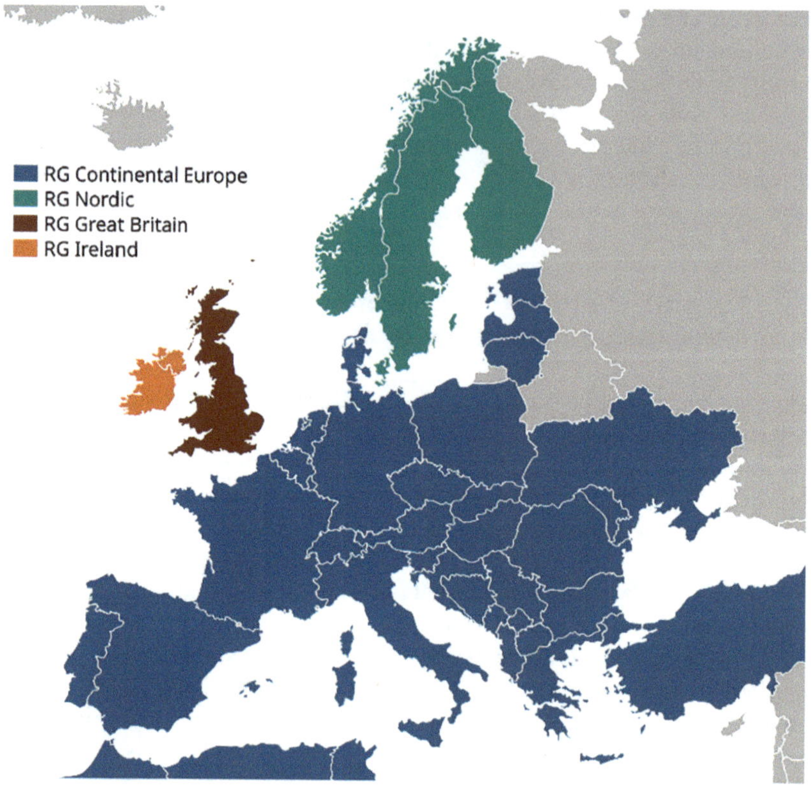

Fig. 5.7 Synchronous zones within the European electricity system (Source: https://en.wikipedia.org/wiki/Continental_Europe_Synchronous_Area)

grid. Within this large region, all the national grid operators together make sure that the grid frequency is maintained by permanently equalising total load with total generation. This continental grid is connected to the synchronous zones in the United Kingdom, Ireland and the Nordic countries through Direct Current (DC) connections. Within each region, Transmission System Operators (TSOs) are responsible for balancing the aggregated load and generation.

In order to better control the frequency of the continental grid and develop the grid infrastructure, the European grid operators increasingly collaborate. Initially, the collaboration, through the Union for the Coordination of Transmission of Electricity (UCTE), was directed at the joint frequency management, the optimal dispatch of generation units and the extension of cross-border connections (UCTE, 2010). In 2008, the European Network of Transmission System Operators for Electricity (ENTSOE-E) was established. This European network of TSOs has strategic objectives to contribute to a European electricity system that is both suited for carbon-neutral generation and secure and efficient (ENTSO-E, 2024).[13] In order to realise this task, the TSOs together work on extensions of cross-border capacity, while also extending the transport capacity within their own zones. In addition, in collaboration with the electricity exchanges (such as EPEX SPOT) and the National Regulatory Authorities (NRAs), they have increased the efficiency of the grid use by, amongst others, the introduction of flow-based market coupling. This means that the clearing of spot markets in various countries is done by simultaneously paying attention to the available grid capacity and the flow of electricity throughout the grid. One of the results of this market coupling is that the available capacity for cross-border trade in electricity has increased significantly, with as result that the spot market prices in the various countries less often deviate from each other.

Besides the increased collaboration between national TSOs and the extension of their tasks, several grid operators have also undergone mergers and acquisitions. The fully state-owned Dutch TSO, TenneT, for instance, acquired one of the German TSOs, previously owned by E.ON, to reach economies of scale in its operation and advantages in the further integration of the Dutch and German electricity market. A similar example is the acquisition of the Belgian TSO (Elia) by the German TSO 50 Hertz (see Fig. 5.3). In 2026, however, the Dutch state sold its shares in TenneT Germany to the German state. The key reason to sell was the large financial burden on the shareholders (i.e. the Dutch state) resulting from the high investment required to facilitate the energy transition in Germany (i.e. the need to expand the transmission grid).

5.4.5 Transitions within Energy-Intensive Industries: The Case of the European Steel Industry[14]

Energy-intensive industries are particularly sensitive to changes in the costs of using energy, either as a result of market developments or measures taken by governments. An example of an energy-intensive industry that has to deal with the high costs of using (fossil) energy is the steel industry. This type of industry is the producer of crucial inputs for many other types of industries, such as the automotive industry, construction sector and manufacturing. The current process of making steel is heavily based on the use of fossil-energy carriers, resulting in high emissions. In 2025, the European steel industry was responsible for about 5% of European total carbon emissions and more than a quarter of the European industrial emissions. In that year, more than 50% of the European steel production was based on the coal-based blast furnace and basic oxygen furnace (BF-BOF) route.

[13] According to European regulation, the ENTSOE is responsible for ensuring a secure and reliable operation of the increasingly complex network, facilitating cross-border development and the integration of renewable energy and enhancing the creation of the internal European electricity market (European Union, 2009).

[14] Source: EEB (2025).

In this route, steel is produced in a number of consecutive steps. A crucial step is making iron out of ore. In the coal-based blast furnaces, this is achieved by removing the oxygen from the ore (which is a mineral consisting of the elements Fe, iron and O_2, oxygen). This removal of oxygen occurs with the help of cokes in high-temperature furnaces. Cokes are made out of coal by removing the gases from it under high temperature. During the process of removing the oxygen from the iron, oxygen molecules react with a carbon molecule in the cokes resulting in CO_2 while this process also generates emissions of NO_x, SO_2 and particulate matter. This way of steelmaking is, therefore, highly polluting for both the global and neighbouring environment. Not only the process of making iron out of the ores, but also that of making cokes, results in carbon emissions. Per ton of crude steel, the carbon emissions are about 2.3 tons, with the majority (1.4) resulting from the process of ironmaking in the blast furnaces, 0.7 ton through the production of cokes and 0.2 ton in the final process of steel-making. On top of this, there are also carbon emissions resulting from coal mining, which are estimated at about 0.7 ton per ton of crude steel.

Because of cap within the EU ETS, court cases, as well as societal pressure to reduce carbon emissions, the European steel industry needs to undergo a fundamental transition. This transition entails a shift from coal-based production to near-zero emissions alternatives. Technically, the carbon emissions of making steel can be reduced in various ways. The iron can be directly produced from the ore by using natural gas, hydrogen or a blend of these gases. If the hydrogen is generated with renewable electricity, the resulting iron can be a near-zero emissions iron. Other options to reduce the carbon emissions in the process of making steel are the use of scrap iron and electric arc furnaces based on renewable electricity or a combination of electric smelters and basic oxygen furnaces.

Economically, however, the transition to these near-zero-carbon alternatives is challenging because of the high costs (in particular those of renewable hydrogen), limited availability of infrastructures for electricity and hydrogen and the fact that the steel market is a global market.[15] The latter means that the European steel industry is not only competing with companies within, but also with large competitors from Asia and the Middle East. Although these regions are also transitioning towards low-carbon emissions technologies, this occurs at a slower pace. As a consequence, the global competitors can operate at lower costs when the European steel industry is transitioning to near-zero emissions alternatives.

To what extent the steel industry is able, economically, to make the transition depends on two factors: the willingness of customers in the automotive industry, construction business and manufacturing to pay a premium for steel produced with significantly lower carbon emissions, and governmental regulations. The latter refers to policy measures at different levels. At the local level, the local circumstances of a steel company, such as access to electricity and/or hydrogen grid, play a role. Relevant policies at the national level refer to, amongst others, tariffs for using the electricity grid, existence of support schemes as well as rules regarding minimum amounts of low-carbon steel in end-products, such as cars. Finally, at the

[15] See e.g. ING (2024).

international level, the economic feasibility of transitions in the steel industry are affected by international differences in costs. These differences refer to energy prices and costs related to climate policy. An example of the latter is the EU regulation regarding differences in carbon costs between Europe and countries outside Europe (see Sect. 4.6). In the EU Emissions Trading System (EU ETS), the so-called Carbon Border Abatement Costs (CBAM) scheme is introduced which is meant to protect (particular) European industries, such as the steel industry, from non-European competitors facing a lower carbon price.

An important aspect to realise is that if the transition of the European steel industry into near-zero emissions production is not successful, the production of the steel may be moved outside Europe, while European customers will continue to use steel. Such a carbon leakage would imply that there are not many benefits for the climate, while European economies suffer the costs of the steel producers leaving Europe. This also implies that changes in major industries are not only the responsibility of the companies involved, but also other stakeholders, such as customers and investors.

5.4.6 Transition within Heat Users: The Case of the Dutch Horticultural Farmers

Another example of an energy-intensive industry is the Dutch horticulture under glass, which is one of the major suppliers of vegetables and flowers in international trade. This production is relatively energy-intensive because of the local climatological circumstances (i.e. relatively cold) and the wish to also produce the products during seasons with less daylight and lower outside temperatures. As the use of energy is a major contributor to the costs of the horticultural farms, which operate in competitive international markets, they face a strong economic incentive to reduce their energy use as much as possible. As a result, their energy consumption has been strongly reduced over the past decades. In 2000, the average use of primary fuels (in particular natural gas) was equal to almost 45 gas equivalents per m^2, while this was less than 25 in 2024 (see Fig. 5.7). As the physical production per m^2 also strongly increased, the reduction in energy use per unit of product was even stronger.

The decline in energy intensity was the result of a variety of measures and changes. The energy demand was reduced by optimising the design and scale of the warehouses and using other materials. On top of that, the primary fuel use was reduced by more efficiently converting it into heat through Combined Heat Power (CHP) installations. By also using the electricity of these installations, for instance to illuminate the warehouses during winter season which raises the production, the energetic efficiency is increased. The CHP installations are also used to produce CO_2, which fosters the growth of the plants, resulting in a higher physical production.

The liberalisation of the electricity market enabled the horticultural farmers to operate in the electricity market. By being flexible in using their energy assets, they can respond to short-term price volatilities. When the electricity price is expected to be high in the day-ahead or intraday market, they can produce more electricity and sell it on the market. The heat which is produced can be stored in (water) buffers to

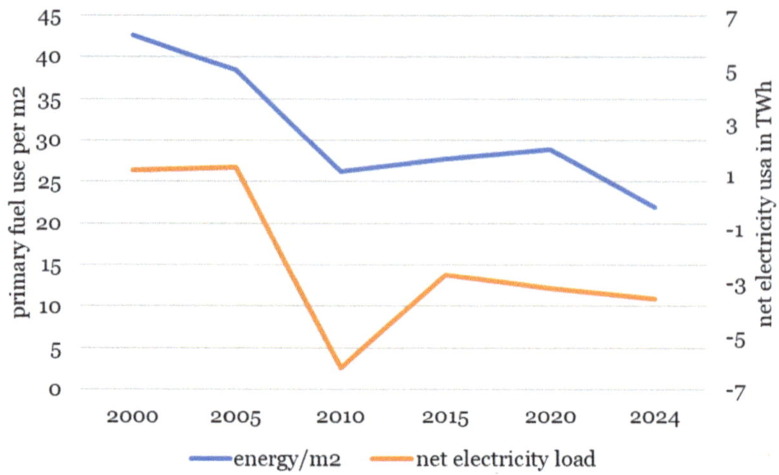

Fig. 5.8 Primary fuel use (in natural-gas equivalents) per m^2 and aggregated net electricity load in the Dutch horticulture-under-glass industry (in TWh), 2000–2024 (Source: Smit (2025). Note: the energy use is corrected for differences in outside temperature)

be used later on, for instance, during the next day when electricity prices may be lower because of a higher production by solar PV. In this way, the farmers have become, next to their horticulture business, significant players in the electricity market, mainly as providers of flexibility. As a result, the horticultural-under-glass industry has become a net producer of electricity (see Fig. 5.8).

The transitions within the horticulture on glass industry resulted not only from market threats and opportunities, but also from policy factors. In the past, the industry could benefit from a special treatment within the tax scheme on natural gas. As this industry has a strong internal collaboration, they were able to be treated together as a large gas user, which enabled them to make use of the much lower gas tariff for large industrial users. This favourable treatment will be gradually phased out by 2035, which gives the industry an even stronger incentive to reduce their use of natural gas.

The further reduction of gas use is partly pursued by using other sources of energy. Horticulture farmers are increasingly making use of heat that is produced elsewhere. Partly this is residual heat coming from industry and electricity producers, but heat is also being produced as geothermal heat. By developing joint infrastructures for the transport of heat, local heat markets are being developed, such as in the main horticulture region, the Westland. This heat market is meant to provide individual farmers the flexibility to deviate from contracted use of the heat infrastructure. The contracts between farmers and the transport-infrastructure developer give the latter the certainty that the investments can be recouped (addressing the so-called hold-up problem; see Sect. 4.6.7), while the flexibility offered by market systems makes that the former are more willing to conclude such contracts.[16] In the future, this heat grid may be further developed by connecting other types of heat

[16] Through the market platform, individual farmers can resell unused transport capacity, or buy more capacity than what is in their contract.

producers, such as from the industry in the Port of Rotterdam which can supply residual heat, as well as other types of heat users, such as residential areas in neighbouring cities as The Hague and Leiden.

5.4.7 Transitions within Financial Institutions: The Case of Central Banks

Financial institutions play a key role in modern economies as they are responsible for the monetary policy, organisation of financial transfers within the economy, financing investments and providing insurance. These roles are conducted by several types of institutions. One of the crucial institutions are the central banks.

Central banks are responsible for the monetary policy, which primarily means they take care of price stability. In addition, they may also be responsible for managing economic fluctuations.[17] The key tool of central banks to realise these macroeconomic objectives is adjusting the supply of money. By changing this supply, for instance, by buying government bonds, they can influence the short-term interest rates, which indirectly affect the long-term interest rates. These interest rates are crucial variables in the assessment of investments by economic agents. A higher interest rate, for instance, translates into higher costs of capital, which reduces the net present value (NPV) of an investment (see Sect. 3.3.3). A higher interest rate also translates into a higher discount rate, which is, for instance, used to calculate the LCOE of energy technologies (see Box 2.5). In particular, capital-intensive technologies, such as wind turbines, solar PV and nuclear power plants, are relatively sensitive to the discount rate.[18] By stabilising the economy, which has a downwards effect on the interest rate, central banks can contribute to (investments in) energy systems. In this way, they enable banks, for instance, to engage in project finance of renewable-energy projects (see Box 5.5).

Another crucial task of central banks is to monitor the stability of the other financial institutions, in particular banks. When banks are financially robust, they are more resilient against sudden shocks in the economy, which in turn contributes to the stability of the economy. In this respect, central banks increasingly pay attention to climate-related risks and to what extent banks are able to deal with them.[19] Here, we can distinguish between physical risks and transition risks.

The physical risks are related to nature degradation and biodiversity losses, which are caused by climate change. The European Central Bank (ECB) (2025) shows, for instance, that the output losses in the agricultural sector in particular can be 30%–40% in a scenario with a long period of drought, but also other industries, such as water supply and construction, are vulnerable to climate-related risks. By

[17] This paragraph is based on IMF, https://www.imf.org/en/about/factsheets/sheets/2023/monetary-policy-and-central-banking.

[18] This is due to the fact that for these technologies, the discount rate mainly affects the revenues, while for technologies with relatively more variable costs, such as a gas-fired power plant, also the future operational costs are affected.

[19] See e.g. the policy of the European Central bank: https://www.ecb.europa.eu/press/pr/date/2026/html/ecb.pr260116~4b4a05a179.en.html.

incorporating such risks in financing decisions, banks can reduce their own vulnerability. This can, for instance, be done by charging high-risk premiums for loans to companies or investments which face higher climate-related risks. In this way, banks also affect the (investment) decisions made by other economic agents.

Transition risks are related to the changing economy as a result of climate policy. When governments implement, for instance, a carbon-emissions trading scheme which restricts the amount of carbon emissions, fossil-based activities will become less profitable. When a bank continues to finance such activities, it may negatively affect its own financial stability. By incorporating such risks in their financing decisions, banks may, for instance, charge higher interest rates to fossil-based companies in comparison to companies that are less vulnerable to risks related to climate policy.

Box 5.5 Project Finance of Renewable-Energy Projects

When a project developer wants to realise a renewable-energy project, it needs capital to finance the investment (Raikar & Adamson, 2025). Investments can be realised as part of a portfolio of projects of a company. In that case, the financing is done through so-called corporate finance, which means that a company attracts capital in order to pay for the various types of projects. An alternative way of financing is so-called project finance. In this approach, a special-purpose vehicle (SPV) is established that is only directed at realising the project. This entity has so-called sponsors, which are parties that provide a particular amount of equity. The risk for the sponsors is limited to the size of this equity, which means that in case of default (i.e. the SPV cannot fully comply with all financial obligations), the sponsors are not responsible for losses above the amount already injected in the SPV. This characteristic is called non-recourse.

The majority of the required capital for an investment in renewable-energy projects is provided by providers of debt capital (i.e. lenders, banks). Because of the non-recourse characteristic, they can only reduce their credit risk (i.e. the risk that the borrower is not able to repay the loan and pay the interest) by conducting extensive analysis of the project and concluding detailed contracts. The analysis refers to many different aspects, such as the technical characteristics of the project, the construction process, contracts with suppliers of maintenance services and contracts with off takers of the energy produced. The fact that such extensive analysis and detailed contracts are needed to mitigate the risk for lenders has as a consequence that project finance is mainly applied to projects which can be well defined. Another consequence is that the transaction costs are relatively high.

The advantage of project finance is that it allows sponsors to provide equity without facing too much financial risk. The creation of an SPV also helps to create a clear governance structure and to manage the risks related to the project through well-defined contracts. Because of its advantages, the use of project finance for realising renewable-energy projects has strongly grown over the past decade. The share of low-emissions projects in financing new generation assets by banks has internationally grown from 71% in 2015 to 96% in 2024 (IEA, 2025).

5.4.8 Transitions within Energy Retailers: The Case of European Retailers

Before the unbundling of European gas and electricity systems, retailing activities were conducted by vertically integrated companies. Since then, various types of retailers have been established, varying from retailers as subsidiaries of holdings which are also active in other commercial activities such as generation and trade, and retailers which are fully specialised in that activity. As one of the results, the number of retailers in most European countries has increased significantly, as is illustrated for a number of countries in Fig. 5.9.

The activities of retailers have also changed. Initially, after the creation of energy retail markets, they were strongly engaged in price competition, but gradually the focus shifted to other parameters of competition, such as the supply of new types of products and services, like advice on energy savings and enabling households to provide flexibility to the electricity market.

Energy retailers still are, however, the intermediate parties connecting residential energy demand with the energy supply on wholesale markets. As their activities primarily consist of concluding contracts on wholesale markets and linking them with contracts with residential users (and other small users), their main role is to deal with financial flows and risks between suppliers and users. Depending on the preferences of users, their contracts can be differentiated according to various dimensions aside from the price of energy. Examples are the duration of the contract, the link to spot prices in the wholesale market and how the energy is being produced. Hence, retailers are increasingly not just selling energy to residential customers, but energy produced in specific ways, such as renewable energy in general, or more specifically, wind or nuclear energy. They also typically offer different

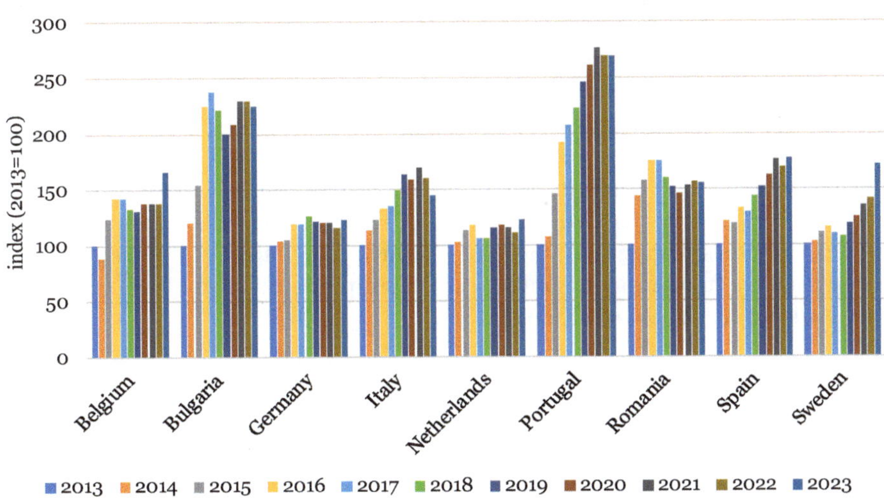

Fig. 5.9 Index of number of energy retailers in a number of European countries, 2013–2023 (2013 = 100) (Source: Eurostat)

types of contracts, such as fixed-price contracts for a specific duration. On top of that, they are increasingly offering additional services to their clients, such as helping them reduce their energy consumption by facilitating home insulation. The promotion of energy efficiency helps to reduce the energy consumption and may result in lower carbon emissions and lower dependence on the import of fossil energy. It also helps to reduce the vulnerability of households against high and volatile energy prices. The competition within retail markets stimulates retailers to diversify their offers, for instance, by providing services for energy-efficiency improvements and flexibility provision, to obtain higher market shares or profit margins. Therefore, one may state that the presence of a competitive retail market reduces the need for government policies to stimulate households to use less energy.

Note, however, that several groups of households, such as low-income households, face significant barriers to improving the energy efficiency of their homes due to financial constraints and, in the case of tenants, limited decision-making authority.[20] As a result, even in a competitive retail market, many households risk being left behind, which may require specific government measures to overcome these hurdles (see also Sect. 4.5).

5.4.9 Transitions within Individual Residential Households

The changes in the role of energy retailers are related to the fact that residential households have become a different type of agents as well. Before the liberalisation of electricity (and natural-gas) markets, energy was seen as a basic commodity which was provided by utilities. Households were connected to the grid and could use the electricity when they needed it, and once per period households received an invoice for this utility service. One can say that during those times, households were just passive consumers who did not interfere with the production, transport, storage or trade of electricity.

Since the liberalisation of electricity markets, the way residential households treat electricity has changed significantly. The first change was the ability to choose their energy provider, with which more providers entered the scheme with increasing variation in types of contracts, as we discussed in the previous section. Since a number of years, more and more consumers have become active producers (so-called prosumers) by installing solar PV on their rooftop, facilitated by support schemes, such as netting (see Box 5.6). An increasing number of households are using batteries in order to raise their use of self-produced electricity and become more independent of the electricity market.

[20] The situation in which tenants are responsible for the costs of energy use, while the investments in energy efficiency of buildings is the responsibility of the landlords, may result in the so-called split-incentive problem. After all, the latter group has to make the costs of insulation, while the former group will enjoy the benefits. From an empirical evaluation of the German housing market, however, it appears that there is not a significant gap in energy efficiency between rented apartments and apartments used by their owner (Singhal et al., 2025).

All these increased activities at the household level contribute to the development of distributed energy systems. By this is meant that the production, transport and use of energy occur on a relatively narrow spatial scale and that households and small-and-medium-sized companies become active participants. This development is enhanced by technological innovations, such as smart meters and home energy-management systems, which enable consumers to actively steer the charging times of electric vehicles and home battery systems, thereby shifting demand to periods with lower electricity prices or grid costs.

In order to contribute to the mitigation of climate change, households also become actively involved in reducing their energy consumption. In countries with a high heating demand during the winter, insulating houses can be an effective measure to reduce the use of fossil energy. Another option increasingly applied by households is replacing their heating system based on gas boilers by a system based on electrical heat pumps.

Besides being participants in energy markets, residential households are also citizens who may influence the development of energy systems in other ways. One of these ways is through elections on local, regional, national and/or supranational levels. In democratic societies, depending on constitutional rules, they have the right to vote for representatives in controlling and legislating bodies (e.g. parliament) or for those with executive powers (e.g. president). In this manner, citizens can influence the policy measures implemented by the latter.

Box 5.6 Fairness and Efficiency of Solar PV Support for Residential Households

In the societal debate on energy transition policies, fairness is often mentioned as a crucial condition for a successful transition (see also Box 2.9). The concept of fairness can be separated into distributional, procedural and recognitional fairness. Distributional fairness refers to the extent to which the various individuals are negatively and/or positively affected by something, such as a policy measure. Procedural fairness refers to the extent to which the various individuals have been able to participate in the process of decision-making, while recognitional fairness refers to the attention that has been paid to (possible) negative effects of something for others.

In theory, each of these aspects of fairness seem to be rather clear, but in practice it is more challenging to determine what a fair situation is. It appears that the assessment of fairness is related to the perspective and circumstances of the agents involved. If, for instance, a fair distribution of the economic consequences of energy transition is important to households, you would expect this would hold for both costs and benefits. However, when people are confronted with costs of the energy transition, they seem to be more inclined to complain about fairness than when they are confronted with its benefits.

To illustrate this point, we can refer to the Dutch netting scheme for solar panels for residential households. It appears that this scheme resulted in significant distributional consequences in the Netherlands (Masciandaro et al., 2025).

(continued)

Box 5.6 (continued)

Households that have installed solar panels on the roof of their house benefit as they can cancel out their electricity consumption with their own electricity production on an annual basis. This implies that they receive the end-user price (including residential taxes) for their production, while other producers of electricity have to sell their electricity on the market at much lower prices (i.e. the wholesale price). In addition, under the netting scheme, households with solar panels are not confronted with fluctuating electricity prices. That means they receive an average price for their production, while on the wholesale market the electricity price is generally quite low during hours when the sun shines and the solar PV installations produce. For retailers, this implies that they receive electricity from residential households with solar PV during hours when electricity has a low economic and commercial value (due to the low market prices), but that they have to supply them with electricity when the sun does not shine and, hence, the electricity price is much higher. Consequently, retailers face significant costs due to the netting measure. When retailers pass on these costs to all their customers, the households without solar PV face costs which are caused by households with solar PV. The latter group of households also benefit from significant reductions in their energy tax (since this is charged based on the net annual consumption, which can be very low or even negative due to the installation of solar PV). Consequently, the government receives much less tax revenues, which is a loss for society, including households without solar PV.

Although this netting scheme offers a clear example of an uneven, and maybe unfair distribution of the costs and benefits of an energy-transition policy, the netting scheme was very popular among Dutch households, and in particular homeowners. They did not complain about the unfairness of passing on the cost of the support scheme to households without solar PV, while the latter were less aware they were financing the netting scheme. When the abolishment of the scheme was announced by the Dutch government, homeowners protested, as that was seen as unfair.

Note that the unequal distributional effects are not completely gone when the net-metering scheme is abolished. Such effects still remain when the annual metered energy consumption is taxed. After all, because of such taxes, homeowners have an incentive to maximise the consumption of their own production, as that results in less metered consumption. Households without solar PV do not have that option and, hence, they pay relatively more energy taxes.

In addition to these institutionalised opportunities to affect, amongst others, energy transition, households can influence the realisation of projects by making use of legal procedures (e.g. objecting against decisions by a local authority) or by participating in social protests. As the latter can hinder the realisation of energy-transition projects, governments and other involved stakeholders may try to manage citizen participation. An example of the latter is the so-called Pact for Engagement (European Commission, 2024), which includes principles for how to manage public involvement in the development of investments in energy infrastructure (see Table 5.2).

Table 5.2 Pact for engagement: ten guiding principles for public engagement for the development of energy-infrastructure projects

Nr.	Principle	Description
1	Early involvement	Inform public stakeholders about the necessity of the project, before the planning of the project has started
2	Education and awareness	Provide information to the public regarding the project
3	Transparency	Involve the public in decision-making by providing them information regularly and asking feedback
4	Accountability	Project developers and decision makers need to be transparent about their actions
5	Meaningful engagement, inclusiveness and local benefit sharing	Public stakeholders should be able to participate in an active and equitable way, including the option to establish rules for local-benefit sharing
6	Mutual respect and trust	Realise a process of open communication and collaboration
7	Consistent application	The engagement with public stakeholders should continue during the full period of project development
8	Long-term commitment	Encourage long-term collaboration between project developers and public stakeholders
9	Conflict resolution	Implement clear mechanisms for addressing and resolving conflicts
10	Continuous improvement	The process of public engagement needs to be regularly reviewed and adjusted when necessary

Source: European Commission (2024)

5.4.10 Transitions Within Local Energy Communities and Cooperatives

The further decentralisation of energy systems can also include changes in the way households and small businesses interact with others. Instead of having contracts with retailers, who act as intermediate parties between the wholesale market and residential end-users, the latter can engage in local energy communities or energy cooperatives. Energy communities are local groups of stakeholders who want to organise their energy systems together. Energy cooperatives refer to a specific type of organisation by which citizens together develop and participate in renewable-energy or energy-efficiency projects. In 2024, there were over 9000 energy communities in the EU, with in total more than 1.5 million citizens involved.[21]

The success of local energy communities is related to their size, i.e. the number of participants. In large communities, it is more complicated to manage and coordinate the interests of all participants. The crucial aspects of such management include trust building, conflict resolution and coordination (Das & Teng, 2002). All these aspects refer to controlling the social exchange between group members.

One may wonder about the reasons for such communities or cooperatives to pursue such objectives. They might wish to raise the ability of citizens to participate in the decision-making as well as in the benefits of energy projects, as is formulated by REScoop, the European federation of energy communities.[22] Other motivations might be related to the ambition to contribute to the overall reduction in carbon emissions, to be less dependent on others, to raise the security of supply or to be less vulnerable to volatile international energy prices.

Some of the local energy communities want to be energy neutral, by which they mean that on an annual basis the aggregated consumption of the community is compensated by its aggregated production. In a single moment of time, however, the community may still be a net consumer of energy. In physical terms, energy communities remain connected to the larger system as long as they are connected to the grid. A more stringent objective of a local energy community would be to become fully independent of other regions for the supply of energy. This would mean that at every single second, the energy consumption in the region needs to be supplied by production in that same region.

In theory, local energy communities may pursue such objectives, but the question is how efficient this would be. After all, when a local community is completely responsible for managing its own energy needs, the options to do this at a low cost are much more limited than for energy systems functioning at a much larger spatial scale. For instance, a region that has good spatial conditions for wind turbines may have much less favourable conditions for solar panels or biomass production. Therefore, in an isolated regional energy system with a limited number of production technologies, one has to make more costs to assure there is sufficient capacity, while in a larger system, it is possible to rely on other production facilities. Moreover, in a smaller region with a lower number of stakeholders active in the system, there may be more concerns about the degree of competition and incentives for individual stakeholders to operate efficiently.

Hence, from a cost perspective, it seems to be more efficient to pursue energy systems operating at a larger spatial scale with more technologies and more different stakeholders. Because of this, existing energy communities are generally still connected to the grid, which also means that these communities in most cases only affect how the flows of energy are administratively dealt with, not how the energy

[21] Interreg Danube Region, Recent Survey Highlights Potential of Energy Communities in the EU. Website: https://interreg-danube.eu/news/recent-survey-highlights-potential-of-energy-communities-in-the-eu.

[22] See https://www.rescoop.eu/.

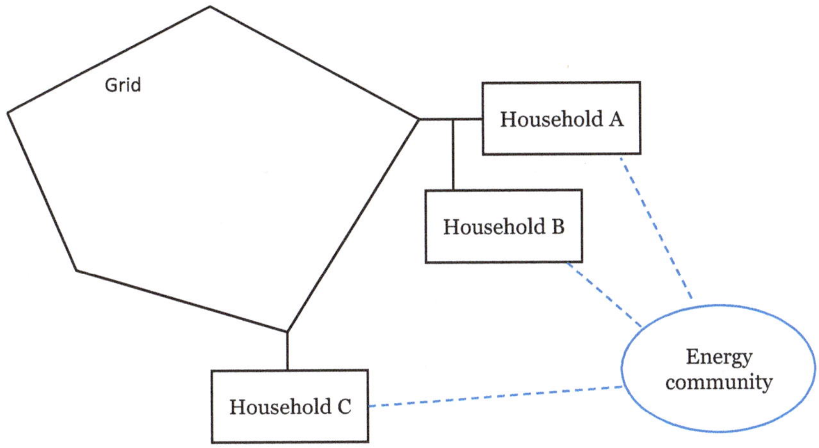

Fig. 5.10 Stylised example of energy community of households connected to different parts of the grid

really flows. This also implies that communities cannot easily contribute to addressing grid congestion issues, as therefore communities need to be in the same part of the grid. Figure 5.10 illustrates this through a stylised example. Households C and A may exchange electricity administratively through the energy community they participate in, but that would not change anything about the net usage of the grid. When households A and B, however, adapt the patterns of their production and consumption patterns,[23] this may result in a lower usage of the higher level of grid where they are both connected to. Hence, energy communities which operate locally may have an impact on the net grid usage on a higher level of the grid. However, this only results in a real benefit for the electricity system when there is actual congestion. When there is abundant capacity in the local part of the grid, which is the case most of the time, such a harmonisation of the grid usage is not useful.

The benefits of energy communities, therefore, mainly exist in terms of increased participation of local stakeholders, in particular residential households, in developing local renewable-energy projects or energy efficiency. The stakeholders participating in these communities may also enjoy benefits like savings on taxes as a result of a lower net annual energy consumption. However, such benefits come at the expense of lower tax revenues for the government, which means that tax benefits for a community do not reflect real benefits at a societal level (see also Box 5.5).

5.5 Conclusions

In this chapter, we have seen that energy systems consist of a wide variety of stakeholders which play different roles and have different interests and objectives. The stakeholders respond to changing circumstances in markets, policies and society by

[23] For example, household B consumes when the solar panels of household A generates electricity.

taking various types of decisions. All these different types of decisions by the various types of agents contribute to the constantly changing energy systems, as we have seen in Chap. 2. When governments have the objective to change energy systems, for any of the reasons discussed in Chap. 3, they have to do this through influencing the decisions of economic agents. This can be done through various types of policy measures, as we have discussed in Chap. 4.

In this chapter, we have seen that economic agents respond to policy measures, but also to other external factors, while they also have their own objectives. We have seen that various types of stakeholders make different types of decisions, varying from becoming more global or less global, more or less reliant on fossil energy, focusing on one market or expanding the scope of their operations, and increasing the collaboration with others or become more focused on their own business. All these actions are, more or less, influenced by energy-transition measures taken by governments, but the strength of this influence depends on how strong the other factors behind stakeholder decisions are.

Some agents also have as an objective to contribute to changes in the energy system, for instance, by making it less fossil-based or more resilient. This is, however, challenging as other agents will respond to the resulting changes in energy systems, which may neutralise the effects of individual actions. Actions by individual stakeholders can have an impact on the overall energy transition when they are able to change the circumstances that other agents are facing. This can, for instance, be done by developing new technologies or new products, which may enable others to reduce their use of (fossil) energy.

Exercises

1. The development of energy systems results from the activities of various kinds of stakeholders. To what extent is it needed that these shareholders share common views regarding the future development of the systems?
2. Firms in energy supply chains make quite different (strategic) choices regarding their further development, even if they operate in the same economic environment. What does this mean?
3. Give an example how a transition on firm level can be neutralised on industry level by responses by other firms.
4. How can an individual firm successfully contribute to a transition on industry level?
5. To what extent can a growth in local energy communities be seen as a further decentralisation of energy systems?

References

Barani, M., Löffler, K., del Granado, P. C., et al. (2026). European energy vision 2050 and beyond: designing scenarios for Europe's energy transition. *Renewable and Sustainable Energy Reviews, 225*, 116074.

Climate Action Network (CAN) Europe. (n.d.). *Towards a truly green vision for Europe's energy system.* https://caneurope.org/towards-a-truly-green-vision-for-europe-s-energy-system/

Copenhagen Infrastructure Partners. (n.d.). Powering the future—a vision for Europe's energy system in 2050.

Das, T. K., & Teng, B. S. (2002). Alliance constellations: A social exchange perspective. *Academy of Management Review, 27*(3), 445–456.

European Central Bank (ECB). (2025). *Nature at risk: implications for the euro are economy and financial stability: economic and financial risks stemming from degradation of ecosystem services.* Occasional Paper Series, no 380.

EEB. (2025). The State of the European Steel Transition, March 2025.

ENTSO-E. (2024). Strategic roadmap; prepare the future and manage the present. February.

European Commission. (2024). Report from the Commission to the European Parliament and the Council on the functioning of the European carbon market in 2023, COM(2024) 538 final.

European Network of Transmission System Operators for Electricity – ENTSO-E. (n.d.) website: https://www.entsoe.eu/

European Union. (2009). Regulation (EC) No 714/2009 of the European Parliament and of the Council of 13 July 2009 on conditions for access to the network for cross-border exchanges in electricity and repealing Regulation (EC) No 1228/2003.

Freeman, R. E., & McVea, J. (2001). A stakeholder approach to strategic management. Darden Graduate School of Business Administration, University of Virginia, Working Paper no. 01-02.

IEA. (n.d.). *Net zero emissions by 2050 scenario*; website: https://www.iea.org/reports/global-energy-and-climate-model/net-zero-emissions-by-2050-scenario-nze

IEA (Ed.). (2025). *World energy investment 2050* (10th ed.). IEA. https://www.iea.org/reports/world-energy-investment-2025

ING. (2024, 23 August). *Steel's green makeover: Swapping coal for gas and scrap.*

Interreg Danube Region. (n.d.). website: https://interreg-anube.eu/projects/nrgcom/news/recent-survey-highlights-potential-of-energy-communities-in-the-eu

Masciandaro, C., Mulder, M., & Kesina, M. (2025). Distributional effects of the Dutch net-metering scheme for residential solar panels. *Energy Economics, 151*, 108891.

Raikar, S., & Adamson, S. (2025). *Renewable energy finance; theory and practice* (2nd ed.). Elsevier Academic Press.

Rentier, G. (2025). Institutions and the energy transition; a comparative analysis of decarbonization pathways in European countries. University of Utrecht (PhD thesis).

REScoop. (n.d.). *The REScoop Model.* website: https://www.rescoop.eu/the-rescoop-model

Shell. (n.d.). *Annual report 2024.*

Singhal, P., Sommer, S., Koestner, K., & Pahle, M. (2025). Split-incentives in energy efficiency investments? Evidence from rental housing. *Resource and Energy Economics, 82*, 101488. https://doi.org/10.1016/j.reseneeco.2025.101488

Smit, P. (2025). Energiemonitor van de Nederlandse glastuinbouw 2024. Wageningen University & Research. Rapport 2025-150.

UCTE. (2010). The 50 year success story—evolution of a European interconnected grid.

Concluding Remarks 6

6.1 Defining Energy Transition

In talking about energy transition, the attention generally is on physically changing energy systems. Reducing the use of fossil energy by installing wind turbines and solar PV panels, as well as improving the efficiency of energy use, are common examples of this approach to energy transition. These types of activities are becoming increasingly important, looking both at the policy objectives of many governments and the changes occurring in energy systems all over the globe. However, defining energy transition in this way offers a too narrow perspective, which is less helpful in defining actions which can contribute to realising an energy transition in an effective and efficient manner. Based on this approach to energy transition, one may conclude, for instance, that renewables have to be supported by governmental subsidies, while actually for the profitability of investments, subsidies may not be needed or that such investments may not contribute to addressing societal problems.

The reason that the common perception of energy transition is not very helpful for defining appropriate policy measures is that stakeholders in energy systems are continuously making various types of decisions, including the way they produce energy and the efficiency of their energy use. These decisions are affected by several external circumstances, such as market prices, technological developments and (other) government policies, while also the characteristics of the stakeholders themselves, such as their preferences, type of activities and locations, may change. The ongoing decisions by all the stakeholders result in constantly changing energy systems, which differ significantly among regions and countries, as we have seen over the past centuries.

Because so many factors play a role, the outcomes of the developments in energy systems cannot be foreseen. This also implies that formulating clear objectives for future energy systems, regarding for example the industrial structure or type of energy systems that should be used, does not make much sense. Instead, it is more

M. Mulder, *Economics of Energy Transition*, Studies in Energy, Resource and Environmental Economics, https://doi.org/10.1007/978-3-032-29010-6_6

useful to analyse to what extent individual decision-makers (e.g. firms and households) can make the best decisions. Therefore, the maxim chosen for this book is the one formulated by the French author Antoine de Saint-Exupéry: 'as for the future, your task is not to foresee it, but to enable it'. This maxim fits very well with the economic approach of energy transition. From an economic perspective, energy transition is not defined in terms of a particular outcome of the changes in energy systems, but in terms of the process.

Economically, energy transition can be defined as the interventions by governments in the decisions individual stakeholders of energy systems make, to influence the development of these systems. Departing from the theoretical economic notion that stakeholders (in principle) pursue their own interests which, when a number of conditions are met, results in the maximum welfare of society, governments should only intervene when one or more of these conditions do not hold. In the latter case, we are talking about market failures, which are fundamental shortcomings in the way stakeholders interact with each other regarding the allocation of (scarce) commodities. From this follows that governments should only pursue an energy transition, i.e. influencing the decisions of economic agents in energy systems, when market failures are present.

6.2 Assessing Arguments for Energy Transition

Instead of starting with an analysis of the presence of market failures in energy systems, this book assessed the arguments which are often put forward for pursuing energy transition. These arguments are related to the three general objectives of energy policy: security of supply, affordability and sustainability. Related to the security of energy supply objective are the policy concerns regarding the depletion of fossil-energy resources and the dependence of a country (or region) on the import of energy. The policy objective regarding affordability of energy is often translated into concerns about the volatility and prices of energy. Regarding the sustainability of energy, the policy concern is in particular directed at the climate effects of the use of fossil energy. These concerns are used as arguments to pursue an energy transition. For each of these arguments, we have analysed to what extent they really refer to a fundamental shortcoming in energy markets which may call for government intervention.

For these four arguments, we concluded that in particular the one related to the environmental effects of the use of fossil energy refers to a clear, fundamental flaw in energy markets which calls for policy intervention. Market parties do not have incentives to take climate-change effects of using fossil energy into account because of their long-term and global nature. The arguments related to the depletion of fossil-energy resources and import dependence are less clearly related to market failures, as markets appear to partly address these issues. For instance, higher perceived scarcity of resources results in higher energy prices, which gives incentives to market parties to respond. A similar mechanism exists for the risk of a higher import dependence resulting in higher prices in the future. For both issues, however, market parties may not be fully able to capture all risks, which can be a reason to implement government measures to influence the decisions of stakeholders in energy systems. The argument of affordability of energy is the least clearly related to the presence of market failures, as high and volatile market prices may be an indication of well-functioning markets, although they may also result from a lack of liquidity or presence of market power in these markets. However, from a distributional (fairness) point of view, governments can have a reason to intervene in energy systems in order to protect vulnerable households or particular (energy-intensive) industries against too high prices.

6.3 Determining Appropriate Policy Measures

Purely the fact that a market failure exists is not a sufficient reason to implement any type of government intervention, as some interventions can generate more harm (i.e. costs) than benefits. Therefore, for any type of market failure, one should clearly analyse which types of government interventions (i.e. energy-transition measures) are most effective and efficient, while fairness considerations should also be taken into account.

In order to address market failures in exploration, development and production of natural resources, governments can intervene by fostering the distribution of information regarding the characteristics of natural resources, promoting competition in the upstream business, internalising the externality of a too rapid depletion through financial or regulatory measures, and redistributing the resource rents through financial measures or public ownership.

The market failures related to import dependencies, which in particular refer to geopolitical risks, can be addressed through subsidising domestic production or imposing regulatory constraints on imports. The most efficient policy measure, however, seems to be facilitating the resilience of an economy, for instance, by promoting the diversification of import routes and enabling economic agents to flexibly respond to supply shocks.

To address high and volatile energy prices, governments should be hesitant to intervene in energy systems as that would not mitigate the underlying problem of high costs or scarcity, but reduces the ability of markets to solve this problem itself. As far as vulnerable households are concerned, it seems to be more efficient to make use of specific income-related measures or measures directed at reducing their energy use to help them to cope with high and volatile energy prices. Supporting energy-intensive industries to deal with (extremely) high energy prices can be considered out of distributional concerns (e.g. consequences for local employment) or concerns about security of supply (e.g. consequences for supply of crucial commodities).

The market failure consisting of the negative climate impact caused by the use of fossil energy can be addressed in several ways, at least in theory. Imposing a carbon tax is a straightforward measure, but in practice many issues arise, in particular in relation to economic consequences for industries and distributional effects. Support schemes can be very effective in promoting particular (low-carbon) technologies, but are subject to the risk of free riders, rebound effects and inefficient designs. Regulatory standards can also be very effective, but require the government to have a strong information position. Emissions-trading schemes, which combine regulatory obligations with financial incentives, can be both effective and efficient. When such schemes are implemented, interaction with other policy measures, such as carbon taxes, renewable subsidies or regulatory constraints may reduce the overall efficiency of these policy measures. Because of the policy incentives to make energy systems less based on fossil energy, economic agents may want to use low-carbon energy carriers for which infrastructures have to be developed. When the development of these infrastructures suffers from hold-up problems, governments can reduce the financial risks for involved stakeholders through support schemes or public participation.

From the above analysis, it appears that from an economic perspective, energy-transition policies can consist of a variety of measures. As policy measures can influence each other, one should also take into account the interaction effects.

6.4 Exploring the Role of Stakeholders

The governmental measures to intervene in energy systems can only be effective through the impact on the decisions of all the various stakeholders. We have seen that these stakeholders do not only respond to policy measures, but also to other external factors. Under the influence of these factors, and depending on their own characteristics and objectives, stakeholders make various decisions, such as their level of international orientation, degree of specialisation, reliance on fossil versus renewable energy sources and the type of collaboration with other agents.

Stakeholders also influence each other, and in that way, they may also contribute to an energy transition. Actions by individual stakeholders to change energy systems face the problem that their impacts may be neutralised through the responses of other agents. Actions by individual stakeholders to change the overall energy transition can be successful, however, when they are able to change the circumstances other agents are facing, for instance, by developing new technologies or products.

6.5 Interacting with Other Disciplinary Approaches

This book has shown how the economic discipline can contribute to understanding the factors affecting energy transition and formulate concrete recommendations not only for governments, but also other stakeholders. This contribution is based on a clear theoretical framework and the presence of operational tools which can be used to systematically analyse the need for energy-transition policies, and how such policies can be designed in the most efficient and effective way. The economic perspective is, of course, only one of the relevant perspectives, and for a full understanding of how to realise energy transition successfully, other disciplinary perspectives need to be taken on board as well.

Appendix A: Technical Definitions and Characteristics

A.1 Energy Units

To express the amount of energy, the International System of Units is used. The most common units are the following:

Base 10	Prefix (symbol)	Prefix name	English name	Decimal
10^{18}	E	exa	quintillion	1,000,000,000,000,000,000
10^{15}	P	peta	quadrillion	1,000,000,000,000,000
10^{12}	T	tera	trillion	1,000,000,000,000
10^{9}	G	giga	billion	1,000,000,000
10^{6}	M	mega	million	1,000,000
10^{3}	k	kilo	thousand	1000
10^{0}				1

So:

- 1 PWh = 1 thousand TWh = 1 million GWh = 1 billion MWh.
- 1 EJ = 1 thousand PJ = 1 million TJ = 1 billion GJ

Relationships between energy units:

- 1 GJ is equal to 0.28 MWh and 1 MWh = 3.6 GJ.
- 1 ton of crude oil is 7.33 barrel and has an energy content of 10 million kilocalories or about 42 GJ or 11.7 MWh. Hence, 1 MWh of oil is equal to (7.33/11.7=) 0.62 barrel of oil, and 1 GJ of oil is equal to (7.33/42=) 0.175 barrel of oil. Hence, an annual consumption of oil of, for instance, 200 EJ (i.e. 2 billion GJ) is equal to (2 billion × 0.175=) 35 billion barrels of oil, which is equal to about 95 million barrels per day.
- 1 ton of oil equivalent (toe) is defined as the energy content of 1 ton of crude oil and 1 ton of coal equivalent (tce) is defined as the energy content of 1 ton of coal, which is equal to 7 million kCal or 29.3 GJ or 8.2 MWh. Hence, one tce is equal to 0.7 ton of oil equivalent (toe).
- 1000 m^3 of natural gas is equal to 35.17 GJ or 9.8 MWh of energy. Hence, 1 GJ of natural gas is equal to 28.4 m^3, which implies that, for instance a global con-

M. Mulder, *Economics of Energy Transition*, Studies in Energy, Resource and Environmental Economics, https://doi.org/10.1007/978-3-032-29010-6

sumption of 140 EJ (i.e. 140 billion GJ) is equal to (140 billion × 28.4/1 billion=) 3976 bcm (billion cubic metres).
- 1000 kg of hydrogen is equal to about 126 GJ or 35 MWh of energy.
- For more detailed information on conversion factors, see for instance: https://www.eia.gov/energyexplained/units-and-calculators/energy-conversion-calculators.php

A.2 Technical Characteristics of Fossil-Energy Carriers

The precise chemical characteristics of coal, oil as well as natural gas vary significantly among all the various types of these energy carriers, depending on the origin of their resource base:[1]

- The share of carbon in coal can vary from 60% to 98% (based on weight). Other chemical components of coal are hydrogen, oxygen, nitrogen, sulphur and inorganic residues. Depending on the composition, coal is categorised into four categories: anthracite, bituminous, sub-bituminous and lignite, with the former having the highest carbon content.
- The share of hydrocarbons (i.e. combination of carbon and hydrogen) in crude oil varies between 50% and 95% (based on weight). By refining, the oil molecules are separated through distillation into different hydrocarbon fractions, such as gasoline, kerosene and fuel oils.
- Natural gas as it is produced consists of various hydrocarbons, in particular methane (CH_4), but also hydrocarbons like ethane (C_2H_6) and propane (C_3H_8). The natural gas that is transported and delivered to end-users primarily consists of methane and ethane, as the other hydrocarbons and elements are removed from it. The share of methane varies among the different types of natural gas, resulting in so-called high-calorific gas (i.e. with high methane and energy content) and low-calorific gas.

In statistics, the average CO_2-emission per unit of energy is used, such as:

- 1 MWh of hard coal (anthracite) includes 0.35 ton of CO_2.
- 1 MWh of crude oil includes 0.264 ton CO_2.
- 1 MWh of natural gas includes 0.2 ton of CO_2.

For more information on carbon content of energy carriers, see for instance: https://ourworldindata.org/grapher/carbon-dioxide-emissions-factor.

A.3 Transport of Energy Carriers

- Coal is a solid and is internationally transported through vessels.
- Oil is a liquid and is internationally mainly transported through vessels, but also through pipeline systems.

[1] Source: https://chemed.chem.purdue.edu/genchem/topicreview/bp/1organic/coal.html.

- Natural gas is a gas and can be transported both through pipeline systems and as a liquid. In the latter case, the gas is made a liquid by lowering the temperature, which results in so-called Liquefied Natural Gas (LNG). As a liquid, natural gas can be efficiently transported over long distances through vessels.
- Hydrogen is also a gas and can be transported through pipeline systems, but through cooling or conversion into, for instance, ammonia, it can be (internationally) transported as a liquid.
- Electricity is energy that results from rotating magnetic fields and is transported through mediums (so-called conductors) such as cables made out of copper or aluminium.

A.4 Capacity Versus Energy

- The ability to produce energy is expressed as capacity and can be measured in terms of MW. The energy which is actually produced is expressed in MWh, which depends on (a) the capacity and (b) the time in which that capacity is used to produce energy.
- The capacity of solar panels is typically expressed in P_w, which refers to the maximum capacity when the solar radiation conditions are optimal.
- The actual production of a technology in comparison to the technical possible production is expressed through the capacity factor. The capacity factor (*cf*) is defined as the ratio between the gross energy production measured in, for instance, GWh in a year (G^{prod}) divided by the net capacity measured in GW (G^{cap}) times the number of hours in a year (=365 days × 24 h/day):

$$cf = \frac{G^{\text{prod}}}{G^{\text{cap}} * 365 * 24}. \tag{A.1}$$

A.5 Flexibility

Flexibility can be defined as the ability of capacities to change the level of production or consumption of energy.

- At the level of technologies, this refers to the ability of, for instance, a power plant to increase or decrease production (i.e. ramp up or ramp down) with a particular speed.
- At the level of economic agents, flexibility refers to the ability of, for instance, an energy consumer, to change the level of consumption (upward or downward) with a particular speed.

- At the system level, flexibility refers to the ability of the system to remain in balance, which is a crucial condition for electricity systems, but also (albeit to a lesser extent) for natural gas, heating and hydrogen systems.[2]

A.6 Measurement of Emissions

- Emissions of CO_2 are expressed in tons of CO_2 and tons of C. One ton of C is equal to 3.67 tons of CO_2.
- Emissions of the various types of greenhouse gases can be aggregated by using information on the Global Warming Potential (GWP) of each gas. By multiplying the GWP for each gas with the amount of emissions (in tons) per gas, emissions are expressed in terms of CO_2-equivalents (CO_2-eq). See Box 3.6 for more information.

[2] See, for instance, the definition of flexibility in the power sector given by Eurelectric: 'Flexibility in the power sector refers to the ability of an energy system to adjust both power generation and consumption in response to signals from the grid, or the market, to ensure security of supply and avoid blackouts' (https://www.eurelectric.org/in-detail/what-is-flexibility-in-the-power-sector/).

Appendix B: Definition of Scope 1, 2 and 3 Emissions

Activities of economic agents can result in carbon emissions through different mechanisms. When they use fossil energy, for instance by burning gas for heating or using gasoline to drive a car, this immediately results in carbon emissions. These emissions are called Scope 1 emissions. Hence, this category of emissions refers to the emissions which are directly caused by agents. This also implies that this type of emissions can be directly controlled by agents themselves.

Economic agents also indirectly cause emissions, in particular through the use of energy carriers which generate emissions at the source. This holds for electricity, heating and cooling. Although the direct use of electricity, heat and cooling does generally not result in carbon emissions, these emissions may occur when these energy carriers are produced. When electricity is generated by a coal or gas-fired power plant, the use of that electricity causes carbon emissions at the source, i.e. the power plant producing the electricity. The same holds for heat that is produced as a residual product of an industry that uses fossil fuels. This category of emissions is called Scope 2 emissions.

Next to these two categories of emissions which are related to the production process of agents, there are also emissions which result from other activities or other parts of the supply chain. These activities include, amongst others, the transport of the products, the travel of employees, the use of the products and the generation of waste. This category of emissions is called Scope 3 emissions.

These three categories of emissions are helpful to discuss the accountability for emissions and determine which types of actions can be taken by what agents to reduce the emissions. An agent can reduce its own (Scope 1) emissions by increasing the efficiency of its energy use or by replacing its use of fossil fuels by renewable energy or electrification. In the latter case, the reduction of Scope 1 emissions may result in higher Scope 2 emissions. In order to reduce the latter, an agent can, for instance, conclude a contract for the purchase of renewable electricity. Scope 3 emissions are generally the most difficult to reduce, given the dependence on other stakeholders. Examples of mitigating measures are the implementation of recycle programs for its products or measures which reduce the waste production during the production process.

M. Mulder, *Economics of Energy Transition*, Studies in Energy, Resource and Environmental Economics, https://doi.org/10.1007/978-3-032-29010-6

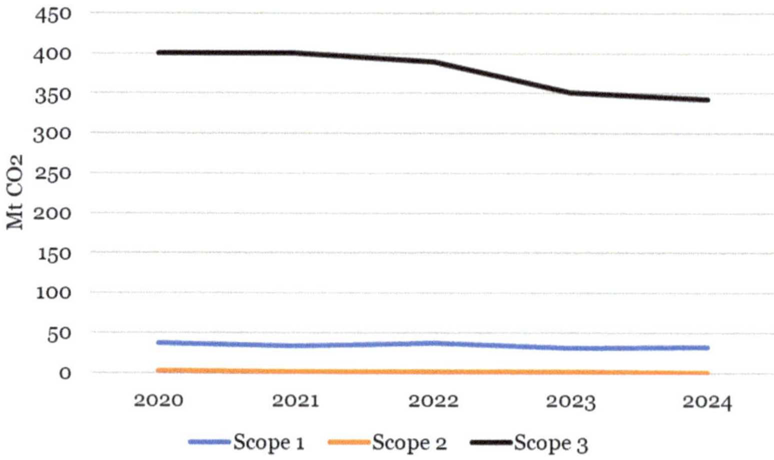

Fig. B.1 Scope 1, 2 and 3 emissions of TotalEnergies, total per year, 2020–2024 (Source: totalenergies.com)

The magnitude of Scope 3 emissions is generally much higher than the ones for Scope 1 and 2. This holds in particular for firms that are active in the fossil-energy industry, as Fig. B.1 shows (as an example) for TotalEnergies. The majority of the emissions related to the activities of this company occur when its products (like gasoline) are used by its customers.

Appendix C: Price Elasticities of Demand and Supply Curves

C.1 Linear Demand and Supply Curves

The impact of changes in demand and supply on market prices depends on the price elasticity of both curves.[1] The demand curve ($D(p)$ can, for instance be assumed to be a linear function of the price:

$$D(p) = Q_d = a - bP. \tag{C.1}$$

where Q_d stands for demanded quantity, a for the so-called intercept (i.e. the price independent component of demand) and b is the degree to which the demand changes if the price (P) changes.[2] The parameter b is also called the slope of the demand curve. The higher the slope, the greater the price sensitivity, all else being equal. The parameter b is generally positive, which makes that the demand curve is downward sloping: the higher the price, the lower the demand. The slope of the demand curve is related to the price elasticity of the demand (ε_d), which is defined as the relative change in demand in response to a relative change in the price:

$$\varepsilon_d = \frac{\frac{dQ_d}{Q_d}}{\frac{dP}{P}} = \frac{dQ_d}{dP} * \frac{P}{Q_d}. \tag{C.2}$$

This price elasticity is related to the slope of the demand curve as the expression dQ/dP is the first derivative of the demand curve ($D'(p)$:

$$D'(p) = \frac{dQ_d}{dP} = -b. \tag{C.3}$$

Using the above formulas, it appears that

[1] See e.g. Varian (2003) for a more in-depth discussion of price elasticities.

[2] Note that graphically it is common to show the inverse of the demand curve, where price depends on quantity instead of the other way around.

M. Mulder, *Economics of Energy Transition*, Studies in Energy, Resource and Environmental Economics, https://doi.org/10.1007/978-3-032-29010-6

$$\varepsilon_d = -b * \frac{P}{Q_d} = \frac{-bP}{a - bP}, \quad \text{(C.4)}$$

and from that follows that

$$b = -\varepsilon * \frac{Q_d}{P}. \quad \text{(C.5)}$$

Equation (C.4) shows that the higher the slope, i.e. the steeper the demand curve, the greater (i.e. the more negative) the price elasticity for any price quantity ratio, while Eq. (C.5) shows, the other way around, that a larger (absolute value of the) elasticity makes that the slope becomes larger as well.

The degree to which supply responds to changing demand conditions can be expressed by the price elasticity of the supply curve. The flatter this curve (in a P-Q plot, i.e. a plot with P on vertical axis and Q on horizontal axis), the more price sensitive the supply is and the stronger the response of supply when the price changes. Mathematically, a linear supply curve can be formulated as:

$$Q_s = c + dP, \quad \text{(C.6)}$$

consisting of a price-independent amount of supply c and costs which are expressed in terms of the market price P through the parameter d. This equation can be rewritten in the inverse supply function:

$$P = e + fQ_s, \text{where } e = -\frac{c}{d} \text{ and } f = \frac{1}{d}. \quad \text{(C.7)}$$

Equation (C.6) shows that (if d>0), the quantity supplied is a positive function of price (i.e. the higher the price, the more will be supplied), and also a positive function of a, as a steeper slope indicates that the supply will increase more strongly at a given increase in the price. From the inverse supply curve (see Equation (C.7), we learn that its slope (in a P-Q plot) is equal to the opposite (i.e. $1/a$) of the slope of the standard supply curve (a). Hence, a higher value of a means that the slope of the inverse supply curve becomes smaller indicating a higher responsiveness, and vice versa.

Just as for demand, also for supply elasticities can be determined. In case of the linear supply curve, the supply elasticity (ε_s) is determined by:

$$\varepsilon_s = d * \frac{P}{Q_s} = \frac{dP}{c + dP} \quad \text{(C.8)}$$

C.2 Demand Curves with Constant Price Elasticity

When linear specifications are used for a demand and supply curve, the price elasticity also depends on the intercept. Using the above specification of the demand function, the price elasticity is precisely −1 when $p = a/2b$. If the price exceeds this value, the absolute value of the price elasticity will be >1 (i.e. the demand curve is price elastic) and when the price is below this value, the price elasticity will be ≥0 and <1 (i.e. the demand curve is price inelastic).[3] Consequently, at very high price levels and low quantity levels, the linear specification of the demand curve can result in unrealistically high values of the price elasticity, and the opposite holds for situations with very low prices and high quantities. In order to have a demand curve which better reflects the actual price responsiveness, the specification should be a bit different, i.e. non-linear.

In order to have a constant price elasticity, the slope of the demand curve should change when prices and quantities change. The formula for a demand curve ($D(p)$) with a constant price elasticity, no matter what the price and quantity are, is the following:

$$D(p) = Q_d = a * p^{-x}. \tag{C.9}$$

The first derivative of this demand curve is:

$$D'(p) = -xa * p^{-x-1}. \tag{C.10}$$

Substituting the value of this derivative into the formula for the price elasticity and inserting the demand curve in this expression as well, results in the following expression for elasticity:

$$\varepsilon_d = -xa * p^{-x-1} * \frac{P}{Q_d} = -xa * p^{-x-1} * \frac{P}{a * p^{-x}} = -x. \tag{C.11}$$

This shows that, in this formula of the demand curve, the opposite value of power x determines the constant price elasticity, which is independent of the levels for price and quantity. As an example, using the values of 10 for a and various values for $\boldsymbol{x}$ results in the following (inverse) demand curves with a constant elasticity. At every price and quantity level of these curves, the price elasticity is equal to −0.5, −1 or −1.5, respectively. It is clear that the higher the value of x, the greater (i.e. the more negative) the price elasticity, the more convex to the origin the demand curve is (Fig. C.1).

[3] Hence, in case of a linear demand curve, the slope is constant, but the price elasticity is different at different values for price and quantity.

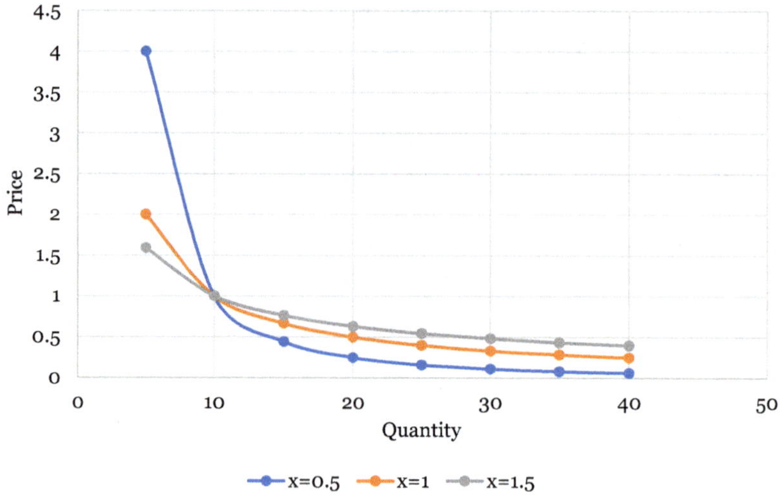

Fig. C.1 Different demand curves with each having a constant elasticity

Appendix D: Classroom Experiment in Emissions Trading and Energy Transition: Example of Results of One Application

D.1 Introduction

The classroom experiment on emissions trading and energy transition, developed by the author of this book, is meant to help participants obtain a better understanding of the functioning of a cap-and-trade emissions-trading scheme and how that scheme interacts with a support scheme for particular carbon-mitigating technologies. The experiment also helps students to better understand the conditions for market efficiency and how efficient markets can have various distributional outcomes. The experiment is conducted in two groups: both groups have about an equal number of participants and receive the same options to reduce emissions. One group, however, has lower costs for particular reduction options than the other group, because that group in question received subsidies (without knowing). The objective for all participants is to comply with the environmental regulation, which entails they are not allowed to emit more than the number of allowances they can hand over. In this appendix, the results of one application of this experiment are presented. This application was conducted with a group of 13 staff members from an energy consultancy in Spring 2026.[1]

D.2 Number of Reduction Options per Group and per Type

Group A consisted of 7 members, Group B of 6. Both groups had similar reduction options, which consisted of energy saving, installing an onshore wind park, installing an offshore wind park, installing solar panels on the roof of houses and installing a solar park. The costs of the various options ranged from 1 to 10 euros per ton.

[1] Since 2016, the author of this book has played this game about 50 times, with various types of groups with in total 6 to about 50 persons. As the experiment is conducted in two subgroups, the sizes of these groups varied from 3 to about 25 persons. It appeared, that even in large groups, efficient market outcomes can be reached when some group members take on the role of coordinator, while small groups can have difficulties to operate efficiently when there is a lack of communication or understanding of the rules of the game.

M. Mulder, *Economics of Energy Transition*, Studies in Energy, Resource and Environmental Economics, https://doi.org/10.1007/978-3-032-29010-6

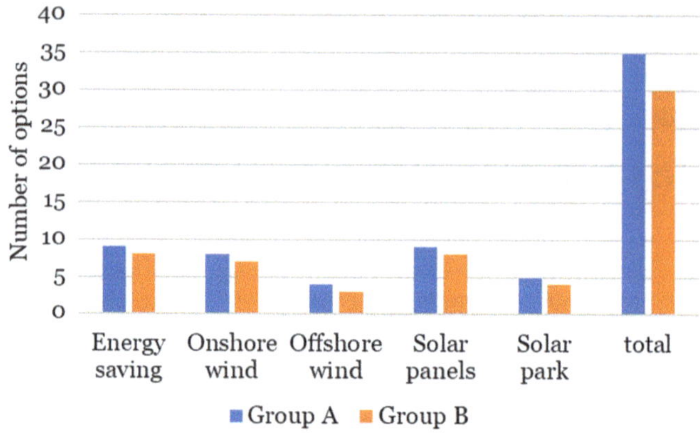

Fig. D.1 Number of reduction options per type, per group

Every participant received five reduction options, which means that in Group A, there were 35 reductions available and in Group B 30 (see Fig. D.1). Each option could be used to reduce emissions by 1 ton.

D.3 Emissions Reduction

At the start of the experiment, it was stated that each participant emitted 6 tons. This means that the initial emissions were 42 tons in Group A and 36 in Group B (blue bars) (see Fig. D.2). In both groups, the total emissions had to be reduced by 50%, which meant that the emissions cap in Group A was 21 tons, and in Group B 18 tons (green bars). At the end of the experiment, it was found that Group A reduced 1 ton more than needed to meet the cap, while in Group B, the remaining emissions were equal to the cap (grey bars). Although in Group B, emissions reduction was cheaper due to subsidies, they did not reduce more. Instead, in Group A, one participant was motivated to exceed the required reduction due to her concerns about climate change. That participant could have sold an allowance to someone else, but she was unwilling to do, fearing that the other participant would reduce less.[2]

D.4 Costs of Emissions Reduction

As Group A did not receive subsidies for particular technologies, the costs of emissions reduction were significantly higher than in Group B. When the participants could only use their own reduction options, the average costs of being compliant

[2] In other groups, it sometimes occurred that a person, who really wants to contribute to emission reduction, realizes all its (five) reduction options, but gave the two redundant allowances for free to someone else, as the person was not interested in making money. During the discussion after the game, the person realized that there was no net effect of its effort on the overall emission reduction.

Fig. D.2 Initial, allowed and remaining emissions, per group

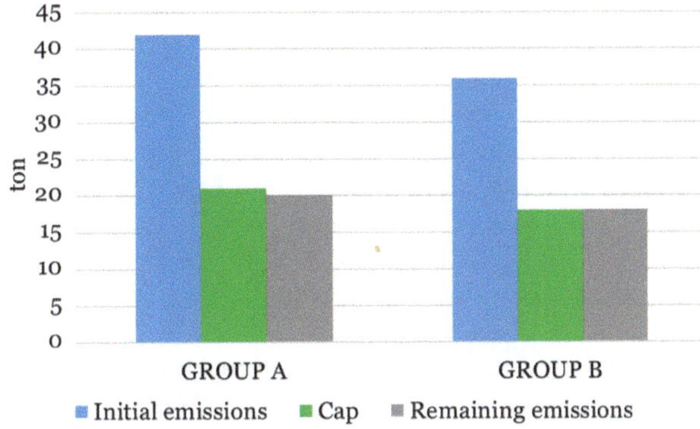

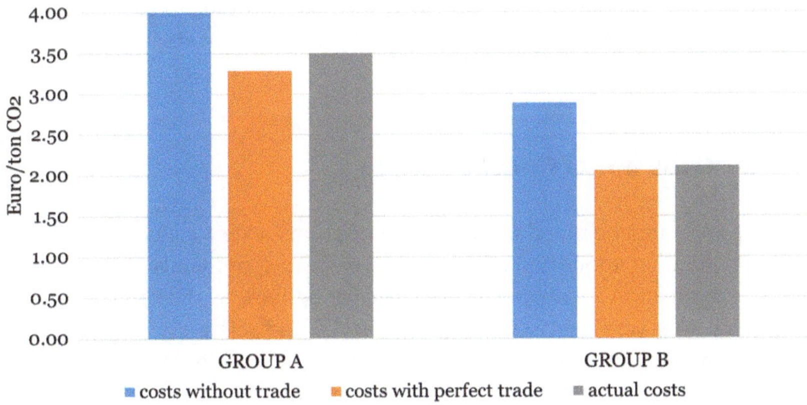

Fig. D.3 Costs of emissions reduction: without trade, in case of perfect trade, and actual, per group

would be 4 euro/ton in Group A and 2.9 eur/ton in Group B (blue bars) (see Fig. D.3). If, in both groups, perfect use was made of the opportunities for trading in allowances, the average costs per unit of reduction would be significantly lower in both groups (orange bars). It appeared, however, that in both groups, the realised average costs of emissions reduction were higher than the theoretical minimum (grey bars). For Group B, this was entirely due to not perfectly using the available cheapest reduction options, while in group A, it was also related to the additional emissions reduction.

The efficiency of the emissions reduction can be measured by how closely these reductions align with the marginal-abatement costs curve (see Fig. D.4). This curve shows the amount of emissions reduction that can be achieved at the various cost levels, starting with the lowest on the left. Both groups were quite efficient in using the cheapest options before a more expensive option. This is reflected by the red curve overlapping the blue curve. We can also see that, in both groups, there was an unused cheaper option (5 euro/ton in Group A and 4 euro/ton in Group B), while a

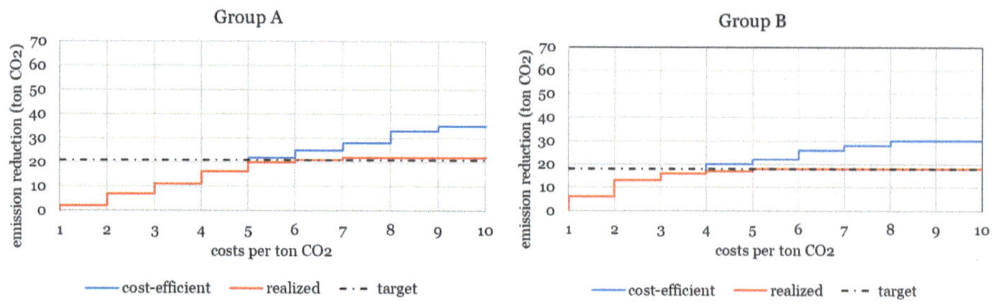

Fig. D.4 Use of reduction options in comparison to marginal-abatement costs curve, per group

more expensive option was used (7 euro/ton in Group A and 5 euro/ton in Group B). In the discussion, it became clear that the respective participants did not have a full overview of the available remaining reduction options. This shows the importance of transparency for the efficiency of markets.

D.5 Distributional Consequences

Although group members had quite different options, everyone could benefit from trade, no matter if someone had only expensive options, or mainly cheap options. In Group A, participant A3 had relatively expensive options, as their remaining capital without trade was very low, while participant A4 had relatively cheap options, as their remaining capital without trade was quite high (see Fig. D.5). However, both benefitted from trade. The latter follows from the fact that their remaining capital after the experiment (orange bars) was higher than would have been the case without the option to trade (blue bars). From the distribution of capital, we can see that participant A2 was the one who reduced more than needed, without selling the redundant allowance, which resulted in a lower amount of capital. In Group B, also, almost everyone benefitted from the presence of the trade mechanism.

The discussion also revealed that the distribution of total benefits of trade (green bars) depends on how participants set up the trade, what the negotiation power is of individual group members and to what extent individual members are willing or eager to engage in negotiation. An important outcome is that the different attitudes of people towards trade and profit maximisation behaviour affects only the distributional outcomes, but hardly the overall efficiency of trade (i.e. the total cost reduction due to the ability to exchange allowances).

We also see that in Group B, the remaining capital was larger than in Group A, which was due to the fact that the former group received subsidies for particular technologies. Hence, subsidies are a form of wealth transfer, but do not necessarily affect the overall emissions reduction when a cap-and-trade mechanism is in place.

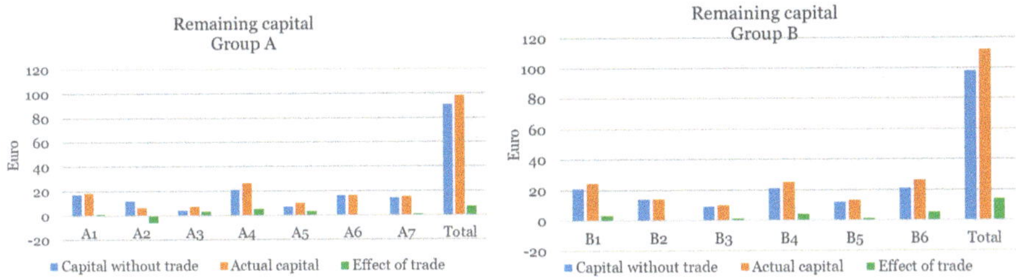

Fig. D.5 Capital per player, before and afterwards, per group

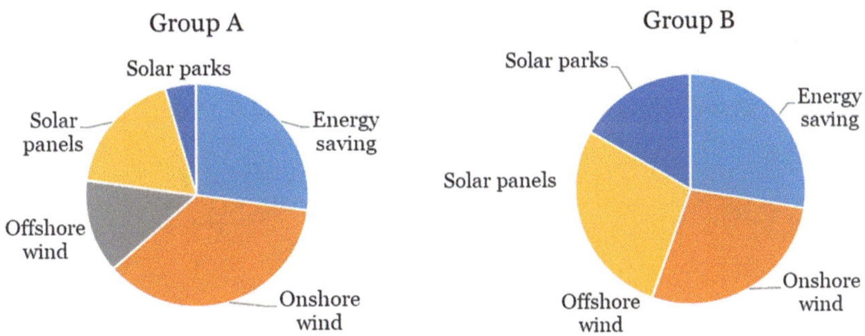

Fig. D.6 Relative usage of the various reduction options, per group

D.6 Technological Choices

Subsidies for particular technologies do, however, affect the choices participants make. Group A did not receive any subsidy, while Group B had lower costs for solar panels and solar parks because of subsidies. As a result, Group B made significantly more use of solar panels and solar parks to reduce their emissions (see Fig. D.6). Hence, subsidies for particular choices affect the technology choices of participants.

D.7 Concluding Remarks

All the above results were based on the decisions made by the participants themselves. The only information they received upfront is that they should reduce their emissions, view their budget as if it were real money, and that they would have the opportunity to exchange allowances. No further information was provided. Often, participants asked whether the objective was to make profit, but that question was always answered by saying that everyone is completely free to pursue their objective, as long as everyone is compliant.

A crucial element of the classroom experiment is the joint discussion of the results afterwards. This discussion helps the participants to better understand their own decisions during the experiment, how markets (in general) and a cap-and-trade market function and how they interact with support schemes. Many participants learned that transparency contributes to higher efficiency, that high efficiency can be achieved with various distributional consequences, that emissions reduction is almost entirely determined by the number of allowances, and that subsidies for particular technologies reduce compliance costs (i.e. lower costs per ton of emissions reduction) and affect the technological choices, though they do not affect the magnitude of emissions reductions.

Appendix E: Answers to Exercises

E.1 Chapter 1

1. The production costs of primary energy carriers are only related to the technologies needed to produce them, but the production costs of secondary and tertiary energy carriers are also related to the costs of using primary or secondary energy carriers.
2. Sector coupling refers to the technical and economic relationships between the supply chains of different energy carriers.
3. A successful realisation of energy-transition projects depends on many factors, such as engineering, economics, finance, legal, spatial and social factors. Ignoring one of these factors may result in delay or suboptimal design of a project.
4. In the economic perspective on energy transition, attention is focused on the choices economic agents, such as firms, other types of organisations and consumers, make in relation to the supply, transport, storage or use of energy. By understanding the factors that influence such choices, governments are better able to determine how these choices can be influenced so that energy systems move in a particular direction.
5. Energy transition may result in various, large changes in how energy systems are organised, but these changes are the outcome of many decisions made by a large number of agents. Prescribing how the energy system should change is impossible when societies are organised in a decentralised manner. It is, therefore, more effective to influence the decisions of individual agents.

E.2 Chapter 2

1. In the common approach to energy transition, the focus is on achieving a particular outcome, but this does not give any information on how that outcome could be realised, and what would be the most efficient way to do so.

M. Mulder, *Economics of Energy Transition*, Studies in Energy, Resource and Environmental Economics, https://doi.org/10.1007/978-3-032-29010-6

2. Behavioural economics shows that the choices of economic agents are not always rational (in an economic sense), such as how they depend on the design of policy measures. By taking such insights into account, the effectiveness of policy measures can be increased.
3. The energy intensity of economies depends on the efficiency of using energy in different types of activities, and the share of these activities in the economy. Changes in the latter are called structural changes.
4. Changes in energy systems result from changes in the choices made by economic agents, such as using more or less energy for a particular objective. These changes in energy use are related to several factors, including the costs of using energy. The price elasticity of demand measures how the use of energy changes in relation to a change in energy prices, while the price elasticity of supply measures to what extent the supply of energy changes when the price of energy changes.
5. An inelastic supply means that the supply of energy does not strongly respond to changes in the price of energy. The formal definition is that in case of an inelastic supply, the price elasticity of supply is less than 1.

E.3 Chapter 3

1. When economic agents want to conclude contracts, they should know who may be interested and against what conditions. When economic agents have information on all other agents, they can make their best decision. When information is lacking, it is more likely that the best possible deals (i.e. contracts) will not be closed.
2. Public goods are goods that are non-excludable and non-rivalrous. By the former aspect, it is meant that no one can be excluded from enjoying that good, while non-rivalrous means that the use of that good by one agent does not affect its availability for others. Because of these characteristics, economic agents are not able to force consumers to pay for such goods, and therefore, private parties will not provide such goods. Hence, coordination among agents or government regulation is needed to secure the provision of such goods.
3. The fact that natural resources are not unlimitedly available is not a shortcoming of markets, but a fact of life. Markets are institutional devices to coordinate the allocation of commodities, such as natural resources. When all the information on these resources is freely available to everyone, and no agent has the power to influence market outcomes, one can conclude that markets take care of the fact that the resources will at some point be exhausted.
4. A high import dependence may spill over into geopolitical dependencies, and if market parties do not sufficiently pay attention to the costs of such dependencies, it can be viewed as a market failure (i.e. a negative externality).
5. Energy markets based on fossil energy sometimes result in periods with high price volatility, but the same holds for markets mainly based on renewables.

These price volatilities can result from scarcity situations when demand exceeds the available production capacity.

E.4 Chapter 4

1. A regulatory constraint can be effective when it precisely prescribes what an economic agent should (not) do, but this can be inefficient when it leaves less room to that agent to choose the cheapest option.
2. If economic agents are well informed about the current level of (proven, probable and possible) reserves, they can better estimate how scarce the resource is, and hence, what the resource rents are and what the profitability of new exploration activities could be.
3. This can be done by facilitating extension of transport and storage infrastructure, both nationally and cross-border, which enables economic agents to respond more flexibly to price and supply shocks, as well as by promoting energy-efficiency measures, which makes economic agents less vulnerable to such shocks.
4. Volatile and high prices result generally from scarcity within a market and the inability of supply and/or demand to respond quickly in the short term. A strong price increase, therefore, has as a function to inform and incentivise economic agents that the market is tight and that more response is needed. Using strategic reserves may suppress this role of volatile and high prices, making things even worse. Strategic reserves may be useful, however, when there is a real shortage in which markets cannot clear.
5. In a cap-and-trade emissions trading scheme, the size of the emission reduction is determined by the cap on emissions, which means that adding other policy measures, like support for renewables, results in a so-called waterbed effect. This can be useful, nevertheless, when the resulting decline in the emission price makes it politically more feasible to further reduce the cap.

E.5 Chapter 5

1. As shareholders differ in their roles, interests, knowledge, information position and objectives, it is not feasible, but also not necessary that they share a common view on the future development. What is crucial is that everyone is correctly informed about the situation in energy systems. Most of the time, this is done through market prices, but when markets do not exist or cannot find an equilibrium solution, government (or joint) coordination may be needed to inform the involved agents, such as in the case of infrastructure development.
2. Firms may make different choices because they have different preferences and backgrounds (e.g. expertise and experiences), while they can also make different assessments of threats and opportunities. Such a decentralised economic system contributes to welfare of society, as it makes it possible to optimise the use of

inputs (i.e. capital, labour, energy, knowledge), while there is a higher likelihood that the various innovation activities result in successful new discoveries.

3. A firm can decarbonise by selling its fossil-fuel activities, like coal-fired power plants, to another company. As a result, the former firm can report having less carbon emissions, while on the level of industry, there is no change at all.
4. For instance, when a firm invests in innovation to reduce the costs of insulating houses, this may incentivise homeowners to invest more in insulation, which reduces their energy consumption for heating and makes them less vulnerable to high energy prices, while they also contribute to the mitigation of carbon emissions.
5. In economic sense, decentralisation of energy systems refers to at what level decisions are being made. When households are becoming more active players by installing solar panels on the roofs of their houses and responding to dynamic retail prices, this can be clearly understood as a further decentralisation. However, when households communicate more with each other through energy communities, this is not a further decentralisation when such communities mainly refer to other ways of administrative organisation, which (partly) replaces the organisation through retailers and other intermediate parties.

Index

M. Mulder, *Economics of Energy Transition*, Studies in Energy, Resource and Environmental Economics, https://doi.org/10.1007/978-3-032-29010-6

Kolibri 360 GmbH
Ferdinand-Jühlke-Straße 7
99095 Erfurt, Deutschland
produktsicherheit@kolibri360.de